"I really found my faith when I learned that the government was opposed to the film. If NASA took the time to write me a twenty-page letter, then I knew there must be something happening." **Steven Spielberg**

Important Note from the Publishers and the Editorial Board: Two new books by Maximillien de Lafayette are published each month.
To learn about all his current and forthcoming books, please check regularly:
www.amazon.com
www.ufozetareticuli.com
www.maximilliendelafayettebibliography.com

Covers Design and Pages Layout-Maquette: Maximillien de Lafayette. Senior Editor: Carol Lexter. Photos' and Graphics' Templates: Robert Howard. Art Production: Solange Berthier and Fabiola Rossi. Pagination: Joy Elliot. Series Editor: Shoshanna Rosenstein. Media: Germaine Poitiers. Series Art Director: Patrique Dreyfus. Montage and Photoshop: Daniel Iliescu.

*** *** ***

ISBN: 9781434843074. Date of Publication: February 20, 2008.

A PUBLICATION OF TIMES SQUARE PRESS AND ELITE ASSOCIATES

<u>PUBLISHED AND DISTRIBUTED BY AMAZON.COM COMPANY</u>
PRINTED IN THE UNITED STATES OF AMERICA

NEW YORK ▪ CALIFORNIA ▪ WASHINGTON, DC ▪ PARIS ▪ LONDON ▪ TOKYO

ZETA RETICULI AND ANUNNAKI DESCENDANTS AMONG US
Who Are They?
Hybrids And Genetically Created Humans Who Are Ruling The Earth

---

Maximillien de Lafayette

Author of

From Zeta Reticuli To Earth: Time, Space And The UFO Technology
Inside A UFO: Alien Abduction, Hypnosis, Psychiatry, Quantum Physics and
Religions Face to Face
Extraterrestrials-US Government Treaty And Agreements
Biographical Encyclopedia of People in Ufology and Scientific Extraterrestrial
Research: People Who Matter

Edited by
Carol Lexter, Shoshannah Rosenstein and Germaine Poitiers

*** *** ***

A PUBLICATION OF TIMES SQUARE PRESS & ELITE ASSOCIATES INTERNATIONAL
PUBLISHED AND DISTRIBUTED BY AMAZON.COM COMPANY
2008

Acknowledgments and Gratitude

For their enormous contributions, articles, comments, generosity, and guidance, I am deeply grateful to:

Dr. Ilil Arbel, Rabbi Mordachai, Monsignor Maroon, Cheik Ahmad Al Huseini, Joy Elliot, Patrique Dreyfus, Dr. Richard Boylan, Dr. William Birnes, Dr. Michael E. Salla, Dr. Zecharia Sitchin, John Stokes, late Dr. Carl Sagan, Prof. Sam Chang, Dr. John Chen, Dr. Kurt Rosenstadt, Dr. Gisele von Guntenbergersen, Lyssa Royal Holt, Alex Collier, Dr. David Jacobs, Branton, Nick Pope, Dr. Lynne Kitei, Helen Littrell, Jean Bilodeaux, Pamela Stonebrooke, Louise Compton, Nigel Watson, Barbara Tandory, Chris Rutkowski, Dr. John Dreher, Shoshanna Rosenstein, Dr. Carol Lexter, Michele Bugliaro Goggia, Victor Martinez, Bill Ryan, Michael Lindemann, Len Kasten, Tim Swartz, Linda Moulton-Howe, Mark Pilkington, Dee Finey, Sal Rachel, Estelle Nora Harwit Amrani, Dr. Al Mutawalli, Dr. Erica Doserholm.

The Author

Table of Contents_____

Excerpts from the book: Revelations of an Anunnaki's Wife: Christianity, The White House, and Victoria's Hybrid Congressman Son. Chapter 1...73

Chapter 2: History and Civilization of Zeta Reticuli and other Extraterrestrials...81

Chapter 3: Galactic Family: Zeta Reticuli and Physical Genotypes...97

Chapter 4: Theories and Findings About the Descendant of the Anunnaki and Aliens' Races Still living Among Us...115

Chapter 5: The Reptilian Bloodlines on Earth: The Breathing Descendants Among Us...141

Chapter 6: The Real Truth of How Humanity Began...193

Chapter 7: The Origins and Beginning Of the Human Races From The Anunnaki To The Present...221

Chapter 8: Extraterrestrials, Humans and their Genes/DNA Close Relationship...229

Chapter 9: The Anunnaki's Super Physics, Science And Genetic Engineering...237

Chapter 10: Adam and Human Longevity and Anunnaki DNA...247

Chapter 11: Extraterrestrials Among Us...253

Chapter 12: The Remnants of the Anunnaki Among Us. Why are they here?...275

Chapter 13: The Star People: Races, Categories and Intent...293

Chapter 14: Anunnaki's Descendants And Remnants Among Us, And Aliens Behind World Government...301

Chapter 15: Sex With Aliens...313

Chapter 16: Project SERPO...337

Chapter 17: The Truth...381

***   ***   ***

IN THIS SERIES (15 BOOKS)
BY MAXIMILLIEN de LAFAYETTE
Read more at
www.ufozetareticuli.com & www.maximilliendelafayettebibliography.com

Probing and analyzing the secret events, chronicles, files and dossiers of governments, organizations, societies, and powerful people. A collection of the most important theories, concepts, essays and analyses by top scientists, theologians, investigators, philosophers, media, believers and skeptics. From UFO, and the assassination of President Kennedy to time/space travel, parallel universes, Jesus Christ, Maria Magdalena, immortality, quantum physics, and the hidden world of the occult.

The series is a prism of the reflections and opinions of highly regarded scientists, philosophers and investigators.

The author presents summaries of their theories and opinions. It should please both the believers and the skeptics. This series is an essential reference tool and guide to the secret world of UFOS, extraterrestrials, the greatest conspiracies, cover-ups and controversies of our time.

Published (2007-2008):
- **1-**From Zeta Reticuli to Earth: Time, Space And the UFO Technology. (400 Pages)
- **2-**The Biggest Controversies, Conspiracies, Theories and Coverups of our Time: From the Secret Files of Science, Politics, The Occult and Religion. (400 Pages)
- **3-**Inside A UFO: Alien Abduction, Hypnosis, Psychiatry, Quantum Physics and Religions Face to Face. (400 Pages)
- **4-**UFOs and the Alien Agenda. The Complete Book of UFOs, Encounters, Abduction And Aliens Bases On Earth. (400 Pages)
- **5-**Extraterrestrials Agenda: Aliens' Origin, Species, Societies, Intentions and Plan for Humanity. (400 Pages)
- **6-**The Anunnaki's Genetic Creation of the Human Race: UFOs, Aliens and Gods, Then and Now. (400 Pages)
- **7-**Extraterrestrials-US Government Treaty and Agreements: Alien Technology, Abduction, and Military Alliance. (400 Pages)
- **8-**Biographical Encyclopedia of People in Ufology and Scientific Extraterrestrial Research: People Who Matter. (740 Pages)
- **9-**Zeta Reticuli and Anunnaki Descendants Among Us: Who Are They? (400 Pages)
- **10-**UFO-USO and Extraterrestrials of the Sea: Flying Saucers and Aliens Civilizations, Life and Bases Underwater (400 Pages)
- **11-**Revelation of an Anunnaki's Wife: Christianity, The White House, And Victoria's Hybrid Congressman Son. (400 Pages)

En route: (February-March 2008)
12-Thematic Encyclopedia of Ufology and Extraterrestrial Research (740 Pages)
13-World Who's Who in Ufology and Study of Extraterrestrial Civilizations (400 Pages)
14-Ulema: Code and Language of the World Beyond (400 Pages)
15-Map of the After-Life: Where And How You Continue Your Life After Death (400 Pages)

FROM ZETA RETICULI TO EARTH
Time, Space And The UFO Technology

About the book: Anyone who thinks that our universe is a simple one, where two and two always add to four, and where all we needed to know we had learned in the proverbial kindergarten, lives in denial. This is a very complex universe and just a glimpse into the works of such greats as Albert Einstein, Niels Bohr, or even the early visionaries like Leonardo da Vinci or Emanuel Kant, will shake anyone's complacent world view after a few minutes of reading.

As human beings, we seek comfort. Perhaps we are finding it in religion; perhaps we look for it in the teachings of Kabbalah or New Age. We feel the need to know, to understand, because if we do not we cannot be comfortable and may even be scared. And the factions of conservative religions, atheism, science, spirituality, evolution supporters, creationists, etc., clash and fight, each honestly convinced that their own views are the only correct ones, and the rest of the world must be persuaded to follow that path.

But to read, understand, and enjoy this book, try to adopt the one and only state of mind that would allow it: *for a few hours, try to be an agnostic*. Adopt the one tenet of the true agnostic, which is, very simply, the admission that you simply don't know. That you cannot know, because you are three-dimensional while the universe is multi-dimensional. That you are willing to open your mind to the possibilities – and perhaps enjoy the freedom and liberation that such attitude can bring.

This book has everything, and it does not take a judgemental stand. It reports, discusses, and engages the reader in fruitful lines of investigation and independent thought. From time travel to UFO phenomena, from modern physics and the role of the astronauts and the military to blatant cover-ups and controversies, from the views of the most distinguished scientists and thinkers of our time to sceptics and scoffers, it simply covers the field in the most complete way one can hope to find in a single volume.

The book can be read from beginning to end and be greatly enjoyed by any intelligent reader. However, some of us may have a pet topic. Perhaps you are fond of cover-ups? Perhaps, specifically, presidential involvement? You will find a chapter about it. Eisenhower, Bush, Clinton, Truman? They are there. Interested in Element115? Hard to find, right? Well, here you will find it in detail. Travel exceeding the speed of light? Of course. Relationship with Zeta Reticuli? Right here. And you don't have to be a believer. Part III will support the opposition. This is a spectacular book, written in a language that all of us can understand, but never talks down. It will enlighten and entertain and give you food for thought and reflection for years to come. And if I may indulge in a cliché – it may change your life!

*** *** ***

THE BIGGEST CONTROVERSIES, CONSPIRACIES, THEORIES AND COVERUPS OF OUR TIME

From the secret files of science, politics, the occult and religion

- "To dare to write such a book is a risky affair. Maximillien de Lafayette who wrote it got to be exceptionally brave, an idealistic or totally crazy. This book could jeopardize his life. This is not the first time Mr. De Lafayette writes about a delicate and dangerous subject. He did it once before when he authored "Extraterrestrials-US Government Treaty and Agreements." But he must be protected by some powerful organizations to come forward and present those facts about secret and influential people and governments who control the world and our life. Once you start to read this book you will not be able to put it down. An amazing, revealing and explosive book. Get your copy. It will take you to the world of conspiracies, greed, power, and world domination. Probing and analyzing the secrets, events, chronicles, files and dossiers of governments, organizations, societies, and powerful people."- New York Monthly Herald

- A collection of the most important theories, concepts, essays and analyses by top scientists, theologians, investigators, philosophers, media, believers and skeptics.

- From UFO, the assassination of President Kennedy to time/space travel, parallel universes, Jesus Christ, Maria Magdalena, immortality and hidden world of the occult. The book is a prism of the reflections and opinions of highly regarded scientists, philosophers and investigators.

- The author presents summaries of their theories and opinions. It should please both, the believers and the skeptics. This book is an essential reference tool and guide to the secret world of the greatest conspiracies, cover-ups and controversies of our time.

INSIDE A UFO

Alien Abduction, Hypnosis, Psychiatry, Quantum Physics and Religions Face to Face

This book is a prism of the opinions and theories of the most brilliant minds of our times, and an expose of the thoughts and findings of skeptics, believers, therapists, psychiatrists, psychologists, UFOlogists, scientists, astronauts, governments' officials, and the abductees.

It contains an astonishing variety of topics, including but not limited to:

- Alien abduction.
- Portraits and profiles of alien abductees and their experiences.
- Sleep paralysis, false memories, trauma and regression hypnosis.
- Aliens' telepathy, intentions and agenda.
- UFO technology; space/time travel possibilities and paradoxes.
- Description of the aliens' societies, families, physiognomy.
- Surgical operations performed on abductees.
- Interviews with leading authorities in the field.
- Types, categories and origin of aliens.
- Conspiracies, cover-ups, and alleged governments contacts and treaties with aliens.

*** *** ***

UFOS AND THE ALIEN AGENDA

The Complete Book of UFOs, Encounters, Abduction And Aliens Bases On Earth

The book includes multi-varied topics and in-depth articles including but not limited to:

- UFOs: Complete history, conspiracies, cover-ups, security threat, defense, and government secrecy
- National Security and UFOs
- What the U.S. government knows about unidentified flying objects
- UFOs as a threat and the evidence
- The reasons why the government might have chosen not to disclose the ET reality: The 65 reasons
- A correlation between nuclear devices and UFOs
- Reverse engineering alien technology at United States government facilities
- Extraterrestrials' agenda. Cosmic top secret
- The plot thickens at Area 51 and Hangar 18
- Seeing UFOs at Area 51
- United States acquisition of advanced technology and interaction with alien cultures
- Report on the motivations and activities of extraterrestrial races
- A typology of the most significant extraterrestrial races interacting with humanity
- 57 extraterrestrial races known to the U.S. military
- Very first communication between aliens and the United States
- Setting up the first written protocol and the signing of a treaty between aliens and the United States government
- First set of the treaty and a know-how technical book given by aliens to Eisenhower and American scientists.
- The first alien hostage at Holloman AFB;
- "KRILL": The first book on aliens' technology written by aliens and given to the US military and US space program.

EXTRATERRESTRIALS AGENDA
Aliens' Origin, Species, Societies, Intentions and Plan for Humanity

An explosive book! Everything about the aliens' agenda, including in-depth articles about (to name a few):

- Historical chronology: The era of "modern" interaction with non-human terrestrial and non-terrestrial entities
- The United States air force and the central intelligence agency exercised complete control over the 'alien secret
- Plans were formulated to defend the earth in case of invasion
- The impact of UFOs and their occupants on religion
- Given their technological superiority, why don't hostile alien forces just take over the planet?
- What about military abductions?
- Can anything be done to stop the alien agenda?
- There are artificial humans who are manufactured by alien forces
- Alien threat response security
- Earth may be a combined multi-alien race
- The symbols of nature and evolution and ETs

*** *** ***

THE ANUNNAKI'S GENETIC CREATION OF THE HUMAN RACE
UFOs, Aliens and Gods, Then and Now

The most comprehensive published work on the Anunnaki and their impact on the human race. Wealth of information and in-depth articles on so many topics, including, but not limited to:

1-ETs' role in human development
2-God and the extraterrestrials
3-The mystery surrounding Jesus and the Sons of God
4-The extraterrestrials are responsible for genetic intervention in the modern era
5-The 'God' of the Old Testament, Yahweh/Jehovah, is in fact an "intermediary god" or extraterrestrial
6-How the Anunnaki created us genetically
7-The real story of Nibiru (Planet X)
8-We created you. We came from space
9-The truth behind human origins
10-The alien gods were genetic engineers
11-The Nephilim an ancient race of half-breed humans... And much much more...

*** *** ***

EXTRATERRESTRIALS-US GOVERNMENT TREATY AND AGREEMENTS
ALIEN TECHNOLOGY, ABDUCTION, AND MILITARY ALLIANCE

An explosive book! It details all the agreements and treaty signed between the United States and Aliens from Zeta Reticuli and other planets. Complete disclosure of the articles of the SECRET TREATY.

What aliens wanted from us, and what the US Government gave them? What did we receive in return? The book discusses an infinity of fascinating subjects including: 1- How secretly NASA and US astronauts dealt with UFOS, 2- President Eisenhower 1954 meeting with extraterrestrials, the first United States contact, and treaty with extraterrestrials, points and agreements of the treaty, 3- The formulated plans by the United States and Russia to defend the earth in case of invasion, 4- The whole story of MJ-12, 5-Aliens agenda and purposes on earth.

Biographical Encyclopedia of People in Ufology and Scientific Extraterrestrial Research: People Who Matter

- The world's largest and first biographical encyclopedia of the most important people, ufologists, scientists, researchers, writers, believers and skeptics of all time.
- Their life, times, career highlights, theories, opinions, work, books and contributions.
- Including interviews and historical analyses of ufology from its dawn to the present.
- Followed by Volume 2 (740 pages) and the Yearbook (400 pages).
- A total of 1,880 pages!

*** *** ***

UFO-USO And Extraterrestrials Of The Sea: Flying Saucers and Aliens Civilizations, Life and Bases Underwater

- Comprehensive list of sightings and encounters, including dates and charts.
- List of alll known bases, locations, description, roles and functions.
- Extraterrestrial civilizations and aliens living and operating underwater.
- USO and the United State Navy face to face: Secret reports, sightings and encounters.
- How USOs operate, fly and hide.
- Why USOs are there? Purpose and agenda.

*** *** ***

REVELATION OF AN ANUNNAKI'S WIFE
Christianity, The White House, And Victoria's Hybrid Congressman Son.
Co authored by Ilil Arbel, Ph.D.

The amazing autobiography of Victoria, an Anunnaki wife in her own words...no channeling, no trances, no séances. Direct data by and rapport with Victoria in person. Including explosive revelations about:

- Major UFOs-Extraterrestrials incidents and threats inside secret military bases,
- Governments' involvement with 2 particular alien races,
- Description of the world of extraterrestrials,
- The Anunnaki's community, societies and families
- Description of life on Zeta Reticuli,
- Description of the habitat on Planet X,
- Victoria-Alien husband love story, and wedding ceremony,
- Victoria's voyage to Zeta Reticuli,
- Victoria's personal involvement with her alien in-laws, and the leader of the Anunnaki,
- Victoria's hybrid congressman son and the major role he will be playing on the arena of world politics,
- Dwight Eisenhower's direct contact with extraterrestrials,
- The Vatican's secret files on UFOS, extraterrestrials, Christianity-Alien entities connection,
- Jesus Christ's life after the crucifixion; his trip to Marseille, his family, children and their bloodlines, and his wife Mary Magdalene,
- Victoria's take on channelers, contactees, abductees, ufologists, and charlatans,
- Earth's future, multiple universes, interdimensional beings,
- Anunnaki's existence and civilization on earth: Past, present and future.

*** *** ***

ULEMA

CODE AND LANGUAGE OF THE WORLD BEYOND

About the book: This is NOT a book on magic, occultism, channeling, spirits, and communicating with the dead! Simply because the author does not believe in "such things" as he put it bluntly.

The book is far deeper and more complex. It has roots in science, power of the mind, and transmutation of thoughts and visions into mental rapport with Ulemas who communicate with terrestrial beings through codes and secret language known to very few. It is hard to categorize the content of this book, since it does not belong to the commonly known aspects and teachings of "new age", Eastern philosophy, mind-body concepts, meditation, Zen, Yoga, spirituality, "energy", and similar disciplines.

For years, the author was reluctant to put in writing what he has discovered and learned from a secret group of scientists, philosophers and inquisitive minds who believe in a parallel world, and the scientifico-mental powers of the mind.

They are the ULEMAS; they do not teach religion, nor impose any moral doctrine.

The ULEMA hold a secret; the ultimate knowledge of at least one world beyond the one we know. In this book, the author tries to explain their thoughts, and attempts to introduce us to some codes and techniques they use to communicate with far more advanced "cosmic presence."

No! They are not UFO, extra-terrestrials, or the spirits of the dead.

They are the manifestation of an "intelligence" the human race can benefit from.

This book can change the way you understand the world you live in, and open your eyes to "unseen powerful and positive intelligence" that surrounds you, lives around you, and could change your whole life.

*** *** ***

The Author: Maximillien de Lafayette

International best-selling author, Maximillien de Lafayette wrote 117 books, 7 encyclopedias, and several world premiere musicals (One play was produced at the John F. Kennedy Center for the Performing Arts in Washington, D.C., USA.) De Lafayette is fluent in 7 languages, an expert linguist-historian of modern and ancient Middle/Near East languages, tribal dialects, and comparative history. He authored numerous authoritative books and encyclopedias such as, the 4 volume-"The 10 Language Universal Dictionary", the 10 volume- "Anthology and History of French Literature", "Encyclopedia of the 21st Century: Biographies and Profiles of the First Decade", "Biographical Encyclopedia of People in Ufology and Scientific Extraterrestrial Research", the 20 volume "World Who's Who in Jazz, Cabaret, Music and Entertainment", and "The Book of Nations".

For 25 years, De Lafayette has been researching subjects pertaining to space, time, gravity, multiple universes and "Space civilizations", and exchanging dialogues and rapports with scientists, and authorities in the field, from around the globe. He just finished writing a most unusual book "ULEMA: Code and Language of the World Beyond."

A multi-lingual, a syndicated columnist, a world traveler who has visited 46 countries, studied and taught comparative civilizations, international law and social systems for two decades; de Lafayette is in a privileged position to write this book. His columns, articles and books are read by more than 20 million readers in 135 countries, and his work has been translated in 17 languages. At 13, he published his first book; a collection of poems in French, hailed by members of the L'Academie Française as a masterpiece. Said book was translated in English by Dr. John Chen, Laureate of the United Nations/UNESCO, and former member of The White House Presidential Convention on Library Science and Information Services.

His latest international best-seller is "Entertainment: Divas, Cabaret, Jazz Then and Now". It hits the top chart, the world's 25 most popular items on the international market of Amazon. Uk.com on November 17, 2006. In addition, he has 3 international bestsellers, and two #1 bestsellers in Europe. Lawyer by trade, de Lafayette practiced international law for 20 years and served as legal advisor and counsel to several world organizations and governments in Europe and the Middle East. In the early eighties, he created the neo-cubism progressive movement in Europe, and was hailed as one of the pioneers of progressive abstract art in the 20th century. Visit a website dedicated to his paintings: www.maximilliendelafayette.com The author can be reached at:

delafayette@internationalnewsagency.org

Books by Maximillien de Lafayette

Read more about these books, description and reviews at your local library, Amazon.com, Barnes & Noble and other booksellers, and distributors websites worldwide.

Books on UFOs and Extraterrestrial Civilizations:

Published:
1-From Zeta Reticuli to Earth: Time, Space And The UFO Technology
2-The Biggest Controversies, Conspiracies, Theories and Coverups of our Time. From the secrer files of science, politics, the occult and religion
3-Inside A UFO: Alien Abduction, Hypnosis, Psychiatry, Quantum Physics and Religions Face to Face
4-UFOs and the Alien Agenda: The Complete Book of UFOs, Encounters, Abductions And Aliens' Bases On Earth
5-Extraterrestrials Agenda: Aliens' Origin, Species, Societies, Intentions and Plan for Humanity
6-The Anunnaki's Genetic Creation of the Human Race: UFOs, Aliens and Gods, Then and Now
7-Extraterrestrials-US Government Treaty and Agreements: Alien Technology, Abductions and Military Alliance
8-Biographical Encyclopedia of People in Ufology and Scientific Extraterrestrial Research. Volume I
9-Zeta Reticuli And Anunnaki Descendants Among Us: Who Are They?
10-UFO-USO and Extraterrestrials of the Sea: Flying Saucers and Aliens Civilizations, Life and Bases Underwater

11- Hybrid Humans and Abductions: Aliens and Government Experiments

En route: (Books, study-guides, Who's Who, and encyclopedias on ufology, hypnotherapy, hypnosis, abduction, channeling, and aliens' cultures)

1-Biographical Encyclopedia of People in Ufology and Scientific Extraterrestrial Research. Volume II. Coming in March 2008
2-Thematic Encyclopedia of Ufology and Extraterrestrial Research. Coming in March 2008 (740 pages)
3-Ulema: Code and Language of the World Beyond. Coming in March 2008 (400 pages)
4-Map of the After-Life: Where And How You Continue Your Life After Death. Coming in March 2008 (400 pages)
5-World Who's Who in Ufology and Study of Extraterrestrial Civilizations. Coming in April 2008 (740 pages)
6-Revelation of an Anunnaki's Wife: Christianity, The White House and Victoria's Hybrid Congressman Son

***   ***   ***

In other fields:

1-Washington Does Not Believe in Tears: Play Their Game Or Eat The Blame!
2-What Foreigners Should Know About Liberal American Women
3-The Nine Language Universal Dictionary. (New Edition: The Ten Language Universal Dictionary
4-Anthologie De La Literature Française (Anthology & History of French Literature)
5-The Dating Phenomenon In The United States: Great Expectations or Justified Deceptions
6-Marmara the Gypsy: Biography of Baroness Myriam de Roszka (The script of the original play at the John F. Kennedy Center for the Performing Arts.)
7-One Hundred Reasons Why You Should And Should Not Marry An American Woman: Take Him to the Cleaners, Madame!
8-The United States Today: People, Society, Life from A to Z
9-Causes Celebres from 2,000 BC to Modern Times
10-The World's Best and Worst People
11-How Psychologists, Therapists and Psychiatrists Can Ruin Your Life in Court of Law in America
12-International Encyclopedia of Comparative Slang and Folkloric Expressions
13-Encyclopedia of Science of Mind: Religion, Science, and Parapsychology
14-Essay on Psychocosmoly of Man, Universe and Metalogics
15-The Social Register of the Most Prominent and Influential People in the United States
16-How to Use Easy, Fancy French & Latin to Your Advantage and Impress Others
17-How People Rule People with Words: From speechwriters and tele-evangelists to lawmakers and politicians
18-How to Protect Yourself from Your Ex-Wife Lawsuits
19-Divorces for the Highest Bidders
20-The International Book of World Etiquette, Protocol and Refined Manners
21-Bona Fide Divas & Femmes Fatales: The 700 Official Divas of the World
22-How Not To Fail In America: Are You Looking For Happiness Or Financial Success?
23-How to Understand People's Personality and Character Just by Looking at Them
24-The Art and Science of Understanding and Discovering Friends and Enemies
25-New Concise Dictionary of Law for Beginners
26-Comparative Study of Penal Codes As Applied In France and Great Britain
27-How to Understand International Law
28-La Pensee Arabe Face Au Continent Europeen
29-Beyond Mind & Body: The Passive Indo-Chinese School of Philosophy and Way of Life
30-New Approach to the Metaphysical Concept of Human Salvation in the Anthropological Psychology of Indian Religions
31-Worldwide Encyclopedia of Study and Learning Opportunities Abroad.
32-World Who's Who In Contemporary Art
33-World Who's Who in Jazz, Cabaret, Music and Entertainment

34-Thematic Encyclopedia of Cabaret Jazz
35-United States and the World Face to Face
36-Music, Showbiz and Entertainment
37-Entertainment: Divas, Cabaret, Jazz Then and Now
38-Showbiz, Pioneers, Best Singers, Entertainers and Musicians from 1606 to the Present
39-Best Musicians, Singers, Albums, and Entertainment Personalities of the 19th, 20th and 21st Centuries
40-Entertainment Greats From the 1800's to the Present: Cinema, Music, Divas, Legends
41-You, the World, and Everything Around You
42-World of Contemporary Jazz: Biographies of the Legends, the Pioneers, the Divas
43-Living Legends and Ultimate Singers, Musicians and Entertainers
44-People Who Shaped Our World
45-International Register of Events and People Who Shaped Our World
46-United States Cultural and Social Impact on Foreign Intelligentsia
47-Directory of United States Adult and Continuing Postsecondary Education
48-Comprehensive Guide to the Best Colleges and Universities in the United States
49-The Best of Washington: Its People, Society, and Establishments
50-Credentials Academic Equivalency and New Trends in Higher Education Worldwide
51-How Foreign Students Can Earn an American University Degree Without Leaving Their Country
52-Comprehensive Guide to the Best Academic Programs and Best Buys In College Education In The United States
53-How to Learn Seven Thousand French Words in Less Than Thirty Minutes
54-Comprehensive Guide to the Best Colleges and Universities in the U.S. (Alternative Education)
55-World's Best and Worst Countries: A comparative Study of Communities, Societies, Lifestyles and Their People
56-World Encyclopedia of Learning and Higher Education
57-How Much Your Degree Is Worth Today In America?
58-Worldwide Comparative Study and Evaluation of Postsecondary Education
59-Thematic Encyclopedia of Hospitality and Culinary Arts
60-Five Stars Hospitality: La Crème de la Crème in Hotel Guest Service, Food and Beverage
61-Hospitality Best & Worst: How to Succeed in the Food and Hotel Business
62-Encyclopedia of American Contemporary Art
63-Encyclopedia of Jazz: Life &Times of the 3.000 Most Prominent Singers &Musicians (V. 1)
64-Encyclopedia of Jazz: Life and Times of the 3.000 Most Prominent Singers and Musicians (V.2)
65-Concise Encyclopedia of American Music and Showbiz
66-The World Today: Headliners, Leaders, Lifestyles and Relationships

67-Evaluation of Personal and Professional Experiences: How to convert your knowledge and life experiences into academic degrees.

68-Contemporary Art, Culture, Politics and Modern Thought

69- Maximillien de La Croix « Mistral », Life and Times of Maximillien de La Croix de Lafayette

70-International Rating Of Countries in Higher Education And Comparative Study of Curricula, Degrees And Qualifications Worldwide

71-Alternative Higher Education

72-Dictionary of Academic Terminology Worldwide

73-Fake Titles Fake People

74-How to Use Greek, Latin and Hieroglyphic Expressions and Quotations to Your Advantage and Impress Others.

75-The Best and Worst Non-Traditional and Alternative Colleges and Universities in the United States

76-Directory of United States Traditional and Alternative Colleges and Universities

77-The Non Traditional Postsecondary Education in the United States: Its Merits, Advantages and Disastrous Consequences

78-Lafayette's Encyclopedic Dictionary of Higher Education Worldwide

79-Academic Degrees, Titles and Credentials

80-Independent Study Programs

81-America's Best Education at a Low Cost

82-Fictitious Credentials on Your Resume

83-Distance Learning

84-New Trends in American Higher Education

85-Directory of United States Postsecondary Education

86-Directory of United States Traditional and Alternative Colleges and Universities

87-National Register of Social Prestige and Academic Ratings of American Colleges and Universities

88-The Book of Nations

89-The World's Lists of Best and Worst

90-The Ultimate Book of World's Lists, Volume I

91-The Ultimate Book of World's Lists, Volume 2

92-Biographical Encyclopedia of the Greatest Minds, Talents and Personalities of our Time

93-Encyclopedia of the 21st Century. Biographies and Profile of the First Decade

94-Hospitality and Food Best and Worst: How to Succeed in the Food and Hotel Business

95-The Biggest Controversies, Conspiracies, Theories & Coverups of our Time, Vol. I

96-The Biggest Controversies, Conspiracies, Theories, & Coverups of our Time, Vol. II

97-Ulema: Code and Language of the World Beyond

98-The 1,000 Divas and Femmes Fatales of the World

99-140 Years of Cinema

100-Ulema: Code and Language of the World Beyond

101-Map of the After Life: Where And How You Continue Your Life After Death

Encyclopedias:

1-International Encyclopedia of Comparative Slang and Folkloric Expressions
2-Encyclopedia of Science of Mind: Religion, Science, and Parapsychology
3-World Encyclopedia of Learning and Higher Education
4-Worldwide Comparative Study and Evaluation of Postsecondary Education
5-Thematic Encyclopedia of Hospitality and Culinary Arts
6-Encyclopedia of American Contemporary Art
7-Encyclopedia of Jazz: Life & Times of 3.000 Most Prominent Singers and Musicians
8-Concise Encyclopedia of American Music and Showbiz (2 Volumes)
9-Encyclopedia of the 21st Century. Biographies and Profile of the First Decade
10-Biographical Encyclopedia of the Greatest Minds, Talents and Personalities of our time
11-Biographical Encyclopedia of People in Ufology and Scientific Extraterrestrial Research: People Who Matter and Most Important Figures
12-Thematic Encyclopedia of Ufology and Extraterrestrial Sciences (En route)

Dictionaries:

1-The Nine Language Universal Dictionary: How to Write It and Say It in Arabic, English, French, German, Italian, Japanese, Portuguese, Russian, Spanish (4 Volumes)
2-How to Learn 7,000 French Words in Less than Thirty Minutes
3-Lafayette's Encyclopedic Dictionary of Higher Education Worldwide
4-Dictionary of Academic Terminology Worldwide
5-How to Use Easy, Fancy French & Latin to Your Advantage and Impress Others

*** *** ***

Prologue

Sons of God And Daughters of Men Mating?

Early Extraterrestrials-Zetas-Reptilians-Anunnaki and Earth's Women Offspring

How did it start? And for what purpose?
Was it a one-time intercourse?
A one night stand?
An on-going sexual relationship?
A real marriage?
Did the women of the Earth who had relationships with extraterrestrials give birth to normal human babies?
Or did they produce hybrid, half-hybrid, humanoid or extraterrestrial babies?
What about the bloodlines of these babies?
Any descendants or remnants living today among us?
If yes! Who are they? Where are they? And what are they doing now?
Are they the Reptilians? Illuminati? Shape-shifters? Draconians? Aliens at Area 51 and Hangar 18? Extraterrestrials living underwater?

Many writers, abductees, and military men who claimed to have worked with aliens in secret military bases reported that extraterrestrials did not have genital organs, so how did they mate with women from Earth and made them pregnant?
What did they use to fertilize their eggs?
How do we explain this Biblical sentence: "And it came to pass, when man began to multiply on the face of the earth, and daughters were born unto them"?

Some Biblical scholars (avant garde or not) claim that the Sons of God were the fallen angels the Bible talked about. Those were the followers of Satan who rebelled against God. They fell to earth, saw the very beautiful women living on Earth, seduced them, and boom kaboum, the women got pregnant, and gave birth to Giants, as simple as that! Another group of theologians and doctors of the Church explained it in the most ridiculous and naive way. They say that all men and women of this world are the descendants of Adam and Eve. And this happened a few thousands years ago. Just imagine 2 people created 6 billions, and populated the whole earth!

To many, this explanation is one of the man history's silliest soap operas. But to millions of believers, this explanation is the ultimate truth – Gospel Truth –
And if it is true that "we were created in the image of God" as written in the Bible, then, I have to say that God is not a very good-looking fella, because our ancestors (the very first or early human race specimen) were the ugliest thing walking or crawling on the face of Earth next to the Dinosaurs and crocodiles. Obviously, those who wrote the Bible did not know much about forensic science, archeology, anthropology and DNA.

There is also this group of theologians who argues that the Sons of God were from Seth's lineage, and the daughters of men came from Cain's lineage. Consequently, something very wrong or extraordinary must have happened during the genetical process to produce the Giants' race.

We should not forget the big bang theoricists and cosmologists who ascertain that humans are made out of cosmic dust. They are absolutely sure that even your 1965 Corvette's dash board, the tires of your bicycle and M&M candies...all are made out of the same dust.

St. Luke traced back Jesus to Adam, who had been described as "The Son of God." In Corinthians 11:7, St. Paul said: "Man was made in the image of God, and woman was made in the image of man." History has revealed that St. Paul did not think much of women. He considered them inferior to men and would not allow them to preach the gospel. Same beliefs and same attitude were adopted by the Catholic Church for centuries. This is why the Gospel of Mary Magdalene was ignored by the early doctors of the Church, the bishops of Constantinople and the Vatican. So for now, we can put the theory of St. Paul to rest.
Ironically, and according to many experts in the field of extratrerrestrials' studies, including those who claim to have been contacted by aliens, extraterrestrial entities, and especially the Anunnaki themselves, women were highly regarded, and were considered as the "Source of Creation." I wish if St. Paul could hear this!
According to Victoria, the Anunnaki and Zetas found women on earth to be more honorable than men. But also, these claims and theories can be easily contested.

*** *** ***

How much do we really know about the Anunnaki and Zeta Reticulians (Zetas)? And especially about their genetic creation of the human race?
What kind of documents and data have been used by ufologists to write all those *ad infinitum* articles about these enigmatic extraterrestrial entities?

What sources and reference tools did authors and ufologists use to narrate on the subject?

Is there any unshakable proof to ascertain to the identity and existence of extraterrestrials, and their highly propagandized agenda?

Those questions should and must to be answered by rational, unbiased, and alert persons. But this is not so easy, because extraterrestrial-ology and Ufology are not yet established or defined as a bona fide academic field. And any person who pretends to know the answers is a Fool!

*** *** ***

The vast literature on the Anunnaki and Zeta Reticulians (Zetas) was originated and fed by:

1-Dr. Zecharia Sitchin's original and pioneering theories. (Stimulating)

2-Abductees who told their alien abduction stories under the effect and influence of regression hypnosis. (Possible but also doubtful)

3-Contactees who described aliens' encounters and what happened to them. (Some stories could be genuine but almost 95% are nonsense.)

4-Regression hypnosis practitioners, hypnotherapists analyses and findings summaries. (Subject to debate, however they are reliable IF the hypnotherapist is not misleading, misguiding, influencing patients and clients. Suggestion manipulations on the part of hypnotherapists, and false memories are deceiving and even dangerous.)

5-Personal statements and sworn affidavits by scientists who claim to have worked with aliens in secret military bases and laboratories. (Many should be taken seriously.)

6-Translations of ancient texts, parchments, terracota and clay tablets found in Babylon, Sumeria, Mesopotamia, Phoenicia, Egypt and other parts of the world, including Central Africa. (The texts are authentic. The translations are accurate. But the primordial question remains: Is it mythology? A galactic fable? Ali Baba tale? Or a solid historical document and unquestionable chronicles of the human history?)

7-Military men who worked with aliens in secret underground military bases. (Many reports were absolutely true. However, a great number of reports and reproduced documents were fake.)

8-Information received by channelers. (I don't know about that!? I have doubts when a channeler reveals information for a price. This reminds me of a gypsy woman who is reading your palm or predicting your future under the tent of a Hungarian circus for $5.95)

9-And now, the *piece de resistance*! Should I call it *un coup de theatre*: Revelations by an Anunnaki's wife by the name of Victoria. Do I believe her? YES!

*** *** ***

Grosso modo...plenty of stuff, stories, reports, tales, data, affidavits, testimonies, documentaries and most recently, video tapes about UFOs and extraterrestrials. But how accurate these information, reports and data are?

And how credible and reliable are the witnesses and ufologists?

I will try to answer some of these questions in this book.

There are so many things I want to share with you in this book, to name a few:

- Revelations of Victoria; a hybrid woman who married an Anunnaki;
- New discoveries about the early cities of the Anunnaki and the Igigi, who were the first creators of the human race;
- Mind-boggling findings about the interaction between the Phoenicians and the Anunnaki;
- Revolutionary theories and concepts pertaining to the 46 primitive and different quasi-human races;
- Stories about humans who had sex with extraterrestrials;
- The early remnants of the Anunnaki;
- The descendants of the Anunaki who still live among us;
- The degree and extent of the veracity of Mr. Zecharia Sitchin's theories about the Anunnaki, and their genetic creation of the human race;
- How extraterrestrials evolved beyond the sexual reproduction process;
- What the Zeta Reticulians (Zetas) are doing now?;
- Claims about famous reptilian leaders who disguise as humans;
- The bloodlines of extraterrestrials on earth;
- How the Cabal controls the human race and operates from the shadows outside the public domain;
- The real truth of how humanity began;
- The future of the human race;
- And of course, the hottest conspiracies' theories.

Once again, I ask myself: Is there any unshakable proof to ascertain to their identity and existence?

Those questions should and must to be answered by rational, unbiased, and alert persons. But this is not so easy, because extraterrestrial-ology and Ufology are not yet established or defined as a bona fide academic field.

Also, I will be exploring and presenting the theories, opinions, public statements and most revealing articles on all these subjects as "crafted" and advanced by some of the most colorful and captivating figures in Ufology and the paranormal cosmos.

Needless to say, I am merely reporting, and just like you, I am questioning these revolutionary ideas and theories; some are disturbing, revolting, frightening, while some others are entertaining and fun. I had to include them in this book, because they constitute the very fabric of ufology.

They are NOT mine.

I do not advance any theory, nor do I pretend to present an explanation to these intriguing events and mysteries in the history of humanity, simply because I do NOT know. And once again, I would like to remind you that I am NOT an ufologist. I do not belong to any UFO's group, nor do I wish to do so. Simply, - and as usual – I am presenting my books as a prism of the most advanced ideas, theories and concepts in the field, leaving you the reader to come up with your own perception and conclusions.

There are zillions of fantastic opinions and theories advanced by highly respected university professors, physicians, scientists, archeologists, psychiatrists, historians and top military men that have shaped a global vision and a collective interpretation of the history of the creation of man on earth. Some thinkers were right, other were pompous and ridiculous. Some theories deserve sincere attention, while others raise a red flag. Ironically, history has showed us that the most unorthodox yet truthful and beneficial theories and concepts of the day were always the first to be ridiculed and the last to be recognized by the scientific community. Nevertheless, they were finally recognized and entered mainstream science, after so many lives were destroyed, outstanding scientists were ridiculed, and illustrious careers were completely jeopardized and annihilated by ignorant debunkers and arrogant skeptics, including top scientists.

In the field of ufology and paranormal, imagination is fertile, and the galactic Pantheon is full of deities, supreme beings and extraterrestrials who mesmerize us. Their stories, influence, interaction with humans and their paramount role in shaping human destiny are told by contactees, abductees, messengers, prophets, lunatics, honest believers, and visionaries. Who to believe and who to discredit? It is a hard call. Especially when those incredible stories come sometimes from highly educated individuals, astronomers, astronauts, astrophysicists, university professors and unusual and credible human beings who revealed impressive knowledge and a very high level of scientific information only known by and to the world's greatest scientists.

This book explores these issues.

But what does the ordinary person think about all these phenomena?

A simple, ordinary, honest, and down-to earth person? You will be amazed!

Here is something to sink your teeth in:

One person posted this question on a website:
"Aliens (the Gray's in particular) living under ground for many years. Do you know anything about them?

And here are some of the most colorful answers by respondents (Unedited):

1-Asker's reply: They want to assimilate into our culture and take over the world. They live on our essence. They are our descendants from the future. They are dying out because of genetic experiments that went wrong and trying to keep themselves alive by breeding with their ancestors (us). They are from another dimension. They have been interacting with us for millennia, hence all the stories of fairies, gnomes etc. They are from Zeta Reticuli.They have a mining colony here for fuel for their craft.They are demons. Or maybe some or all of the above. Take your pick.

2-Pink Princess' reply: Stop it that is the most ridiculous question I've ever heard.

3-Mint Jul's reply: This is a new one on me. Aliens discovered living underground like H. G. Wells' Morlocks in The Time Machine who emerge on the hours of darkness for nightly raids on the encampments of the Eloi, who live above ground!? Sounds like pure science fiction to me. Are there any photographs taken by potholers who have stumbled across them?
Or (like the planet Nibiru) has no-one actually seen them?
I thought the Grays were supposed to (allegedly) live on planets surrounding the star Zeta Reticuli and abduct people and take them there.
Why would they do that, one wonders, if they were here already, and could just pop down a nearby rabbit hole to be back among their own kind?
Of course we don't know anything about them because those of us who are here because we are interested in astronomy believe they don't exist. It is those who believe that they exist who will know what there is to know and it is them you should be asking. Tell us what they say and we will subject it to intelligent scrutiny.
Normally, that is the last thing that anyone with psuedo-scientific ideas wants, so I suspect that they won't be very forthcoming! Better still, invite the Grays (if you are in touch with them) to contribute to Yahoo! Answers and then they can tell us themselves...

4-Peg Palmeri's reply: according to Silvia Browne they are now amoung us and even high up in the government and they aren't grey anymore- they look just like us.

5-Dedak's reply: I live in Nevada, and lived in Californa for a long time as well, there is so much open space, like take the drive from LA to LV, you can drive a good hour and see nothing. With all that open space, in the middle of no where, if the Greys wanted to, they could likely have an above ground base and no one would ever find it.

I believe I've seen 3 Gray's before, not going to get into that story now because I don't want to look like a joke to those that don't believe in them, but I'll go on to say I think they're just here to study us, and our planet.

The way I see if, it there are able to get from there to here, if they wanted to hurt us or take over our planet, there's nothing we could do to stop them, and they would have done it by now. Our weapons are to the point we can destory life on our planet, and they know it. They could even be taking DNA to clone life on a different planet, or on their ship either for space zoos or to give us a new start somewhere else if we do end up killing ourselves off.

Or, Earth might mean nothing to them at all, and they only use us as a truck stop in space, and the Grey left behind are like gas station workers to them. I still say, if they where bad, they would have already taken over.

6-Fast Eddy's reply: I don't know what nonsense you have been exposed to, to believe that there are aliens under ground. Anyway assuming for a moment it was true then there are only 2 reasons why some ET's would want to visit us.

a) They are scientists and want to study an intelligent life form. The reason that they were here at present times was probably to see if humans were intelligent enough not to kill themselves with weapons of mass destruction or causing climate disasters, etc. They would want to understand if and how a complex society finds methods for selfcontrol.

 b) They were even meaner than humans and as they spread throughout the universe they would occupy every inhabitable planet they can find.

At the moment they would just figure out how to get rid of us, if we don't take care of this ourselves. Guys, there are really more important questions to be asked and answeres to be found. Quit worrying about ET's and start thinking about the real problems this planet has.

7-John R's reply: First of all the Gray's as you call then, have not lived under ground, they live in cities much more advanced than you can think of. When they visit Earth, they are studding us just like we study the insects and other things on the Earth and things we brought back from the moon. They do not contact us because they have been shot at many times.

8-Miyuki's reply: No one really knows about such stuff...because it does not exist. Where did you hear it?

There are many con men who write ridiculous books to make money.

*** *** ***

So, how should we approach these subjects?

To believe <u>everything</u> an abductee, a contactee, or an ufologist tells you is foolish. To not believe <u>anything</u> at all is equally stupid.

Hardcore skeptics are annoying.

UFOs' cult followers are simple-minded.

Flat-earth argumentative minds are ignorami.

Governments' official spokesmen about these phenomena always hide something, and that something is sometimes EVERYTHING.

Scientists who still believe that the shortest distance between two points is a straight line are limited in their thinking, and should eat wet sponges for breakfast.

Theologians who still preach the dogma of medieval ages are as narrow-minded as the hole of a donut.

So what is the final word?

The final word is: Open your mind and accept the possibility that some day, some of the most important ideas, teachings and beliefs we have learned in schools that have shaped our understanding of the universe and ourselves will change completely, as we discover new scientific frontiers, and acquire a higher level of spirituality, wisdom, goodness and cosmic awareness. And this includes the scenario of UFOs and extraterrestrials with all its close shots, fade in, and cuts.

Sir Francis Crick, the Nobel laureate, says there are an estimated 100 billion galaxies in our universe and he believes there are at least one million planets in our galaxy that could support life as we know it.

I predict that within 10 years, humanity will make a Global Contact with advanced civilizations we thought they never existed, or it was impossible to reach or communicate with.

***   ***   ***

CHAPTER 1
VICTORIA AND HER ANUNNAKI HUSBAND

Victoria's first letter. Summary of her letter

- Jesus did not die on the cross!
- Mary Magdalene and Jesus fled to Marseille, where they settled permanently and had children.
- The Quran did not descend on Mohammad from Heaven. Mohammad learned it from a Christian ascetic monk in the desert. This monk was known in the area as "Raheb Bouhayrah"
- Moses never left Egypt. Not only there had never been an Exodus of the Israelites, but Moses, who was a pure Egyptian, enjoyed an illustrious career as a general in Pharaoh's army. Incidentally, he married a woman of a Hyskos origin.
- Communication with extraterrestrials cannot be done through channeling. It is impossible!
- The United Stated government and scientists from Europe will discover new planets and extraterrestrial habitat before 2012.

Victoria's second letter. Summary of her letter

- The first creators of the human race: The Igigi
- The Igigi were great mineralogists
- The early 13 faculties of the quasi-human race
- The Anunnaki taught humans who to speak and how to write
- "Women of the Light": The early female-form on earth
- 46 different races of humans and quasi-humans populated the earth.
- Sumerians, Ashurians, Hyskos, and Phoenicians are the direct descendants of the Anunnaki
- Early remnants of the Anunnaki.
- The language of the Anunnaki is currently being used by American scientists and researchers who work in secret American-Aliens military bases
- Early remnants of the Anunnaki.

- The written language of the Anunnaki
- The differences between the Anunnaki, Nephilim, Elohim, Anakim, Zeta Reticulians and other extraterrestrials.

Freemasons, Illuminati, Trilateral Commission, military uniforms in secret underground bases, UFOs, and the Anunnaki-Zeta Reticuli symbol/insignia

The "Triangle" is also a negative force

Our human ancestors borrowed many words from extraterrestrial languages, and learned the secret 7 powerful names of God

Extraterrestrial lexicon is in use by military personnel in secret bases in the United States

Early names of the Hebrew God were of an extraterrestrial origin

Extraterrestrial families are the origin of the hybrids and extraterrestrial human beings living among us today

Sinharmarduchk's twin sister came all the way to earth to help me choose a dress

Additional revelations by Victoria

*** *** ***

VICTORIA AND HER ALIEN HUSBAND

Excerpts from the book: Revelations of an Anunnaki's Wife. Christianity, The White House, and Victoria's Hybrid Congressman Son

By Maximillien de Lafayette and Ilil Arbel

This story was recently sent to me in a letter. As soon as I opened it and read the first few lines, I knew this was extraordinary, and as I kept reading I realized it was explosive. I feel it is my duty to bring the knowledge it gives to everyone, and indeed the writer gave me permission to publish her story, as long as her privacy is maintained. Since I only know her as Victoria, which is not her real name, nor do I know her address, keeping this condition would not be difficult. Some of the readers may be shocked, others may feel elated, but no one who will read it will be able to ignore the facts and their interpretation. I am printing the letter as it was sent – no editing, no comment. Let Victoria speak for herself.

Victoria's first letter. Summary of her letter:

- Jesus did not die on the cross!
- Mary Magdalene and Jesus fled to Marseille, where they settled permanently and had children.
- The Quran did not descend on Mohammad from Heaven. Mohammad learned it from a Christian ascetic monk in the desert. This monk was known in the area as "Raheb Bouhayrah"
- Moses never left Egypt. Not only there had never been an Exodus of the Israelites, but Moses, who was a pure Egyptian, enjoyed an illustrious career as a general in Pharaoh's army. Incidentally, he married a woman of a Hyskos origin.
- Communication with extraterrestrials cannot be done through channeling. It is impossible!
- The United Stated government and scientists from Europe will discover new planets and extraterrestrial habitat before 2012.

Dear Mr. de Lafayette:

After much soul-searching, I have decided to write to you. Because of my unique experience, I have read many books about the Anunnaki, but your book, *The Anunnaki's Genetic Creation of the Human Race* was the one nearest the truth, and I appreciated its spirit of investigation and non-judgmental attitude. However, there is much in there which is incorrect. The wrong material was based on articles and statements of American Ufologists, and unfortunately, they lack the necessary knowledge. Allow me to give you an example.

Most of the people who claim to have met the aliens describe them as three to four feet tall, gray, and possessing big, dark, bug eyes. This is not the case. Some of the aliens do, indeed, answer to this description, but generally they do not, and often they look just like us since they are shape changers. When the alien appears to you, the first thing you notice is dusty light with tiny particles in it. Soon the particles begin to coagulate, to form a center, and suddenly you see the form of small baby. Then, an explosion-like phenomenon occurs, and the shape changes to a grown human, but it is deformed, as if still adjusting itself. For example, his back may overlap his neck, or part of his hips extends far from his body. That lasts a few minutes, and then the shape rearranges itself into a perfectly normal human.

You may wonder how I know, maybe even think I am being arrogant and unreasonable. But this is not so. My certainty is based upon my personal relationship with the Anunnaki, and particularly, with the one who is, to all intents and purposes, my husband, even if our marriage ceremony was non-traditional. I would also like to note that my alien husband does not object to my revelations. In fact, since the year 2012 is almost upon us (and I don't have to tell you the significance of this year) he feels the time has come to be more open about the relationship between humans and extraterrestrials.

The first time the alien appeared to me, many years ago, his eyes looked like glittering light. I could not take my own eyes off them, and could not move, as if I were hypnotized. Then, his eyes calmed down, became normal, and immediately I felt I could move again.

Another claim which I did not find to be true is that the aliens speak to us telepathically. It was nothing of the sort with me. The alien spoke, but that was even stranger than telepathy, because at first he sounded like an old record that was played at the wrong speed – fast, squeaky, scratching. Then the sound adjusted, and the voice became a normal human voice. A very pleasant human voice.

What really upsets me, though, is the idea that all aliens are out to rape, mutilate, and generally harm their abductees. This was not the case with me – exactly the opposite. I have never met such respect, such gentleness, such willingness to accommodate the other person, in any human being. Nor was I abducted in the sense that anything was done against my wishes.

True, I was asleep in my bed, and I woke up in a strange place, but as soon as I got out of my strange inability to move, and Sinharmarduchk adjusted his voice, he immediately reassured me I was a guest, that I could go home any minute I chose to, and that all he wanted was to tell me certain things he felt I should know. I could see no reason to object, seeing here was an opportunity to learn so much, and that no harm would come to me. Besides, Sinharmarduchk was so incredibly handsome and charming, I rather enjoyed his companionship and did not see any reason to cut my visit short. Therefore, I expressed my gratitude for the invitation, and was ready to listen.

The first thing Sinharmarduchk told me, after introducing himself, was indeed a shock. He informed me that I am a descendant of the Anunnaki! That I am really and truly one of them. While shocking, it made a strange sort of sense. You see, Mr. de Lafayette, I did not really know my birth parents. I was adopted in infancy by a wonderful couple who made excellent parents and loved me very much. I would have known I was adopted even if they had not told me, because here I was with olive skin, black hair, and dark brown eyes, while my parents, who came from England, were both blond. When I expressed a wish, as a teenager, to find out who my birth parents were, they tried to help, but we did not have much luck, so I gave up. All the information was locked up and unavailable.

Therefore, when my new alien friend informed me that my ancestry went back to the relationship between the early Anunnaki and the "daughters of man," I was shocked, but not for long. Apparently, I was born in Iraq, and my birth parents were Ashurians, who are Middle Eastern Christians, related to the Syriac, who still speak Aramaic among themselves. "Would you like to speak your own language?" asked Sinharmarduchk, smiling, his large, black, Anunnaki eyes full of humor.

"Of course," I said. "But it would probably take years to learn, right?"

"Wrong," said Sinharmarduchk. He looked into my eyes, and his own eyes started acting as before, with the hypnotic glittering light. I felt paralyzed again, but only for a few seconds. Then it stopped, I shook myself, and to my utter disbelief found myself talking and understanding a language that I have never heard before.

"Will I forget it as soon as I go home?" I asked.

"No, it is my gift to you. You can now read it, too." I was thrilled. From then on we always speak Aramaic between us.

Anyway, I have so much to tell you, Mr. de Lafayette, so possibly my own story is of less importance than the revelations and knowledge I acquired from Sinharmarduchk. The Anunnaki live for thousands of years, and their understanding of history is very deep. We, who live such short lives, make many historical mistakes, even when written records are available. Take, for instance, the issue of Jesus and the crucifixion. I was raised a Presbyterian, and my parents took me quite often to church. It had become a habit and I never questioned or even thought about the Crucifixion. Well, imagine my surprise when Sinharmarduchk told me that Jesus did not die on the cross! I hope I am not upsetting anyone, but the real story involves the existence of two tombs. Apparently, two disciples planned it all out with Jesus' mother and with his wife, Mary Magdalene. One of them gave Jesus a rag soaked in something that made him sleep.

Later in the day he was indeed stabbed with a spear, but not fatally, and at sunset the soldiers assumed he was dead and took him down. The two disciples that had arranged the matter wrapped him with a shroud, and took him to a faraway cave to hide him and help him recover, but then they took the bloody shroud and left it in the tomb everyone expected him to be in. He was never there, and in the morning, the other disciples, or anyone else interested in him, assumed he left the tomb and left the shroud there, thus giving rise to the story of the resurrection.

They took Jesus secretly to Phoenicia, where he fully recovered, then put him and his wife on a Phoenician boat that went to Cyprus. Eventually, they fled to Marseille, where they settled permanently and had children. Jesus worked in his profession, a handyman (he never really was a carpenter, this is a translation mistake), lived peacefully, and avoided all matters of religion for the rest of his life. His descendants lived in France, and perhaps some of them still exist, I really don't know.

"Does that story bother you?" asked Sinharmarduchk. "Not at all," I said. "I am no longer a religious person, and I would much rather know the truth than live in ignorance." Sinharmarduchk smiled with appreciation. Apparently he liked to see that I kept an open mind.

Also, another major revelation about other great religions such as Islam, Sinharmarduchk told me that the Koran, the holy book I really admire and respect, did not descend on Muhammad from Heaven, but he learned it from a Christian ascetic monk in the desert. This monk was known in the area as "Raheb Bouḥayrah" meaning, priest, or monk, of the lake. After all, Muhammad could not read and write, as is well known. He had to remember by heart what the priest told him on a weekly basis.

Also, I must tell you that Moses never left Egypt. Not only there had never been an Exodus of the Israelites, but Moses, who was a pure Egyptian, enjoyed an illustrious career as a general in Pharaoh's army. Incidentally, he married a woman of a Hyskos origin, connected to the royal house, whose name was Lady Nefert.

Probably you are not very religious, and will not pay attention to these details, but would you be interested to learn about very influential politicians from different countries, and belonging to different faiths, who manipulate the fate of humanity, and even very ordinary people, through an international organization headquartered in Europe? I am willing to give you their names, and a detailed description of their political and economical agenda. Please believe me, that you see them almost every day on television, where they fight each other verbally, when competing for a public office or an election. But as soon as this public charade, or masquerade, is over, they go to their secret meetings to decide the fate of nations.

"I have to tell you something personal," he said gently. "I think you are ready for it. Twelve years ago, we met for the first time. We fell in love." This did not exactly surprise me, since I found him extremely attractive, but I was at a loss to understand why I did not remember our previous meeting, and asked him about it.

"You would have remembered, but you have asked me to wipe out the memory – for a while, at least. You see… you were a very young girl, not yet in college. We were together for a while, and you became pregnant…You told me that you cannot as yet handle the burden, would rather, if possible, get on with your life…but you could not abandon the baby if you remembered him. I explained to you that this was, really, a very good decision. I had important plans for our son."

Well, the plans were astounding. Sinharmarduchk had a family in mind, a wonderful couple that he wished would adopt our son, belonging to a very powerful Washington dynasty. He wanted our son to be raised as a politician, to learn the ropes, and eventually become an important member of government. The couple he had in mind was also descendants of the Anunnaki, decent, intelligent, and longing for a child. To make a long story short, he manipulated their minds to believe that the woman had given birth to this infant, and rearranged the paperwork so that the birth certificate would say so. The lady actually came out of a hospital carrying the infant, accompanied by her proud husband, and the whole hospital crew also had their minds manipulated to believe the events. He took care to do the same with the couple's friends and relatives. Manipulating minds and events is something the Anunnaki can do very well.

"So where is the child now?" I asked Sinharmarduchk.

"He is going to school in Washington, doing very well. Our son will grow up to be a credit to us."

Now I understood my life so much better. This must be why I never married, why I even disliked dating. Deep in my brain I knew I was married to this wonderful, spiritual, kind individual, and anyone else would never do. I do not want to weary you with personal details, but of course Sinharmarduchk and I acknowledged our married state. We could not live together on a regular basis, since he had to spend much of his time on his home planet, Zeta Reticuli, and I could not follow him because my body would not withstand such a trip. My husband promised me a very long life, and most important, that as the years go by I will develop the necessary physical attributes that would allow me to visit his home planet, which indeed I have done a few times in the last thirty years. We had a daughter, which is very different in her interests from our son, who is now a senator. She is a linguist, and the number of languages she speaks is astounding. I am very proud of her.

*** *** ***

I am now sixty years old, but of course age mean nothing to anyone who is married to an Anunnaki. I look considerably younger, and my husband, who knows so much, promises me that not only I shall live a very long life, but that death itself does not exist. When we die we move on to another dimension, giving up our earthly bodies, and where we go is very much influenced by our thoughts and desires. As my husband promised me, I shall live until he is ready to move on, and then we can spend eternity together. So there is nothing to be afraid of, ever.

There is so much more to tell, but this letter is so long already, I am afraid you will put it aside and refuse to read more. I do hope I have given you something to think about, and perhaps, if you like, we can correspond. It is up to you – I will be happy to be the conduit through which the Anunnaki speaks with humanity.

Mr. de Lafayette, I know you are a very scientific person, and because you have practiced law, as I have found out, you want facts, not fiction. Don't ever believe or let your readers believe that communication with extraterrestrials can be done through channelling, as many people pretend. This is impossible, because they are in different worlds and your thoughts and state of trance could not reach them through certain frequencies. The human thoughts, even though they emanate frequencies and vibes like electrical and radio emissions, they do stop at the end of the solar system, and the mind transmission cannot go beyond that limit. Extraterrestrial have not and would not communicate telepathically. If you show interest in my letter, I will show you step by step, detail by detail, how communication can be done with an extraterrestrial, as my alien husband taught me. They can teach you their language, written and spoken. Why would anyone want to talk telepathically, when they can converse in the extraterrestrial language? So people who pretend to telepathic communication are speaking nonsense. I can stay in constant contact with you to tell you where the Anunnaki descendants live, in what countries, in what cities, and how to recognize them. Also, I might mention that they do come not only from Zeta Reticuli, but from several other planets, as the United Stated government and scientists from Europe will discover before 2012.

Sincerely
Victoria

*** *** ***

Naturally, I agreed to correspond with Victoria. She is, as you can see from this letter, an extraordinary woman with much to tell us. I shall never meet her – her desire for anonymity is too strong – but I have persuaded her to collaborate on a book, based on our correspondence and telephone calls. The book will include so much more information, of course, and will touch on subjects that I believe will be of interest to anyone with an open mind. I can promise you more revelations about world's religions, politics, government conspiracies, the afterlife, spirituality, and history that may seem revised – but is really the truth. And this is just the tip of the iceberg – the book will change your life. I sincerely believe that the chosen title of the forthcoming book "Revelation of an Anunnaki's Wife: Christianity, The White House, and Victoria's Hybrid Congressman Son" is very *a propos*.

Although, I do not agree or disagree with Victoria's statement about the Prophet Mohammad, the origin of the Quran, Jesus' Crucifixion and his marriage to Mary Magdalene, Moses and the Israelites' Exodus, simply because I do NOT know, I found her revelations quite fascinating.

*** *** ***

Victoria's second letter

Summary of her letter:

- The first creators of the human race: The Igigi
- The Igigi were great mineralogists
- The early 13 faculties of the quasi-human race
- The Anunnaki taught humans who to speak and how to write
- "Women of the Light": The early female-form on earth
- 46 different races of humans and quasi-humans populated the earth.
- Sumerians, Ashurians (Assyrians), Hyskos, and Phoenicians are the direct descendants of the Anunnaki
- Early remnants of the Anunnaki.
- The language of the Anunnaki
- The lower class of the Anunnaki are the Nephilim
- The Freemasons' and Illuminati's favorite symbol is the Anunnaki's eye
- Phoenicia borrowed her Alphabet from the Anunnaki
- The 7 positive and powerful names/attributes of the Anunnaki's grand leader.
- American top military scientists working in secret bases use an extraterrestrial lexicon
- Baalshalimroot-An'kgh is the Anunnaki's greatest leader
- Some Anunnaki are 9 feet and could live as long as 400,000 years

The following material is the second letter I received from Victoria. Again, it is in her own words and I will not attempt to change, edit, or even form judgment.

Dear Mr. de Lafayette:

Since you have so kindly shown an interest in my story, I am writing to you again, and this time I plan to give you much more elaborate information. Therefore, I think it may be advisable to separate the material under explanatory titles. This way we will avoid confusion, and present the information in manageable sizes.

The first creators of the human race: The Igigi

The Anunnaki were not the first to experiment with and on humans. Some 145,000 years ago, a different race called the Igigihl or Igigi, were the first extraterrestrials to create quasi-human specimens. At the very beginning of their genetic experiments, the results were catastrophic.

Their creations looked awful – bestial, very ugly, even frightening. This may have happened because the Igigi were more terrestrial explorers than geneticists, and therefore more interested in certain molecules found in terrestrial water, and in various minerals, than in creating a perfectly shaped human race.

The Igigi did co-exist with the Anunnaki, and shared some traits with them, but they were totally dissimilar in their physical shape, and had different intentions as far as the human race was concerned. The Igigi were 245 million years older than the Anunnaki.

At one point in time, they were ferocious toward the early quasi-human beings, treating them very badly, since they considered the early version of human beings on earth as a lower working class without intelligence. Incidentally, the earth was extremely cold and the Igigihl had to cover the human bodies with lots of hair to protect them from the elements. It took the quasi-human race thousands of years to evolve into an early human form, and even then not totally human, but looking like apes. Some of them had bizarre skulls and facial bones. My husband told me that the history and theories of human creation and evolution are distorted by both theologians and scientists.

The Igigi were great mineralogists

The Igigi were highly advanced in mineralogy and minerals transmutation. The Anunnaki were geneticists and engineers with an strong appreciation for esthetics. Therefore, the Igigi created a very primitive form of living beings on earth, exactly as we, the humans, created very unappealing early forms and shapes of robots and related mechanical devices at the dawn of robotics. These robots were functional but not pretty to look at, and the early quasi-humans were not much more than machines with limited mental faculties.

The early thirteen faculties of the quasi-human race

In the genes, molecules and DNA of the early quasi-human race, the Igigi programmed thirteen faculties, or functions. The most important abilities were as follows:

1. move
2. sense danger
3. understand by association
4. memorize
5. see forms and shapes in four colors. These colors were bright yellow, representing gold; grey, representing minerals and rocks; blue, representing the atmosphere, air, and water; and a very strong red, representing heat and blood. Other colors such as green, purple, lilac, etc, were not visible or known to the early and primitive form of quasi-humans.

The Anunnaki taught humans how to speak and how to write

The first genetically created race could not speak, and the concept of Language was completely unknown to them. Thousands of years later, the Anunnaki taught the newly race of humans how to speak, read, and write. The Anunnaki's first genetically created human race was the seed of humanity as we know it; they were the ancestors of modern humans, beginning to populate the earth 25,000 years before the construction of the great pyramids. I am only citing the pyramids as a landmark in human history to give you a chronological perspective. Greater, taller and bigger monuments were erected centuries before the construction of the pyramids, and some ruins can still be found in Phoenicia (Modern Lebanon today) particularily in Baalbeck, and in Mesopotamia (Modern Iraq today).

"Women of the Light": The early female-form on earth

Contrary to all beliefs, including what Judaism, Christianity and Islam teach us, Eve was not created from the rib of Adam. Men were created from an early female form that was "fertilized" by the leaders and the elite of the Anunnaki. They lived in quarantine cities, and had both sons and daughters fathered by the Anunnaki.

Some of the most puzzling sites of these cities, due to their size and functionality, were in Ur, Amrit, Ougarit, Petra (Batra), Tyre and Sidon. Early humans who lived during that era called the quarantined city of these women "The City of Mirage", and "The City of Beautiful Illusion," since the most attractive women from earth lived there. And the quasi-humans who were made out of earth were *not* allowed to interact with these women.

Thousands of years later, the inhabitants of what is today the Arab Peninsula and the lands bordering Persia, the United Arab Emirates, and India, called these women "The Women of Light", and those who were allowed to "mix with them" were called "The Sons of Light". From this early human race, all humans came to life. God had nothing to do with us. In other words, the God we know, revere, and fear today did not create us. Even the word or term "God" did not exist in the early stages of the existence of the human race on earth. Instead "Gods" or "Heavenly Masters" were used. And thousands of years later, those terms were changed to "Giants," "Elohim," "Nephilim," "Anakim," "Fallen Angels," you name it...

46 different races of humans and quasi-humans populated the earth.

Some 300,000 years before the creation of the cities of "The Women of Lights," forty-six different races of humans and quasi-humans populated the earth. The greatest numbers were found in Africa, Madagascar, Indonesia, Brazil, and Australia. These races died out not because of famine, ecological catastrophes, or acts of war, but because of the disintegration of the very molecules and composition of their cells. The Anunnaki created the "final form" of human beings, and we, all the ordinary and normal people, are their descendents.

Sumerians, Ashurians (Assyrians), Hyskos, and Phoenicians are the direct descendants of the Anunnaki

Eusebius, the Bishop of Cæsarea, Palestine, had genealogical records of the descendants of the Anunnaki who became Syriac. At the Council of Antioch in 363 A.D., Bishop Eusebius intended to bring this subject in his "Theophania" to the attention of the members of the Council. But for obvious reasons, no additional information or manuscripts about what happened at the Council were provided.

In the Syriac manuscripts of Zachariah of Mitylene, who frequently corresponded with Eupraxius, two references were made to the Anunnaki as the ancestors of the Ashurian-Syriac. Another bishop by the name of Proterius tried to destroy these letters. Fortunately, two hand-written copies were made, as the tradition of this era dictated, and were saved in the vault of a scribe.

Those letters resurfaced in 1957 in a personal acquisition of Cardinal Maouchi, the Patriarch of the Maronite Church in Lebanon. After of Maouchi's death, those files were kept in the secret vaults of Al-Kaslik Monastery in Lebanon.

The language of the Anunnaki is currently being used by American scientists and researchers who work in secret American-Aliens military bases

The original language of the Anunnaki is still intact and is currently being used by top American scientists and researchers who work in secret American-Aliens military bases in the United States and Mexico.

In 1947, the first attempt was made by American linguists, who previously worked at the OSS (Precursor to the CIA), to decipher it. They tried to compare it with the Sumerian, Hebrew, Armenian and Phoenician Alphabet, languages which are directly derived from the Anunnaki's written language.

The problem they faced and could not resolve were the geometrical symbols included in the written Anunnaki's texts. But in 1956, they cracked down the puzzle. Those mathematical figures hold great secrets regarding an alien advanced technology used for peaceful and constructive purposes. The American military intelligence and what's left from Dr. Fermi's group at Los Alamos wanted to use this alien technology for military purposes.

Early remnants of the Anunnaki.

The earliest among the final terrestrial human race were the Phoenicians, the Hyskos, the Philistines, the very early Etruscans, the earliest Druids, Minoan, people of Mu, and the first inhabitants of Sumeria.

Later on, the Ashuryans resided among the last remnants of the Anunnaki who visited earth and lived there for 600 more years.

After that, the Anunnaki left earth for good, never to return again, except as visitors. One of the reasons for their departure was the discovery of the "tree of life", also known as "The Tree of Knowledge" by humans – a metaphor for the acquisition of knowledge and understanding by the human race, on its own. The acquisition of this supreme knowledge caused the humans to rebel against the Anunnaki.

The written language of the Anunnaki

The Anunnaki have two kinds or styles of languages; one is spoken and the other one is written. The spoken language is the easiest one to learn, and it is used by the Anunnaki's population. The written one is exclusively used in books and consists of twenty-six letters. Seven of these letters represent the planets that surround their star. Many of the Anunnaki's letters cannot be pronounced by Westerners because of the limitation of their vocal chords.

There are seven additional letters that are complete words, and these words represent the attributes of their "Grand Leader." Translated into terrestrial language, the grand leader becomes the creator of energy, in other words, "God."

However, the Anunnaki do not believe in a God in the same sense we do, even though they were the ones who created and originated the early forms of religions on earth.

The god they brought to earth is a vengeful and terrifying god, something that the Gnostics and early scholars of the Coptic Church in Egypt were fully aware of. Their doctrines show their disdain for such a god, and consequently, they called him the "Creator of Evil and Darkness."

Later on in history, the early Gnostics began to spread the word that this earth was not created by the God of the Church, but rather by ab evil demi-god. The early human beings who interacted with the Anunnaki shared similar beliefs.

But they were mistaken, and were intentionally mislead by a lower class of the Anunnaki who hated other extraterrestrials who visited the earth, and particularly by the Igigi who treated humans like slaves and robotic machines.

The differences between the Anunnaki, Nephilim, Elohim, Anakim, Zeta Reticulians and other extraterrestrials.

Scholars like Sitchin and Gardner have equated the Anunnaki with the Nephilim. This is not totally correct. The lower class of the Anunnaki are the Nephilim, although many historians call them sometimes Anakim or Elohim.

The higher class of the Anunnaki is ruled by Baalshalimroot, and his followers or subjects are called the "Shtaroout-Hxall Ain", meaning the inhabitants of the house of knowledge, or "those who see clearly."

The word "Ain" was later adopted by the early inhabitants of the Arab Peninsula. "Ain" in Arabic means "eye".

In the secret teachings of Sufism, visions of Al Hallaj, and of the greatest poetess of Sufism, Rabiha' Al Adawi Yah, known as "Ha Chi katou Al Houbb Al Ilahi" (The mistress of the divine love), and in the banned book *Shams Al Maa'Ref Al Kubrah* (Book of the Sun of the Great Knowledge), the word "eye" meant the ultimate knowledge, or wisdom from above.

"Above" clearly indicates the heavens. Later on, it was used to symbolize the justice of God or "God watching over us." And much later in history, several societies and cultures adopted the "eye" as an institutional symbol and caused it to appear on many temples' pillars, bank notes, money bills, and religious texts.

Freemasons, Illuminati, Trilateral Commission, military uniforms in secret underground bases, UFOs, and the Anunnaki-Zeta Reticuli symbol/insignia

The Freemasons' and Illuminati's favorite symbol is the Anunnaki's eye. And as everything changes in life and takes on different forms and meanings, the "eye" became a "triangle," a very secretive and powerful symbol. George Washington carried this triangle with him wherever he went, and wore it during official ceremonies. If you double and reverse the triangle, you get the Star of David. This very triangle is visible on many extraterrestrial spacecrafts, and on uniforms of military personnel in secret American military bases underground, working on alien technology and propulsion systems.

The powerful Trilateral Commission was founded by David Rockefeller, the Chairman of the Chase Manhattan Bank of New York, in July 1973. It is recorded that in their first board meeting, Rockefeller proposed to adopt the Anunnaki's triangle as the official symbol/logo of this world organization.

According to an official statement issued by the Commission, the principal and official aim of the Trilateral Commission is "to harmonize the political, economic, social, and cultural relations between the three major economic regions in the world." The Commission divided the world into a triangle joining three regions consisting of the Far East, Europe, and North America, all within the perimeter of a triangle.

Basically, the Trilateral Commission aims at controlling the world under the auspices of a centralized American power-group consisting of bankers, financiers, selected political leaders, top military echelon and members of the cabinet from each administration. On February 17, 1953, an American millionaire by the name of Paul Warburg shouted before the Senate of the United States of America: "We shall have world government whether or not you like it, by conquest or consent."

Many members of the Trilateral Commission are descendants of a lower class of an extraterrestrial race. Some passed away, but many of them still live among us. It is impossible for ordinary people to recognize them.

But the good and decent descendants of our extraterrestrial teachers can identify them very easily. In future letters, I will give you their names and explain their plans.

The "Triangle" is also a negative force

When integrated without balance and cosmic harmony (spatial equilibrium) in architectural design and lining up territories, the triangle becomes a negative force on the map. My husband told me that if the three sides of the triangle are separated, such separation can cause serious health problems. The triangle becomes three lines of negative energy.

This energy is not easily detected; nevertheless it runs strong and deep underground. People who live above these lines suffer enormously. In many instances, this negative power or current can negatively affect the present and future of many human beings.

Similar to some Ufologists who can identify UFOs' hot spots on earth, usually above ground, descendants of the extraterrestrials can identify and locate the negative currents underground. Each country has these negative currents or circuits underground. I do not wish to scare you, but I must inform you that some American states are located above these lines; for example, Mississippi, Alabama, the northern part of Washington, DC, and two areas in Brooklyn, New York share this misfortune.

Our human ancestors borrowed many words from extraterrestrial languages, and learned the secret 7 powerful names of God

Many of the Phoenician linguists and early creators of their Alphabet borrowed numerous words and expressions from the higher class of the Anunnaki. Ancient Phoenician texts and poems, recorded on tablets found in Tyre and Sidon, included reference to symbols and words taken from the written language of the upper class of the Anunnaki. Members of an early Anunnaki expedition to Phoenicia taught the Phoenicians how to create their language, and revealed to them the secret powerful names and attributes of Baalshalimroot.

They instructed them not to use these words for ill purposes. Particularly, the word "Baalazamhour-Il" is never to be said, spelled, or written. Later on in history, the Hebrews religiously observed this instruction, and pronouncing the word of name of God became forbidden.

However, the Anunnaki revealed to the Phoenicians and Sumerians seven positive and powerful names/attributes of the Grand Leader. If well used, these words can bring prosperity, good health, and salvation in moments of difficulty. The prophet Mohammad learned these seven words from an early Christian ascetic, a Sahara hermit called Raheb Bouhayra.

Today, Muslims all over the world are aware of these seven words or names. They call them in written Arabic "Asma' Al Lah Al Sabha' Al Housna," meaning the seven lovely names of God.

Those names do not have numerical value or secret meanings as many scholars claim, simply because they were not originally written in a geometrical form.

None of these words appeared in the so-called hieroglyphic measuring tape that the Americans found at the crash site in Roswell. The symbols and geometrical signs Americans found in Roswell were biochemical symbols.

Extraterrestrial lexicon is in use by military personnel in secret bases in the United States

The American top military scientists who work in secret military bases and aliens' laboratories on earth have an extraterrestrial lexicon, and use it constantly.

In that lexicon, or dictionary, you will find variations of Phoenician and Sumerian symbols. Some letters represent maritime and celestial symbols and measurements.

The fact that the Americans are still using this extraterrestrial language should be enough to convince you that extraterrestrials, Anunnaki and Zeta Reticuli descendants, live among us, otherwise why would anyone learn a language that cannot used to communicate with people who speak it and write it?

On some of the manifestos of military parts used in anti-gravity secret laboratories underground in the United States, several letters were borrowed from the "Enuma Elish" of Sumeria and regularly appeared on the top right corner of each document. In the eighties, those Sumerian numbers were replaced by an Americanized version.

Early names of the Hebrew God were of an extraterrestrial origin

It is true that the Sumerian ancient texts and records mentioned names of some of the Anunnaki leaders such as Utu, Ningishzida, Ninki, Marduk, Enki, Enlil, Inanna, but the greatest name of all remains Baalshalimroot, also referred to as "Baalshalimroot-An'kgh." Terah, the father of Abraham, mistakenly worshiped Baalshalimroot-An'kgh.

Early Semites made the same mistake when they worshiped the leaders of the Anunnaki as gods who later became Bene Ha-Elohim, meaning the children of gods. The Anunnaki never introduced themselves as gods.

The words: El Elyon and Yahweh or Jehovah were taken directly from the Anunnaki's written language. The original word was "Yah'weh-El' Ankh" and El Elyon was "Il Ilayon-imroot."

Extraterrestrial families are the origin of the hybrids and extraterrestrial human beings living among us today

The Early Anunnaki who visited earth were extremely tall. Some reached the height of 9 feet, and lived as long as 400,000 years. These Anunnaki did not leave descendants on earth.

Those who came to earth much later, before the regional deluge, and right after that huge Tsunami, left families behind them when they returned home. By home, I mean Nibiru, Zeta Reticuli and Ashartartun-ra.

These families are the origin of the hybrids and extraterrestrial human beings living today among us. It is very important to learn and remember this.

Another important detail, contrary to what many believe that only greys or reptilians live on Zeta Reticuli, the Anunnaki had also occupied vast territories on Zeta Reticuli, and by now you know that they are not the greys or reptilians, as wrongly described in Ufology literature.

Mr. de Lafayette, even though I have given you quite a bit of scientific and historical data, I don't want you to think that this is all I have to say. My relationship with the Anunnaki is personal, loving, and involving family and friends. This book is really about the fact that we must seek similarities and affiliations between sentient beings, rather than always harp on the differences.

My dear sister-in-law, Sinharmarduchk's twin sister, came all the way to earth to help me choose a dress

I want to tell you so much more – I want the world to know about my dear sister-in-law, Sinharmarduchk's twin sister, who came all the way to earth to help me choose a dress for my wedding, and became my closest friend.

I want to tell you all about the guests who came to our wedding – and what a list that was…I want you to know about my nieces and nephews and the other lovely Anunnaki children I met on my own trips to Zeta Reticuli.

We had hours of fun as the children demonstrated their shape-changing talents to me, assuming what they thought would be such frightening or amusing personalities.

So I venture to hope that this is just the beginning of a most profitable and pleasant correspondence, even friendship, even though we can never meet in person.

All the best,
Victoria

*** *** ***

Additional Revelations by Victoria

Victoria is not a magician, a channeler, a medium, a trance expert, an Ufologist, an abductee, a contactee on earth, a regression hypnotherapist, a Roswell fan, a wacko, or a UFO's hunter. She does not lecture on these subjects, nor sell extraterrestrial and flying saucers' gizmos, gadgets, toys and T-Shirts. She has never made a penny selling UFO's stories. She will never appear on TV and radio talk shows, nor does she give interviews. She does not have a website, and she does not respond to inquiries or engage in forum about extraterrestrials. She never sought fame or fortune from all this! And you will never know about her true name and identity.

Would these facts be enough to take her revelations and words into consideration? Absolutely!

Then, let's listen to Victoria. Maybe we can learn something new or remarkably revealing not readily available in best selling books, silly alien abduction stories, and unrealistic theories. Here are the most important revelations in Victoria's own words, and as directly communicated to me. No! Not through channeling, but via letters, regular mail and telephone calls.

Publishers' Note: The life and biography of Victoria are written in-depth in "Revelation by an Anunnaki Wife: Christianity, The White House, and Victoria's Hybrid Congressman Son", authored by Maximillien de Lafayette and Ilil Arbel. Published by Times Square Press and Amon.com Publishing Company. The book is already written. The authors are still waiting for Victoria's revision. The book shall be made available to the general public by mid March 2008. Check with www.amazon.com

Some of Victoria's Revelations:

1- All our spoken languages derived directly from extraterrestrial languages.

2- Many of the spaceships we see in our skies were constructed 1,000 years in our future. Victoria never used the term UFOs

3- Many of the spaceships we see in our skies were here on earth thousands of years before the human race existed on earth.

4- The greater number of spaceships come from underwater; straight from seas and oceans.

5- The Anunnaki created the priesthood system and hierarchy on earth.

6- Two different extraterrestrial races created us; the Igigi and the Anunnaki.

7- Humans coined the term "God." The early human race created the idea and concept of "God." And later on, priests and so-called prophets propagated the idea.

8- The Pleiadians created the Atlanteans and taught them very advanced technology and science. Later on the Lyrians visited Atlantis and Lumeria and befriended the Atlanteans and Lumerians.

9- Humans cannot contact extraterrestrial using their current technology and their rudimentary tools and devices, including the most advanced ones. They need to learn more about time and how space changes beyond the solar system. However, very few scientists on earth succeeded in contacting extraterrestrials, only because extraterrestrials who visited earth taught them how to do so. The learning process began in 1947.

10- Even if humans could land on planets inhabited by extraterrestrials, they would not be able to understand what they see and what they hear. Because space and time exist simultaneously at different vibrational levels. The human mind is not equipped nor programmed to fully understand the multiple dimensions of these planets. These dimensions cannot be clearly explained or understood in terrestrial terms.

11- Extraterrestrials do NOT hang out in the woods, get lost in the desert, or hide behind rocks as many humans claimed. Those claims are ridiculous.

12- Extraterrestrials are equipped with a very sophisticated communication device they always carry with them wherever they travel. There is no way or any possibility that extraterrestrials would get lost on earth or become disoriented as many witnesses and contactees claim. The device is small, and the size-shape are interchangeable. It has multiple functions and a very wide range of capabilities. It sends and receives beams and coded messages. It also functions as a spatial and inter-planetary navigation tool. If intentionally directed toward a human, the device releases a beam capable of paralyzing any living creature.

13- Upon encountering humans, extraterrestrials do NOT pronounce one word and walk away as some contactees reported. When they contact or encounter a human being, they usually complete sentences and engage into a dialogue, even though - sometimes – the dialogue is short and their request is firm.

14- Extraterrestrial spaceships rarely crash. If damaged, they are repaired INSTANTLY if accompanied by a mother-spaceship, or are in the company of a formation. Singular extraterrestrial craft could crash. This occurs when the craft is traveling "alone." The truth is that many extraterrestrial spaceships constantly travel our skies without being noticed by humans, because they are surrounded by an "invisibility shield." Consequently, they remain undetected. This "inivisibility shield" prevents the spacecraft from crashing. The shield could malfunction for numerous reasons, including electro-magnetic discharges, and anti-gravity protection failure. This happens ONLY in our solar system.

15- Extraterrestrials are capable of speaking and understanding many languages, including our own. They assimilate and "compute" words and sentences with mathematical formulas and numerical values. Some extraterrestrials have limited vocal chords capabilities, but they can very quickly acquire additional vocal faculties by rewinding sounds and vibes. Contrary to what many contactees and others said, extraterrestrials from higher dimensions do not talk like computerized machines. They have their own language but also they can absorb and assimilate all the languages on earth in a blink of an eye via the reception and emission of a "spatial memory."

16- Extraterrestrials do NOT ask for human help to repair their damaged ships. Always a large mother-ship accompanies their spacecrafts for full technical support. The mother-ship is usually very big and enormously spacious. One of its main characteristics is "housing" a large number of spacecrafts. So-called damaged spaceships are repaired in hangars located inside the mother-ship, usually found at the lower level of the interior of the mother space-ship. Consequently, so-called damaged spaceships do not need to land on earth to be repaired.

17- Extraterrestrials are capable of speaking and understanding many languages, including our own. They assimilate and "compute" words and sentences with mathematical formulas and numerical values. Some extraterrestrials have limited vocal chords capabilities, but they can very quickly acquire additional vocal faculties by rewinding sounds and vibes. Contrary to what many contactees and others said, extraterrestrials from higher dimensions do not talk like computerized machines. They have their own language but also they can absorb and assimilate all the languages on earth in a blink of an eye via the reception and emission of a "spatial memory."

18- Extraterrestrial damaged ships are never repaired manually on earth. Usually, aliens' spacecrafts are self-repaired above ground while flying. A damaged spaceship is never visible to the human eye. And if this incident occurs, the spaceship releases a substance from a section under its "belly". This substance is quickly coagulated as soon as it touched the surface of the earth. And in no time, it disintegrates, leaving no trace. It is important and very useful to remember that extraterrestrial spaceships do NOT fly as wrongly and mistakenly described by humans; they "jump", so to speak for lack of proper terms. They reach destinations by traveling through "aerial lines and curves" incomprehensible to humans. They belong to an infinite time, rather to a limited space. And when they appear in our skies, they adopt a zigzagging pattern for sharp turns and for speed acceleration. If they want to stand still, they hover "motionless" and in complete silence.

19- Extraterrestrial spaceships do NOT use engines, propulsion systems or fuel. Almost all of them use two "devices": 1-An antigravity module for traveling inside the solar system and for landing. 2-A space/time apparatus for galactic travel. The human mind can not understand how these two "devices" work. Therefore, humans can NOT reverse the engineering of extraterrestrial crafts, unless taught by extraterrestrials in person. In addition, humans need very advanced repair tools, material and spare parts found only outside the solar system. Therefore, no scientist on earth has ever succeeded in deciphering and learning how to fly or repair an extraterrestrial scapeship.

20- Extraterrestrial spaceships dot NOT use engines, propulsion systems, or fuel. Almost all of them use two "devices": 1-An antigravity module for traveling inside the solar system and for landing. 2-A space/time apparatus for galactic travel. The human mind can not understand how these two "devices" work. Therefore, humans CAN NOT reverse the engineering of extraterrestrial crafts, unless taught by extraterrestrials in person. In addition, humans need very advanced repair tools, material, charts and spare parts found only outside the solar system. Therefore, no man, no scientist on earth has ever succeeded in deciphering and learning how to fly or repair an extraterrestrial scapeship.

21- Many of the extraterrestrial spaceships we see in our skies come from our future. The word "future" is used because this is the only word found in human vocabularies that can be used to interpret and describe the appearance or manifestation of an extraterrestrial spaceship. The humans call them "spaceship." In fact, they are "timeships." Outside the solar system, time and space are not found or defined separately. In fact, there is no time, and there is no "physically limited" space in the outer galaxy. The human mind is incapable of understanding this, yet! In the future (human/terrestrial interpretation), scientists on earth will eventually figure it out.

22- The Creation is made out of millions of dimensions, parallel universes, future universes, humans with multiple doubles sharing an infinite space.

23- The extraterrestrial "Nordic" race descended on Phoenicia. They settled for 600 years in the regions of Byblos, Sidon, Tyre, Batroun, Afka, Anjar and Baalbeck. The early Phoenicians were the descendants and remnants of extraterrestrials. The Lyrians and Anunnaki also lived in Phoenicia named the land "Loubnan." Later, the early Israelites, the tribes that lived in Palestine, before the arrival of the Hebrews, and the Accadians in Iraq, Syria, and Northern Jordan began to use the word "Loubnan" which means in their languages "White."

24- The extraterrestrials called the land "Loubnan" because of the striking snowy mountains of Phoenicia. For centuries, humans considered the Phoenicians to be a Semite people. They were not Semite. They were taller than their neighbors. They had white skin, blue eyes and blond hair. You can still find these physical traits on the figurines and statues of their kings, queens and gods in archeological sites and museums around the world. The Anunnaki came much much later. The early Lyrians were there first. But the Anunnaki were the extraterrestrials who taught the Phoenicians many secrets about the sea and how to sail the high oceans. The Phoenicians received their first Alphabet from the Anunnaki. The first version contained two parts. Part one had 28 letters divided into 4 categories, and each category had 7 letters. The letters in these categories were used in arts and literature. Part two had 23 letters, 56 measures and 7 numerical values; they were used in alchemy, metals transmutation, architecture and maritime sciences. This helped them to draw and understand maps. Some of these maps represented the global surface of Earth (lands and waters.) This was an amazing accomplishment for humanity, because these lands and waters could be seen ONLY from the sky. Another great gift bestowed by the Anunnaki were the hexagram, the square and the compass; essential tools for masonry and architecture. This constituted the masonry secret of the Phoenicians. The descendants of the early Phoenicians inherited these treasures and knowledge and revered them as celestial symbols. They created secret orders and fraternities to preserve and protect these secrets. One of the most recognizable one is the "Hiram Brotherhood", also known as the world first Freemason Rite. Hiram, the Phoenician king created the world first Freemason Lodge, and King Solomon was second in command. The Anunnaki's square and compass became the symbol of the Phoenician Free-Masonry. King Solomon married one of the daughters of king Hiram. And the first structured social-military alliance was formed in the region: The alliance of Hiram and Solomon. The Phoenicians of Tyre and Sidon built the temple of Solomon using the tools given to them by the Anunnaki and which they have inherited from their ancestors who learned science, technology, arts, language and architecture from the Anunnaki. The Anunnaki did not stay long in Phoenicia. In fact, the Anunnaki did not stay very long in the Middle and Near East; the land of Iraq, Syria, Jordan, Palestine and Lebanon. They were disappointed by the demeaning behavior, greed, violence, ingratitude, lust for power of humans, and left earth for good. Today, Freemasons have adopted the Anunnaki-Phoenician square and compass as their symbol.

*** *** ***

REVELATIONS OF AN ANUNNAKI'S WIFE
Christianity, The White house, and Victoria's Hybrid Congressman Son

---

Note: This is the book I wrote with Ilil Arbel, Ph.D. about Victoria. It is her autobiography. It is her life story, relationship/marriage with an Anunnaki, her hybrid congressman son whom she predicted one day will become the president of a powerful country, description of her alien in-laws, the planet of her alien husband, and her revelations. It is Victoria on Victoria and her alien husband in her own words. The book shall be made available by March 20008.

Chapter 1 Of The Book

February 1965, Maine

At this time of year darkness fell early, and the roads were not busy on that extremely cold night. I was enjoying the drive despite the snowy and slippery conditions because I was so young, and just having a car was a novelty and an adventure. I was going home after an afternoon's study at a good friend's house. We planned to prepare for our high school finals, but we were so excited about the prospect of college, that we could barely concentrate. Both of us applied to the archaeology/anthropology department of a well-known New York university, and were so thrilled with the fact that our parents would allow us to spend four years on our own in the huge and exciting city. As I cautiously wound my way, I was dreaming about myself in New York, wearing sophisticated clothes and drinking coffee at some marvelous little places, when I noticed that a large vehicle, possibly a lorry, was blocking the road at a little distance. I could not make it out clearly, so I drove carefully until I was about fifteen feet or so behind it. I was considering going to the vehicle to see if the driver needed help, when I suddenly noticed a bright, yellow shaft of light moving from the vehicle toward me. It was a dusty sort of light, with particles moving in it at a random motion, much like a sunbeam through a window on a summer afternoon, but brighter and highly visible against the dark evening. I stared at the light, trying to figure out what it could possibly be, until it stopped just in front of my car. The little particles stopped moving in their crazy random way, and instead, started to coagulate, moving toward the center in a rather orderly way. Mesmerized by the movement, I cannot tell how long it took, but I think only a few minutes. The particles at the center formed a globe, while the rest of the shaft of light was clean and empty of particles.

Then, a sudden visual but silent explosion took place in the center – there is really no other way to describe the phenomenon – as if the center exploded into fireworks. Then, the fireworks rearranged themselves into the shape of a baby!

Suddenly I was afraid. Before I saw the baby form, it could have been a natural phenomenon of some sort, but when this shape took place, no reasonable explanation existed. I looked at it, not knowing what to do and feeling trapped, since I could not drive away and escape. Then, the baby form started growing. It expanded, changed, filled out the shaft, and seemed to be a grown-up man. But the man was deformed. Part of his back overlapped his neck, his hips jutted away from his body, and the face was blurred. My heart was beating so quickly that I felt it would explode, too. The fear almost paralyzed me, and then everything became even worse. The man rearranged himself and became normal, and stepped out of the shaft of light. The shaft remained where it was, waving gently and illuminating the man. He waved at me, in a friendly and normal fashion, and moved toward my car, but I still could not see his face since the light was behind him. Realizing it, the man waved his hand in a circular motion, the shaft of light moved to his side, illuminating the most handsome face I had ever seen.

However, the eyes in that perfect face were not normal. They seemed to glitter, so brightly that I was not able to make out their color. I could not take my own eyes off them, as if hypnotized, and was not able to move at all, as if my limbs were made of iron. Then the glitter died down, and I could see that his eyes were very dark, almost black in the golden light, and very large, much like my own. As a matter of fact, the man's olive skin and black hair were exactly like mine.

"I hope I have not frightened you, Victoria," he said. Kind words, but I did not even notice that he knew my name, because his voice was so horribly alarming. It was much like one of those old records you played on an old-fashioned turntable – if you put it on the wrong speed, it became fast, squeaky, and scratchy, very unpleasant. He stopped, made some elaborate movements with his hands, and spoke again, this time with a very pleasant, normal human voice. "I am sorry. I am out of practice, and these changes and adaptations of my normal form into human shape and sound can be tricky."

I found my voice. "Human shape and sound? Who are you? What are you? And what do you want of me? Yes, you scared me a lot – I should think you could have changed before I came and then stopped me in a simpler way, rather than do this dramatic appearance, like a grade B horror movie?" I was infuriated, but astonishingly, no longer terrified. At the time, I could not understand why I was not paralyzed with terror. Now, of course, I know that part of my mind was willing to accept it, which makes sense in the light of the events that followed, and the secrets that were told. But also, let's face it, perhaps I was also influenced by the mysterious stranger's great looks... teenage girls *can* be silly about very handsome men.

The stranger laughed at my defiant words, but rather kindly, not at all in a mocking way. Later, he confessed that he was quite relieved that I was annoyed rather than horrified to a point of fainting or shrieking helplessly. "You are right. I should have thought about a nicer way to meet you.

I apologize...Anyway, to answer your very reasonable questions, my name is Sinharmarduchk and I am an Anunnaki. I come from Zeta Reticuli."

Anunnaki. I have heard this word before, in school, something from ancient history. I did not remember too well. Zeta Reticuli could have been in China for all I knew. Never heard of it.

"Well, I am pleased to meet you, Mr. Sin... Mard... Sorry, I can't say your name too well."

"No wonder. It's quite a name, I suspect. But my friends call me Marduchk," said the apparition, his teeth gleaming by the light of the shaft.

"My name is Victoria... wait, you just called me by my name. I was too confused to notice. You know me?"

"Of course I know you. I came specifically to meet you. We have a small job for you to do, if you agree to cooperate with us."

"What sort of job?" I asked suspiciously.

"I wonder if I can tell you without some preparation," he said. "It has something to do with who you really are."

"I see," I said. "So you know I am adopted. You know a lot about me, Marduchk. It's a little disconcerting."

"I know more than you think, to be honest, but no, you should not worry about it. Naturally, when you want someone to perform a very important task, you try to learn something about them, right?" said Marduchk. "And yes, I do know you were adopted."

Indeed, I was adopted in infancy by a wonderful couple who made excellent parents, and loved me very much. I would have known I was adopted even if they had not told me, because I had olive skin, black hair, and eyes that were so dark as to be almost black, as I mentioned before. My parents, whose ancestors came from England, were both blond. A couple of years ago I expressed a wish to find who were my birth parents, and my adoptive parents tried their very best to help, but we did not have any luck. Wherever we turned, all the information was blocked, deleted, or carefully hidden somehow. We finally gave up, and I was not too troubled about it after all. I had such a good life at home, I knew I did my best to find out, and not succeeding, I decided to just forget about the whole issue and go on as usual. I must say my parents were much relieved, they were afraid I would mope about it.

"So do tell," I said.

"You were born in Iraq," said Marduchk. "Your birth parents were Ashurians, who are Middle Eastern Christians, related to the Syriacs, who still speak Aramaic among themselves."

"That would explain the difficulties we had finding my birth parents," I said.

"I have something to tell you about them, too," he said. "The reason why I was sent to meet you was that your DNA is very rich in Anunnaki genes. All modern humans have Anunnaki genes, since the original human race, as you know it, was the product of the Anunnaki and what was the human race in ancient times, but some people, in certain areas of the world, maintained a stronger pool. Many live in Iraq, of course, since it exists on top of the Sumerian and Babylonian civilizations."

"I am an Anunnaki? Like you, then?" I have to admit that while this may be shocking to some, to me it sounded like a wonderful fairy tale. Besides, having common ground with this gorgeous guy was not so bad...

"Well, yes, you are, to a large extent."

"And you chose me specifically for some splendid job?"

"I don't know if you will find it splendid. Well, maybe you will, since it involves some courage and some sacrifice."

"Maybe you want me to be a spy? Or an agent? Hunt bad aliens that fight good aliens like you?"

"Nothing like it. Sorry. It's totally different."

"Am I the first one to be chosen?"

"Oh, no. We have to employ many people. We always contact many women, since women are paramount in our experiments, much more important than men, I am afraid. But you were selected for this particular task, that is, if you agree." I rather liked hearing how important women were in the Anunnaki's plans. Usually, I felt women had to always fight for their rights.

"Why are you employing humans, anyway? What is the connections between the Anunnaki and us?"

"We are your creators. The Anunnaki's first genetically created human race was the seed of humanity as you know it, the ancestors of modern humans, beginning to populate the earth 25,000 years before the construction of the great pyramids. Contrary to all of your beliefs, including what Judaism, Christianity and Islam teach you, Eve was not created from the rib of Adam. Men were created from an early female form that was 'fertilized' by the leaders and the elite of the Anunnaki. The women lived in quarantined cities, and had both sons and daughters fathered by the Anunnaki. Thousands of years later, the inhabitants of what is today the Arab Peninsula and the lands bordering Persia, the United Arab Emirates, and India, called these women 'The Women of Light', and those men who were allowed to mix with them, including their sons, were called 'The Sons of Light.' From this early human race, all humans came to life."

"What about God and his creation?" I asked.

"God had nothing to do with us," said Marduchk. "In other words, the God you know, revere, and fear today did not create you. Even the word or term 'God' did not exist in the early stages of the existence of the human race on earth. Instead 'Gods' or 'Heavenly Masters' were used. And thousands of years later, those terms were changed to 'Giants,' 'Elohim,' 'Nephilim,' 'Anakim,' 'Fallen Angels,' you name it..."

"So the Bible was not entirely right," I said, reflecting on my Sunday School lessons.

"Some is right, some is myth, some is fable," said Marduchk.

"This is fantastic," I said. "Scary, though."

"As a matter of fact, it should not be scary. Some day I will tell you how much there is nothing to fear, how much we are all the children of the universe and of eternity, and how we can look forward to eons of joy and peace. But we can't go into it now. We must concentrate on our task."

"So you still take an interest in our affairs?"

"Yes, even though at some point you rebelled against us... but then again, don't all children rebel against their parents, and the parents still love them? We do love you, Victoria."

"What do I have to do?" I was not going to refuse, even though I was a bit scared of what was to come. I knew that if I refused, he would go away and contact someone else, and I did not want to lose him. I was already beginning to fall in love, even though of course I did not know it.

"Have a baby," he said simply.

"WHAT?" I screamed. "I am only eighteen years old! I can't get married and have babies! I am going to college next year!"

"You don't have to get married. You don't have to raise the baby. We have plans for this baby. We just want your genetic material, always with your permission."

"Plans? For my baby? Doesn't a baby need a mother? Are you people as cruel and as mad as to deprive a child of his mother?"

"This baby has to grow to be a pivotal figure in the government of this country. He is important for world peace, for recovery from hunger and want, for freedom. He has a great task ahead of him, which I can already tell you he will fulfil admirably, since I am able to see a great deal of the future, though not all, not that which requires free will. Therefore, we have a couple in mind who will adopt this child. Both belong to very powerful Washington dynasties, they are longing for a child, and they are decent and intelligent. They will be extremely kind and loving to their child. What's more, I am going to manipulate their minds. They will believe that the baby is their birth child, that the woman has actually given birth to this child. I will change all the records, rearrange the paperwork and the birth certificate, and at the right moment the woman will come out of the hospital, carrying the infant and accompanied by her proud husband. The whole hospital crew will have their minds manipulated to believe all these events."

I was quiet, thinking. Marduchk was quiet, letting me mull over it. Finally I said, "My goodness, the things you can do... Anyway, if I agree, I have a condition."

"Which is?"

"You said you can manipulate minds. If I agree, I want you to make me forget the whole incident, until I am ready to face the situation. I cannot bring myself knowingly, consciously, to give away my baby; I simply cannot perform such an act. But I can see that it is needed, and in addition, for some reason I simply can't bring myself to refuse. Can you do that?"

"It will be very easy," said Marduchk. "And I can revive your memory when you have accomplished everything you want to do, and we can meet again and take up our lives from there. We can even decide at what age you would want to do it. Would you feel more comfortable if we got married first?"

"You want to marry me?" I felt elated, in my teenage way.

"Yes, I do," said Marduchk in the most matter of fact way. "I am, after all, going to be the father of this baby. And I know we will be very happy together, if you accept."

He was going to be the father of this baby. One way or another, Marduchk was to remain a permanent factor in my life, if I accept. If I don't accept, Marduchk will disappear from my life, and make me forget this has ever happened.

Why did he matter so much to me? And why did I trust him so implicitly? He was almost a hallucination, and yet I did trust him, completely. But marriage? That was the issue.

"No," I said decisively. "I am too young to marry. When we meet again, if we feel we want to do that, then we shall. I suspect I will want to marry you very much, but let's wait on that. However, I will take up the task. I accept it."

"That is wonderful," said Marduchk. "As for the marriage, I promise you I will not change my mind; an Anunnaki never does. And you will know your own mind then."

"But how can I disappear for the nine months of pregnancy? I can't let my parents know, they will be horrified."

"You don't have to," said Marduchk. "For us, past, present, and future are all one and the same. I will take you away on my machine to Zeta Reticuli, where you shall spend the time quite happily with my sister and me, and when I have the baby safely in my arms, and you are well and on your feet, I will return you to this car, one second after our current conversation. You will know nothing, forget it ever happened, drive home safely, and get on with your life. And ten, twelve years from now, you will have a little surprise. We will then see how good I was in my brain manipulation..."

"I hope I really do forget," I said. "If I have bits and pieces of memory intruding on me it would be so confusing. And yet, I have to give everything up for so long. This is all so confusing."

"I have an idea that might cheer you up," said Marduchk. "How would you like to speak your own language, Aramaic?" His smiling, large, black Anunnaki eyes were full of humor.

"Of course, I would love to, it would be wonderful," I said. "But it probably will take years to learn, right?"

"Wrong," said Marduchk. He looked into my eyes and his own eyes started acting as before, with the hypnotic glittering light. I felt paralyzed again, but only for a few seconds. Then it stopped, I shook myself, and to my utter disbelief found myself speaking and understanding a language that I have never heard before.

"Will I forget it as soon as we part?" I asked, enjoying speaking in Aramaic.

"No, it is my gift to you. You can now read and write it, too. It will be great for your college studies, considering the subject you have chosen. You will believe, and tell your teachers, that you have learned it on your own when you were in high school, in preparations for your classes, from various books. These books are now on your shelf, at home, I just placed them there. They look well used." By now, I was not even surprised that Marduchk knew what subject I was about to major in. Incidentally, Marduchk and I always speak to each other in Aramaic, and such a pleasure it is to be able to share something that is so close to our emotional core.

"Very well, let's get on with it" I said, rather bravely getting out of the car. We walked toward his vehicle. I must admit I felt very important... again, girls can be so silly sometimes. I did not really grasp then that so many women have been approached, over the centuries, for such important tasks; significant motherhood is a universal pattern.

Still, looking back, I am so happy I followed my instincts, trusted Marduchk, and helped shape humanity in my own little way. And how rewarding it was for my own life as well, I can't even begin to tell.

*** *** ***

April 1977, New York (Synopsis)

What happened next? Victoria tells us about her life on earth, and how at age thirty she was reunited with Marduchk and married him in the Anunnaki style. The memory of her happy nine months on Zeta Reticuli is restored, including how she had to adjust by taking special medications to even be able to see building and plants and people on Zeta Reticuli, due to the heavy atmosphere that makes it impossible for normal human eyes. What supernatural faculties were given to her by developing her innate Anunnaki gifts. She was taught to understand how to navigate time and space, and study any historical period by simply going there, she could learn any language almost instantly, and most important, she was able to understand something we as human cannot grasp – our own relationship with eternity. She now knows, not by faith like us, but with scientific certainty, that she will live hundreds of years, that she can be any physical age she chooses, that death does not exit, and that any person can spend eternity with the ones he or she truly loves. And that, she says, is just the tip of the iceberg. She has so much to tell, it will really take a book, perhaps more... stay tuned to her revelations!

Author's Note: Victoria's revelations were dictated and given to us in Aramaic, Hebrew and English. Languages we understand perfectly. On many occasions, a large portion was presented in a language totally unknown to us. And Victoria did apologize for that. With a delightful smiling voice, she said: "Sometimes, I cannot control it...This was the language my husband taught me...The An'hkh; the Anunnaki's language." For the fun of it, I asked her to write down one sentence in An'hkh. She did. I compared it with Phoenician and Hebrew, and I found few similarities, but the pronunciation was different. Many letters and words could not be pronounced by a person who did not learn ancient Hebrew, Aramaic and Arabic from CHILDHOOD. The vocal cords of Westerners do not have the range or the faculties to produce the sounds of many of the An'hkh words and letters, including the 3 Semite languages. In Hebrew, two letters exist that are pronounced differently by two groups in Israel: the Ashkenazi and the Sephardic. These are the letter Chet and the letter Ain. The Ashkenazi have only one Chet and one Ain. The Chet sounds like the Hebrew Caf, and the Ain sounds like Aleph. An American Jew, unless taught from early childhood by a Sephardic parent or teacher, will speak like an Ashkenazi. The Sephardic, particularly in Israel, pronounces the Chet and the Ain in a more guttural fashion, employing the throat muscles or the vocal cords in a totally different fashion. The Israeli Sephardic pronunciation of these two letters is proof positive that the language of the Anunnaki was preserved, at least in some fashion, by their descendants, since the Anunnaki used these same letters in their language, and pronounced it in the Sephardic way.

CHAPTER 2
HISTORY AND CIVILIZATION OF ZETA RETICULI AND OTHER EXTRATERRESTRIALS

- History of Zeta Reticuli as channeled by Lyssa Royal Holt
- The Zeta Reticuli identity was created from crisis
- The evolution of Zeta Reticuli's race does not really occur linearly
- Planet Apex: The ancient origin of the Zeta Reticuli race
- Their population was decreasing, and began turning to cloning techniques
- They began altering their genetics so that when new babies arrived they could be part of the underground ecosystem.
- They deliberately manipulated their body type to suit their underground environment
- They no longer allowed emotion in their lives
- Extraterrestrials playing a big role in abduction come mostly from the original Apex planet
- A good number of them live on earth...among us
- Originally, the Zetas lived on Planet Apex, and were called Apexians
- A small number of Zetas went to the Lyran system
- Their brain and pupil grew larger
- Planet Apex remains in the Reticulum star system.
- Their technological advancement allows them to evolve physically
- Victoria, the wife of an Annunaki's comments and revelations
- More theories about Zeta Reticuli aliens
- Their home system
- Description of their physiognomy
- Activity
- Organization

- Friend/foe
- Cooper's theories and beliefs
- They have evolved beyond the sexual reproduction process
- The Zetas swim in the mixture and absorb the nutrients through their skin.
- Characteristics
- **Bellatrax Grays**
- Orion Grays
- All Grays
- Pleiadeans of the five
- Draco Mothmen
- Deros/Teros

*** *** ***

History and Civilization of Zeta Reticuli

History of Zeta Reticuli as channeled by Lyssa Royal Holt

Lyssa Royal Holt is a world famous author and channeler. Her lectures, seminars, channelings, books and tapes deal with subjects pertaining to ufology, extraterrestrial civilizations, aliens' cultures and contact, and supreme beings. She is highly respected by peers and UFOs' researchers. Consequently, she has been recognized as one of the main, major and original source of information on extraterrestrials, and particularly aliens from Zeta Reticuli and the Anunnaki race. Lyssa Royal Holt channels the group consciousness Germane and Sasha, a Pleiadian female. She currently lives in Arizona, and frequently organizes groups' tours and trips to sacred sites.

The Zeta Reticuli identity was created from crisis.

According to Lyssa Royal Holt, for a clearer understanding of the Zeta Reticuli, one may study the history of their species. This will answer many questions about the Zeta psyche and belief systems. The Zeta Reticuli identity was created from crisis. This idea may account for their baffling methods of communicating with humans. Presented in this chapter is a brief history of the Zeta Reticuli, channeled from Germane. Audience questions highlight some of the fascinating historical data that is available as we search deeper into some of the aspects of the visitor phenomenon.

Germane: The primary goal of sharing the history of the Zeta Reticuli with you is so it can allow you to see some parallels between their civilization in the past and yours in the present. There is quite a bit of similarity.

The evolution of Zeta Reticuli's race does not really occur linearly

Though the evolution of their race does not really occur linearly, we will place this story in a linear format. We begin "back" hundreds of thousands of years ago in the Lyran system. The roots of the humanoid race in your area of the galaxy emerged from the Lyran system. The Zeta Reticuli are no exception.

Let us begin in the Lyran system back when civilization was flourishing and new cultures were exploding throughout the cosmos. The range of cultures these early humanoids created was vast.

Planet Apex: The ancient origin of the Zeta Reticuli race

There was one planet we have called the Apex planet that we will refer to as the ancient origin of the Zeta Reticuli race.

This Apex planet was very similar to Earth. The beings on Apex were a mixture genetically just like you are, because the early Lyran races had already begun to colonize. Apex became a melting pot for the genetics of the Lyran races. Therefore their society manifested a great deal of individuality and unpredictability. These qualities were even more pronounced than upon present-day Earth.

There were those who were pacifists. There were those who were warriors. There were those who were technologically oriented and those who rejected technology in favor of an inner spirituality. Every polarity one could imagine was played out on this Apex planet even more dramatically than it is played out on your Earth plane.

Their culture flourished for many thowsands of years. However, beneath the surface of the mass consciousness there was a great deal of disharmony because the spiritual growth of the planet did not parallel the technological growth of its inhabitants. The gap began to widen. On the surface of the planet cataclysm began – severe toxicity and severe radiation from atomic blasts even more destructive than on your planet today. There was much pollution. The atmosphere began to deteriorate and plant life was shortly thereafter unable to produce enough oxygen to continue the cycle of carbon dioxide/oxygen which kept the ecosystem balanced.

There were those within the system who were aware of what was happening. They began taking measures to preserve life. They built underground shelters and prepared themselves for the total destruction of the planet's surface. They didn't know whether this was going to occur, but they wanted to be safe. They knew they had a safety margin and that if they were prepared, their race would survive. They began learning to use alternate energy sources that could be used underground without any dependency on sunlight or oxygen from the surface. Thus they created a world that would be totally independent from the surface ecosystem.

Preparation stretched out over many generations. They were farsighted, for they were certain this change needed to occur. They paced themselves and moved slowly. They began to see that they were evolving at such a rapid rate that the Apexian cranial size was quickly increasing. The natural birth process became difficult, for the cranial size was expanding more quickly than the female pelvis could accommodate. Thus there were many deaths during childbirth – of both the mother and the child. Since what you call caesarian delivery was not part of their belief system, they were certainly facing a species crisis.

Their population was decreasing, and began turning to cloning techniques

They were faced with a dilemma. Their population was decreasing. It became obvious that they had to prepare for planetary catastrophe as well as the possible death of their own species. They thus began turning to cloning techniques so they would not be dependent on the birth process.

Then they could actually reproduce their species in the laboratory without the need for the reproductive act, conception, or natural birth. They assumed this knowledge would take care of them and they would be ready for anything.

The Apexians did attempt to reverse some of the conditions that were occurring on the planet's surface before they took shelter underground. However, it had progressed too far. Many Apexians were dying from various diseases resulting from radiation or air pollution. They knew this was the time to move beneath the planet's surface.

Gradually, individuals wrapped up their business on the surface of the planet and began to inhabit the underground cities. This was a great shock to many. Imagine knowing that you could never look at the sky again...that you could never lie under the stars...that you would be trapped in a rock environment for the rest of your life. Imagine the fear and sorrow these people were experiencing.

Eventually, they all were moved underground. They had to learn how to adapt. Through their cloning capabilities (which they had been working on for at least 100 of their years), they began to understand how a body could adapt to an environment such as this.

They began altering their genetics so that when new babies arrived they could be part of the underground ecosystem.

This entailed restructuring bodies so they could absorb frequencies of light beyond the visible spectrum and then change these frequencies into heat. This required a completely different way of body functioning and a new way of teaching the body to absorb nutrients. The bodies began learning to ingest nutrients from some of the luminiferous rocks underground. They had brought from the surface luminiferous plants as well. They studied these plants (which were hlorophyll-based) and allowed themselves to incorporate these qualities into themselves.

All of this occurred over a span of hundreds of years. Many Apexians died. There were successes as well as failures. They eventually got to a point where the population growth leveled out as the death rate decreased. The methods by which they were taking in nutrients and recycling into the ecosystem became symbiotic and balanced. They knew they could survive this way for an indefinite period of time.

While this was occurring under the surface of the planet, profound changes were occurring on the surface. The Apexians did not realize that the planet's toxicity had set a chain reaction in motion. Severe radiation had begun breaking down the planetary energy field on a subatomic level. This created an electromagnetic warp in the time/space fabric surrounding the Apex planet. While they were underground, Apex actually shifted its position in the time/space continuum because of this dramatic subatomic energy breakdown.

Time and space is very much like Swiss cheese. A planet in one location is connected through a series of multidimensional networks or passageways to other areas of your galaxy.

When this warp began around their planet, the planet was moved through the fabric of time/space to another time/space continuum – which was a significant distance from their point of origin. You have labeled this area the Reticulum star group. The Apex planet was inserted in the Reticulum system around one of the faintest stars is that star group. This occurred simply because the planetary shift followed the fabric of time and space. The underground Apexians were totally unaware of this as they continued with their lives under the surface. They continued saving their species.

If something such as this occurred on Earth, there would be various factions of people living underground who would have no communication with each other. These factions could develop very different cultures over hundreds of years. This is what occurred on Apex. These different factions represent the different variations that have been viewed in the Zeta Reticuli groups. Some individuals say they are very negative; others say they are very benevolent. But it really isn't as black and white as that.

They deliberately manipulated their body type to suit their underground environment

Over the hundreds of years that they were underground, they deliberately manipulated their body type to suit their underground environment. They allowed themselves to become shorter in stature than they originally were so they could make better use of the cavern space. It was merely a conservation effort. Because they were not procreating physically, their reproductive organs atrophied.

Their digestive tracts atrophied because they were no longer taking in solid nutrients. They had mutated to allow themselves to take in nutrients through the skin. Their eyes adapted to the environment through the pupil mutating to cover the entire eye. This allowed them to absorb certain frequencies of light beyond the visible spectrum. They had to do this in order to make optimal use of their underground environment. This description of their changes is a general one, since different factions would have made slightly different alterations to their genetic structure.

They no longer allowed emotion in their lives

During this time, they evaluated what they had done to their planet. They concluded that emotions were largely responsible, so they no longer allowed emotion in their lives. They also vowed that they would no longer allow diversity in their culture. Thus they deliberately bred out variations in emotional reactions to differing stimuli. They were adamant that their passions would no longer rule them. They began creating a neurochemical structure in which every external stimulus produced the same reaction in every person.

They felt this would allow them to integrate into one people and eliminate the warring and passion that had ruled their culture in the past.

Generally speaking, the separate underground factions followed the same reasoning. Most of them adapted themselves biologically in much the same way. This was a natural progression – they were following an equation. But the differences in the factions were more noticeable in their philosophy orientations.

Each faction had differing points of view about their own sense of self. The ones you now call Zeta Reticuli are the more benign and benevolent beings. There are those we can term the "negative Zeta Reticuli" who stemmed from a faction that was interested in gaining power. They carried this desire from their Lyran roots into their mutation. There were other groups whom you have named "the Greys" who were from this Apex world but had slightly different genetic structures.

Extraterrestrials playing a big role in abduction come mostly from the original Apex planet

You will find that the extraterrestrials playing a big role in your abduction literature come mostly from this original Apex planet. This is why there is so much controversy over who is who. Though they have the same lineage, their orientations and motivations are quite varied.

Eventually the Apexians realized that enough time had passed that they could return to the surface of the planet. The atmosphere had not totally regenerated (thus their time on the planet's surface was limited), but they did allow themselves to emerge. When they did, they had quite a shock.

Observing the star field, they knew the planet had shifted its position in the cosmos. The stars were very different. The astronomers who had been plotting the heavens during the seclusion were astonished. They realized then what they had done.

The more benevolent Zeta Reticuli now were firmly committed to becoming one people and finding out what they had lost during the time they were underground. Thus they diligently learned about the folding of time and space.

They didn't even know where they were. They wanted to find out what had happened. They wanted to learn about themselves through other cultures. It was also their desire for no one else to ever do to themselves what they had done. At this time, that was their primary motivation.

The other more negative or self-serving groups also emerged on the surface of the planet and realized what they had done. The negative Zeta Reticuli group allowed themselves – with the technology they had in the past – to build ships and move to other planets in the Reticulum system where they built their culture.

Others of the self-serving orientation allowed themselves to explore the universe, setting up colonies in several systems including Orion (Betelgeuse) and the Sirius trinary system.

Have any of these beings on Apex been reincarnationally connected with Earth?
Reincarnationally speaking, a good number of them are upon your planet now. Many of these Apexians who died out were somewhat opposed to the idea of manipulating the Apexian genetic structure. But at the same time, they were adamant about not creating pollution and toxicity and knew the Apex planet had to change. So they have incarnated all through the galactic family – especially whenever they saw a planet coming to the brink of the same kind of destruction they had created in their past. It is their wish to share their knowledge of what occurred in their past so that others will not need to recreate it.

Originally, the Zetas lived on Planet Apex, and were called Apexians

So the Zetas are not indigenous to the Reticulum system?
Correct. However, after Apex shifted into the Reticulum system, the Zetas had many thousands of years of evolution. They have been there so long that Apex is only a dim memory to them.
If the Apexians had spacecraft, why didn't they leave Apex when the catastrophe was occurring?
They could have left had they desired. Understand the nature of their being: They were pioneers; they had the same motivations and passions as the individuals who colonized your America. Even when the pioneers were faced with Indian attacks, they did not want to leave. The Apexians saw this as a great challenge. They felt that by going underground and changing their species, they would heal their past.
They felt they would not recreate it again.

A small number of Zetas went to the Lyran system

The majority of them felt that if they left and went somewhere else, they would continue to recreate the pattern. Some of them did leave and went to other planets in the Lyran system, but only a small number. For the most part, the individuals who were committed allowed themselves to stay, feeling that this was an opportunity for them to heal their society.

Their brain and pupil grew larger

You were saying that the pupil of the eye mutated to cover the whole eye. Does the pupil also grow larger through expanded consciousness?

In their case, yes. The brain was growing larger and therefore the eye structure as well as their desire for knowledge facilitated the enlargement of the pupil. But they also genetically manipulated it as well. Over a long period of time it would have occurred naturally because the surface area of the eye was not large enough to take in all of the light they needed. Also, the Lyran beings who were their forefathers had larger eyes than the Earth human.

Planet Apex remains in the Reticulum star system.

Did the Apex planet move back to its original location once they began healing themselves?

No. The planet still remains in the Reticulum star system. The underground caverns are still home to many of them, though for the most part a good number of them spend time in space on their ships.

Is it possible in our time that our world could create something like this?

Yes, it is. In your current development and use of atomic power, it is not possible, but should you continue using your knowledge of atomics for more destructive means without allowing yourself to evolve from atomics to something else, then you could create that scenario.

Understand that there is a certain evolutionary scale (on average) that a civilization will follow.

You are now at the stage of playing with the nuclear or atomic energies.

There is a natural evolution from atomics that moves you away from the danger point. You are at the point now of almost deciding to move away from the danger scenario.

You are still deciding whether or not you are going to take the natural evolutionary process away from atomics.

Their technological advancement allows them to evolve physically

Most of the Zeta Reticuli that we interact with today are quasi-physical, almost approaching nonphysicality. How did they get to that state? Was it simply the great length of time they've been focused on developing themselves?

The length of time has something to do with it, yes. But also it was because of their technological advancement, which allowed them to evolve themselves physically. They have allowed themselves to evolve to the point where they are on the brink of becoming nonphysical. However, they do not wish to leave physicality because there is still something they think they need to learn.

Never forget that there are different factions of the Zeta beings. Some of them are very altruistic. There are others who are here purely for their own reasons and those reasons can be either positive or negative or any shade in between. As an overall idea, they want certain things from you they feel they lack.

You see, they think they have made some mistakes in what they have eliminated through cloning. They are now trying to watch you and learn how they can successfully integrate these things within themselves.

In a sense we can say that you are their past as well as their future.

It is as if at every corner they turn, they face you.

You represent their past; you also represent their only hope for a future.

Victoria's Comments/Revelations:

Note: Victoria, the wife of an Anunnaki seems to confirm a large part of what Lyssa Royal Holt revealed through "Germane". However, minor nuances contradict Holt's revelations. Victoria told me that me the following:

- The Zeta Reticuli identity was not created from a crisis as stated by Lyssa Royal Holt.

- The evolution of their race evolved interdimensionally by cloning themselves and fertilizing their own genes.

- On other planets, more advanced extraterrestrial civilizations multiply and prosper through the development of brain's waves and thoughts frequencies. They did not need to use cloning, or to immigrate to other planets in order to survive, for they did not encounter insurmountable ecological or spiritual catastrophes.

- The Lyran system consisted of 9 planets and 13 moons.

- No gravity law applied to that system.

- 7 of these planets had an atmosphere similar to the atmosphere of the Earth.

- There is a particular extraterrestrial race which resembled the human race (more on this later.) This race had white skin, and alien males were tall, almost 9 feet. Women were 7 feet. Many ufologists and chanellers confuse them with other extraterrestrial races, including the "White Talls."

- Inhabitants of adjacent planets of higher level of civilization and technology never built underground shelters. Their technology allowed them to surround their planets with anti-pollution shields. Underground shelters are solely used by a race of inferior or very limited scientific/ technological level and resources like Earth.

- They did alter their genetics but, not for survival purposes or for intra-planetary travel/immigration readiness. The alteration came as cause and effect; much needed to reach a higher level of awareness and scientific advancement.

More Theories about Zeta Reticuli Aliens

According to the ufologists group "alien monstruous", Zeta Reticuli extraterrestrials are known as The Greys Type A. The group continues:

Their home system:

Zeta Reticuli Greys come from Zeta Reticulan, the 4th planet out from Zeta2 Reticulum, near Barnard's Star, which is a neighboring star system to Orion. The constellation Reticulum is a fairly small collection of faint stars, of which zeta is barely visible to the naked eye even though it is relatively close to us at approximately 40 light years. The dim point of light known to us as Zeta Reticuli is actually a binary star system, and its two stars, Zeta Reticulum and Zeta2 Reticulum, are each very much like our own yellow sun. It is not visible in the northern hemisphere.

Their day is 90 hours long and the year is a little over 432 of our days long. Travel time to that location is about 91 days by Reticulan jumpcraft. Are both stars in the Constellation Reticulum in the Southern Celestial Hemisphere.

These greys have their best-known bases in New Mexico and Nevada but are also known to have bases in many countries of the world.

Description of their physiognomy:

The most commonly seen grey is around two to four feet tall, very slender and delicate looking, small beings and light weight, extremely penetrating black slanted eyes with no pupils, almost vestigial mouth and nose, a very large head with a pointed chin. The skin color varies from dark grey to light grey, tan to tanish grey, white to pale white. They have no hair on their bodies. They have evolved beyond the need for reproductive systems or digestive systems and reproduce by cloning. Their genetics are partly based on insectoidal genetics.

Activity:

Their science deals largely with the study of other life forms and genetic engineering. They have supposedly had a part to play in the alteration of human genetics over thousands of years. It seems that they may be trying to cross breed with humans in order to create a "mixture race" that would be better than either.

Organization:

There social organization is similar to ants with a very rigidly defined social structure but they are technologically advanced and seem to be in a conquest mode. There seem to be two main social classes. One is the more hawkish and is more abrupt, crude and blunt. The more dove-like ones are more refined and capable of a more business-like behavior towards humans, and prefer to use more "diplomatic" behavior to gain control over humans. This type of Grey is what I believe is being referred to as the "Orange" class of Greys. These greys are servants to a master race of reptilian-type aliens and are trying to prepare the earth for their arrival by gaining control over the earth through many means. They tend to enjoy the feeling of freedom they have on earth, away from their masters and would desire the help of humans in confrontations with the reptilians.

Friend/Foe:

They seem to be emotionless (by human standards) and therefore are seen as cruel in their treatment of human beings. They are able to take human lives without any regard for that individual. They apparently can use certain substances of the human body for their sustenance and therefore appear to be carnivorous in regards to humans.
This could apply to physical or mental fluids, an experience reported by many abductees that felt like being "vampirized" as aliens would use their fear as a recreational drug.

Cooper's Theories and Beliefs

ZETA RETICULI GREYS

Small Zeta Reticuli Greys come from Zeta Reticulan, near Barnard's Star, which is a neighboring star system to Orion. They are very short (about 3 1/2 to 4 feet tall), grayish silver in color and have no sexual or digestive parts to their bodies. They are created through a cloning process of alien genetic engineering. They are an ancient race and have reproduced themselves for thousands of years. They have very limited facial features.

They have large eyes, a very small slit for a mouth and no nose to speak of. The eyes are large almond-shaped and black.

They have evolved beyond the sexual reproduction process

They have evolved beyond the sexual reproduction process so that all sexual organs and their digestive tracts havetotally atrophied. They are no longer capable of eating or indulging in sexual activities. They are a close relative to the insect family. The Zetas are the ones involved in the cattle mutilations.

They absorb certain substances from parts of the cattle that stabilize them during the cloning process. This can be placed under the tongue to give sustenance and stability for some time. It is a substance that comes from certain mucus membranes: The lips, nose, genitals and rectum, and also from certain organs. These glandular substances serve as nutrients in lieu of eating.

Resting the substances under the tongue is not the only way they get nutrition. You may have noticed that the cattle mutilations generally result in all the blood being drained from the body.

The Zetas have in their bases canisters and vats in which animal and human organs float along with a purple liquid to hold these parts in suspension.

The Zetas swim in the mixture and absorb the nutrients through their skin.

They use hydrogen peroxide in both the absorption and elimination process. The hydrogen peroxide also helps to preserve the liquid and organ mixture to keep it from spoiling. They have no digestive tract and eliminate through the skin. To eliminate, they need to pass the substance through some part of their body, much the same way plants eliminate through their skin or outer shells. They use hydrogen peroxide for helping with that elimination as well.

The Zetas have also been referred to as the Little Green Men because they tend to turn a shade of green when they have not received sufficient food.

When they are in this state, they are very vicious.

Characteristics

The cloning of these aliens can be done quite quickly, reproducing synthetic replicas. They have a technology that is much beyond that of humans and that has led to the agreements with the United States government whereby exchanges of these techniques could occur. The Zeta Reticuli Greys are not masters of their own fate. They are, rather, subservient to a reptilian race of people from their home planet. The Zetas seek, but are fearful of, freedom from their masters.

They seem to have some desire to work closely with humans in an effort to retain the freedom they have on earth, which they have never experienced before. In their desire to retain that freedom from their reptilian masters, they would hope to play the role of being masters here on earth, or at least having enough control so as to be safe from slavery by any other species. The Zetas are of two social classes, one being hawkish, the other more dove-like. The more dove like Zetas are more refined and capable of more business like behavior toward humans, while the other type is more abrupt, blunt and crude in their directness.

The Zetas desire the help of humans in an expected future confrontation with the reptilian masters who are expected to follow soon, within the next 20 years.

This refers to the so-called asteroid that is on its way toward earth.

It is housing approximately 30 million reptilian aliens.

It has, however, temporarily diverted its path as it moves into the constellation of Draco.

BELLATRAX GREYS

They are the short Grey, which is shorter than the Zeta Reticuli, is from a star system near the Orion constellation, near the shoulder of the figure in a star system called Belletrax. They are shorter, much like dwarves (about 1 1/2 feet tall). They are more indirect, but just as vicious towards humans as the Zetas. Both the Bellatrax Grays and the Zeta Reticuli Greys are related genetically from the same root race and look very much alike except for size.

ORION GREYS

They are the tall Greys; big-nosed Greys. They have large noses and stand about 7 or 8 feet tall. They are based in the Aleutian Islands and recently were witnessed in a park in the Eastern part of Russia. These creatures are hostile, but less vicious toward humans. They tend to try to influence through the use of political controls. They have certain powers and technologies that allow them to perform actions that appear miraculous. In the Russian incident, a woman whose leg was deformed was picked up by these Orion Greys and was released thousands of miles away. Her leg was healed. The aliens did not heal her leg. They transplanted a new leg onto her body. The Orion Grays give the impression that they are benevolent towards humans, but they are heavily into genetic engineering.

They use humans as guinea pigs to conduct various experiments.

They have grown arms and legs and other body parts in a formless matrix made from human flesh. A leg may grow out of a torso, hands might grow from the middle of the torso's stomach. All this is done through the injecting of certain genomes into flesh and the application of electromagnetic charges. In this way they can grow human body parts to help deformed or injured humans, or for their own purposes of food and sustenance.

They are interested in controlling the masses of the earth through certain negotiated agreements with those in power.

ALL GREYS

The Greys are all, to some degree, influencing human history at this time. The nature of the Greys, especially the Zeta Reticuli and the short Greys, is that they do not have deep emotional feelings or compassion.

They are very calculating, cold intellectuals and see humans as being inferior. They look at humans much the same way a farmer looks at his cows. They understand the passions and compassion of humans to the degree it is observable by them. But they do not have feelings.

These aliens are on the equivalent human level of cannibals. They see humans being an inferior species. They are carnivorous. The Zeta Reticuli Greys feed upon glandular secretions of humans and are quite capable of killing people for that secretion, or abducting humans and extracting the secretions for themselves. The genetic manipulation is one way that the aliens see as evolving and saving their dying race.

In a sense, humans are suddenly the saviors of the souls of the aliens. But at least it is a way that humans may have an influence on the aliens.

This is not the first time that a civilization has attempted to absorb an enemy rather than defeating it.

While the enemy invader may assume that they are taking over, they are in fact being absorbed. The Tartars invaded Russia and within a hundred years were absorbed into Russian society.

PLEIADEANS

"Pleiadeans of the five", those from the Pleiades are entities who are distant relatives of humankind. They are related to and are the forefather race of the genetic creation of humankind. They are of a higher spiritual development than most people on earth at this time. They have a kinship towards humans, and are essentially the only aliens who can to be trusted by humans.

They have blonde hair and fair skin. They are allied with the Intergalactic Space Confederation. That doesn't mean that all entities of human appearance in space craft can or should be trusted, for there are humans from this planet from various governments who are working for the Zeta Reticuli Grays. Some from the Pleiades are subordinates to the Grays, having been abducted as children or offspring of the abductees.

They have been raised and trained by the Grays as servants.

The humans from the Pleiades have made several earth contacts, but in recent times have suspended visitations to earth.

The government was told that this was because of a space law that states that the destiny of a people shall not be interfered with unless it threatens themselves or others in the galaxy.

If the threat of nuclear war became strong enough, these entities indicated that they might interfere, but only to the degree of reducing that threat. That could also set up a conflict between the Pleiadeans and the Zeta Grays, to whom a limited nuclear war is seen as beneficial. Since the humans have made an agreement and pact with the Zeta Greys, even though there were warnings by the Pleiadeans against this, there is now a "hands off" policy. The Pleiadeans feel that the humans have made their bed and now they must lie in it. It is not likely that humans will be rescued from planned events simply to make things easier for humans to overcome the masters they have agreed to work with.

DRACO MOTHMEN

In the constellation of Draco, there is another race of entities which has in the past visited Earth. They are 8-foot-tall, dark, nocturnal aliens who appeared around graveyards and parks. They have red eyes that glow in the dark and wings to fly. They are referred to by us as Mothmen. They are also the source of legends of the past relating to gargoyles and Valkeries.

Even some qualities of vampires have been taken from the qualities of this creature -- the ability to fly and nocturnal habits. The Mothmen have no particular influence on earth at this time other than as causing panic and a cause for curiosity.

They are mostly hidden underground and do not wish to attract attention.

DEROS/TEROS

There are also underground civilizations of non-humans that have been referred to as Deros and Teros. The Teros are friendlier and help keep the Deros, who are more demented, from having excessive power. They live underground in tunnels, cities and sometimes under the sea. Most of the legends of the past of leprechauns and trolls refer to these non-humans from the inner earth. The Deros are competitors with the Greys, but they have similar qualities and cannot be trusted.

CHAPTER 3
GALACTIC FAMILY: ZETA RETICULI AND PHYSICAL GENOTYPES

- Germane's overview of extraterrestrial genotypes
- The Zeta Reticuli civilization and physical characteristics of the Zetas
- Description of the entities
- What the Zeta Reticuli are doing?
- Do they themselves have a genetic future? And what is it?
- What do these various races think about us when they see us physically? How do they feel about us?
- Do they like our physical appearance? Do they dislike it? Are they neutral or is it a curiosity?
- Information about the physical genotypes of your galactic family
- The Lyrans
- Lyran Giants
- Lyran Redheads
- Are we speaking of what their current state is also?
- Did they have any spiritual or energetic relationship to the few red-haired Pleiadians?
- Did these red-haired people naturally evolve as red-haired, or was there intentional manipulation somewhere along the line?
- Colloquially speaking, did they carry a chip on their shoulder?
- Redhead and Caucasian subgroups
- Darker-Skinned Lyrans
- Would it be a completely different genetics from the Lyrans?
- This group is Lyran-based and the group you'll talk about later would not be considered Lyran?
- Birdlike Lyran subgroup
- Catlike Lyran subgroup

- If they're Lyran-based, then we're talking millions of years ago that these developments started separately from our branch, right?
- Eyes of the extraterrestrials who have communicated with you.
- So why do our eyes appear to be so small in comparison to the rest of the family?
- Are there other lines of Lyran evolution that have nothing to do with us historically, that literally branched off into other parts of the galaxy?
- The Vegans
- So some of the Eastern Indians are extremely dark brown in contrast to the skin color of some of the African groups that are very black, almost coal black?
- Humanoid-Type Vegans
- Nonhuman-Type Vegans
- The Pleiadian civilization
- These light brown eyes you keep mentioning, would they appear at first to be gold?
- So reports of golden eyes would actually be these light brown eyes, as opposed to our standard brown eyes?
- Emotional temperament of the Pleiadians
- Is the potential similar; is the basic emotional structure similar?
- The Orion civilization
- This would be the body types with the very high copper content that is due not only to the genetic line but the diet?
- And they do tend to be aggressive, to leave their mark?
- Is there enough genetic similarity that natural cross-breeding is possible?
- The Sirian civilization
- Cetaceans don't represent a genetic heritage in the human family through Sirius

*** *** ***

Galactic Family: Zeta Reticuli
Germane's Overview of Extraterrestrial Genotypes

The Zeta Reticuli Civilization and physical characteristics of the Zetas

Description of the entities:

Germane via Lyssa Royal Holt: We'd now like to talk about the entities that you know of as the Zeta Reticuli. The physical characteristics of the Zeta Reticuli that you are already aware of is 3-1/2 to 4-1/2 to, in some cases, 5 feet tall, generally bald, frail-looking, larger-headed in proportion to the body, large eyes that seem to have no lid, very small (if any) nose, mouth and ears. We have given you the story about the Zeta Reticuli. To encapsulate it here, they were a civilization very much like you who went on a path of (in some ways) self-destruction, a specie crisis. They caught it before they were annihilated. However, they found themselves sterile. They performed genetic engineering, cloning, etc. to change their species and so you have the Zeta Reticuli you see today.

We will tell you that the base genetics of the Zeta Reticuli before they went through their species crisis and transformation was that of human-type Vegan heritage. Their civilization, when it went through the change, required them to alter their body structure into what they are now. This accounts for one of the reasons why they are here and interested in your genetics, because they are looking for an aspect of their original genetics to reinsert into themselves because of what they perceive they've done wrong during their transformation - namely, breeding out emotions. If they were to time-travel, which they can do, and go back to their past, they would only be gathering genetic data before their crisis. To them, that genetic data is inferior; they do not want that. They look to other races who have Vegan forefathers for some of the Vegan DNA that has been adapted through experience to a more expanded state of being. Your planet is one of the places. There are Vegan codes active here, and at this point just about everyone on your planet carries both the Lyran and Vegan codes. You've intermixed so well. When they are taking genetic samples from you, they are looking mostly for Vegan (but some Lyran) genetic codes that have been strengthened and adapted from their original state on Vega millennia ago. So this is why, to them, you are so important - because you carry locked in the cells of your body what they think is their only future.

You on Earth, more than anything else, have served as a genetic repository, a genetic storehouse for the galactic universe, for your galactic family. In some ways you've been earning interest on this DNA you've been storing, because it's a lot more valuable now than it has been in the past. Individuals are now coming back to explore that greater value and that is what the Zeta Reticuli are doing.

What the Zeta Reticuli are Doing?

Do they themselves have a genetic future? And what is it?

They are creating their genetic future as they go along. In some way (and we speak a little bit loosely here) they have no future other than what they deliberately manipulate. According to the laws of species evolution, they should have transformed out of physicality already. Since they are not running according to the standard laws of species evolution, their future is what they make it. They could annihilate themselves tomorrow by simply pulling up all of their laboratories and leaving, never enhancing their own genetics, and eventually dying off. They could do that, but they don't want to. They don't want to leave this reality without resolving the things they feel they need to resolve, and so they will keep themselves physical until they do so. And as we've stated before, they understand that you have invited them and that you are also getting something out of your interactions with them; it's not a one-way street. We would say at this point that what you are getting out of your interactions with them is much more valuable than you've ever realized, much more valuable than we've ever told you. It's essential.

What do these various races think about us when they see us physically? How do they feel about us?

There are different emotions. Imagine being an interracial couple; imagine being an Asian woman and a black man creating a child. As you watch the child grow, you can very clearly see, at least physically, the African attributes and the Asian attributes and you can watch them expand and grow and interweave with each other. They know themselves so well at this point that when they watch you, they can see not only the physical attributes you have, but the emotional and mental attributes, even the spiritual attributes, and they can pinpoint themselves within you very clearly. To some, it's a shock; it's painful to come here because you are very clear mirrors for them. To others, coming here is the only way they can see themselves.

Do they like our physical appearance? Do they dislike it? Are they neutral or is it a curiosity?

When you have traveled the universe as much as many of these races have, it's not a matter of liking or disliking appearances, because you've seen very strange things. It's like a sense of deja vu when they see you. There is something very familiar about you, and yet there's something very alien - something that frightens them very much. They are drawn to you and they are also frightened - and that is where growth lies. With that, we will thank you for your wonderful questions. There will be more information on this in the future. We're just laying the groundwork here. We'd like to take this opportunity to thank each and every one of you for the gifts you have given. Not only to your reality, to your forefathers, but mostly to yourselves, because those gifts will bear much more valuable fruit than you can yet see.

Germane chanelling: Greetings to you. It is a pleasure to be here once again. We would like to give you information about the physical genotypes of your galactic family. This is information you have been asking about for quite some time and we would like to provide you at least the foundation of this information so that you may build upon it in some of your future work.

Information about the physical genotypes of your galactic family

The Lyrans

We are going to start with the group called the Lyrans. We are going to give you some basic information about the various subgroups that have existed within their races and allow you a more expanded point of view, perhaps, on the diversity of your forefathers - which, of course, is reflected in the diversity you have upon your world. We will then bring in the Vegan civilizations, because they are instrumental in forming some of the other galactic races as well. Starting, then, with the Lyrans (going back chronologically), the first expression of physicality that could be considered Lyran would be somewhat small - smaller, in fact, than your present average human.
But as the culture grew, as their experiences and genetic structures began changing, their physical characteristics began expanding as well.

Lyran Giants

We're going to give you some of the primary groups that were very active in space exploration because those are the ones that matter the most to you, since they are the ones you had contact with. First is the genotype that we will call the Lyran Giants These entities (physical like yourself, of course) existing in third and fourth density, were Caucasian in type. They were primarily of light skin, light eyes and light hair; the darkest hair would be a medium brown, which was somewhat unusual. The physical body would be likened to the mesomorph, which is basically a well-balanced, muscular body. The height would be anywhere from six to nine feet tall, depending upon the group of entities we are speaking of, the smallest being at the six-foot range (female as well as a male). These entities developed this size from long periods of genetic development on a planet with higher gravitational fields and a denser electromagnetic envelope, also present in the solar system in general. This added to the creation of a more hearty, shall we say, entity. These entities are reflected in some of the Greek mythology and in some of the biblical stories of giants. This is one of the groups that your civilization still has a cellular memory about.

This particular group was one of the primary groups that began forming a God-worshipper relationship with you. Do you follow so far? This is one of the reasons for some of the expressions in your religious art and architecture (which has very large doors and windows); this patterning with this particular racial structure was very deep within the human psyche. These were the original gods – or at least the ones that made the biggest impression on you.

Lyran Redheads

There is another race that has branched off from this giant race, the red-haired Lyrans. Their hair was red to strawberry blonde in color. The skin tone very, very fair; these entities had a difficulty exposing their skin to certain frequencies of natural light, due to the planet they sprang from. Some of these were also giant in stature, though there were some who were average human size. Eye color was generally light to what you would now consider green, though it is a different quality of green than you see upon your world. These entities were some of the first Lyran pioneers. (Pioneers is a very kind word, for there are many worlds that consider the red-haired ones to be the invaders, marauders and the basic havoc-wreakers of the Lyran genotype.)

Are we speaking of what their current state is also?

Well, to some degree we are speaking about the distant past as they interacted with your earth plane. These entities still exist but are much fewer in number. We would say that your closest mythological remnants are in your Norse mythology - Vikings etc. Some of that mythology was about actual Earth beings who were either influenced by or interacted with this red-headed Lyran strain. This is not a very common interaction on your world, not as common as that of the giants, but common enough to have made it into your mythology.

Did they have any spiritual or energetic relationship to the few red-haired Pleiadians?

Apparently there's a remnant of a red-haired group in the Pleiades.
Yes, there would be genetic connections, most certainly. And if there is a genetic connection there is always an energetic connection.
It's hard to think of someone living in the Pleiades who would be violent. But if that aggressive tendency somehow channeled into other areas...
It's channeled into excitement. The Pleiadian version is much more watered down. (We can get to that later on if you wish.) But the purebred red-head was very aggressive, violent, passionate and, to some degree, very rebellious. They saw the giant Lyran race as their parents, and they were rebelling against that idea. They were rebelling because they felt that the morality of the giant race was being impinged into their reality. We do not perceive this was the case, but this was another expression that needed to be experienced in your galactic family.

Did these red-haired people naturally evolve as red-haired, or was there intentional manipulation somewhere along the line?

There were those from the giant race who left and went exploring. The primary group colonized one specific planet and over generations adapted themselves to the planet. They adapted to the specific mineral content of the planet as well as the atmosphere; the specific wavelengths of the planet's atmosphere caused the mutation to lean toward the more red tinge. That, in combination with the more rebellious attitude, began to create a specific sub-genotype.

So that particular race must have felt somehow slighted within the family. Colloquially speaking, did they carry a chip on their shoulder? Did they feel they had something to prove?

We would say that's pretty accurate, yes. We say this a little lightly, but this is the story of your entire galactic history. Most groups splintered off because they did not agree with the mother group. In this way most of your experience as a galactic species is based on conflict/disagreement and the attempt at rightfulness.

Redhead and Caucasian Subgroups

So far you have the giants and the redheads. And within the redheads you have two subgroups - one giant-sized, one average-sized. Also within the Lyran you have a broad type we would call Caucasian who are light-skinned, light-eyed (the darkest eyes were perhaps a light brown, but that is uncommon), hair ranging from almost white to a light brown (but anything in the brown range was unusual). These entities' body types would be anything from ectomorphic, (thin) to the mesomorphic (muscular). This is the broadest category. Most of your genetic forefathers were from this Caucasian category. Your diversity began with some red-head influence as well as some giant influence, but those are secondary compared to the Caucasian influence, which is primary.

In terms of actual internal structure, that information is unnecessary, for it is lengthy and not all that pertinent right now. The desire we have for communicating this information is not so much for the raw data, but for your understanding of how your planet has achieved such a group diversity. So we will stick to the external appearances rather than the internal makeup.

Darker-Skinned Lyrans

There was one other group, a humanoid type that is more rare, but it has had interactions with your world as well. This was Caucasian in features but the skin is more of a light chocolate, very uniform throughout the whole body. You would consider it a very pleasant, appealing shade. The eyes are brown, not black, although some were green; and the hair was not black but dark brown. This group had influence on your planet in the area of India, Pakistan, etc.

That was their primary area of interest in their visits here.

None of the races now on your world are pure extensions of any of these races; just about every race on your world has had some mixing.

However, this last race, which we will call the darker skinned Lyrans, were considered pacifists. Their psychological makeup was one of extreme passivity, peacefulness. One may even call them lackadaisical, because it was very difficult to get an emotional reaction out of them. You will find some of these individuals mentioned in some of your Sanskrit literature from ancient times. In a moment we will talk about the Vegan influence. However, we want to make it clear that this last group, the darker-skinned Lyrans, is not the same as some of the Vegan genotypes we will speak of, who have a different genetic structure.

Would it be a completely different genetics from the Lyran?
This group is Lyran-based and the group you'll talk about later would not be considered Lyran?

Birdlike Lyran Subgroup

Yes. They might look similar in appearance, but the base genetics is different. There is a need to express some of the other forms that have expressed their energy through the energy of Lyran that are humanoid, meaning mammalian, but whose appearance is different from what you know as humanoid. This has also accounted for some of your mythology. There is one group of entities who are mammals, yet are oriented toward Lyran principles (Lyra being the mother group), and whose features are very different from humanoid. One particular group resembles what you call alien. The body type of these entities would be what you call ectomorph, very thin, almost frail and birdlike. The facial structure is more angular, sharper, resembling a bird, though these are still mammals. The eyes are birdlike. The hair is not feathered, but is of a different quality that can resemble feathers, if you are not touching it or in close proximity to it. It was also ceremoniously adorned in a certain way that made it look like feathers. This was not intentional but simply their own expression. These entities are very cool and intellectual. They consider themselves primarily scientists, explorers and philosophers. They do not engage in galactic politics, but they do travel and visit.

They have had interaction here on your Earth during some of the most influential civilizations; Sumerian, Egyptian.

There was interaction in what you call the Indus Valley. These entities have entered, in a backhanded way, the mythology of your people. They are not bird creatures; they are mammals who are birdlike in appearance. We have not talked about these entities at all up until this point because we've limited our discussion to what matters to you now on the Earth plane. This is a curiosity, but at least for now they do not represent something significant you need to look at to continue your own unfoldment.

Catlike Lyran Subgroup

One other Lyran subgroup is also mammal and what you would consider to be humanoid - but whose physical appearance resembles what you call the feline kingdom on your world. They are not cat people, but humanoids who have catlike qualities. They are very agile and strong. The nose is not predominant but catlike, if you can imagine the nose of a cat. The ears are neither human nor catlike but somewhat of a cross, a little pointed, not very much, but a little. The mouths are very gentle and small. (Many times when extraterrestrials look at the human face, to them the human face is overwhelmed by the mouth.) These catlike entities have very small, delicate and what you would call dainty mouths.

The eyes are very pronounced, large and catlike, with a second lid. Again, these qualities developed from the specific environment they have placed themselves within over generations. They do not have fur. However, there is a protective layer of what you could consider peach fuzz over the skin because of the harsh ultraviolet radiation on their indigenous planet - it simply protected the skin. Any primitive interaction with these entities on your world may report that they are cat people - they are not.

They are humanoid.

So early on, the development of these two groups took a different direction than ours did.

If they're Lyran-based, then we're talking millions of years ago that these developments started separately from our branch, right?

Oh, yes. They are not so much involved in your human drama. This has not been from a denial of the Lyran dysfunction and conflicts. It is simply that their excitement has gone in other directions, and they've evolved in those directions. They have had contact with you every once in awhile.

They recognize that you are all part of a family, at least genetically. And there are individuals within their societies who often project to you on an astral level simply to keep the lines open for communication. But for now there has been no necessity for a lot of interaction between your cultures.

Eyes Of The Extraterrestrials Who Have Communicated With _____You._____

There's a point we would like to make here about the Lyran, Vegan and other extraterrestrial civilizations as well who have communicated with you. It is about their eyes. Primarily the eyes are accentuated, whether it be through the tilt, the shape, the size, the color or their reflectivity. They are usually very pronounced. If you search through your mythologies, many civilizations have accented the eyes – most notably the Egyptian civilization. This did not start out as an adornment but as an imitation of the gods, as an attempt to make humans more godlike, as an attempt to revere the gods.

Over time there has been a loss of the connection to why the eyes were accentuated?
It was originally because of the gods.

So why do our eyes appear to be so small in comparison to the rest of the family?
If you remember the stories we've told about the genetic manipulation in the creation of Homo sapiens, the Lyrans did not want to create you as them. They had some definite issues about creating you equal with them. So one of the choices was in the creation of the eyes – to give you more a simian eye quality. You understand what we mean by simian?

To retain the simian quality?
To retain the simian eye quality, the ape, which to some degree is one of the most painful things they've done to you, because when you look in the mirror your cellular memory remembers simian.
If you had the eyes of the gods when you look into your own eyes, you would see God.

Interesting. When we look in the mirror we see to the past, whereas they see to the future, at least symbolically, the genetic response?
Yes. That was the intent originally, so that you would always be looking behind you, never looking forward. When the Sirians took over the project from the Lyrans it was too late to change it. So to some degree the Sirians encouraged your practice of accentuating the eyes as a remembrance of God so you would not forget your forefathers. They have done a lot through the ages to stimulate memory in you so that you would never ever forget.

Are there other lines of Lyran evolution that have nothing to do with us historically, that literally branched off into other parts of the galaxy?
Oh, yes. But the majority of Lyran evolution is tied with you. For instance, the birdlike and catlike entities we have spoken of have their own affiliation with other groups. They are a part of the developmental evolution of other civilizations. It is important that we stress here once again that the Lyran basic genetic structure is the mother of all in this case.

However, we recognize Vega as being a significant enough emergence that it can take on its own genotype as well. Those entities who from the very, very early days of Lyra branched off in other directions, began through their own experiences, through their own evolution, to form their own unique genotypes.

*** *** ***

The Vegans

There's less variation in the Vegan genotypes than in the Lyran. The primary subgroup of Vegan genetics is what we would call standard Vegan, averaging approximately six to seven feet tall (males and females), darker skin, non-Caucasian type.

Generally speaking, the skin layers are thicker with fewer layers. The skin is not as soft as human skin, is much tougher, able to withstand high levels of ultraviolet radiation and heat as well as cold. A much sturdier and more durable humanoid being. Generally, the hair of any Vegans who have hair will be primarily black, and the range of shades will be standard black as a midpoint to a light to dark brown (which is unusual) and an even darker black with a greenish tinge. That range frequently varies.

What is interesting to note is that, depending on the various Vegan race, some have no hair at all, some have very little hair and some have full heads of hair, depending on the individual race.

The skin tone will be anywhere from light brown (almost beige) to very dark brown – what you would call on your planet (using your own terminology) either negroid or Indian (your native people) – anything in that shade range.

So some of the Eastern Indians are extremely dark brown in contrast to the skin color of some of the African groups that are very black, almost coal black?

Yes. Generally speaking, the coal black is a quality of your Earth that was bred here. It is very unusual out there. Also you will find that the skin will have more of a wrinkled quality – not always, but some will.

Humanoid-Type Vegans

We're basically going to break up the Vegan genotypes into only two categories. One is humanoid and one is nonhumanoid and these are appearances only, not genetic structures. What we have described to you previously as Vegan is of the humanoid type. Generally you're going to find in the humanoid group that the eyes are very striking.

The average eye of the standard Vegan humanoid group has a very large, dark pupil and iris.

The eyes are generally a little angled but still large, and they retain a lid. So it's not like the Zeta, who appear not to have a lid. If they walked down your street they would be very unusual looking, but you would not necessarily think they were alien. They would definitely attract your attention; you might think they had some type of birth defect. The eyes of these Vegans are very striking, and were even more instrumental in getting the attention of the humans than the Lyran's eyes. It was simply the contrast between the darkness of the skin and the whiteness of the eye outside the pupil and iris that made it more striking. Of course, those with darker hair and eyelashes seemed to have a black outline around their very large eyes.

Many of the other groups we will talk about stem from this Vegan group, most notably the Orions. It is a very broad category we've been describing, the human type group in the Vegan genetic structure.

Nonhuman-Type Vegans

The second group – nonhuman-type Vegan – is still humanoid, still mammal. When we say nonhuman we are talking about appearance. The appearance of these particular entities can either be insectlike or reptilian. (These are your labels that we apply to the physical appearance of these particular entities.) Generally speaking, you will find that the range of skin color will apply the same as the human type. However, there are some groups who not only have a greenish tinge to the hair but also to the skin. It's not very pronounced; we don't want you to think we're talking about some type of green monster. We're talking about a basic humanoid entity with a copper base in the skin and bloodstream that gives it a greenish tinge. The eyes are very large and may or may not have a second lid, depending on the planet of origin. They have a very small nose and a pronounced jaw in some cases. The jaw can either be thrust forward (which would give it a reptilian look) or downward (which would give it an insect look). We are talking about humanoid-type entities. We call this group nonhumanoid type only because of the appearance – they are still mammals.

These entities have had communication on your Earth plane with you and have been responsible for some of the stories that circulate about reptilian monsters or cold-blooded aliens, etc.

(When one is in fear, when one encounters the unknown, one often exaggerates the experience.)

These entities are genetically connected to you. They still procreate as mammals.

The base genetic structure is reflective of the template from which your galactic family expresses itself, so they are still part of your family.

There is more to say at some point about these particular entities, but for now we simply want to present this idea for those of you who have had a curiosity about what this reptilian stuff is about.

They are not insect; they are not reptilian; they are humanoid and mammalian. They simply do not look the same as you do. These two groups, then – the Lyran and the Vegan genotypes – are instrumental in how the rest of your galactic family expresses itself genetically. We will now mention the other primary groups of the galactic family and show you where their genetic heritage lies.

The Pleiadian Civilization

The most obvious is that of the Pleiadians. The Pleiadians splintered off from the Lyran group, some going directly to the Pleiades from Lyra, others going to Earth and mixing their genetics with the Earth genetics for themselves, then going back to the Pleiades to join some of the other Lyran splinter groups there. The standard Pleiadian is a mixture of the different genotypes we've talked about.

Generally, a Pleiadian will manifest anywhere from blonde to even some black-haired, or very dark-brown-haired strains. The eyes are generally light blue to a light brown – Caucasian. Generally, they are Caucasian. They can range from very petite (five feet tall) to very large (sometimes seven feet tall – rare, but possible). You can see how some of the recessive genes that they brought from their Lyran heritage (the giants, for instance) may manifest in a body.

So the Pleiadian group, in terms of the Caucasian type, is very diverse.

These light brown eyes you keep mentioning, would they appear at first to be gold?
Yes.

So reports of golden eyes would actually be these light brown eyes, as opposed to our standard brown eyes?

Yes, it is not like your standard brown eyes. When we are talking about eye color, in no way are we talking about what you know as eye color. What you see of your own eye color is only how your eyes reflect light in this reality. If you are vibrating at a different rate or if you are in another plane of reality, all color quality changes, because the laws governing light reflection change and the quality of reflected light changes.

So we can describe this only broadly. There are other colors of eyes, but if we told you lavender eyes, you would picture what lavender looks like and then your perception of what we're saying would be very wrong. So we keep this information very standardized. There's really no need to go further into the Pleiadian genotypes because they reflect the Lyran groups very much. Some are combinations; some are redheads; some are very light-skinned. Pleiadian physical expression is basically dealing with Lyran genetics and, in some cases, Lyran and Terran genetics.

Is that complete?

Emotional temperament of the Pleiadians

Can you talk about the emotional temperament of the Pleiadians, the similarities or dissimilarities within their own groups and in comparison to us?

Is it similar to ours, and is there variance of emotional temperament within the Pleiadian groupings?

Their emotional bodies are much more harmonious, though, understand that where they are today came from their denial of negativity. We've talked to you about that already, so that's nothing new. You, on the other hand, deny both negativity and positivity in an attempt to be neutral or nonfeeling. That is what a greater portion of your reality attempts to do. Now, to some degree this is an attempt at balancing what you see as your forefathers' energies, because obviously whatever they did didn't work for them, since they were still in conflict. So you are bound and determined not to do what your forefathers did in just about every way.

The Pleiadian emotional structure is now not repressing negativity, for the most part.

However, who they are today is because of their repression of negativity.

So to some degree that's how something that is actually a negative thing (repression) can turn into a growth process that can eventually lead to the growth that is sought.

Is the potential similar; is the basic emotional structure similar?

Oh, yes. We would say, more than any of the other races we've talked about with you. The emotional similarity between the Pleiadians and yourselves is most pronounced. One of the biggest reasons for the difference is simply the differences in your reality. If, let's say, several thousands of years ago, Pleiadians from that era came and lived on your world today, they would have become you emotionally.

But with their evolution, that would not occur.

The Orion Civilization

The Orion civilization is primarily 89% Vegan in nature. Of that 89% Vegan genetics, we would say that 75% is of the human-type, Vegan-based genetics. The remaining 14% would be considered nonhuman-type Vegan genetics. Therefore, your stories of reptiles from Orion, although they are embellished somewhat (usually by the emotional body), are accurate because there are those nonhuman-type entities with Vegan-based genetics living within the Orion system (or have in the past) that account for those stories. Primarily it is Vegan in nature.

This would be the body types with the very high copper content that is due not only to the genetic line but the diet?

Yes, most definitely. Your bodies here on Earth are based on water and though theirs have water as a primary substance to some degree, a certain oil or fatty content lubricates the body, the skin. Kind of like the idea of the engine in a car; the gears turn because of the oil. One thing we want to mention is a uniqueness in the eyes of Orions. Through very strict spiritual training, which includes diet, ceremony and certain psychic experiences, various priests in the Orion system can change their eye color to a very vivid blue. Some of your people have had encounters with these Orion-type entities with very sharp blue eyes. If anyone has, it is most likely that the entity they are contacting is a priest of some sort, for the eye color is not natural at birth but is attained through a type of spiritual path. We told you that 89% of the Orion entities are Vegan in nature. The remaining 11% are of a Lyran stock. We would say that of that 11%, 90% are of the light-brown-skinned people we've talked about and the remaining 10% are of the Caucasian-type Lyran – light hair. They are rare, but of course if you're talking about several billions in population, then that could account for a goodly amount of people.

And they do tend to be aggressive, to leave their mark?

Yes, generally that is the common theme. These are the most common physical attributes of these Orion entities. Getting a little esoteric for a moment, as you get into the rarified vibrations, as you're getting into higher levels of fourth density, the physical appearances really become very malleable and not all that important. What we're talking about is the third density and early fourth density characteristics, because that's when the genetic differences are very marked, very apparent.

Is there enough genetic similarity that natural cross-breeding is possible?
Yes, absolutely.

What about between the Lyran and the Vegan types?
We would say that if you took a random Lyran and a random Vegan, there is a 60% chance that the birth would be successful without any alteration whatsoever.

What would the result look like?
In some ways like a typical ethnic person on your planet. Now we're getting into the idea of the breeding on your planet. There have been two lines active on your planet. The royal houses of Vega - which actually have changed hands and are now the royal houses of Sirius, but are the Vegan genetics - and the royal houses of Lyra. Your interbreeding with each other throughout history has been an attempt at unifying those houses. So it stands to reason, then, that any crosses between the two out there would primarily be successful with very little manipulation.

*** *** ***

The Sirian Civilization

This brings us to Sirius. Sirius, being a primary star, in some ways a dimensional doorway for a lot of consciousness, is very diverse. So we would like to make it known here that the Sirians of which we speak are the Sirians of your history, the Sirians who were part of your genetic project on Earth. There are so many Sirians on many different levels (mostly existing in the Light realms) that we don't want you to get confused with what we are talking about - those who were part of the genetic creation on Earth of Homo sapiens.

This Sirian race we are talking about - we'll call them the Sirian gods - stemmed from Vega. So the primary genetics of Sirius is a Vegan stock - darker skin, but anywhere from very light brown to very dark brown. They have a lot of the Vegan qualities, including the very pro-nounced eyes, the large, slightly angled eyes. The particular Sirian gods who had interacted with your planet, having spent a lot of time with the Lyrans who were also part of the genetic project, had done some interbreeding themselves. So these Sirian gods began through time to take on a lot of qualities of the Lyrans. Some began to have lighter skin, some began to be more diverse in their genetic makeup.

It got to the point where the interbreeding between the Lyrans and the Sirians was so mixed that the only way to denote a Sirian would be through their belief structure rather than their physical appearance. Since our focus right now is not the genetic project on Earth, we will be very brief with this.

The ultimate attempt was to join the royal houses of Sirius and Lyra.

Throughout time on your planet, since the prototypes of Adam and Eve were created, this attempt has been made with the belief that a more advanced type of human being could be created. This is still going on; it's not so much now the physical attributes attempting integration but rather the belief structures themselves. Because the Sirians gods were of Vegan heritage, it stands to reason that some of them may have had some of the genetics of the nonhuman-type Vegan entity, which would mean that some of the Sirian gods appeared to be nonhuman, whether that seemed insect or reptilian (though they were mammal, like you but with a different appearance).

That accounts for some of the stories.

Anything more about Sirius before we move on?

Sirius, like Vega, has an extremely bright sun; so bright that if we were to look at it, even at the probable orbits of the planets, it could cause instant blindness, being thousands of times brighter than our sun. I can understand how their sun conditioned the Vegan body, and the Sirian sun may be even harsher. So I'm wondering if some of the aquatic references could not have been due to some elaborate genetic engineering done in the Sirian system just to survive - or is this a distortion of the mythology?

The idea of the cetacean connection on your planet (meaning that cetaceans represent Sirius consciousness) is more a Terran than a Sirian representation. Though there are cetacean creatures in your galactic family, the creation of the cetaceans here was deliberate for Earth. It did not come from somewhere else.

Thus the types of cetaceans you have on your planet evolved with some help; you can see that by examining the skeletons of dolphins and whales. They have finger and toe bones in their fins.

They have a rudimentary humanoid skeleton that has been adapted for their environment.

What you're saying is that Cetaceans don't represent a genetic heritage in the human family through Sirius?

Correct. But they do represent a genetic alternative. It was desired that genetic alternatives would be present for those who wished other experiences. There is a lot more we could talk about regarding this; however, we want to keep it focused in a certain direction. If you want questions on this at another time, please feel free to ask.

*** *** ***

114

CHAPTER 4
THEORIES AND FINDINGS ABOUT THE DESCENDANT OF THE ANUNNAKI AND ALIENS' RACES STILL LIVING AMONG US

- The unrevealed and secret history and origin of the aliens known as the Anunnaki
- Ancient Arabic, Pre-Islamic Era Document Related to the Anunnaki
- The forbidden secret book of the "Ultimate Knowledge"
- A key sentence: "Wa Ma Khalaknah Lakoum, Ja'a min Al Anna-ki"
- Most important reference to the Anunnaki: Wa Fi Baalaback, Rafat Al Aliha (Elohim) Al Annah-Ki HAJARAT AL HOUBLAH Bi Soura Ghayrou Mar Iya...Al Malakout"
- Importance and meaning of the stone "Pregnant Woman"
- Children in Ohio may be taught life was created by aliens
- Collier and Moraney theories
- 13 families from Sirius B and Nubiru, were living here on the planet
- The first melding between the primate genes and the human species was 28,731,007 BC
- The Magi interbreeding resulted in the cultures such as "Ivory Hebrew", the "Mayan", the "Celts", and the "Aryan" races
- The Reptilian Race...The Serpent Race
- All our languages derived from extraterrestrial languages
- There was a race of human beings prior to the Sumerians called the "Annunites"
- Moraney: They controlled the human race by controlling the water supply
- The Magi created the class system and priesthood on earth
- The Pleiadians, Lyrians, Vegans, Centaurians and human beings

- Lyrian beamshipsThe craft carried 3 beings aboard, one of whom introduced herself as MenaraThe ship was constructed 300 years in our future
- Vegan beamships…Vegan origin…Vegan ancestry
- DAL universe beamships
- The DALs are a handsome Nordic-looking race
- Lyrians were the original ancestors of our branch of our lifestream of evolution
- Lyrian history
- The new wave of Pleiadians and the creation of the Atlantean civilization
- The Lyrians believe that Creation itself is the First Cause, not that a Creator created it.
- The Bawwi extraterrestrial race
- The Lyrians produced and developed a civilization with advanced technology here on Earth.
- Their home planet atmosphere is very similar to ours
- Their skin…Their hands…Their gardens…Their schools…Their professions
- They need to adjust time and vibrational state in order to contact us and we would have to do the same
- The Pleiadians have more ground stations in use on our surface. One of them is in the United States
- Their time is altered slightly
- The large "mother-ship" in solar orbit
- Other extraterrestrials come from an atmospheric planet about 10 light years from Earth, a planet which they call Iarga
- Description of the Planet Iarga
- Another contact with extraterrestrials from planet near Epsilon Eridani
- Another contact involves the smaller hairless alien creatures with white skin, large domed heads, large eyes and small facial features
- These extraterrestrial creatures came from Zeta 1 and Zeta 2 Reticuli
- The Cygnusians
- Extraterrestrials are under the authority of a confederation of planets headed by a high council in Andromeda
- Non-physical beings who exist in a different kind of energy form
- The strange being who said "Muurrrg" to Meier
- Comments by Victoria

***   ***   ***

Theories And Findings About The Descendant Of Aliens' Races Still Living Among Us

The unrevealed and secret history and origin of the aliens known as the Anunnaki

---

1-Ancient Arabic, Pre-Islamic Era Document Related to the Anunnaki

One fascinating version of the unrevealed and secret history and origin of the aliens known as Anunnaki was detailed in the "Ulema" Arabic book of "Shams Al Maaref Al Koubra" (Sun of the Great Knowledge). The book called the Anunnaki "Annah-Ki."

I have read and studied it for years. In the seventies, I translated the book from ancient Arabic to Greek, but I was not allowed to publish it.

This secret book was banned by Muslims and the Maronite Church in the Near/Middle East, because the authors were thought to be "Jin", "Afreet", and "Spirits"; celestial beings who manifest themselves to humans in multiple forms according to their wishes and needs. Those entities are mentioned in Pre-Islamic era literature, in early Coptic and Armenian religious texts, in the Quran and in the official Maronite mass prayers book in Lebanon and Syria. So, there is no fabrication about their existence.

The forbidden secret book of the "Ultimate Knowledge"

This secret book teaches the forbidden language of the spirits of the lower and higher dimensions of heaven. Later on, I will use the term "Aliens" instead of "Spirits".

Every Muslim Sheik in the region has heard about this book and secretly wished if he could put his hand on it, because it reveals great secrets and the "Ultimate Knowledge."

"Ultimate Knowledge" means the secret knowledge of the creation of the human race, its relation with "Al Khalek" (The Creator), and a very particular language used to call upon "Al Arwah" (The spirits), and "Mala-Ikah" (The Angels). The book was presented to me by Mr. Farid Tayarah, who was "Nakeeb Al Sahafah Sabikan", (The former president of the Press Syndicate of Lebanon). Mr. Tayarah was also the president of the Masonic Lodge, number 18 located in the "Bastah" Muslim area of Beirut, 50 feet away from the school "Kouliyat Loubnan" (Lyceum of Lebanon), owned and operated by the very well-known, Father Hannah Al Fakhouri, a Maromite priest, scholar and author of scholastic books on Arab literature.

Intentionally, I am giving you all these details and names to anchor the veracity of my story. Once again, let me repeat that "Shams Al Maaref Al Koubra" (Sun of the Great Knowledge) is the most sought and most treasured book in the history of Oriental Christianity, Islamic world, the Middle East, Near East and Anatolia.

A Key Sentence:

In chapter 13, I read this phrase: "Wa Ma Khalaknah Lakoum, Ja'a min Al Anna-ki".
Verbatim: And what WE have created for you, came from the Anunnaki.
It is interesting and mind-boggling to me, to have seen this book in the hands of Mr. Tayarah, a devoted Muslim Sunni, for the book sharply contradicts the teachings of Islam, the message of the Prophet Mohammad, and his "Hadith Sharif" (Holy Dialogue and Speech of the Prophet.) The book was Mr. Tayarah's most precious possession. At that time, Mr. Tayarah was 53 year old.
This very book was frequently used in ceremonies and meetings of the Freemasons of "Al Bastah Lodge." I knew this for a fact, because for a short period, I joined the lodge and attended numerous Freemasons' meetings in the third floor of the building housing the Lodge. Another astonishing phrase of the book goes like this: "Anzalou Al Hayat Ala Al Ardi". Verbatim: And they (Anunnaki) descended life on Earth. Also, the book ties the Anunnaki to the existence of the early giants who inhabited the earth and built immense buildings and temples in Baalbeck, a city in Lebanon, now occupied by Muslim Shiha and Hizboullah Party.

Most Important Reference to the Anunnaki:

In chapter 21, I read this phrase, probably this is the <u>MOST important statement and reference about the Anunnaki's presence in the ancient Middle East and their system of building cities on Earth</u>: "Wa Fi Baalaback, Rafat Al Aliha (Elohim) Al Annah-Ki HAJARAT AL HOUBLAH Bi Soura Ghayrou Mar Iya...Al Malakout".
In a following sentence, the words: Baa'Al, Malak, Malek and Mala-Ikah were used. Those words are primordial and revealing. I will explain their enormous importance and how they categorically refer to the Anunnaki.
These two sentences are extremely important, because:

- 1-They contain Arabic, Aramaic, Hebrew, Syriac, Sumerian and Phoenician, and Canaanite words; all in the same sentences. Quite unique "cocktail" of languages in one single sentence.
- 2-They explain in three words how the Anunnaki built up enormous buildings and lifted up in the air blocks of stone exceeding several thousands tons.
- 3-They locate the precise region where the Anunnaki first settled in the Near East long before they flourished in Iraq.
- 4-They cite "HAJARAT AL HOUBLAH" which is the world's largest and heaviest piece of sizzled/carved stone ever to be found or moved on Earth! Incidentally, Dr. Zecharia Sitchin mentioned this stone in his books. I have personally seen this stone in Baalbeck, Lebanon.

Explanations:

Let's go back to the first sentence, translate it and analyze each word of it.

"Wa (***and***) Fi (***In***) Baalaback, (***Baalbeck***) Rafat (***Lifted up***) Al (***The***) Aliha Baa'hl (***Gods***) Al (***The***) Annah-Ki (***Anunnaki***) HAJARAT (***Stone***) AL (***The***) HOUBLAH (***Pregnant Woman***) Bi (***With***) Soura (***Way or Fashion***) Ghayra (***Without***) Mar-Iya (***Being Visible or Could be Seen by the Naked Eye***)... Elihim (Plural of **Eli** meaning: ***The Gods***) Al (***The***) Malakout (***Paradise or Heaven, or Kingdom of Gods***).

So, the full sentence becomes word for word:
And in Baalbeck, lifted up the Gods Anunnaki stone of the pregnant woman with a way without being visible or could be seen by the naked eye...The Gods of the heaven.

Linguistic composition of the sentence:
Wa is Arabic
Fi is Arabic
Baalaback or Ba'al Back is Phoenician, Hittite, Canaanite
Rafat is Arabic
Al also *El* or *Il* is Hebrew, Aramaic, Arabic, Phoenician
Hajarat Houblah is Arabic
Bi is Arabic
Soura or *Sourat* is Arabic, Hebrew
Ghayra is Arabic
Mar-Iya is Arabic
Elihim or *Ilahi* is Hebrew, Aramaic, Arabic
Malakout or Malkoot is Aramaic, Hebrew, Phoenician, Canaanite, Arabic

---

In the ancient world, historically, traditionally, religiously, epistemologically and linguistically, when one word or one name is pronounced the same way (Or close to) or meant the same thing in many different languages, this is an indication that this word or this name reflects a major importance, since the meaning was understood by several people from so different civilizations and populations. Thus, the inclusion of several words from different languages in the same sentence reveals an extremely important message. Those who wrote the sentence wanted so many people from so many cultures and nationalities to understand it.

Note: Jews who lived in the region, pronounced Annunaki: Anahk. The "hk" to be pronounced Ek. In Arabic, the "hk" is pronounced the same way you pronounce "Jose" in Spanish.

Very Important Extraterrestrial Site in Baalbeck

Importance of the Baalbeck ruins and the stone "Pregnant Woman"

Baa'lbeck, or as the Lebanese and inhabitants of the region say and write it is "Baalbeck." In their native tongue, spoken Arabic is "Baalback." In the written Arabic (Language of the book) is: Baalaback.

I have visited the area numerous times, and I have spent a few weekends there as the guest of Mr. Ahmad Al Huseini, a Muslim historian, a dear friend and one of my students. Also, I spent several days on the very sites of the Roman ruins and what is left from the plateau of the temple of Jupiter where "Le Festival International de Baalbeck" took place for several years; it is an international festival of Lebanese traditional and modern music, and Lebanese famous "Dabkeh" (Dance like the Greek Sirtaki) as a guest of the leading singers and dancers of the festival, and director of the festival; remarkable people like Fayrouz, Sabah, the Rahbanis, Kegham, Nasri Shams El Dine, Philemon Wehbe and Wadih Al Safi.

I knew them all. In other words, I know the sites and the people extremely well. Especially the alleged UFO's landing plateau and main temple of the Anunnaki. I am calling it temple for now, but in fact it is an edifice/mining lab known to and used by Sumerians, Babylonians, Phoenicians, Hittites, Hyskos, Egyptians, Nubians, Greeks, Romans, Anatolians and Arabs.

Practically, I lived there for a while, and I was able to conduct intense research, exchange documents, talk to the local historians, treasures hunters, mediums, Spiritists, topographers, charlatans, and colorful and unusual characters who were directly involved with alien races and extraterrestrial entities that have landed in the area and built enormous buildings in Baalbeck.

What I have learned about UFOs and extraterrestrials of Baalbeck did not come to me from reading UFOs books published in the United States, and so-called channelers who receive their information via trance, séances and silly creatures talking to them from outer space.

What I have learned is enormously important, because it originated from the direct source, and I love to share with you some "notions" and "items", but not the whole story, because I can't.

"Hajarat Al Houblah" as nicknamed by Arabs and Lebanese, means the "Stone of the Pregnant Woman." In ancient times, the Sumerians and Phoenicians (Ancient people of Lebanon) called it the landing and launching platform for extraterrestrial beings and their birds' flying machines. The ruins of Jupiter Temple at Baalbeck offer a spectacular site; rows and rows and rows of 605 tons stone (each!) perfectly lined up, carved symmetrically with absolutely perfect edges, supporting gigantic columns.

These stones are almost 25 times heavier, bigger and larger than any carved and transported stones in recorded history. Today, no technology in the world can lift or move such heavy weight.

But this is not the most amazing aspect of the site. On a higher platform, more stones exceeding 925 tomes (each) retain a wall. Still, this is NOT the strangest thing on the site.

On the top of these monstrous stones, there are layers of perfectly carved stones exceeding 1,150 tons each.

You need to line up 35 persons side by side, and shoulder to shoulder to cover the length of each stone! It is mind-boggling.

Not very far from the standing columns, rests the mysterious "Hajarat Al Houblah", the biggest and heaviest carved stone of all. One of its ends is buried in the ground, and the other end stands up, barely touching the ground.

Under the stone, there is a deep ditch. Local legend has it that in ancient times before the Muslims conquered Lebanon, this ditch was the entrance to a secret underground passage leading to a city inhabited by the "Jins" and an alien race.

The cavern or underground entrance was excavated by the conquering Islamic troops and later on totally covered – and hidden – by the Arabs. Residents of the area claim that the Muslims found secret manuscripts containing alchemy instruction and formulas for metal transmutation into gold.

The instructions were written in two languages; The Anakh or Annackh (Anunnaki) language and Sumerian language. Not very far away, a mosque underground tunnel linked the buried end of Al Houblah stone to a mine, commonly referred to as an underground city inhabited by a strange-looking non-human race who were in the business of "manufacturing creatures and beings."

According to Dr. Zecharia Sitchin: "The Maronite Christians who for generations deemed themselves custodians of the site (before they were displaced by the Shiite Moslems) told legends of the "giants" who had built the colossal platform. I found the answers in the ancient Sumerian texts, and related them in *The Stairway to Heaven* and *The Wars of Gods and Men*.

The great stone platform was indeed the first Landing Place of the Anunnaki gods on Earth, built by them before they established a proper spaceport.

It was the only structure that had survived the Flood, and was used by Enki and Enlil as the post-Diluvial headquarters for the reconstruction of the devastated Earth. It is the only structure on Earth from before the Flood."

The year is 1974: By pure coincidence, in the basement of the National Museum of Beirut, Monsignor Maroon, a Catholic priest and scholar brought my attention to a Phoenician tablet found in Ougarit in 1946, and which was completely forgotten, or perhaps unnoticed by the curator and historians.

I went to the museum, because the director general/curator called me and asked if I could help in the final cataloging and shipment of hundreds of tablets and terracotta pieces to a safe place, far away from Beirut.

The museum has been constantly bombarded by Palestinian militia, because Christian Maronites fighters known as Al Kataeb (Phalanges or Phalangists) used part of the museum as an ammunition depot, and as a military command center on the so-called "The Green Line" dividing the Capital Beirut in two zones: The Christian zone and the Muslim Zone.

The museum's director general/curator introduced me to the Monsignor who was a distinguished linguist, and an authority on the history of the religions of the Near/Middle East. The Monsignor was helping the curator in identifying, cataloging and assigning a brief title to each historical piece, because he was fluent in Aramaic, Syriac, Hebrew, Arabic, French, Greek, Latin, Phoenician and Sumerian languages. Almost 90% of these ancient tablets were Roman, Phoenician, Sumerian, Hittite and from the era of the Crusaders.

While numbering the ancient plates, Monsignor Maroon tapped gently on my shoulder and said: "Read this! Fascinating...Did you know this?" I looked at the tablet, read a few lines and with the help of the Monsignor's integral translation, I kept on reading and reading... And I was stunned! The tablet told the story of "Adon" (Adonis), a Phoenician god, who was also worshiped by the Greeks and the early Hebrews who referred to him as "Adonai", (Lord in Hebrew) and the original "Yahweh." *

Adonis was the lover of "Ashtaroot" known also as "Astarte" and "Aphrodite". Adonis was killed by a jealous god who was in love with Ashtaroot. Following his death, the river "Nahr Ibrahim" turned into a river of blood. The last two lines of the tablet described Adonis as a "traveling handsome god" who descended on earth aboard "a circular disc resembling the sun to fertilize the earth." Worth mentioning here, the striking similarities with Biblical accounts:

1- The "Ibrahim River": The Jews use "Abraham". The Arabs and people of the area use "Ibrahim" instead. Both names refer to the same biblical personage.

2- The Ibrahim River turning into a river of blood echoes the story of one of the biblical plagues.

3- Yahweh was also called Adonai or Adoni by the Hebrews. And the Phoenicians called their god "Adon."

4- Hebrews, Phoenicians and Sumerians...all of them wrote about gods descending on earth to "fertilize the earth" and "fertilize" women of the earth, thus giving birth to a new breed of humans.

The tablet clearly identified "Adon" as an extraterrestrial creator. You might say that all these stories are nothing by mythology. Sure, it is mythology. But everything in our human existence started with a mythological tale, and the Anunnaki as brought to the Western world by Dr. Sitchin were the product and subject of what you might call a Sumerian mythology. But look now to what happened to this Sumerian mythology that took the world by storm; it became the foundation of the most advanced historical, archeological and scientific theories of all time.

---

* Adonis is derived from the ancient Canaanite "Adon". It is the Semitic meaning of "Master" or "My Lord" in Hebrew. In their prayer, the Jews pronounce "Yahweh' (YHWH) as "Adonai." It is directly derived from the Phoenician words: "Adon" and "Adonis." Also, the Hebrew, Aramaic and Arab words: "Eloi", "Elohak", "Eloh", "Elahona", "Elohaino", "Eli", "Elah" and "Allah" derived from the Phoenician "El".

*** *** ***

Children in Ohio may be taught life was created by aliens

In March 2002, The Herald Sun, Columbus, Ohio, wrote: "Children in Ohio may be taught life was created by aliens under an education package designed to ditch Darwin's Theory of evolution. The US state is considering adopting the "intelligent design" theory that life is too complex to have simply evolved – as the Darwin Theory suggests. Therefore says the package, life must have been designed by some supernatural being, maybe God, maybe aliens."

Collier and Moraney Theories

13 families from Sirius B and Nubiru were living here on the planet.

According to Alex Collier, (from his essay on the Reptilians) when the extraterrestrials were here in force - that is, during the time referenced in the Bible where it says the Sons of God married the Daughters of Man, they bred and mated with their human wives. Out of this came offspring, half-breeds. There were at that time, within the last 5,000 years, predominantly 13 families from Sirius B and Nubiru, who were living here on the planet.

These were the tribes of En-lil, Marduk, Enki, etc. They all had offspring. Those from Nubiru were a tribe that came about as a result of a "marriage" between some groups between Sirius B and Orion. It was in essence a "royal marriage" between groups that formed a "tribe". This "tribe" was called Nubiru. The word Nubiru, in the ancient Sumerican language, means "between two peoples". I know Sitchin calls it something else. The offspring were not allowed to go with the extraterrestrial parents when they left the Earth, because they were considered "half-breeds". The reason they were viewed like this by the extraterrestrials was because of their Terran genetics, which contain certain genes from the primate race.

The first melding between the primate genes and the human species was 28,731,007 BC

According to Moraney, the first melding between the primate genes and the human species was 28,731,007 BC, and there have been many prototypes. In fact, they just found another prototype in Portugal that is estimated to be 780,000 years old. They will discover more. In fact, start looking for some major discoveries in Nigeria.

Apparently, there is a tremendous amount of extraterrestrial technology buried in Nigeria that has not been tapped yet.

When the extraterrestrials left, the real ET's, they left certain types of technology behind. The Indian Veda's discuss some of this technology. They didn't care. They had science teams who were constantly inventing new things, and as they got new technology they discarded the old. Well, it was the Magi, the half-breeds who left these technologies.

There were 13 major families that were considered under the heading of Magi. Does that number ring a bell?

The Magi interbreeding resulted in the cultures such as "Ivory Hebrew", the "Mayan", the "Celts", and the "Aryan" races

The members of these 13 families on earth contain the genetics of both Terran and extraterrestrial races that formerly tyrannized the Earth. They were basically left in charge. Some of them were actually Pharoahs. The Magi interbreeding resulted in the cultures we today recognize as the "Ivory Hebrew", the "Mayan", the "Celts", and the "Aryan" races. Now, while all of this was transpiring on the surface of the planet, underground there was another extraterrestrial race that had been here - a race that has been here for hundreds of thousands of years.

The Reptilian Race...The Serpent Race

They are, of course, the reptilian race, which the Bible refers to as the "serpent race". Serpent men are still here, and they can't stand the radiation of the sun. They haven't been able to live on the surface of the planet since the last major war that occurred here approximately 450,000 years ago. They are basically hyperborean in nature. They have control of the planet at depths from 100 to 200 miles down. That's their turf, and no one contests that. That is why when people go into the inner earth, they enter via the poles. They do not go through the crust, because these reptilians simply do not like humans.

They consider us to be "fleas" on the surface. Again, prejudice as a concept has its origin in extraterrestrial perspectives.

All Our Languages Derived From Extraterrestrial Languages

All of the concepts involving languages and social structures for human societies were introduced by extraterrestrial sources. All of the languages that we have on the planet have their origins within the structures of extraterrestrial languages. The letters and their numerical values.

There was a race of human beings prior to the Sumerians called the "Annunites"

Moraney: They controlled the human race by controlling the water supply

From Moraney's perspective, "Adam and Eve" were in fact two human tribes that were created. I know the Bible refers to "Adam" as a singular person. This is not accurate. According to Moraney, there was a race of human beings prior to the Sumerians called the "Annunites", and they were named after the chief scientist who the Sumerian's called the "God" Anu. The name of "A-dam", as far as these people were concerned, was originally "Anu-dam". That word meant workers in the mines. Like everything else, we get the "Cliff notes" version of what really was the case.

I (Alex Collier) asked Moraney how the extraterrestrials were able to control all the populations. Apparently, there were groups of hundreds of thousands of people in areas all over the planet. Moraney said that it was very easy to control the population by controlling the water. He said that primary control was through technology, but the single most important control mechanism for a race as primitive as ours was control of the water supply. You have to have water.

This leads me to share something with you that I started to share earlier. Two weeks ago, Bill Clinton signed a presidential directive, number 28, which is legislation that has been put into the Federal Register. It did not go to Congress for approval. They withheld it for two weeks, only giving the legislation 14 days of review before it became law.

It is called the River Heritage Act. He is taking ten of the largest rivers in the United States and declaring on behalf of the Federal Government that ten miles on each side constitute a "world heritage protection site".

Now, why would he do this? On the entire planet, 2.5% of the water is fresh water that is fit to drink. Now, 78% of that 2.5% is right here in North America.

The Great Lakes.

Are you getting the picture?

126

The Magi Created the Class Systems and Priesthood on Earth

Now, the Magi created class systems around themselves: Priesthood. You can read about this priesthood's in Sumerian and Egyptian lore. Every major religion has these. The priesthood's of the Magi were known as the "Naga", and I know that is a name that has been thrown around a lot. The Naga constituted the priesthood. They are like the international bankers today, who are the new "priesthood", in a sense, for the extraterrestrial controllers. Everything in your life revolves around money. Everything. My reason for bringing this up is to show you how history is constantly repeating itself. Our race has been stuck in a cycle of doing the same thing over and over again, and getting "screwed" over and over again. Maybe now you will be able to take a step back and see the "games" and the political mind sets that are coming down again. Folks, it's right there. I want you to know something, and I mean this with all my heart. There are people that say, "you know, Alex, if you think this way you will create it". Well, you know what? I don't think this way, and it's being created anyway. The reason it's being created anyway is because of apathy. People don't give a damn, because they are so busy just "surviving". Well, you are going to have to try and make room for more than just "survival" in your life. You're going to have to do this. There is only one semi-free nation on the planet. The United States. If we loose it, there is nowhere for us to go, and I will tell you this: I refuse to serve two masters! I refuse. You can't do it.

The Pleiadians, Lyrians, Vegans, Centaurians and Human Beings

According to the writers and researchers of the group of the whipnet org., the Pleiadian extraterrestrials presently visiting and lending a hand to we of Earth are part of a larger Confederation of Planets involving a lifestream of human like forms almost identical to ourselves. Other extraterrestrials in this group are the Lyrians, Vegans, and DAL Universe entities (and probably the Centaurians too.)

The text of this article was obtained from "UFO Contact from the Pleiades", by Wendelle Stevens, and includes most of the text from Chapter 11 "Other Cosmonauts" and some from Chapter 12 "Re- Investigation", in which the whipnet org reorganized and combined. The book mainly concerns the Billy Meier case of the 1970's, in which Meier was visited numerous times by the Pleiadian extraterrestrials. (The "I" in the text below refers to Stevens, the investigator.)

Lyrian Beamships

In 1977 a new and different spacecraft landed on the drive in front of the Meier home and he went out to investigate. There he saw a circular disk-shaped craft with a high cupulo on top sitting about 1 meter above the ground on a very coherent straight-sided beam of white light.

The disk-shaped lower part of the strange craft was of a bright matt silver color and was rotating slowly in a counterclockwise direction. The rim, or edge, of the disk about 60 cm thick, was squared off into vertical sides which seemed to consist of myriads of small flapper vanes mounted vertically, and which moved from right to left and back again through a 90 degree arc in a rhythmic sequence. A 3 meter diameter underflange of the base of the craft projected down about 20 cm below the lower disk surface and was also squared off on the sides. The intense white light which seemed to support the ship was projected down vertically from this lower flange. Inside of the intense white light Meier could see a cantilever stair of 5 steps descending from the lower center of the craft to the ground surface. Back to the rim, he could see that as it rotated slowly and the vertical flapper vanes moved back and forth, an aura of rainbow colors was thrown off to the sides around the rim.

The 7 meter diameter main disk structure was about 1.5 meters measured from top to bottom, and the lower surface showed more of a curve than the upper.

On top of that a 2.5 meter diameter cupulo with 1 meter vertical sides having 8 bulging hemispherical windows set into them, rose to a 70 cm thick rolled static ring having about the same 3 meter diameter as the bottom underflange of the base.

This part was a luminous orange color and a bright yellow-white light shown from the "windows".

The top of this cupulo structure blended into a smooth curved dome of some kind of colored dark glass. It looked like glass and has a smooth finish but he could not see any reflections in its surface.

The craft carried 3 beings aboard, one of whom introduced herself as Menara

This craft carried 3 beings aboard - one of whom introduced herself as Menara, from a place in the heavens near the star system Lyra. She said that her native planet has a population of 14 billion and belongs to a confederation of planets. She said that her people work closely with the DALs and the Pleiadians on certain things, and that those intelligences were aware of her activities here. Another member aboard the ship was identified as Alena. They were both darker skinned and had long slender forms. The Lyrians have more than one racetype of beings on their planet.

Menara said that her ship could travel in time as well as space and offered the mind boggling note that her ship was constructed 300 years in our future but that it had been in use for over 250 years already.

It appears that there is an ascending order of technological development here. The Pleiadians say their technology is about 3000 years in advance of ours but that the DALs are about 350 Earth years of technology ahead of them, and that they are assisted technologically by the DALs.

Now we have a race of beings from Lyra who seem to be several thousand years ahead of the DALs, who help the DALs and the Pleiadians in certain respects.

This may give us some clue to the kind of guidance offered us by the Pleiadians. The contact with the beings from Lyra is also continuing and more landings have taken place, including another landing in snow 12 cm deep, where the characteristic circular landing track was melted through the snow and ice clear to the ground.

Vegan Beamships...Vegan Origin...Vegan Ancestry

In a passing conversation on another matter, "Billy" casually mentioned the Vegans, beings who come here from the direction of the constellation Vega. Further inquiry developed the information that the Vegan technology is only about 250 years ahead of that of the Pleiadians, and that they also are in contact with the DALs, and were in fact assisted by the DALs just as were the Pleiadians.

The Pleiadians, the Vegans, the DALs and the Lyrians all belong to the same lifestream, which also includes us! There are others not known to Meier and not elaborated upon by these entities. The being identified as Alena returned at another time in her own ship, having signaled Meier telepathically in advance. She arrived in still another style of spacecraft which Meier had not seen before. She explained that she, and others like her, come from a planet in the star-system Vega, which is a part of the constellation Lyra as viewed from here.

The Vegans are darker in color still than the Lyrians, and look a little like Hottentots except with higher cheekbones and more triangular faces.

The Vegans, as explained to Meier, are really descended from the early Lyrians also, as are the Pleiadians and us. Their ancestry is a little older than that of the Pleiadians.

The Vegans arrive at our surface in 8 meter diameter circular craft that land, or rather hover, on a coherent beam of plasmic energy 40 to 50 cm above the ground. This plasma efflux flows downward only 30 to 40 cm and then curls out and up in an almost ring-like coil.

129

The efflux looks more like a very definite length curtain of bluish-white flame with a ring around the bottom, except that it flows constantly. Meier says that the efflux looks like it comes out of a hatched grating of very heavy metal mesh inside the circular bottom surface. The ship has a raised dome of transparent material in many pie-shaped sections, or else it is one piece with transparent ribs that rise vertically and meet at the top. The cupulo is surrounded at the base by a smooth brushed silver ring of a stainless steel color. From this ring plate to the rim of the ship the upper surface skin is fluted with the sharper creases up. The bottom of the craft has a smooth stainless steel-like finish from the perimeter of the plasma efflux up to the rim. The rims do not come together but have a narrow gap which is filled by a circular small-fluted plate of very peculiar shape. Instead of being truly circular like the rims of the disk-sections, it has a 4-lobed shape as viewed from above. This fluted plate rotates rapidly in a counter-clockwise direction between the rims. The rapidly rotating fluted section gives off an orange glow.

Dal Universe Beamships
The DALs Are A Handsome Nordic-Looking Race

Exactly how the DALs fit into the relationship is not clear at this time. They are a handsome Nordic-looking race so like northern European Caucasians that they could pass in conventional clothes on our streets unnoticed. The DALs arrive in circular disk-shaped spacecraft also but their ships have a little lower profile and land flat on the ground on a flat-surfaced bottom. The bottom has 3 light colored rings and 2 dark colored rings and a dark center in the flat surface of the bottom which was not explained. (Meier succeeded in photographing a DAL spacecraft at about 16:00 in the afternoon on 3 July 1964 as it flew over the Ashoka Ashram on Gurgoan Road at Mehrauli, near New Delhi, India.) The next section up is a lighter metallic rim that rises almost vertically to a dark metallic rim that joins another light colored metallic piece which forms the upper disk flange to the raised cupulo in the center.

The DALs can also breathe our atmosphere directly and do not need environmental headgear to debark from their ship.

Exit and egress from the DAL ship is through the canopy section of the dome which raises on a rear hinge arrangement.

The cabin of the ship Meier was allowed to inspect, and has seats for three. He had photographed this type of ship earlier. It is also about 8 meters in diameter.

Lyrian history

This was all becoming a little confusing and so the Pleiadians offered a brief history to get it into perspective. According to the explanation offered, the Lyrians were the original (to us at least) ancestors of our branch of our lifestream of evolution.

Many thousands of years ago their civilization in Lyra reached a high technological level and they began to travel in space. They were free-will creatures and had control of their destiny. At a certain point in time they fell into disagreement and divided into factions with different ideaologies and different goals and objectives. They eventually went to war and destroyed much of their society and ruined their home. Escapists seeking to avoid the anticipated outcome fled from their native system and found homes in star systems that we call the Pleiades and the Hyades. They also went to nearby Vega. In a few thousands of years they had raised those societies to high technological levels and once again were able to travel in space. Some of the Pleiadians of Lyrian ancestry, on their travels, discovered our planet and its nascent life evolving in a very hospitable atmosphere. They stayed and settled briefly in later Lemuria and early Atlantis, some even mixing with Earth creatures and becoming Earth men. Those who remained apart and did not mix soon produced highly evolved technologies here and they designed and built many wonderful machines and devices, and created comforts and conveniences of all kinds. Again they came into conflict and the society became polarized into two camps, each possessing marvelous technologies.

Eventually they went to war and terrible destruction resulted. Those who could, escaped to other regions of space and started all over again. Some of those beings are now also visiting us occasionally.

The New Wave Of Pleiadians And The Creation Of The Atlantean Civilization

A long time later a new wave of Pleiadians arrived to check on the descendants of their ancestors who survived the terrible war. They found survivors and again they mixed with them and assisted Earth humanity in getting control of its assets and producing a new technology. This society became the later Atlanteans who raised their sciences to levels that produced air and undersea travel before that civilization was also destroyed by surface war on Earth.

The modern Pleiadians are descendants of the peaceful faction that settled in the star group which astronomy gives that name. The Vegans visiting us now are descendants of another peaceful group that settled a planet in the Vega System.

The descendants of the Lyrians, long evolved beyond the conflict stage, are now interested in our welfare and feel a special responsibility toward us since we reflect the earlier warlike tendencies of themselves.

They lost much in their history of conflict and destroyed themselves several times, and lost their great technological advances each time. According to the story, they even settled another hospitable planet in our solar system, the 5th one from the sun, which was actually destroyed in a war of nuclear weapons that got out of hand there. This is part of their concern about how we will use our nuclear sciences now. These Lyrians are now being helped and assisted in certain ways by their human cousins in the Pleiades and Vega and others. So we see that although the Lyrians are much older in evolution, they are only a little ahead of the others in some technologies and are behind in others, and are being assisted along the way by their cousins. Thus it is that so many human-like extraterrestrials are appearing in the same age in time. Some are actually linked in evolution and do apparently have a common source. Our re-emerging technology attracts their attention now and they are here to observe and assist according to our will choices.

The Lyrians believe that Creation itself is the First Cause, not that a Creator created it.

The Lyrian races began evacuating their home planet over 22 million years ago, and they have peaked out and migrated from there more than once. They believe that Creation itself is the First Cause, not that a Creator created it. They see creation as Universal Knowledge, Universal Wisdom, Universal Spirit. They told Meier that there are milliards of creation forms known to them. They also told him that our earliest society on Earth was copied from the early Lyrians visiting Earth. They were here and observed physical life on Hyperboria, a mythical first continent encompassing all of the land mass at that time. This was before Earth humans began physical evolution. Descendants of these Lyrians came again later and assisted the budding societies of the next epoch and gave Lemuria and Atlantis their names.

The Bawwi Extraterrestrial Race

There were other beings from another system called Bawwi who also visited the Earth at that time. The Bawwi were a race of beings 2.5 to 3 meters tall. There were once beings visiting Earth who were 7 to 8 meters tall. They had feet 90 to 93 cm long and fossil tracks should still exist. On what we now call Easter Island there was a special race of very big people an unimaginable 10 to 11 meters tall. They were not entirely physical. Whole histories of Hyperboria, Agartha, Mukulia and Atlantis have been described by the Pleiadians. On an extended visit in space, Meier was shown another atmospheric planet with life in an earlier stage of evolution. He saw dinosaur-like creatures, a stocky primitive man wearing skins and steep pyramids in the distance in a very misty golden atmosphere. He was told that this planet would be 770 light years from Earth.

The Lyrians produced and developed a civilization with advanced technology here on Earth.

According to the Pleiadian account, the Lyrians left their system as rebels and settled in the Pleiades and the Hyades. They later came to Earth and mixed with Earth man. Earth men then lived in the remnants of the earlier single continental land mass now known as Hyperboria. These beings produced and developed a civilization with advanced technology here on Earth. They became involved in a war among themselves here and a faction left and proceeded to Erra in the Pleiades, and others went to another planet in our solar system, an atmospheric planet the 5th from the sun, which they called Malona. They settled on this planet and mixed with the human life-form there.

The Lyrian descendants who settled Earth and Malona both were a war-like race and they carried their warlike tendencies with them. The Malonans ended up destroying their planet in a terrible atomic holocaust. Will we do the same?

The surviving Lyrians left for many thousands of years.

Subsequent generations came back in another age and again fell to fighting among themselves and again they left.

This was repeated still once more, and now the descendants of those are again observing Earth and the surviving descendants of their ancestors. The Lyrian rebels have now reached a higher spiritual level of being and no longer indulge in conflict and war.

Their ancestors are responsible for the racial variety now found on Earth. So we see that we and the Pleiadians, and the Vegans, and some other Adamic beings who come here from the Hyades, are all in a sense Lyrian descendants, and we are linked by a common heritage.

The current Lyrian visitors, with their higher spirituality, are here trying to undo some of the effects left by their earlier less spiritual ancestors.

Their home Planet Atmosphere Is Very Similar To Ours

Their skin...Their hands...Their gardens...Their schools...Their professions

The older Lyrian ancestors due to their underdeveloped spirituality fell into stagnation and lost much of their technology. The Pleiadians are now helping them back on their way to the marvelous technologies they once had. The Vegans, also descendants of the old Lyrians, are too helping the Lyrians to recover some of their old advanced sciences and introducing them to some new ones. The Pleiadians have been helped much by the DALs and are passing some of this on to the Lyrians, and are in turn being helped by the Lyrians in other ways. Although the Pleiadians appear very healthy by our standards, they are affected by our atmosphere. Not enough that they have to use environmental suits but they do have sinus problems from prolonged exposure in our air. Their home planet atmosphere is very similar to ours but we have more pollutants in our air. They say that after prolonged living in the purer conditions of the spacecraft they are even affected, to a much lesser degree, by their home planet's atmosphere.

Their hands are very similar to ours but finer and more flexibly articulated. They have fine skin on their hands. All Pleiadians have small gardens and work them with their own hands. It is a part of maintaining contact with their Creation.

They each work two hours per day in their factories - mostly overseeing automated machines and robots. They are all educated in a great many sciences. The Pleiadians go to school until they are in their 70s. In 10 years of school they reach an educational level equivalent to a 25 year old college graduate here.

Everyone must be thoroughly familiar with 12 to 20 professions.

They need to adjust time and their vibrational state in order to contact us and we would have to do the same

They do not marry until they are at least 70 years old. They mature in body in 12 to 15 years. They do not marry until they have completed their chosen education. The median age for those who do marry is about 110 years. Both parties must pass strict mental and physical examinations before they are permitted to marry. They are not required to marry and many do not. In birth they rely on natural partrition with no anesthetic. They find that their brain chemistry is changed by anesthesia. The force of will of the baby is affected and will be reduced to some degree. Life on Erra is peaceful and harmonious.

Everyone strives for his very best for the good of all. If we were to go to the Pleiadian's home planet, Erra, we would not see much because the life and civilization and all its works exist in a slightly different dimension and time frame.

Their time is altered slightly

Their time is altered slightly which also affects their vibrational state of being. They must adjust this time and vibration a little in order to contact us and we would have to do the same to perceive their native existence.

The Pleiadians say that every human has a direct responsibility to help every other one to grow in consciousness. Creation requires every unit of life, within itself, to constantly grow forward. Each unit has this responsibility as well to every other unit. The unexpected thing, which after all really should not be unexpected, is to find reason and logic in the interrelationship of all these odd events.

The Pleiadians have more ground stations in use on our surface. One of them is in the United States

I wondered why all of this activity in only one place in the world, and was then told that Switzerland is not the only location where this activity is taking place. The Pleiadians even told Meier that they have more ground stations in use on our surface, one in the United States and one in the East.

In a discussion of the Pleiadian ground station in the Alps, which is presently headed by Quetzel, one of Meier's frequent contacts, I learned that that station has been in existence for over 70 years! It is in a closed valley between high peaks and has no roads in or out, being inaccessible from the surface. It is fully protected and cannot be seen from the air. While we were on the subject of Pleiadian facilities, I was determined to find out more about the large "mother-ship" in solar orbit, and again I was reminded of the reason for not volunteering information.

The large "mother-ship" in solar orbit

There isn't enough time to discuss all that one could. The discussion of the "mother-ship" took almost half a day and we had barely scratched the surface. Basically, it is not just 10.5 mile sphere in space, but an assembly consisting of one such sphere, 3 smaller several mile diameter spheres joined to the central one 120 degrees apart and below the central one, and a smaller control pod one half to three quarter mile in diameter mounted on a long extension 3 to 4 miles or more above the main sphere. The whole construction is close to 35 km long.

This is entirely built up and assembled in space and is not dependent on any planet. The three lower spheres contain the manufacturing facilities and numerous factories, repair shops, and food production and processing centers for the whole colony.

The larger central sphere contains all of the living quarters, parks, recreational facilities, and the spacecraft hangar decks. The small upper pod on a long narrow extension is the central control and communication center for the whole ship.

Other extraterrestrials come from an atmospheric planet about 10 light years from Earth, a planet which they call Iarga.

Description of the Planet Iarga

But these cousins in the human line of evolution are not all that are here observing us either. There are a number of others so engaged. We have been working for over two years on another UFO contact case that began in July of 1967, one of the heaviest UFO activity periods recorded in modern times, and is still going on. These extraterrestrials come from an atmospheric planet about 10 light years from Earth, a planet which they call Iarga. It has a diameter and mass greater than that of Earth, and the acceleration of gravity at the surface is stronger. The atmosphere is much denser than ours. They said an Earth, human would be pelted to death in the rain on their planet. The speed of rotation is slower making the days and nights longer, but reflected sunlight from the regular twilight can brighten certain nights. Because of the thicker atmosphere and higher air pressure at the surface, which is even a different composition than ours, Iarga knows no bright sunlight and sees nothing of moons and stars. Green predominates as the atmospheric color. The creatures there are a little larger than us are look quite different. They are very stockily built. Their ship and its equipment and furnishings give evidence of a very highly advanced technology.

Another contact with extraterrestrials from planet near Epsilon Eridani

Another contact that has been going on since October of 1969, and still continues, involves a lifeform from another atmospheric planet orbiting a sun some 20 light years away near the star we call Epsilon Eridani. We believe the star indicated to be 82 Eridani as this is a G5 star quite similar to our own sun which is in spectral class GO and is about the right 20 light years distance away.

136

Another contact involves the smaller hairless alien creatures with white skin, large domed heads, large eyes and small facial features

These creatures were larger, like 7 to 7.5 feet tall, and were covered with wrinkled skin and had very large arms with 3 fat fingers on the end. The skin has plates and wrinkles, something like crocodile skin. They had strange faces and a large mouth and very large ears, but they, like the Iargans demonstrated a highly advanced technology. Still another recurring contact case we are working on more recently, involves the smaller hairless alien creatures with white skin, large domed heads, large eyes and small facial features. They have slightly built bodies and are only about 4 feet tall. [These extraterrestrials are the ones now commonly known as the Greys.] Their ships are marvelous machines and they have wonderful devices aboard but they don't seem to be a great deal more advanced than us in some respects. Their technology seems to be just beyond ours, like we might conceivably build such devices in a few more hundreds of years of time.

These extraterrestrial creatures came from Zeta 1 and Zeta 2 Reticuli

These creatures say that they come from the twin suns which we call Zeta 1 and Zeta 2 Reticuli, and that they have been operating here and studying Earth and its creatures for decades. It is said that their large eyes are very light sensitive and for that reason they tend to only come to the surface of Earth at night.

We have just begun investigations into another recurring contact case nearer to our home here in Arizona that has also been going on for many years and involves an extensive transmittal of highly technical evidence of a most advanced nature. We believe that this sort of contact is going on in all countries all over the world if we would just make the effort to identify the cases and spend a little money to properly investigate them.

We are in fact being invaded by alien intelligences on a grand scale, who generally do not seem to be hostile, but we should be aware of it and its possible effects on our lives and our future.

The Cygnusians

Extraterrestrials are under the authority of a confederation of planets headed by a high council in Andromeda

---

Non-physical beings who exist in a different kind of energy form

> These beings [the Pleiadians and most of the other human-like races mentioned earlier] all come under the authority of a confederation of planets in our sector of space headed by a High Council which sits in Andromeda - non-physical beings who exist in a different kind of energy form. The Cygnusians, information on which we encountered in our last investigative trip, are also under the jurisdiction of the High Council in Andromeda, but they belong, with others, to a different stream of evolution.

The strange being who said "Muurrrg" to Meier

I asked Meier if he could tell me any more about that strange being he met in the woods near his home on one of his contacts, the one that said "Murrg" - "Muurrrg", and he repeated that story with more details this time. The contact took place quite nearby. The creature, wearing a kind of spacesuit, had large bulging eyes, very wide spade mouth, no hair, and a dark oily-looking skin, possibly even wet-looking.

It approached him slowly with open hands held in front as if showing that it was not carrying weapons to attack. The creature stopped in front of him and stared for a number of seconds and pronounced the words, waited a few more seconds and then turned away and walked slowly into the night.

A short time later Meier asked Semjase about this and she showed surprise and offered to check into it. She subsequently informed him that the creature was from a planet in the star picture Swan (Cygnus), that the creature's spacecraft was damaged on entry into our atmosphere, and that it was seeking assistance.

It's name was Asina. It's distress signal (now this is amazingly logical) was picked up by the Pleiadians and they sent a Pleiadian party to help the Cygnusians out. While the Cygnusian spacecraft was being repaired, Semjase brought Asina back with her on a contact with Meier and he was then able to communicate with the being telepathically. The Cygnusians are from a different evolution and little of the exchange was understood.

There are many more cases like this that have such an abundance of information and evidence in them that a hoax of this magnitude would be too costly for any but a very wealthy person to afford.

Meier has met representatives from most of these places mentioned so far, at one time or another, and in some cases several times, and still other beings too.

Now it becomes a little clearer and the whole fantastic program of contact makes sense.

We are simply the younger brothers in an ongoing stream of life and intelligence, and are being visited, in this case at least, by our Kind who are a little way ahead and are interested in the welfare and development of their species.- As reported by Walter D.

Comments by Victoria

Victoria told me that some of the contacts and incident mentioned by Meier could be true. However, the following notes should be taken into consideration when we hear a story about humans' contact with extraterrestrials, and especially non-physical entities:

- 1-Extraterrestrials do NOT hang out in the woods.
- 2-Extraterrestrials do NOT pronounce one word and walk away. When they contact or encounter a human being, they usually complete sentences and engage into a dialogue, even though - sometimes – the dialogue is short and their request is firm.
- 3-Extraterrestrials do NOT ask for human help to repair their damaged ships. Always a large mother-ship accompanies their spacecraft for technical support.
- 4-Extraterrestrial damaged ships are never repaired manually on earth. Usually, aliens' spacecrafts are self-repaired above ground while flying. A damaged spaceship is never visible to the human eye. And if this incident occurs, the spaceship releases a substance from a section under its "belly". This substance is quickly coagulated as soon as it touched the surface of the earth. And in no time, it disintegrates, leaving no trace.
- 5-It is important and very useful to remember that extraterrestrial spaceships do NOT fly as wrongly and mistakenly described by humans; they "jump", so to speak for lack of proper terms. They reach destinations by traveling through "aerial lines and curves" incomprehensible to humans. They belong to an infinite time, rather to a limited space. And when they appear in our skies, they adopt a zigzagging pattern for sharp turns and for speed acceleration. If they want to stand still, they hover "motionless" and in complete silence.

CHAPTER 5
THE REPTILIAN BLOODLINES ON EARTH: THE BREATHING DESCENDANTS AMONG US

- David Icke's theory on extraterrestrials' bloodlines on earth
- Icke: 33 of the Presidents of the United States are related, and can be traced back to the bloodline of Charlemagne
- "Non- humans" came to this planet and mated with the beings on planet Earth.
- They can" shape-shift" to be able to look like human beings
- The Reptilians supposedly set up all the organized religions on earth
- Let's have a major serious investigation of "where have all the disappearing children gone?"
- The Space Station and the Space Program questions
- How do all these billions of dollars being spent on the Space Station and space probes benefit the 6 billion poor human "slaves" on this planet?
- Those that are familiar with the Illuminati understand how the Illuminati work.
- Are they Reptilians?
- Go inside the government of the U.S.A, the British Royal House of Windsor, the Vatican, the Illuminati, the House of Rothschild and the Rockefellers, Morgans, Ford's, Duponts, Carnegies, Bushs...
- In between "worlds": The Reptilians and other entities are manipulating our world by possessing "human" bodies
- We must break the "time" circle to free ourselves from the domination of the Reptilians among us
- Genetic corruption: The Reptilians and their allies have corrupted Earth DNA with their own
- Reptilians, The Mormon Church, Illuminati and DNA Data Banks
- Reptilian entities and Illuminati bloodline families

- Icke: UK's Queen Mother and Elizabeth Bowes-Lyon are controlled by the Reptilians
- A race of interbreeding bloodlines, a race within a race in fact, were centered in the Middle and Near East
- The Babylonian Brotherhood
- The Sumerian texts demolish the official version of events and all organized religions
- There were other extraterrestrial races at large on the Earth, and still are
- Subterranean races living among us
- Icke: The Serpent Race, the Anunnaki, is controlling this world by 'possessing' certain bloodline streams
- From the book "Trance Formation of America": Cathy O'Brian was sexually abused by Gerald Ford, Bill Clinton and George Bush
- Icke: I know other people who have seen George Bush shape-shift into a reptilian
- Princess Diana's nicknames for the Windsors were the "lizards" and the "reptiles"
- Queen Elizabeth, Prince Charles, their Illuminati Brotherhood and Satanic Hierarchy: Draconians, Grays, Anunnaki and Reptilians
- The "Planet of Light" is the home planet of the Illuminati
- The 2001 secret treaty between, extraterrestrials, Illuminati and humans
- The Reptilian connection
- The Sumerian clay tablets, African Zulu shaman, Credo Mutwa, Reptilians agenda and hybrid bloodlines
- The Windsor-Bush-Piso Bloodline: The Reptilian Mammalian DNA combination allows them to "shape-shift"
- Religion has been one of the most effective weapons of the Illuminati and the reptilian bloodlines.
- Icke: George Bush, Henry Kissinger, and a stream of the other Illuminati "big names" are reptilian shape-shifters
- One of the locations of this reptilian group is the star-system Draco
- UK shape-shifting queens
- Arizona Wilder and David Icke said: Sacrificial rituals involved Tony Blair, George Bush, Bill and Hillary Clinton, Henry Kissinger, Marquis de Libeaux, UK Queen and Queen Mother
- Diane Gould, head of the US Organization, Mothers Against Ritual Abuse, also confirms this theme.
- I have seen Prince Charles shape-shift into a reptilian
- All humans have reptilian DNA. That's what the story of Adam was about.
- The Montauk Project is under the direction of a Reptilian/Draco
- The Merovingians
- The Reptilian bloodline includes a long line of famous and powerful people in history, to name a few

- Who or what are the Gods that genetically enhanced man?
- Non-terrestrial life forms (ET's) capable of inter-stellar and inter-dimensional travel
- We do know that there are Lesser Gods of many species, including reptilians
- This interbreeding occurred between the human race and this reptilian group within a race.
- Hybrids became demigods and middle men between the gods and humanity
- Who are the "Illuminati" and are they associated with the reptilian bloodline?
- The true illuminati are a closed circle of inter-married bloodlines originating with the first Radically Altered Genetic Units.
- Are there enhanced genetic humans who are the descendants of a race of Lesser God reptilians and human women? Yes.
- The illuminati, within a few elite bloodlines, already control your world.
- The Illuminati know that modern traditional religions are a fabrication.
- Yes, certain members of the illuminati do have contact with extraterrestrial beings.
- Reptilian programs
- The Reptilians did 'exist', said the voice, but they were holographic thought projections of the Matrix
- The existence of projected holographic phenomena is now supported by science
- It works like this
- The Reptilian "sentient programs" did not have human emotion
- The Nephilim were producing human animal hybrids
- Alien Entities, spirits and non-physical remnants on earth summoned by Arab occultists and Ulemas
- Dr. John Dee, a court astrologer for Queen Elizabeth summoned alien-like entities
- Are the bloodlines of past, present and future leaders of the world already decided upon, and predetermined by aliens?
- Descendants and remnants of aliens among us: Origins, their planets, stars, current civilizations and where are they today?
- 1-Arianni
- 2-Atlantides (Tyrrhenians)
- 3-Canaanites (Atlantis/Lumeria)
- 4-Carians (Phoenicians)
- 5-Fallen Angels
- 6-Horus (Sirius)
- 7-Lyraens
- 8-Vegans
- 9-Nordic (Scandinavian countries, Russia)
- 10-Maldekians
- 11-Andromedans
- 12-Reptilians

- 13-Pleiadians
- 14-Pegasians
- 15-Anunnaki
- 16-Zetas (Zeta Reticulians)
- 17-Dracos (Draconians)
- The Alpha Draconians and Lyrans
- Nordic Humans from Lyrae. The ancestors of humanity
- The black race is indigenous to Earth, and developed to Homo sapiens through the periodical insertion of DNA
- Sirian humans
- Relations among Martians, Maldekians, Andromedans, Reptilians and Pleiadians.
- Andromedans: Our Moon is an artificial moon. It originally came from a star system in Ursa Minor, called Chauta.
- Pegasians: Member name in the Galactic Federation: Pegasus Star League.
- Location
- Distance from earth
- Life form type
- Physical appearance
- Special traits and abilities
- Average amount of sleep needed
- Language
- Mother ship and other crafts
- Elohim and Maldek
- Reptilian bloodline and Island of Malta
- Nephilim
- Nibiru and Eridu
- Sirius Reptilians: They are only borderline humans

*** *** ***

The Reptilian Bloodlines On Earth: The breathing Descendants Among Us

David Icke's Theory on Extraterrestrials' Bloodlines on Earth

The Forumforg in the Netherlands summarized and intelligently discussed the most vital points of David Icke's theory on extraterrestrials' bloodlines on Earth; a theory that raised a red flag and disturbed powerful politicians and heads of states around the globe. Without fear, the Dutch group widely publicized Icke's revolutionary concepts. Here is a synopsis

Icke: 33 of the Presidents of the United States are related, and can be traced back to the bloodline of Charlemagne!

David Icke talked about a small group that has ruled this planet for thousands of years and have passed on their "rule" from generation to generation through their bloodline. The "rulers" have maintained this bloodline through the intermarriages of the so-called Royal Family monarchies over the course of thousands of years. The so-called "Eastern Establishment" in the U.S.A., and the "European and British Establishment" also intermarry in the same way to maintain their bloodline.

David Icke's points out that all 43 presidents in the U.S.A. are related and that 33 of the Presidents can be traced back to the bloodline of Charlemagne! This possible truth alone should be sending off major alarm bells in your mind. Like this is no coincidence; the odds of this randomly happening are billions to one.

"Non- humans" came to this planet and mated with the beings on planet Earth.

David Icke's theory is that possibly several thousand years ago "non- humans" came to this planet and mated with the beings on planet Earth. Because of their superior knowledge, they were able to expand their "rule" and control this planet to this day. They maintained their special bloodline for these thousands of years through intermarrying amongst themselves.

The Reptilians supposedly set up all the organized religions on earth

David Icke says they can" shape-shift" to be able to look like human beings and at the same time they can look like Reptilians when they're privately out of the view of the public. David Icke explains that this group of Reptilians supposedly set up all the organized religions, monarchies, school systems, science, all the media and everything else they needed to control the masses of humanity over thousands of years. David Icke goes into details about this group being Satanic and performing human ritual sacrifice throughout the course of history and currently "underground" on a large scale to this very day!

Icke said: "Just ask yourself the question: where have all the "missing children" all over the world "disappeared" to?" This is a horrendous question to confront, but the possible answers to this question is so important to face up to, if we are to look at the possibility that a very evil group is actually performing human sacrifice in this world today on a large scale too sick to imagine!

Only the answers to such a question can allow us to stop them, if this is really happening. You may find yourself saying "how could this group be getting away with mass murder and insane atrocities such as these?"

One possible answer is that If you control ALL the major mass media, it can be possible to suppress even this hideous possible truth. Anyone even raising such a question is shown in the media to be just "another one of those crazy conspiracy nuts".

Let's have a major serious investigation of "where have all the disappearing children gone?"

But before passing judgment and dismissing such an "unbelievable" possibility, at least let's have a major serious investigation of "where have all the disappearing children gone?"

If you remember the problem was so great in the U.S.A. that the faces of thousands of "missing children" were put on milk cartons all across the Nation! And yet no President nor anyone in the U.S. government has ever called for a major serious investigation of this out of control potential "mass murder of children" problem.

How do all these billions of dollars being spent on the Space Station and space probes benefit the 6 billion poor human "slaves" on this planet?

Lately there have been several key developments that need questioning and answers. The Space Station has been continually in the process of being built now for probably 20 or so years. Right now it appears to have turned into a large "coalition project" of the US, Russia, Europe, Japan and maybe others. Just how big the Space Station will eventually be or what is the ultimate goal of the space station is not told to the people, nor talked about in the media. But it seems like a lot of work is going on "up there". Plus you have the Mars, Venus, Saturn and other space probes working "up there" at a quickening pace. And you have many sightings of UFOs all over the world, plus all of the crop circle stuff, which are never addressed in the corporate controlled media in any serious way.

Now how do all these billions of dollars being spent on the Space Station and space probes benefit the 6 billion poor human "slaves" on this planet?

How is this benefiting the 30,000,000 human beings, mostly children, who die of starvation every year? There is no benefit.

In fact it is robbing the "slaves" of hundreds of billions of dollars that could be used to help wipe out poverty in the U.S.A. and every other country and to prevent so many millions of humans from dieing of starvation! So one may ask "who is making the decisions as to why all this effort is being done and for what reasons and goals? Who is planning and coordinating all of this? In other words "what is going on up there and for whose benefit is all this for?"

You may find yourself wanting answers to all these questions too! The answers to these questions are of the utmost importance for every human on this planet. "We the People" have a right to know exactly what the space program is all about and the real true goals of such a major endeavor, and who's benefit is all this for? It's definitely not for the benefit of you or I or our fellow 6 billion human beings. Only a few "space tourists" were allowed to fly "up there" for $20,000,000 each, a price definitely out of the reach of 99.9999999% of the human beings on this planet.

Those that are familiar with the Illuminati understand how the Illuminati work.

They take small steps at a time covertly so the masses won't realize what's going on, thereby diverting attention from what they're really up to. Somehow the space program fits into their plan and it would be a good idea for the 6 billion humans on this planet to investigate the agenda of the Illuminati and all their affiliated groups in regards to this.

Are they Reptilians?

Are they really Reptilians as David Icke says?
Are they getting ready to possibly leave planet Earth after they finish destroying this Planet or most of this Planet?
Many good people write about these subjects on Rense, in books and elsewhere, and they sound frustrated and powerless to do anything about this awful situation and get rid of the Illuminati and their associates and stop this sick horrendous manipulation that is destroying our planet and humanity. There is no concerted focused real course of action being taken on a large scale to bring this potentially "unbelievable" situation to the surface so it can be dealt with.

Go inside the government of the U.S.A, the British Royal House of Windsor, the Vatican, the Illuminati, the House of Rothschild and the Rockefellers, Morgans, Ford's, Duponts, Carnegies, Bushs...

Here is a proposal for everyone to consider: To address this situation and take the action necessary to expose what is possibly going on behind the scenes, be it reptilians or whatever; one major way to quickly find the truth is for the people to use a billion dollars of their own government tax dollars to set up a special citizens committee of intelligent unconnected individuals {no one who was or is a government official or connected lawyers or executives of large corporations etc.} to form a special panel and go inside the government of the U.S.A and inside the governments of every European nation, inside the British Royal House of Windsor and the British Parliament, inside the Vatican, inside all the secret groups connected to the Illuminati, inside the boardrooms of the Fortune 500 Corporations, inside the House of Rothschild and the Rockefellers, Morgans, Ford's, Duponts, Carnegies, Bushs etc. etc. By being given the power to go inside these groups, businesses and organizations, this Committee could ask the questions that would enable them to see and observe first hand exactly WHAT IS GOING ON.

And if it is found that "what is going" on is true according to what David Icke and others are writing about, than the People could take action to get rid of the Illuminati and all their associates. This Committee could also seriously investigate the many UFO sightings and crop circles etc. And they could investigate the Space Program and the Space Station and what is going on up there? If such an investigation fails to prove that anything in David Icke's books or the books of so many others, who have written in relation to these subjects, is true, so be it! At least "WE THE PEOPLE" will hopefully know the truth.

If we do not take some form of peaceful action in this direction, we can expect more millions and possibly billions of our fellow human beings to be killed in Illuminati generated wars we cannot even begin to imagine!

So what are you going to do to help save our world and cure this sick reality that "possibly" the Illuminati and their associates in crime are forcing us to live in?

Most people just throw up their hands and say "well what can I do about this?" which is exactly the reaction the Illuminati want you to have. They don't want the People to believe they have any power. They know that there is only a few of them and there are over six billion of us! They know if we ever figure out and are able to see the Illuminati "magic" manipulation then their game is up.

They are finished and we can get rid of them once and for all. So don't just sit there, get up off your chair and start thinking for yourself and do something.

In between "Worlds": The Reptilians and other entities are manipulating our world by possessing "human" bodies

Icke said that the Reptilians and other entities, which are manipulating our world by possessing "human" bodies, operate in frequencies between the Third and Fourth densities. These are referred to as "hidden spaces and planes unknown to man", in the apparently ancient Emerald Tablets, which I quote from in "Children of the Matrix". For simplicity, I refer to this "between world" in my books as the lower fourth dimension.

It is from here that they police our vibrational prison - the Matrix - and seek to addict and restrict us to the dense physical senses. This world was once far less dense than it is today and the "fall" down the frequencies, caused by the manipulation of incarnate consciousness and DNA infiltration, has made it so much more difficult to maintain a multi-dimensional connection while in physical form. We are now in a cycle of change when the vibration of this "world" will be raised out of dense physicality and return to where it once was. In doing so, the Reptilians' ability to manipulate our physical form will be removed and this is why they are in such a panic at this time to prevent this shift from opening the vibrational prison door.

The reptilians and other manipulating entities exist only just outside the frequency range of our physical senses. Their own physical form has broken down and they can no longer re-produce. Thus they have sought to infiltrate human form and so use that to exist and control in this dimension. They chose the Earth for this infiltration because it most resembles in vibration the locations from which they originate. These reptilians are addicted to the dense physical "world" and the sensations it offers and they have no desire to advance higher. Their aim in this period is to stop the Earth and incarnate humanity from making the shift from dense physical prison into multi-dimensional paradise.

149

We must break the "time" circle to free ourselves from the domination of the Reptilians among us

From what I understand, this dense physical world is caught in a manufactured time "loop", in which "time" is a circle, constantly repeating itself. Note that one of the ancient symbols for "infinity" is the snake swallowing its own tail.

The pentagram or five-pointed star, so prevalent in Satanism, is also symbolic of this unbroken "time" cycle, the vibrational prison.

The period we are now experiencing has, therefore, been played out before. We are just at that point again in the repeating circle or cycle, like a rat running on one of those wheels in a cage. No matter how fast it runs, it keeps covering the same ground. What we need to do is break the "time" circle and thus the prison.

We are now in that part of the circle that is most vulnerable to this because of the vibrational changes taking place in this part of the Universe and this is why the control of humans has tightened so rapidly in this period - they are doing everything they can to defend their prison from the awakening of the inmates.

The micro-chip is crucial to that.

Genetic corruption: The Reptilians and their allies have corrupted Earth DNA with their own

These reptilians and their allies have corrupted Earth DNA with their own and this genetic infiltration lies dormant until it is activated by the vibrational fields generated by the Illuminati secret society rituals, and others in the public eye like the carefully designed coronations and official ceremonies of many kinds, including even the UK State Opening of Parliament and certainly those of the various religions.

This activation is now also being inflicted upon the general population through technology on Earth and in space, no doubt, and this channeled entity said that the cloning program is there to develop designer bodies for the reptilians of the "in between world" that would not require the overpowering of an already incarnate consciousness.

Once activated, the DNA opens the body to possession by these reptilians and other beings, and this is what is happening, for example, to Freemasons in the rituals that most of them deliver parrot fashion while having no idea of their vibrational significance. This is why the Illuminati are so obsessed with knowing a person's bloodline. They know which have the potential for this activation and possession and which do not.

150

Reptilians, The Mormon Church, Illuminati and DNA Data Banks

The Mormon Church genealogical data base and now the DNA data banks are designed to identify those with the bloodline. These are the people who are given jobs and roles that serve the Illuminati agenda, while most of them have no idea what is really going on and what they are being used for. Their DNA is then activated and they go through a change of character (a phrase I have heard so many times in relation to such people once they advance in the system) and a very different consciousness takes over their mental and emotional processes.

Icke added: "This is why it is so important for everyone to stay well clear of ritual, no matter how innocent it may appear on the surface. I would include "New Age" ritual in this, too. I don't mean standing in a circle, connecting together and projecting loving thoughts, etc.
I mean carefully constructed ritual that is constantly repeated, as with religious ceremony for example.
I am beginning to realize why I have had a life-long aversion to taking part in ritual of any kind."

Reptilian entities and Illuminati bloodline families

Icke: UK's Queen Mother and Elizabeth Bowes-Lyon are controlled by the Reptilians

Each new generation of the Illuminati bloodline families is exposed to the appropriate ritual to activate their possession by the reptilian entities and so the cycle goes on. The phrase that comes to mind is "...forgive them for they know not what they do."
P.S. Apparently, this DNA infiltration is known within the inner circles of the British royal family as the "family disease". They are actually in fear of it because they know that once it is activated they will be taken over. But of course they are caught in a world of constant ritual and ceremony designed specifically to activate their possession. It is catch 22. Without the ritual they cannot be the royal family, but with the ritual they are activated and possessed.
The thought and emotional processes of the UK's Queen Mother are not those of Elizabeth Bowes-Lyon, the little girl officially born into that body 101 years ago. They are controlled by the reptilian entity or entities, which possessed her after the hybrid DNA activation.

A race of interbreeding bloodlines, a race within a race in fact, were centered in the Middle and Near East

Summary: A race of interbreeding bloodlines, a race within a race in fact, were centred in the Middle and Near East in the ancient world and , over the thousands of years since, have expanded their powers across the globe. A crucial aspect of this has been to create a network schools and secret societies to covertly introduce their agenda while, at the same time, creating institutions like religions to mentally and emotionally imprison the masses and set them at war with each other.

The Babylonian Brotherhood

The hierarchy of this tribe of bloodlines is not exclusively male and some of its key positions are held by women. But in terms of numbers it is overwhelmingly male and I will therefore refer to this group as the Brotherhood. Even more accurately, given the importance of ancient Babylon to this story, I will also call it the Babylonian Brotherhood. The plan they term their 'Great Work of Ages', I will call the Brotherhood agenda.

The Sumerian texts demolish the official version of events and all organized religions

I will refer to the clay tablets, therefore as the Sumerian texts or tablets. They are one of the greatest historical finds imaginable and yet 150 years after they were discovered they are still ignored by conventional history and education. Why? Because they demolish the official version of events...according to (Zecharia Sitchen) the texts say that the Sumerian civilisation...was a "gift from the gods". Not mythical gods, but physical ones who lived among the. The tablets call these gods the AN.UNNAK.KI (Those from Heaven to Earth came), and DIN.GIR (The Righteous Ones of the Blazing Rockets).

The ancient text known as the book of Enoch also calls the gods the "Watchers", as did the Egyptians. The Egyptian name for their Gods, the Neteru, lierally translates as Watchers and they said that their gods came in heavenly boats.

According to Zecharia Sitchin, the tablets describe how the Anunnaki came from a planet called Nibiru (The Planet of the Crossing)... during the early formation of the solar system, Nibiru caused the near destruction of a planet that once existed between Jupiter and Mars. The Sumerians called it Tiamet, a planet they nicknamed the Watery Monster.

They say that it was debris from Tiamet's collision with a Nubiru moon which created the Great Band Bracelet - the asteroid belt which is found between Mars and Jupiter. What remained of Tiamet was thrown into another orbit, the text says, and eventually became the Earth. The Sumerian name for the Earth means Cleaved one because a vast hole was created, they say, by the collision. Interestingly if you take away the water in the Pacific Ocean you will be left with a gigantic hole.

> **There were other extraterrestrial races at large on the Earth, and still are.**

_____Subterranean Races Living Among Us_____

The more I weave together incredible amounts of information, the more it seems to me that we are talking of two distinct situations running side by side. There were other extraterrestrial races at large on the Earth, and still are, as well as the extraterrestrial race which the Sumerians called the Anunnaki and other ancient texts called the serpent race...In their physical expression, the Anunnaki are one of the many inner-Earth races which live underground in catacombs, caverns and tunnels below the surface. A Hopi Indian legend says that a very ancient tunnel complex exists under Los Angeles and this, they say, was occupied by a 'lizard' race some 5,000 years ago. In 1933 G. Warren Shufelt, an LA mining engineer, claimed to have found it.

Today, it is said, some malevolent Freemasonic rituals are held in this tunnel complex. There has been a massive cover up by the authorities of the existence of these subterranean races and where they live. In 1909 a subterranean city which was built with the precision of the 'Great Pyramid' was found by G. E. Hincaid near the Grand Canyon in Arizona.

It was big enough to accommodate 50,000 people and mummified bodies found were of oriental or possibly Egyptian origin, according to the expedition leader Professor S. A. Jordan.

Icke: The Serpent Race, the Anunnaki, is controlling this world by 'possessing' certain bloodline streams

Icke said: My own research suggests that it is from another dimension, the lower fourth dimension, that the reptilian control and manipulation is primarily orchestrated. Without understanding the multidimensional nature of life and the universe, it is impossible to follow the manipulation of the Earth by a non-human force. As open minded scientists are now confirming, Creation consists of an infinite number of frequencies or dimensions of life sharing the same space in the same way that radio and television frequencies do. At the moment you are tuned to the three-dimensional world or third dimension and so that is what you perceive as your reality...It is from one of these other stations or dimensions, that the Serpent Race, the Anunnaki, is controlling this world by 'possessing' certain bloodline streams...

From the book "Trance Formation Of America": Cathy O'Brian was sexually abused by Gerald Ford, Bill Clinton and George Bush

Icke continues: Other people know this as the lower astral dimension, the legendary home of demons and malevolent entities in their black magic rituals...Then there are the experiences of Cathy O'Brian, the mind controlled slave of the United States Government for more than 25 years, which she details in her astonishing book "Trance Formation Of America", written with Mark Phillips. She was sexually abused as a child and an adult by a stream of famous people named in her book. Among them were the US Presidents, Gerald Ford, Bill Clinton and most appallingly, George Bush, a major player in the brotherhood, as my books and others have long exposed.

Icke: I know other people who have seen George Bush shape-shift into a reptilian

Icke wrote: "It was Bush a paedophile and serial killer, who regularly abused and raped Cathy's daughter, Kelly O' Brian, as a toddler before her mother's courageous exposure of these staggering events forced the authorities to remove Kelly from the mind control program known as Project Monarch. Cathy writes in "Trance Formation of America" of how George Bush was sitting in front of her in his office in Washington DC when he opened up a book at a page depicting "lizard-like aliens from a far off, deep space place". Bush then claimed to be an 'alian' himself and appeared, before her eyes, to transform 'like chameleon' into a reptile...I know other people who have seen George Bush shape-shift into a reptilian."

Princess Diana's nicknames for the Windsors were the "lizards" and the "reptiles"

It is clear that Diana knew about the true nature of the royal family's genetic history and the reptilian control. Her nicknames for the Windsors were the "lizards" and the "reptiles" and she used to say in all seriousness: "They're not human"...The brotherhood obsession with Scotland, she said, was because there are many entrances there into inner-Earth where the physical reptiles live...

She said that during the sacrificial rituals the Queen wears a cloak of gold fabric inlaid with rubies and black onyx. The Queen and Charles have their own ritual goblets, inlaid with pecious stones signifying their Illuminati-Brotherhood rank. The Mother Godess says that that queen makes cruel remarks about lesser initiates, but is afraid of a man code-named 'Pindar' (The Marquis de Libeaux) who is higher in the Satanic heirarchy.

Incorporated in this category, are extraterrestrial species such as the Illuminati, Draconians, Grays, Annunaki, and the Reptilians, to name just a few. During the sinking of Atlantis, the technology which projected a protective beam around our planet, was deactivated, as the beam technology sank with Atlantis.

The "Planet of Light" is the home planet of the Illuminati
The 2001 Secret Treaty between, Extraterrestrials, Illuminati and Humans

As stated by David Icke: On Wednesday, 5th September 2001, I was invited as the only white man, to attend a meeting with a representative group of 174 world wide Aboriginal and Indigenous nations in Byron Bay, New South Wales, Australia. At this meeting, a Peace Treaty was entered into between the extraterrestrial species know as the Illuminati, and Earth. The name Illuminati does not come from meaning that they claim to be "the enlightened ones," rather, their name is so, because they are from "The Planet of Light," where they live in a multi-dimensional existence. "The Planet of Light," is the home planet of the Illuminati, and is part of a planetary Star System comprising some 30,000 Illuminati governed/inhabited planets.

It was at this meeting (on 5th September 2001), that we were informed of the then pending World Trade Center disaster, scheduled and planned by the USA government, in six days time (on 11th September 2001). At this meeting however, this pending disaster was described vaguely as "a world changing event, which would occur on the East coast of America."

The Peace Treaty between the Illuminati and Earth Humans, was in exchange for the Illuminati's advanced technology, and we in turn, agreed to share our forthcoming knowledge of our own 3rd to 5th density, (via 4th density), transformation experience.

The Highest Ranking official for the Illuminati, who has been in human form on Earth for the last 50+ years, was present at this meeting (5th September 2001), and from that date onwards, has instructed his People, to commence the clean-up of Earth, of the mind-controlled interference/mess that has been made by a section of their species in the past.

At this meeting, the fourteen (14) keys of knowledge were brought together for the future benefit of Earth humans. Six (6) of these keys were already held by our planet's Aboriginal and Indigenous Peoples, and the remaining eight (8) keys were promised to be brought at this meeting, by the Illuminati's representative, present at that meeting.

This Illuminati hu-man was the Star Person that our Aboriginal and Indigenous People had been waiting for many years, as has been foretold in their "Dreamtime."

The Reptilian Connection

When I (David Icke) reached the point some years ago where I had put together the structure through which a few people control the direction of the world, it was clear that this network of secret societies and covert groups manipulating global politics, business, banking, military, media, and so on, could not have been put together in a few years or decades. It had to go back a very long time. So I began to trace it back into what we call history. I did this in the knowledge that, for some reason, bloodline and genetics were vitally important to these manipulators, the Illuminati or Illuminated ones - illuminated into knowledge that the public never see. I followed the trail back comfortably to the time of the Crusades in the Middle East, the 12th and 13th centuries, that kind of period, and on it went far back into the ancient world and pre-history. There, all over the planet, you find the ancient legends and accounts of "gods" from another world who interbred with humanity to create a hybrid network of bloodlines.

The Old Testament, for example, talks about the "Sons of God" who interbred with the daughters of men to create the hybrid race, the Nefilim. Before it was translated into English, that passage read "the sons of the gods", plural. But the Bible accounts are only one of so many that describe the same theme.

The Sumerian Clay Tablets, African Zulu shaman, Credo Mutwa, Reptilians Agenda and Hybrid Bloodlines

The Sumerian clay tablets, found in what we now call Iraq in the middle of the 19th century, tell a similar story. It is estimated they were buried around 2,000 BC, but the stories they tell go back long before that. The tablets talk of a race of "gods" from another world who brought advanced knowledge to the planet and interbred with humans to create hybrid bloodlines. These "gods" are called in the tablets, the "Anunnaki", which apparently translates as "those who from heaven to earth came."

156

The ancient accounts tell us that these hybrid bloodlines, the fusion of the genes of selected humans with those of the "gods", were put into the positions of ruling royal power, especially in the ancient Near and Middle East, in advanced cultures like Sumer, Egypt, and Babylon. But it happened elsewhere, also, as you will find, for example, in the amazing information provided by the African Zulu shaman, Credo Mutwa, and in the incredible Credo videos, Reptilian Agenda, parts one and two. He tells the same story from the black African tradition that I have uncovered elsewhere in the world.

The accounts of the "serpent race" in ancient cultures are simply endless, and wherever you look and the serpent, reptilian, symbolism in relation to the Anunnaki and other versions of these "gods" is equally widespread. We see this in the Bible, for instance, with the serpent in the "Garden of Eden"- a story which clearly comes from the Sumerian accounts, as does the story of Moses in the bulrushes, a story told about a Sumerian king long before the Bible. This is why I found it so astounding when I was told by Zecharia Sitchin, the best known translator of the Sumerian tablets, that there was no evidence of a serpent race in the ancient world. Of course there is. He also strongly advised me in relation to the serpent race: "Don't go there". Why, when the evidence, ancient and modern, is so enormous?

From these bloodlines has come the origin of the "divine right of kings", the belief that only certain bloodlines have the god-given right to rule. In truth this is not the "divine" or "God" at all. It is the right to rule from the reptilian "gods" by way of your hybrid genetics.

These bloodlines later became the royal and aristocratic families of Europe and, thanks to the "Great" British Empire and the other European empires, they were exported to the Americas, Africa, Australia, New Zealand, and right across into the Far East, where they connected with other reptilian hybrid bloodlines, like those, most obviously, in China, where the symbolism of the dragon is the very basis of their culture.

These reptilian-human hybrid lines became the political and economic rulers of these lands occupied by the European empires and they continue to rule these countries to this day.

The United States of America has been home to hundreds of millions of people since 1776. What's more, these people came from an amazingly diverse genetic pool. And yet, wait for this, the 42 who have become Presidents of the United States are all related!!! Thirty-Three of them alone go back to Charlemagne, one of the most famous monarchs of what we call France.

He just happens to be a major figure in the story of these bloodlines and their expansion out of Britain, France, Germany, and elsewhere.

The Windsor-Bush-Piso Bloodline: The Reptilian-Mammalian DNA Combination Allows Them to "Shape-Shift"

Bush~Windsor~Piso Bloodline; The Rothschilds, Rockefellers, the British royal family, and the ruling political and economic families of the US and the rest of the world come from these SAME bloodlines. This is why the so called Eastern Establishment families of the United States interbreed with each other as obsessively as the European royal and "noble" families have always done. And similar families across the world. It is not because of snobbery, it is to hold as best they can a genetic structure - the reptilian-mammalian DNA combination which allows them to "shape-shift". Witnesses have reported seeing people (most often those in positions of power), transform before their eyes, from a human form to a reptilian one and then back again. You will find much about this in "The Biggest Secret" and Credo Mutwa confirms exactly the same experience in black Africa. Once again, ancient and modern accounts support each other.

The ancient gods of the Indus Valley, the Nagas, were said to have been able to take either human or reptilian form. Former US president, George Bush, incidentally, is mentioned more than any other person in my experience in relation to shape-shifting. This is why his son is being brought through in the 2000 presidential election.

Presidents are not EL-ected by ballot; they are SEL-ected by blood. Al Gore, his "Democratic" opponent in the one-party state, is also from this bloodline. Look almost anywhere in the world in a position of significant power and you will find the same. The reptilian symbolism you see around you with gargoyles, in coats of arms, in advertising, and so on, is all part of this.

These "gods" could not take over the planet openly because there are not enough of them, so they are doing it covertly by appearing human. Movies like They Live, The Arrival (the first, not the sequel), and the US television series, V, tell the story of what is really going on. I urge you to think about watching these movies to get up to speed if you are new to all of this. New World Order and conspiracy researchers also have political and religious belief systems to defend and while they uncover one level of the conspiracy, most reject and even ridicule what I am saying about the reptilian connection. That's fine, but unless they encompass this bigger picture they will never, in my view, understand what is truly happening all around us.

As Ghandi said: "Even if you are in a minority of one, the truth is still the truth". And as a result of the waves "The Biggest Secret" has caused, and the new information, experiences, and accounts the book and this website have attracted from all over the world, there is a growing understanding that this apparently bizarre, crazy, story is actually true. That the world may indeed be controlled by reptilian bloodlines that hide behind apparently human form and it is this understanding which pulls together all the apparently unconnected information on this site into a very much connected whole. Here are some examples:

Religion has been one of the most effective weapons of the Illuminati and the reptilian bloodlines.

If you wish to control a mass population, you have to disconnect them from the true knowledge of who they are and their own infinite potential to manifest their own destiny and control their own lives. You have to persuade them that they are insignificant and powerless so they will live their lives in accordance with that.

This is where religion has been one of the most effective weapons of the Illuminati and the reptilian bloodlines. It fills people with fear of a judgmental God and tells them that unless they believe that the "truth" of all that is can be found in one book or belief system, they are going to hell or will experience other extremely unpleasant consequences.

Different religions have also been wonderful vehicles for dividing and ruling the people through arrogant, self-righteous, inter-religious conflict. The reptilians created the religions for this reason and the key players within them do not even begin to believe the nonsense they parrot to their followers. They just want the population to believe it, so they will be easy to control. This is why you find so many famous "Christian" evangelists, for example, are actually Satanists. Their "Christianity" is just a smokescreen. The suppression of the true knowledge of healing and the domination of drug and surgery-based "medicine" ensures that the human physical body operates at far less than its optimum potential.

This is the reason for the blatant misrepresentation and suppression of the so-called "alternative" forms of healing which have been around for thousands of years longer than modern "medicine". Food additives, fast food, fluoride in the water supplies, the poisons we put on the land and therefore eat in our food and drink in our water, are all suppressing not only our physical health and vibrancy, but, most crucially, our brain functions and intellect. A fully awake, mentally sharp, population is the last thing you need if you want to control them. Thus the reptilian bloodlines also put so much emphasis on controlling "education" and the media. This allows them to feed us a constant diet of brainless crap, like game shows, while the "news" media tells us what the controllers want us to think. Most journalists are so brain-dead themselves, so lacking in understanding of what they are part of, that they, like most of the population, play a part in advancing an agenda they do not even know exists.

Religion is the greatest form of mass mind control yet invented

This is obviously very related to religion, which is, for me, the greatest form of mass mind control yet invented. So is advertising and television. But mind control goes much deeper than that. The Illuminati-reptilian mind-control projects have produced literally millions of mind-controlled robots in endless walks of life, who are programmed to carry out the Illuminati agenda.

There are many electronic ways that this is done today, but one of the key methods is trauma-based mind control. This is where people are traumatized through sexual abuse, violence, being forced to witness and take part in human sacrifice rituals, and countless other horrors. Such experiences activate the mechanism in the mind which shuts out memories of extreme trauma. One expression of this, which many people have experienced, is when they cannot recall the memory of a bad car crash. They can remember before and after, but not the impact. The mind puts an amnesic barrier around the memory so we do not have to keep re-living it. This is a good thing, but the Illuminati have developed methods of using this technique to traumatize a mind over and over until it fragments into a honeycomb of disconnected amnesic barriers. They then program these different fragments of mind (altars as they call them) with different tasks. The tasks are pre-programmed to be activated with a "trigger" word, color, sound, or whatever. Once the trigger is given that programming locks in and the person will do whatever they have been programmed to do. This can be to have sex with a famous politician, which they will not remember; to assassinate someone like John Lennon; to go crazy with a gun in a school, which leads to gun control etc. The concentration camps of Nazi Germany under the supervision of the "Angel of Death", Josef Mengele, were one of the major centers for such experimentation. Mengele was taken to the United States and South America after the war by the Illuminati under the name Doctor Green or Greenbaum to continue his horrific "work".

This manifested as the notorious mind-control project, MK Ultra. The China Lake Naval Weapons Center in the California desert was one of his premier bases of operation.

The most effective time to start this process of creating human robots is before the age of five or six. Hence you have the colossal child abuse networks and the Satanic ritual abuse of children exposed in my books. (Icke's books)

The abuse and satanic ritual abuse of children, and human sacrifice ceremonies
The sacrifices to "the gods" in the ancient accounts were literally sacrifices to the
reptilians and their hybrid bloodlines

Staggering as it may seem, all of the above are massively widespread all over the world. It is happening in your community now, I don't care where you are. I, and others, have been highlighting this for years and now, as you will see on this site, the scale of it, and the famous people involved, are coming to light at last. Partly these rituals and abuse networks are to do with traumatizing people, especially children, but it is far more than just that. Follow the Illuminati-reptilian bloodlines from the ancient world to now and they have always taken part in human sacrifice ceremonies and blood-drinking.

One of the locations of this reptilian group is the star-system Draco

The sacrifices to "the gods" in the ancient accounts were literally sacrifices to the reptilians and their hybrid bloodlines. The story of the blood-drinking Dracula is symbolic of these reptilian "vampires". One of the locations of this reptilian group would appear to be the star-system known as Draco and "draconian" certainly sums up the Illuminati. To hold their human form, these entities need to drink human (mammalian) blood and access the energy it contains to maintain their DNA codes in their "human" expression. If they don't, they manifest their reptilian codes and we would all see what they really look like. "Oh, my God, Mr. President, do you always eat your breakfast from across the room?" From what I understand from former "insiders", the blood (energy) of babies and small children is the most effective for this, as are blond-haired, blue-eyed people. Hence these are the ones overwhelmingly used in sacrifice, as are red- haired people also, it appears.

This is why people like George Bush, Henry Kissinger, and a stream of the other Illuminati "big names" are exposed in my books and as reptilian shape-shifters who take part in human sacrifice and blood drinking. The two go together. There also appears to be a very significant emphasis among the Illuminati-reptilians and their offshoots with pedophilia, which is rampant on this planet.

I would emphasize also before I end here that I am exposing certain reptilian groups behind the Illuminati, not the reptilian genetic stream in general.

There are many of reptilian origin who are here to help humanity to free themselves from this mental and emotional bondage. Indeed, every one of us has a body with much reptilian genetics, including part of the brain called the R-complex, the reptilian brain.

It is merely a matter of degree.

UK Shape-Shifting Queens

Arizona Wilder (a recovered mind control sex slave, like Cathy O'Brien, of Trance Formation of America book) told me how she had conducted sacrificial rituals involving the British royal family, Tony Blair, and famous American Illuminati names like George Bush, Bill and Hillary Clinton, Henry Kissinger and many others.

The highest operative she knew in the Illuminati, she said was a guy calling himself the Marquis de Libeaux ("of the water"). His codename was Pindar, which she says means "penis of the dragon". Arizona told me how the Queen and Queen Mother regularly sacrifice babies and adults at many ritual centres, including Castle in Balmoral, Scotland, where they were staying at the time Diana was ritually murdered in Paris. The royal family involved in human sacrifice was fantastic enough, but here again came the constantly repeated theme. She described how, during the rituals, these people shape-shift into reptiles.

Diane Gould, head of the US Organization, Mothers Against Ritual Abuse, also confirms this theme.

In a telephone conversation about ritual abuse, Diane asked me if I could explain why many of her clients reported that participants in their rituals had turned into reptiles. People might want to dismiss all this, but they should know that, while they close their eyes and their minds, children are being sacrificed all over the world this very day by the reptilian bloodlines --- many thousands of them o the main ritual dates.

Arizona talked about some of her experiences with Queen Mother: "The Queen Mother was cold, cold, cold, a nasty person. None of her cohorts even trusted her. They have names an altar (mind-control program) after her.

They call it the Black Queen. I have seen her sacrifice people. I remember her pushing a knife into someone's rectum the night the two boys were sacrificed. One was 13 and the others 18. You need to forget that the Queen Mother appears to be a frail woman.

When she shape-shifts into a reptilian, she becomes very tall and strong. Some of them are so strong they can rip out a heart and they all grow by several feet when they shape-shift (This is what the lady said who saw Edward Heath, among endless others.) Of the Queen, Arizona said: "I have seen her sacrifice people and eat their flesh and drink their blood. One time she got so excited with blood-lust that she didn't cut the victim's throat from the left to the right in the normal ritual. She just went crazy, stabbing and ripping at the flesh after she shape-shifted into a reptilian. When she shape-shifts, she has a long reptile face, almost like a beak and she is an off-white colour. (This fits many descriptions of the gods and the "bird gods" of ancient Egypt and elsewhere.)

The Queen Mother looks basically the same, but there are differences. She (the Queen) also has bumps on her head and her eyes are very frightening. She's very aggressive...

I have seen Prince Charles shape-shift into a reptilian and do all of the things the Queen does. I have seen him sacrifice children. There is a lot of rivalry between them for who gets to eat eat what part of the body and who gets to absorb the victim's last breath and steal their soul.

I have seen Andrew participate and I have seen Prince Phillip and Charles sister (Anne) at the rituals, but they didn't participate when I was there. When Andrew shape-shifts, he looks more like one of the lizards. The royals are some of the worst. Ok, as far as enjoying the killing, enjoying the sacrifice, and eating the flesh, they are some of the worst of all of them. They don't care if you see it. Who are you going to tell, who is going to believe you? They feel that it is their birthright and they love it. They love it."

"Various high-level Satanists who have escaped from the Illuminati by God's power were eyewitnesses to Satan appearing at the Rothchilds. They testified they witnessed Satan showing up at the Rothchilds as a very beautiful man who can shape shift, (at times his feet would be cloven hoofs). He wears a black tuxedo to gamble and play cards (winnings are sexual victims) and a white tuxedo when present just to socialize. He can also shape shift into a reptilian.

As a sincere researcher, I must report that lots of info about shape shifting reps has confronted me in so many independent places in such a wide variety of historical periods that this bizarre topic must have some importance. I've withheld my findings for years, because I feel quite tentative about my results.

David Icke gives details of this strange topic and his bold views in The Biggest Secret." - Fritz Springmeier (Bloodlines of the Illuminati). It was after the destruction of Atlantis that the reptilians who were now underground decided to re-take the surface [of Planet Earth], but to show themselves would create a lot of fear and panic upon the population. So what they did was start a hybridization program where they actually created a royalty or elite group that infiltrated many cultures and became their leaders. And to this very day they are the leaders and royalty of Europe and much of the wealthy families that control this planet.

*** *** ***

All humans have reptilian DNA. That's what the story of Adam was about.

That's why we have tail bone, skin that wrinkles and peals and a reptilian brain stem. We all have a DNA makeup of 10% reptilian DNA and 90% human DNA.

However the shape shifting (royalty or elite group) human/reptilians have a 50/50 balance of DNA. They need to consume human products to maintain that balance [missing children etc].

The Montauk Project is under the direction of a Reptilian/Draco

A high percentage of American presidents have been shape shifters". (Reference to "The Biggest Secret" by David Icke.)

Stewart Swerdlow, a participant in the Montauk Project, both as a "Montauk Boy" and later as a supervisor. "I worked under the direction of a reptilian/Draco [at Montauk]. The name "Draco" is actually the name of the star system. It is the whole area of the reptilian races. The reptilians were heavily involved in the Montauk project. At Montauk there was a very tall winged reptilian. He was very, very powerful. The reptilians are tired of living hidden lives and they are very anxious to become public once more as they have been in the past. In order to do that they are literally blitzing the media with reptilian like programs and shows, especially for children, and they are preparing adults through electromagnetic transmissions for the public appearance of reptilians.

One of their biggest weaknesses is that they are not very spiritually minded - they don't have a lot of psychic ability - and they rely a lot on technology and controlling others with technology.

The biggest threat to them is people having control of their own minds."- Stewart Swerdlow referring to the Draco/Reptilians.

164

The Merovingians

1-Extraterrestrial-human hybrids,
2-Rameses II,
3-Philip of Macedonia,
4-Alexander the Great,
5-Cleopatra,
6-Ptolemy XIV,
7-Herod the Great,
8-Piso family,
9-Constantine the Great,
10-King Ferdinand of Spain,
11-Queen Isabella of Castile,
12-King James 1st of England,
13-King Clovis,
14-The Dagoberts,
15-The Windsors,
16-Charlemagne,
17-Daniel Payseur,
18-The Morgans,
19-The Carnegies,
20-The de Medicis,
21-The House of Lorraine,
22-The Habsburgs,
23-Geoffrey Plantagenet,
24-King John,
25-Edward Ist,
26-Edward II,
27-Edward III,
28-Queen Victoria,
29-Edward VII,
30-George V,
31-George VI,
32-Queen Elizabeth II,
33-Prince Charles,
34-Princess Anne,
35-Prince Andrew,
36-Prince Edward,
37-Princes William,
38-George Washington,
39- John Adams,
40-John Quincy Adams,
41-Thomas Jefferson,
42-Franklin Delano Roosevelt,
43-George Bush,
44-George W. Bush Jr.,
45-Jeb Bush,
46-The Lords of Galloway,
47-The Comyns,
48-Marie-Louise of Austria,
49-Kaiser Wilhelm II,
50-Maximilian, Emperor of Mexico,
51-King Juan Carlos of Spain.

This bloodline and its offshoots include a long line of pharaohs in ancient Egypt, including Rameses II (1295-1228 BC), who is considered to be the greatest pharaoh of all. He was his country's master architect (sacred geometry) and his name can be found on almost every ancient shrine. The gold mines of Nubia made him rich beyond the imagination. This bloodline also includes the extraterrestrial-human hybrids who ruled Sumer, Babylon, Greece, and Troy, and which, today, rule the world. One common link in this bloodline is Philip of Macedonia (382-336BC),who married Olympia, and their son was Alexander the Great (356-323BC), a tyrant who plundered that key region of Greece, Persia, Syria, Phoenicia, Egypt, Babylon, the former lands of Sumer, and across into India before dying in Babylon at the age of 33. During his rule of Egypt he founded the city of Alexandria, one the greatest centers for esoteric knowledge in the ancient world. Alexander was taught by the Greek philosopher, Aristotle, who in turn was taught by Plato and he by Socrates. The bloodline and the hidden advanced knowledge have always gone together.

This key bloodline comes down through the most famous Egyptian queen, Cleopatra (60-30BC), who married the most famous Roman Emperor, Julius Caesar, and bore him a son, who became Ptolemy XIV. She also bore twins with Mark Anthony, who has his own connections to this line and its many offshoots; this bloodline also connects to Herod the Great, the "Herod" of the Jesus stories, and continues to the Roman Piso family who, as I explain in The Biggest Secret, wrote the Gospel stories and invented the mythical figure called Jesus!!; the same bloodline includes Constantine the Great, the Roman Emperor who, in 325AD, turned Christianity, based on his ancestors' stories, into the religion we know today, and King Ferdinand of Spain and Queen Isabella of Castile, the sponsors of Christopher Columbus, who instigated the horrific Spanish Inquisition (1478-1834) in which people were tortured and burned at the stake for in any way questioning the basis of the religion their various ancestors had created. More than that, the most used version of the Bible was commissioned and sponsored by another strand in the same bloodline, King James 1st of England. Just a coincidence, nothing to worry about! The line of James, according to genealogy sources listed below, can be traced back to 1550 BC and beyond and includes many Egyptian pharaohs, including Rameses II.

The bloodline moved into France and northern Europe through the Franks and Meroveus or Merovee, who gave his name to the Merovingian bloodline, and it continues with the rest of the Merovingian clan like Clovis and the Dagoberts who connect into the elite secret society, the Priory of Sion and the Rennes-le-Chateau "mystery" in Languedoc Provence, Southern France. Many books have been written recently which claim that the Merovingians are the bloodline of "Jesus".

Some of these authors have just been mistaken, others have blatantly sought to confuse and mislead. The Merovingians are a key bloodline, yes, but it has nothing to do with Jesus, who was invented by an earlier family in the same line, the Pisos. Authors like Sir Laurence Gardner (Bloodline of the Holy Grail and a favorite of Nexus Magazine and its owner, Duncan Roads) MUST know this and yet they still connect the Merovingians to "Jesus". Why?

The Merovingians were Goddess Diana worshippers, as are so many in this line to the present day. They founded the city we call Paris and on one of their former sites of Diana ritual, Princess Diana was murdered in the Pont d'Alma tunnel (meaning "bridge or passage of the Moon Goddess") on August 31st, 1997. As The Biggest Secret points out, the Windsors, another Merovingian bloodline, were very much involved in this ritual murder.

From the Merovingians, this bloodline's connections to the present day include: Charlemagne (742-814), who ruled as Emperor of the West in the Holy Roman Empire; a stream of French kings, including Robert II, Philip Ist, II and III, and Louis Ist, II, VI, VII, VIII, VIIII, XIII, IX, XV, and XVI. The latter married Marie Antoinette of this same bloodline and both were executed in the French Revolution. But they produced the son who became Daniel Payseur, who, as The Biggest Secret explains, was taken to the United States where he became the secret force behind the Morgan and Carnegie empires and owned vast amounts of real estate, banking, and industrial holdings.

This bloodline also connects to the de Medici family which supported Christopher Columbus and produced Catherine de Medici, the Queen of France who died in 1589. Her doctor was Nostradamus: It includes Rene d'Anjou, Duke of Lorraine, and the House of Lorraine which employed Nostradamus and Christopher Columbus. The bloodline relatives of the de Medicis and the House of Lorraine, Queen Isabella of Castile and King Ferdinand of Spain, were also sponsors of Columbus when he "discovered" the Americas.

This bloodline also includes the Habsburgs, the most powerful family in Europe under the Holy Roman Empire; Geoffrey Plantagenet and the Plantagenet royal dynasty in England; King John, who signed the Magna Carta; King Henry Ist, II, and III, who were extremely close to the Knights Templar, as was King John; Mary Stuart and the Stuart Dynasty, including King James Ist of England, sponsor of the King James version of the Bible; King George Ist, II, and III; Edward Ist, II, and III, Queen Victoria; Edward VII; George V and VI; Queen Elizabeth II; Prince Charles and Elizabeth's other offspring, Anne, Andrew and Edward; Princes William and Harry from Charles' "marriage" to Princess Diana; US Presidents, George Washington, John Adams, John Quincy Adams, Thomas Jefferson, Franklin Delano Roosevelt, and George Bush are all named in the charts as strands of this bloodline; it was passed on to the year 2000 US presidential favorite, George W. Bush Jr., and his brother, Jeb Bush, the Governor of Florida.

In fact if you go deeply enough into the genealogical research you will find that Aall the presidents are from this line.

Genealogical sources, like the New England Historical Genealogical Society and Burkes Peerage, have shown that 33 of the 42 presidents to Clinton are related to Charlemagne and 19 are related to England's Edward III, both of whom are of this bloodline.

A spokesman for Burkes Peerage, the bible of royal and aristocratic genealogy based in London, has said that every presidential election since and including George Washington in 1789 has been won by the candidate with the most royal genes. Now we can see how and why.

United States presidents are not chosen by ballot, they are chosen by blood! This same bloodline also includes key Scottish families like the Lords of Galloway and the Comyns; Marie-Louise of Austria, who married Napoleon Bonaparte; Kaiser Wilhelm II, the king of Germany at the time of the First World War; and Maximilian, the Habsburg emperor of Mexico, who died in 1867.

On and on it goes into country after country.

This bloodline connects into every surviving royal family in Europe, including King Juan Carlos of Spain and the Dutch, Swedish, and Danish royal lines.

And this is just one of the reptilian bloodlines and just some of its offshoots.

*** *** ***

Who or what are the Gods that genetically enhanced man?

Non-terrestrial life forms (ET's) capable of inter-stellar and inter-dimensional travel

Before you can understand who or what the Gods were who genetically enhanced mankind, you must first be able to distinguish between Gods as exalted beings of pure conscious energy containing immense knowledge and power, and "non-terrestrial" life forms (ET's) capable of inter-stellar and sometimes inter-dimensional travel who are also capable of genetic alteration of a living organism, in this case human.

The "Gods" were not an abstract concept to early humans as they are in your world today.

The humans knew and were familiar with them and their abilities and capabilities.

The Gods did not tell man that they were aliens.

And aliens will not tell man that they are Gods.

Man, when he achieves a more evolved state and is free to explore the vast reaches of space, will not declare himself a God to those less evolved that he makes contact with. Man knows that he is man and that God is God. Liars and other misfits of your species are not allowed into your space program. Liars and misfits of other species, where they exist, are controlled just as they are on your world. And the Gods do not lie.

Gods do not need craft to travel the vast expanses of their domain. They are beings of pure energy. Using their vast knowledge of the properties of energy and matter, they can manifest physically at will within any aspect of their domain. That which Mr. Sitchin interprets to mean "rocket or spaceship" actually means "from the heavens or a specific aspect of heavens."

Gods do not travel in rocket ships; they come from the heavens, or more precisely, at very specific aspects of the heavens.

In your terminology, Gods exist in hyperspace, or the space between dimensions. The Gods do not behave like the Gods of Mr. Sitchin's material. If the Gods behaved that poorly, there would be no need for Gods. Man already behaves like that. The structures that the ancient Gods instructed Man to build were not space ports or landing pads. They were temples. The Gods ordered the temples built, not because the Gods needed or wanted them, but because Man needed them. The Gods do not physically live there. It was a place where Mankind could go to be in the spiritual presence of the Gods.

Humans still have some resemblance of that form today, but the function is totally missing. For the Radically Altered Genetic Units, it was literally a place to stand in the presence of the Gods and commune according to the manner that the Gods had established. The temples also reminded the masses that there is a God, and of all the things that they had been taught by the Gods. It was a reminder, not a place of worship.

That unnecessary practice was added at a later time. This does not discount the fact that Earth has been visited by extraterrestrials throughout its history, but the aliens are not the genetic creators of man. For those of you who believe ancient human sacred text of certain origins, you believe that God is an exalted human. I can extrapolate that to mean that you believe that only an exalted human form can be God.

By further extrapolation, I can surmise that although God created the heavens and the Earth, and an unimaginable host of beings therein, only His human creations on this Earth are acceptable to be resurrected and reside with Him forever in His heaven.

This, loosely interpreted, means that of all God's creations, only humans have a soul. To interpret this absolutely correctly according to the exactness of those ancient texts, only human males have a soul.

This also means that if humans who accept this premise were faced with the possibility that this was not true, and that there are many Creator Gods, and even more Lesser Gods who serve the Creator God, they would vehemently reject that truth.

I believe the classic human term for such material and its source is called "Demonic". Yet, after all of the fanatical racial prejudice throughout human history, your own science and medicine have concluded that there is absolutely no genetic difference in the human species, regardless of ethnic background or sex.

It is equally arrogant and unfounded to believe that all other "Gods" are anything other than an exalted form of some other species.

If any member of another species has evolved to the stature of a "God", with the prerequisite knowledge and power that such a state requires, we believe that such a being is deserving of our respect, regardless of species.

Unfortunately, this truth, based upon the very human principle of exclusivity, is the very reason that the human species remains quarantined and denied access to the Universal family at large.

We do know that there are lesser Gods of many species, including reptilians

We do not know the origin of the Creator God of this Grid Existence. We do know that there are Lesser Gods of many species, including reptilians, within this Grid Existence. The species of extraterrestrial beings are nearly as varied as the species of your world. If you go far enough back, you discover that an extraterrestrial race has interbred with humanity. This is the reptilian race. I suggest strongly in the book that those we call the Ananaki (in the Sumerian Tablets) are actually a reptilian race.

This interbreeding occurred between the human race and this reptilian group within a race.

I am not alone in this. Dr. David Arthur Horne has written a book, "Humanity's Extraterrestrial Origins", and has made the same connections that I have. I make these connections, not just from intuition, but from a tremendous amount of ancient and modern evidence that shows that this reptilian connection travels right through these thousands of years to the present day. Some of these references to serpents and dragons are obviously symbolic, not the least, the Kundalini energy and other things, but when you look at the evidence, there is a tremendous number of literal references to serpent people - serpent gods. When you do the research, again, into the area where this seems to have happened in the Caucasus Mountains, in what we now call Turkey, Iran and Iraq, which we called Sumer and Babylon, and into the plains of Egypt (the area particularly around the Caucasus Mountains seems to be the place where these bloodlines came out).

This interbreeding occurred between the human race and this reptilian group within a race. Now, I don't see the reptilian genetic stream as negative in itself - quite the opposite - it's just this particular group within it.

Hybrids became demigods and middle men between the gods and humanity

The Sumerian Tablets and many other accounts, all over the world, talk about the fact that these hybrids became the demigods, the middle men and women between the gods and humanity. If you look at some of the history of Iran, the earliest kings were called the serpent kings, and they became kings as a result of their genetic structure and their family bloodlines. Humans must recognize the blatant contradictions and falsehoods of their beliefs, and become open to the real possibilities of "Creation" and "Evolution."

Who are the "Illuminati" and are they associated with the reptilian bloodline?

"The Illuminati, the clique which control the direction of the world, are genetic hybrids, the result of interbreeding between a reptilian extraterrestrial race and humanity many thousands of years ago. The centre of power is not even in this dimension -- it is in the lower fourth dimension, the lower astral as many people call it, the traditional home for the "demons" of folklore and myth. These fourth-dimensional reptilian entities work through these hybrid bloodlines because they have a vibrational compatibility with each other. This is why the European royal and aristocratic families have interbred so obsessively, as do the so-called Eastern Establishment families of the United States, which produce the leaders of America.

Every presidential election since and including George Washington in 1789 has been won by the candidate with the most European royal genes. Of the 42 presidents to Bill Clinton, 33 have been genetically related to two people, Alfred the Great, King of England, and Charlemagne, the most famous monarch of what we now call France. It is the same wherever you look in the positions of power... they are the same tribe!"

The following is a quote from Manly P. Hall, 33° Mason, author of "The Secret Destiny of America."

"There exists in the world today, and has existed for thousands of years, a body of enlightened humans united in what might be termed, an Order of the Quest. It is composed of those whose intellectual and spiritual perceptions have revealed to them that civilization has secret destiny...The outcome of this 'secret destiny' is a World Order ruled by a King with supernatural powers.

This King was descended of a divine race; that is, he belonged to the Order of the Illumined for those who come to a state of wisdom then belong to a family of heroes-perfected human beings."

The true illuminati are a closed circle of inter-married bloodlines originating with the first Radically Altered Genetic Units.

They were the first established divine Priest/Kings, originating from the times of the beginning of the human species. As reported in ancient texts and sacred oral tradition, these enhanced humans are the product of natural breeding by races of Lesser Gods and human females. Beings of Extraterrestrial origin within your Grid Existence, with insignificant exception, have not been permitted to intermingle with or alter the genetics of any sentient species, in accordance with the directives of a seed planet.

The "Greys" are the only exception to that directive, as their genetic splicing has no significant impact on the spontaneous evolution of your world. As one race of Lesser Gods, the reptilians have the ability to transmute into whatever incarnate form they desire.

Their intermingling with the daughters of Man on Earth is no less awkward or conspicuous than the appearance of the "serpent" to Eve in the Garden of Eden.

Just as the Virgin Mary was "overshadowed" by the "Spirit of God" (a "Shining One") to produce Jesus, so it was and is with the breeding of all enhanced beings who are the offspring of the Lesser Gods.

This process is normal for the conception of both Christ and Melchezedek beings, having the ability to self-actualize generally at puberty to full knowledge and empowerment.

The enhanced genetics of the Priest/Kings passed to descendants by normal breeding between two enhanced genetic beings will pass the potential for the enhanced genetic abilities, but will not necessarily ensure that those gifts are either dominant or active.

Anciently, enhanced genetic units that were about to assume positions of authority and power were "initiated" by rituals prescribed to awaken any such latent enhanced gifts. This was called "King-making".

Are there enhanced genetic humans who are the descendants of a race of Lesser God reptilians and human women?
Yes.

Is it true that the illuminati still intends to take over the world?

The illuminati, within a few elite bloodlines, already control your world. It seems clearly evident that any social order that is founded upon a system of exchange, that whom ever controls the system of exchange controls the social order. Although the royal bloodlines of many nations has been usurped, the clandestine power of these many of these families and their allies is still quite evident in your world today if you know where to look.

The Illuminati know that modern traditional religions are a fabrication.

Are the illuminati, aside from their genetic origins, associated with any other Gods or aliens? Since the illuminati understand that there are many universes and many worlds, and the truth concerning not only their own enhanced genetic origins, but the enhanced genetic origins of all mankind and other sentient beings as well, they also know that modern traditional religions are a fabrication. This means that although they accept a Creator God just as most humans do, their gods predate all modern religious belief.

Yes, certain members of the illuminati do have contact with extraterrestrial beings.

Yes, certain members of the illuminati do have contact with both other earthly sentient species and extraterrestrial beings. Are you saying that the secrets of the illuminati, the secrets of other sentient life on earth, and the secrets of extraterrestrial species' visitations to earth are inter-related? The most evolved members of the inner circles of the illuminati are most definitely aware of these truths and are interactive with other species. They are not inter-related in any concrete way, except through awareness and some limited contact. There are no conspiracies to control, enslave or entirely eliminate mankind among these various groups. At the highest levels of the Illuminati and extra-terrestrial intelligence, it is understood that stabilization of your planet must occur through a combination of human environmental and social reform. Some of these reforms, such as human population reduction, human birth control, and worldwide population stabilization by immobilization of transient individuals and groups may be implemented.

The Reptilian Programs

The Reptilians did 'exist', said the voice, but they were holographic thought projections of the Matrix

The ultimate manipulator of the Matrix and its five sense Time Loop, the voice said, was the very fabric of the Matrix itself and its power source was the consciousness trapped within its vibrational walls. The Matrix was a self ware entity that was knowingly manipulating to ensure its own survival by generating the events necessary to produce the fear that empowered it.

Humans were indeed 'batteries' or power stations for the Matrix and we were providing the power to maintain our own prison. The Reptilians did 'exist', said the voice, but they were holographic thought projections of the Matrix very much like the agents or 'sentient programs' that manipulate in the Matrix movies.

They could either operate as a reptilian projection or hide behind an apparently 'human' form, just as the sentient programs morph in and out of different human forms in the movies.

Either way, the Reptilians and other projected agents of the Matrix were not 'real' in consciousness terms; they were projections, thought fields or highly sophisticated software programs.

The existence of projected holographic phenomena is now supported by science

The existence of such thought projected holographic phenomena is now supported by scientific research and experiment, as we shall see. Holograms are projections of energy or 'light' that appear to the observer to be a three dimensional form, but in fact they are a series of codes and wave patterns that only take on the illusion of 3 D when a laser is shone upon them. Or in the case of the holographic projections in the Matrix, when they are observed into illusory reality by the human mind.

It works like this...

As I was told with great clarity in my second ayahuasca experience, the whole of five sense reality is a holographic illusion that only exists in a 'solid' form because the human mind/brain makes it appear that way. The '3 D' world of landscape, seas, buildings and human bodies, only exists in that form when we look at it! Otherwise it is a mass of vibrational fields and codes. In the movies, the Matrix is depicted from the outside as a series of green numbers and codes, while inside it is experienced as the sort of world we think we live in mountains, streets, cars, people and so on. That is a good analogy. I know this all sounds fantastic at first hearing, but these themes are now being confirmed at the cutting edge of scientific research.

The voice said that when the Reptilians absorbed human fear they were absorbing it for the Matrix itself because they are projections of the Matrix. But they were not aware of this. Indeed, the Reptilians, other 'demonic entities', and the Illuminati hierarchy were not aware of who their ultimate master really was the Matrix itself.

The Reptilian "sentient programs" did not have human emotion

The manipulators were also being manipulated. The Reptilian "sentient programs" did not have human emotion, the voice said, because they were just that, 'sentient programs', and are not conscious in the way humans are conscious. "If you programmed a computer to kill children, would that computer have any emotional problems with that?" the voice asked.

No, it would just follow the programming because computers do not have emotion. They do what they are programmed to do. It was the same with the Illuminati and the 'Reptifians' they were, in effect, like highly sophisticated computer software. They were like digital people implanted in the movies alongside human actors. They appear to be the same, but they are not. Unemotional computers can process information faster and more efficiently than human conscious minds in a disconnected state and, in the same way, the sentient program projections of the Matrix have been able to out fox and out think humans. But this can only continue until humanity remembers who it really is and where it really comes from, and reconnects with its true and infinite self.

Then the projected holographic manipulators will have intelligence akin to counting beads compared with human potential and, as I was told, that moment is fast approaching. This is what happened symbolically to the Neo character in the first Matrix movie when he awakened to the illusion of life and death and the dream world he had been living in.

Once he reached that point of reconnected awareness, the agents, the sentient programs, all powerful until then, were suddenly no problem to overcome. In Gen.6 we are told that the angels came down and mated with human women and in turn they women bore giant sons known as the Nephilim.

But this does not explain all the half human and half animals of the past that were worshiped as gods. But if look in the book of Enoch we find a major clue. "And they (the Nephilim) began to sin against birds, and beasts, and reptiles, and fish, and to devour one another's flesh, and drink the blood.

Then the earth laid accusation against the lawless ones." Obviously giant men can not have sexual relations with a fish never mind producing offspring. The early records of the ancient Submersions record that the gods mixed their DNA with mankind in a more scientific way. In other words it was done in a test-tube. This has to be how the Nephilim corrupted the seed of all living creatures on earth.

This is why the flood had to come and clean the slate of this massive DNA meltdown. It also says in Genesis that the angels came down again after the flood to mate and have more Nephilim children who went on to build world empires.

The Nephilim were producing human animal hybrids

It was at this time Israel was to exterminate all the Nephilim tribes around her which were over 20 in the Old Testament. Not only that, they were not only to exterminate all the hybrid women and children, but they were also called upon to kill off all the animals. They were not allowed to eat the animals or take them. If the Nephilim were still corrupting seed, this mysterious action of killing all the animals becomes very interesting. It becomes clear that the Nephilim were at it again producing human animal hybrids.

When the angels came down to mate with women, many of them carried reptilian genes as seen with the Seraphim who were "fiery serpent." Their seed may have produced reptilian Nephilim who then went on to spread their seed among all creatures. From mammals they would produce the giant sized dinosaurs. From fish the giant sea serpents. One of these sea creatures in scripture was called Leviathan who breathed fire. Is it any coincidence that it breathed fire if it carried the DNA of "fiery serpents." known as the Seraphim angels.

I believe that the Reptilians that people encounter today are a product of DNA mixing and mating. Unlike real humans they are known to change their shape to look like humans. They are very intelligent and and appear to walk among us. It is when they become very stressed or angered that they loose the human form and revert back to their original Reptilian form.

Al Gore was seen on a live television feed doing this exact thing. See www.stargods.org/GoreShapeShifted.htm I personally did not see this but a close friend of mine did and I have also come across many other people on the net who saw it too. Apparently according to these people, Al Gore looked very stressed and angry at the time. One day I would like to find a film of it on the net!

In India, human Reptiles are known as the Nagas. Also there have been many reports of people sighting Reptilians in caves. Folklore seems to indicate that there are other reptilian men that live in the earth but cannot come to the surface as the other ones can. They live in the earth as a separate society. For more information refer to the Dulce Book by Branton at: www.title14.com/ufo/dulce/ Divine creatures from the Old Testament, associated with the Cherubim, and later taken to be angels.

The root of Seraphim comes either from the Hebrew verb saraph ('to burn') or the Hebrew noun saraph (a fiery, flying serpent). Because the term appears several times with reference to the serpents encountered in the wilderness (Num. 21.8, Deut. 8.15; Isa. 14.29; 30.6), it has often been understood to refer to "fiery serpents." From this it has also often been proposed that the seraphim were serpentine in form and in some sense "fiery" creatures or associated with fire."

"It is said that whoever lays eyes on a Seraph, he would instantly be incinerated due to the immense brightness of the Seraph. They are described as very tall, with six wings and four heads, one for of the cardinal directions.

One pair of wings are for flying, one for covering their eyes (for even they may not look directly at God), and one for covering their feet (which is almost certainly a euphemism for genitalia). They are in the direct presence of God. In Isaiah's call-vision in the Temple, he sees Seraphim surrounding the throne of God, singing praise to God; the "Thrice Holy" hymn (ch 6).

In this instance they are angelic beings but in the Book of Numbers, seraph-snakes are sent to punish the Israelites. Some of the Seraphim are Metatron, Kemuel, Nathanael, Gabriel, and Lucifer."

What you have read are the opinions, theories and beliefs of Mr. David Icke.

*** *** ***

176

Alien Entities, Spirits, and Non-Physical Remnants on Earth Summoned by Arab Occultists, Spiritists and Ulemas

Court Astrologer for Queen Elizabeth summoned Alien-Like Entities

---

The well-known British occultist, Dr. John Dee, the official court astrologer for Queen Elizabeth I, used to summon alien creatures. But he ceased this practice after the death of the queen in 1603, and retired to Mortlake.

In his fascinating tales, H.P. Lovecraft mentioned a most unusual manuscript titled "The Necronomicon" authored in 750 A.D. by the Syrian Abdul Alhazred. The book was translated into Latin by Olaus Wormius. And later on, from Latin, Dr. John Dee translated it into English.

Almost all the ancient occult and "Spirits" books were originally written in Arabic. The most famous and powerful book on spirits and alien creatures was and still is "Shams Al Maa'ref Al Koubra" (Sun of the Great Knowledge). This book was written by a group of Ulema. In previous chapters, I wrote about this book. Please refer to. It is mind-boggling. The most fascinating part of the book is the large section on the language of the spirits, and celestial symbols and codes given by extraterrestrials to a small number of chosen men, known as the "Righteous Ones", aka "Ulema."

Were the bloodlines of past, present and future leaders of the world already decided upon, and predetermined by aliens?

By using codes and numerical values assigned to letters and words, Ulema were able to predict the future and learn about people who one day will rise to positions of power, including members of congresses, presidents, heads of states and monarchs. It appeared to Mr. Tayarah that the bloodlines of past, present and future leaders of the world were already decided upon, and predetermined by aliens.

Mr. Farid Tayarah who showed me the book, explained to me that religious people thought that the spirits mentioned in the book were "Mala-Ikat" (Angels), while more sophisticated and learned students of Arab magic and spiritism called them the aliens from the 7th heaven or constellation.

Mr. Tayarah also told me that Algebra as used today in our schools derived from the name of "Ahmad Al Jaber"; the famous Arab mathematician and scientist who invented Algebra.

The book explained how "men of science and wisdom" in the Middle East learned math, calculus, map drawing and reading, astronomy, alchemy, medicine and "sacred geometry" from an alien race.

The book also contained reversed names of important people who were part of the bloodlines of extraterrestrials.

The fascinating aspect of these lists is the fact that the book was written centuries before the listees were born.

How did the authors of the book learn about the future leaders of the world, their nationalities and names, particularly when some of the countries mentioned in the book did not exist at the time the book was written, such as the United States, and England in its current form?

Being a linguist and a student of modern and ancient dialects and languages of the Near East and Middle East, I was able to read the book in its entirety. What stunned me most was the detailed description of the "life after death" and how aliens influence and impact the present and future of humans, especially at the time of death.

Another chapter of the book was written in the language of the aliens illustrated with bizarre symbols and geometrical figures. Mr. Tayarah explained to me that these geometrical figures refer to the stars and planets hosting the aliens who descended on earth.

He added that by using a secret configuration, the "learned ones" could point out the precise and exact locations of the aliens' home beyond our galaxy.

Chapters from this book were read at Lodge number 18 of Lebanese Freemasons, located in "Al Bastah", a neighborhood in Beirut.

Coincidently or ironically, the father of H.P. Lovecraft is believed to have read a copy of John Dee's translation at the Grand Orient Lodge of Egyptian Freemasonry in Providence, Rhode Island, where H.P. Lovecraft was born. It seems that Freemasons lodges are vividly interested in these sorts of subjects.

*** *** ***

Descendants and Remnants of Aliens Among Us
Origins, Their Planets, Stars, Current Civilizations And Where Are They Today?

Dee Finey wrote an elaborate essay on this subject. Here are some revealing excerpts.

1-Arianni
2-Atlantides (Tyrrhenians)
3-Canaanites (Atlantis/Lumeria)
4-Carians (Phoenicians)
5-Fallen Angels
6-Horus (Sirius)
7-Lyraens
8-Vegans
9-Nordic (Scandinavian countries, Russia)

10-Maldekians
11-Andromedans
12-Reptilians
13-Pleiadians
14-Pegasians
15-Anunnaki
16-Zetas (Zeta Reticulians)
17-Dracos (Draconians)

Arianni: Admiral Byrd, in his flyover of the North Pole, encountered some inner-earth people called the Arianni. Note the similarity to the word Aryan. Andromodans say these lived on the planet Maldek (now the asteroid belt) and were the lost tribe of Lyrae. They now live underground in Tibet. See Agharta. The Arianni (Arians) are inner-earth people. Note the similarity to the word Aryan. Their space fleet is called the 'Silver Fleet'. They lived on the planet Maldek (now the asteroid belt) and were the lost tribe of Lyrae. Some sources say these are Blond Nordic humanoids who work with the Greys. Said to be captured by the Reptoids and also have implants. They are said to have a tendency to switch their loyalties between the Reptoids and the Confederations of Humans.

Atlantides: They were the Tyrrhenians. They eventually split in half to become the Etruscans and the Carians or Phoenicians.

Canaanites: Descended from Atlantis/Lemuria

Carians (Serpent Sea People of the Atlantean Fire God) Also the Phoenicians.

Fallen Angels: In the 15th century though it was estimated that 133,306,668 angels fell from the Heavens in a total of 9 days according to the Bishop of Tusculum(c.1273), and this was reaffirmed by Alphonso de Spina(c.1460) 133,306,668=36/9 - 1/3 of the angels fell - 133,306,668 x 3 = 399,920,004=36/9

Horus: The Son of God of Egyptian myth was strongly associated with Sirius as in Heru-Sept or "Horus of the Dogstar". One depiction of Horus was as Heru-ami-u, a hawk headed crocodile with a tail ending as a dog's head. He was also portrayed as a jackal or dog/wolf head, as was An or Anu, the royal ldeader of the Anunnaki." Heru=hero-hybrid bloodline and these 'heroes' maybe ruling the Earth at least in part, on behalf ofo the Sirisu 'gods'.

Lyrae: Attacked by the Reptilians (Draco) Survivors dispersed to other locations throughout the galaxy.

Vega (Alpha Lyrae): The brightest star in Lyra; the brightest star in the northern summer sky (forming the northwestern apex of the Summer Triangle), and the fifth brightest star in the whole sky; its name derives from an Arabic phrase that means "the swooping eagle." Vega is a main sequence; a star that has the distinction of being the first star ever to be captured on a photographic plate (1850). At one time, Vega was the pole star and will be so again in about 11,500 years.

In 1983, based on observations by the Infrared Astronomy Satellite (IRAS), Vega became one of the first stars to be discovered with a large luminous infrared-radiating halo that suggests a circumstellar cloud of warm dust. Since Vega seems to be rotating with its pole directed toward Earth, the dust cloud probably represents a face-on disk that may not be unlike the disk surrounding the Sun and that contains the planets. Observations carried out by Helen Walker of the Rutherford Appleton Laboratory, England, and associates, using the Infrared Space Observatory, have shown that the Vegan disk contains particles 200 microns across, or 200 times larger than a typical interstellar dust grain.

In 2002, astronomers announced that two prominent peaks of dust emission around Vega, one offset 60 AU to the southwest of the star, and the other offset 75 AU to the northeast, could be best explained by the dynamical influence of an unseen planet in an eccentric orbit. A massive planet in an eccentric orbit within an in-spiraling dust cloud doesn't create a simple ring like the Earth. Instead, calculations show that an eccentric planet traps dust in two main concentrations at different distances from the star, at positions outside the planet orbit that are generally not in line with the star.

Computer simulations show that this effect appears over a wide range of planet masses and orbital eccentricities. It isn't seen in our Solar System because the orbits of the Sun's planets don't have large enough eccentricities. Since quite a number of known massive extrasolar planets follow highly eccentric orbits, asymmetric dust concentrations may be common features of extrasolar planetary systems. Physical scenarios other than the resonant interactions of a planet might create a dust peak, like the recent collision of very large asteroids. For two such major collisions to happen on opposite sides of Vega at nearly the same time is extremely unlikely, but it can't be ruled out with the current data.

Vega (Alpha Lyrae) has a disk of dust and gas around it, discovered by the IRAS satellite in the mid 1980s. This either signifies planets or that planet that may soon form. The protoplanetary disk, as can be guessed from its name, is believed to be a precursor to the formation of planets but can persist long after planets have been formed if there are no gas giant planets such as Jupiter.

In about 14,000 AD, Vega will take over from Polaris as the North Star, owing to the precession of the equinoxes. A beacon in orbit around Vega was the source of the radio message picked up by the SETI team in Carl Sagan's novel "Contact".

Lyraens: Lyrae is the original star of the Nordic type aliens. The orientation of the Lyraens was agricultural in nature. They were very plentiful and abundant, and lived in peace. The Lyraens are built in a very sturdy way, Caucasian-like, very large. They usually have a light skin, and even though light hair and eyes are the most common, you would sometimes find Lyrans with dark hair. The Lyraens are authority figures. During the times they were most active on Earth they used symbols to depict their group; the most common symbols they used were of birds and of cats. Often throughout history they played a fatherly role, since they were very strict.

You might say they were like father figures. Humans both loved them and feared them, much like they would a authoritative parent. Lyrae was invaded by the saurian type aliens, and the Nordics escaped to Orion, Tau Ceti, the Pleiades, Procyon, Antaries, Alpha Centauri, Barnard Star, Arcturus, Hyades, and Vega as well as dozens of other solar systems. In this solar system, the refugees colonized the planet now called Mars. At that time, it was the third planet in the solar system. A world called Maldek was the fourth planet in this solar system, and was also colonized.

*** *** ***

Alpha Draconians and Lyrans

According to Alex Collier, a large ship came out of a huge craft and approached the planet Bila, and reptilians from Alpha Draconis disembarked. Apparently, the Alpha Draconians and the Lyrans were afraid of each other. The Alpha Draconians were apparently the first race in our galaxy to have interstellar space travel, and have had this capability for 4 billion years.

When the Draconians came and saw Bila, with all its abundance and food and natural resources, the Draconians wanted to control it. There was apparently a mis-communication or misunderstanding between the Draconians and Lyraen humans.

The Lyraens wanted to know more about the Draconians before some kind of "assistance" was offered. The Draconians mistook the communication as a refusal, and subsequently destroyed three out of 14 planets in the Lyraen system. The Lyraens were basically defenseless.

The planets Bila, Teka and Merck were destroyed. Over 50 million Lyraen humans were killed.

Lyssa Royal says: "The remnants of the Draco attack on Lyrae are still seen by today's scientists.

In 1985, a newspaper article stated that scientists are able to observe remnant waves of a blast that fan outward, and emanate from a central part of this galaxy.

They believe this blast to be several million years old and of such intense proportions that the wave is still traveling toward the edge of the galaxy before dissipating. They claim not to have any idea of what created the blast."

There is a race of beings on Sirius A, the humans there, are called the Katayy. They are considered benevolent. There is also animal, mammal and aquatic life on the planet. Many of the human races there are red-skinned. Their ancestry is some of the first Lyraens that escaped with the women and children during the war. In their oceans they have whales, octopus and sharks.

They are a race that is artistic. They have music and are connected to nature. They are builders and not very political. Their governments are based on "spiritual technology", which uses sound and color. It is at this point in history that the Draconians began to look at humans as a food source. This is how old the struggle is between the reptilian and human races. Now, I must make the point that not all the reptilian or human races are "dark". There is a mix. When we start meeting these races, you are going to have to trust your gut instinct.

But, they are coming. The Lyraens, according to Stewart Swerdlow are all blonde-haired, blue-eyed people, with an occasional red-haired or green-eyed person. In Lyraen society, red-haired people were considered very special with extrasensory powers that connected them to non-physical realms.

They were especially desired for breeding purposes. For this reason, red-haired people were kept separate from the rest of the population and even had their own subculture. They were much coveted by the Reptilians, who did not have much psychic ability. For the Reptilians to function in physical reality, they needed physical genetics. The transparent people took genetics from the now physical Lyraens, who had blonde or red hair, and blue or green eyes.

These genetics were mixed with the transparent people's collective energy, thus manifesting physically as the Reptilians. This is why the current Reptilians need the energetics from Aryan-type people to survive on the physical plane. Once the Reptilians were created in the astral, they needed a physical home base from which to accomplish their task. For this, they were taken to many different physical realities in which they could become the dominant species.

Mentally, they were programmed to conquer and absorb all of the races and species that they encountered. Those that could not be absorbed were to be destroyed. The purpose of all of this is to determine the most perfect form in physical reality that can exist in any environment. Think of it as a gigantic, cosmic Survivor contest.

The Reptilians are programmed to believe that they are the superior physical form. Scientifically speaking, Reptilian DNA does not change very much over eons of time. It basically remains the same.

For them, this is their proof that they are already perfect, without any need to adapt. Mammalian life, on the other hand, evolves and changes form constantly to survive. To the Reptilian mind, this denotes weakness and inferiority?

Reptilians are also androgynous, meaning male and female in one body. This is comparable to all non-physical forms that have no gender like God-Mind. For this reason, the Reptilians believe themselves to be more godlike because of their androgyny. Due to their ethnocentric values, they also consider it their right to control and conquer all of space and time. Although the Reptilians operate out of a general group mind, they are separated into seven different Reptilian species, each created to perform specific functions. Over time, the relationship between the Reptilians and the red-haired Lyraens deteriorated such that the Reptilians began to make sacrifices to appease the demons.

Alex Collier says: The Reptilians enjoy human flesh, and human children best, for two reasons. The first is that children don't have the accumulation of pollutants in their bodies that adults do, and when children are put into a state of fear, their energy and field and andrenalin just explodes. The reptilians get a "rush" from this stuff.

Nordic Humans From Lyrae
The Ancestors of Humanity

The black race is indigenous to Earth

The ancestors of humanity were Nordic in appearance, and those of red, brown and yellow skin evolved these distinctions as a result of environmental differences experienced by each respective colony. The black race is indigenous to Earth, and developed to Homo sapiens through the periodical insertion of DNA into their biological systems by other humanoid races (of Lyraen descent).

Humanity is now an intergalactic species and its seed is spread via the system of wormhole transit routes which permeate the cosmos. One major wormhole portal exists in the constellation of Lyrae. Most humanoids inhabiting our corner of the galaxy are descendants of the seven-feet-tall Nordics which came through this portal many millions of years ago. (Earth humans have become shorter as a result of a dramatic increase in the planet's level of gravity, since the end of Atlantis.)

This group primarily colonized the stars of the Lyrae system, and later the Pleiades. A party from the Vega colony shortly settled in the Sirius system.

Sirian Humans

These Sirian humans are usually dark-haired, with white skins because they left Vega at a time before the Vegans evolved into a dark-skinned race. The latter, including an outpost in the Pleiades, were responsible for a colony in the northern section of Atlantis. The descendants of this settlement are now known as the Native Americans. The colonies of Vega and Sirius have long since evolved beyond the philosophy of self-aggrandisement; however, there are several renegade groups active which still retain the old values.

Many of these are working with the secret government, and issue from the past. A theory proposed by Bible scholar I.D.E. Thomas asserts that the race of the "Nephilim" (meaning Giants and/or fallen ones), mentioned in Genesis 6:4 and Numbers 13:33, closely resemble the alien race of the blond Pleiadian Nordics, reported to be eight to nine feet tall. The Nazis attempted to revive this mystical Aryan race in the 1930's and 1940's. Mr. Thomas believes that a hybrid offspring culminated from relations between the Nephilim and the "daughters of man" resulting in increased wickedness upon the earth; and thus evoking God's wrath in the form of the "Great Flood".

Relations Among Martians, Maldekians, Andromedans, Reptilians And Pleiadians

Andromedans: Our Moon is an artificial moon. It originally came from a star system in Ursa Minor, called Chauta.

> Our Moon, according to the Andromedans, is an artificial moon. It originally came from a star system in Ursa Minor, called Chauta. It was one of four moons in a solar system that had 21 planets. Our Moon was brought from an orbit around the 17th planet. It was brought here, with others, during a war.

Our Moon's first location in orbit in our solar system was around a planet called Maldek, which has completely been destroyed during that war and which is now the asteroid belt...Now, apparently, our Moon was one of two moons in orbit around Maldek. The other moon orbiting Maldek we know today as Phobos, which is now orbiting Mars...The beings that were on the Moon in the domed cities were known as Ari-ans - the 'white race'. The Pleiadians apparently were responsible for moving our Moon to an orbit around Earth.

So, the Ari-ans that came here on our Moon were in fact humans from the destroyed planet of Maldek, one of the lost tribes of Lyrae, some of the reincarnated souls of them today are living underground on Earth in Tibet.

According to David Icke, the Reptilians have been following the people of Lyrae from planet to planet in their 'need' to control them and access their psychic powers.

Dan Winters quotes from Lyssa Royal: The remnant Lyraens who colonized other planets formed an alliance against the constant Reptilian attacks.

They called this alliance the Galactic Federation, comprised of 110 different colonies.

The colonies belonging to the Federation wished to maintain their new identities, and no longer associate with the old way.

Together, the Federation colonists managed to repel the Reptilian attacks. There were three primary groups who did not join the Federation.

These three groups were considered extremists, or nationalistic idealists, seeking to recreate the glory of the old Lyraen civilization.

One group was the Atlans, located on a Pleiadian planet.

The Pleiades actually consists of thirty-two planets orbiting seven stars. At that time there were sixteen different colonies of Lyraen descent throughout the Pleiades.

These colonists all wanted to oust the renegade Atlans because they remained independent and did not assist their human cousins. The other two groups were the Martians and Maldekians, who were already at odds with each other.

For this reason, the Reptilians turned their attention toward this solar system with its two human colonies.

In the Reptilians estimation, it would be easy to divide and conquer. The Reptilians love to use comets and asteroids as weapons and ships, using them to travel through the stars. First, they create a small black hole as a propulsion system that pulls the larger planetoid towards its destination. When used as a weapon, they use a particle beam accelerator to create a blast that hurls the comet or asteroid to its target. All of the technology was obtained by the beings from Sirius A.

In this way, they hurled a huge ice comet aimed at Mars and Maldek. The Reptilians, not being very technologically oriented, miscalculated the trajectory. The pull of the gigantic gas planet, Jupiter, pulled the comet off course. The ice comet then headed directly for Maldek. The citizens of that planet asked the Martians for help. Even though they were at odds with each other, they allowed some of the Maldekians to move to the Martian underground. The comet came so close to Maldek that the planet got caught between the gravitational pull of Jupiter, Mars, and the comet. This caused the planet to explode, leaving an asteroid belt between Mars and Jupiter.

The explosion pushed the ice comet close enough to Mars to rip the atmosphere off that planet, leaving only an extremely thin atmosphere. The explosion also pulled Mars further away from the sun.

The comet then continued on toward the Earth. The heat of the sun and the gravitational pull between the two globes forced the watery atmosphere of the Earth to polarize. This polarization pulled most of the ice from the comet to the polar regions of the Earth, thus covering most openings to the inner Earth, while at the same time exposing huge land masses for the first time.

The comet then switched places with Earth, taking up the second orbit from the sun, becoming the planet now known as Venus. The heat of the sun melted the ice on the comet, creating a cloudy covering to this new planet. The Earth was pushed out to the third orbit occupying the previous position held by Mars. The Earth was now ready to be colonized. Most of the surviving amphibians were transported to a new home on Neptune. Some stayed in the newly formed oceans.

The Reptilians who were inside the hollow comet, now Venus, came to the surface of this new world. They built seven domed cities, one for each of the seven groups in the hierarchy. In the mid-1980s one of New Yorks daily papers, *Newsday*, reported that a Soviet space probe penetrated the cloud layer of Venus and photographed seven white domes the size of small cities, all in a row. After a page-long diatribe, the American scientists concluded that this was all a natural formation. The Reptilians drove a large, hollowed out object into Earths orbit to begin the colonization process. This object is now called the Moon.

Conventional science considers the Moon natural, yet it is the only known object in space that does not spin on its axis. The Moon faces the Earth in the same position all of the time, leaving one side in complete darkness. A sonic resonance sent to the surface of the Moon makes a pinging noise like a hollow object.

If the Moon were solid, the noise would sound like a thump or thud. The Moon is hollow. A recent article in an astronomy magazine said that the Moon was being reclassified because it is considered to be hollow.

The Reptilians chose a large continental landmass to begin their civilization on the Earth, now referred to as Lemuria or Mu. This was a vast area in what is now the Pacific Basin, extending from Japan to Australia, and from the coast of California to Peru. The Hawaiian Islands are in the middle of this one-time landmass.

Here, an androgynous Reptilian culture developed. They brought with them the creatures that were their sustenance the dinosaurs. All beings create beneath them animals and plants that are a reflection of the mind-pattern.

Reptilians create dinosaurs, humans create mammals. They are not designed to coexist on the same planet.

Additionally, the thinking process of the Reptilians differs from the human thinking process. Because Reptilians do not evolve rapidly and remain unchanging, their expansion is also slow moving and insidious. It would take several millennia for the Reptilians to decide whether or not they would coexist with humans. After all, Earth was still an outpost far from the centre of the Draconian Empire.

In the meantime, the Martians were now living underground with their hostile Maldekian guests. Something had to be done quickly to prevent them from destroying one another. So, the Martians petitioned the Galactic Federation to remove the Maldekian refugees to another planet.

The Galactic Federation also received a petition from the Pleiadian Council at the same time, asking the Federation to remove the Atlans from their star cluster.

The Federation thusly decided to use the Atlans as a counterbalance on Earth. If the Atlans survived, the Maldekians would also be sent.

The human/Lyraen descendants were literally throwing their own riffraff to the Reptilian colonists on Earth.

In this way, the Federation would get rid of their undesirables. The undesirables would occupy the attention of the Reptilians. The Federation would gain valuable time to build their own forces against the Reptilians.

When the Atlans arrived on the Earth, they colonized what became known as Atlantis. Their continent stretched from what is now the Caribbean Basin to the Azores and Canary Islands, as well as several small island chains reaching up to what is now the East Coast of the United States, including Montauk Point.

The industrious Atlanteans rapidly grew to a large, prospering civilization needing more territory. The dinosaur population was rapidly increasing and becoming dangerous to the human colonists.

The Atlanteans began destroying the dinosaurs to protect themselves. This did not sit well with the Reptilians. Soon major battles occurred on the Earth between the Lemurian Reptilians and Atlantean humans.

At the same time, the Maldekian refugees arrived on Earth.

They created a large human colony in what is now the Gobi desert, northern India, Sumer, and other parts of Asia. The Maldekians attacked the lunar surface where the Reptilians guarded their Earth outpost from invasion. The Maldekians also bombarded Atlantis and Lemuria with laser weapons.

The dinosaurs were wiped out. Additionally, the Martians also attacked the Reptilians from space since they, too, were searching for a Reptilian-free environment in which to live. This might be considered the real First World War on this planet. It was a mess!

The loss of the Martian atmosphere caused by Draco's playing billiards became the "Total Recall" legend (movie about Martian history and the oxygen war). The Draco bases there today still have no hesitation to shoot down a NASA probe, although increasingly as the US government becomes a satellite of the shape-shifters- they begin to let a few Earth probes in.

*** *** ***

Pegasians
Member Name in the Galactic Federation: Pegasus Star League

Accepted into the Galactic Federation: 3.78 million years ago (They were originally a series of special colonies founded by the Sirian Governing Council some 4 million years ago).

Location: The constellation of Pegasus is a vast cluster of over 1,000 stars, located between the constellations of Cygnus and Aquarius.

Distance From Earth: Between 200 and 3,000 light years.

Life Form Type: There are three major types of humanoids located in this star league. The first type strongly resembles the Sirian human in height and appearance and is divided into the same white and blue skin types. The second type is a thinner human type with red or orange skin. The final type is a hybrid formed from the dinoid and second humanoid race.

Physical Appearance: The first type resembles that of the original Sirius B humanoid colonists: the men vary from perfectly formed muscular physiques to child-like bodies, and are 6 feet, 6 inches to 7 feet, 4 inches (1.98 to 2.24 meters) in height, with blonde to light brown hair and light blue to green-colored eyes. The women are extremely voluptuous in appearance and are 6 feet, 2 inches to 6 feet, 8 inches (1.88 meters to 2.03 meters) tall.
They have either extremely pale white or light blue skin. The second humanoid type slightly resembles the first in height and/or body types, except for two major differences.
First, the skin, as well as the hair, is either a light red or a dark orange in color.
Second, the eyes are more cat-like in appearance and the iris is either red or a dark blue. This group originally came from some of the more distant stars in the Lyra constellation. The hybrid third type has a scaly type of skin with more pronounced cat-like eyes that are either red, brown or pale yellow. The body, legs, neck, and arms are more muscular than a human and have a number of thick vein-like protuberances running their length. Each hand and foot ends in 4 thin, long fingers or toes, with a small claw at its end. The males are some 7 to 8 feet (2.13 to 2.44 meters) in height, while the females range from 6 feet, 10 inches to 7 feet, 7 inches (2.08 to 2.31 meters) tall.

Special Traits and Abilities: The beings from Pegasus are known for their prowess as innovators, scientists, and diplomats.

Average Amount of Sleep Needed: One and one-half to three hours, depending on the species.

Language: There are two types of languages spoken. One is slightly toned and harmonic-sounding, while the other is more guttural and coarse.

Mother Ship and Other Crafts: Three types of ships are operating in or near Earth. The first type is a defense ship that resembles a rounded equilateral triangle. Each of its sides is approximately 74 feet (22.56 meters) in length. The second type is a scout ship that is oblong in shape with an average diameter of about 85 feet (25.9 meters). The third ship is a double lens atmospheric command ship that is approximately 1300 feet (402 meters) in length.

*** *** ***

Elohim And Maldek

Used to be the fifth planet from our sun, it is now the asteroid belt. This is where our moon was first orbiting, after it was taken from Chauta in Ursa Minor. Watcher interprets the bible and says this was a planet of Elohim (rebel angels) that was destroyed by God. In Science magazine, Oct 1987, Drs. Cruikshank and Brown discovered organic compounds on 3 asteroids. Since organic compounds need water, and water needs an atmosphere to condense to liquid form, then the planetary body which holds the water would have to be large enough to have the gravity to hold on to an atmosphere. Watcher also says the bible refers to this planet as Rahab.

Reptilian Bloodline And Island Of Malta

Malta, too, was an important centre by 3500 BC and the home of a major mystery school. Under Malta is a vast network of tunnels and magalithic temples where secret rituals took place - and still do. Malta's original name was Lato, named after Mother Lato, the serpent goddess. The Knights Templar secret society was formed in the late 11th century to protect the reptilian bloodline or "Le Serpent Rouge", the red serpent or serpent blood together with their associated order, the highly secretive Priory of Sion.

Nephilim

Race of giants who were morally degraded. Gen 6. Possibly from Lyra or Nibiru. The word means "those who came down." Sitchin links these to people as being from the planet Nibiru. Branton says these were a race of giants who were aligned with a race of pre-Scandanavians who lived on a huge island in the middle of a sea in what is now the Gobi desert. He says they waged a fierce war with the reptoids of Antarctica. (Source: Branton's "Dreamland in the Rockies") In part 7 of Branton's Crim-ram series ("Caverns, dungeons, and labyrinths"), a Paul Doerr mentions in his newsletter "Unknown", mentioned a tradition in Malaysia in the Carolinas, especially Papua.

The tradition says a race of human giants from the lost island of Chamat will one day return from underground. Is Chamat the island from the Gobi desert? Koinonia House says the nephilim were the offspring of the elohim and human females in the days of Noah (see also Gen 6).

Nephilim comes from the Hebrew Naphal which means "to fall" so these were called "the fallen ones."

The B'nai Elohim were "angels of god".

The church viewed the elohim as angels up through the 4th century.

But all the nephilim didn't die during the great flood. Gen 4 mentions "...and after that..." which refers to the sons of Anak, or the Anakim.

The Greek 'titan' mentions they were of both celestial and earthly descent. Hebrew 'satan' is linguistically tied with Greek 'titan'.

Nibiru and Eridu

Sitchin says this is the twelfth planet which orbits our sun every 3600 years. He says these people helped build the pyramids. Their original landing site was Eridu, now in Southern Iraq.

Nibiru has Reptilians on it, living in two factions - the meat eaters, and those who became spiritual and decided that meat eating was not a good thing and are now vegetarian. They battle each other as the meat eaters are cannibalistic.

The term Nibiri, or Nibiru, the alleged home planet of the Annunaki according to the tablets, is derived from the word found in ancient Egypt, Neb-Heru, according to researcher and author Robert Temple. He says that Neb-Heru is clearly described in the Sumerian, Enuma Elish, as a star and not a planet.

Sirius Reptilians

They are only borderline humans

Created to antagonize and test humans. Created on a planet of Sirius A, and placed in the Draco star system. They are only borderline humans. They need the help of humans to manifest in the physical realm. Their vibratory rate is so high, they cannot sustain a physical body on their own. They need the "Aryan" type humans to survive on the physical plane. However, they are programmed to believe that they are the superior race and are perfect because their DNA doesn't change like humans' does.

They are also androgynous - in other words, both male and female in one body which makes them feel even more god-like. Though they operate out of a general group mind, they are separated into seven different Reptilian species, each created to perform specific functions. (See: 'Blue Blood, True Blood' by Stewart Swerdlow)

CHAPTER 6
THE REAL TRUTH OF HOW HUMANITY BEGAN

- A race of interbreeding bloodlines, a race within a race in fact, were centered in the Middle and Near East
- Importance of ancient Babylon and the "Brotherhood Agenda".
- The cabal which controls the human race operates from the shadows outside the public domain.
- The origin of the bloodlines and the plan for the takeover of the Earth began thousands of years with the extraterrestrials
- Sir Francis Crick, the Nobel laureate: There are at least one million planets in our galaxy that could support life as we know it.
- The idea is not to educate, but to indoctrinate
- The Old Testament had many gods and their names were written in plural
- The Sumerian Texts are ignored because they demolish the official version of events and religions
- Sitchin is mistaken in his Nibiru theory, though his main themes about the Anunnaki are correct.
- The Sumerians called Nibiru "TIAMAT"
- The Sumerian Tablets describe the nature and colour of Neptune and Uranus in ways that have only been confirmed in the last few years!
- Sumerian Tablets described the creation of Homo Sapiens
- The Tablets describe how the genes of the Anunnaki and those of the native humans were combined in a test tube to create the 'updated' human
- Humans were up grated some 200,000 years ago
- The Sumerian Tablets name the two people involved in the creation of the slave race: Enki and Ninkharsag
- They described how they created people with major defects and also human-animal hybrids
- The extraterrestrial Anunnaki found the right mix to create the Homo Sapiens and called him LU.LU (One who has been mixed, in Sumerian)
- From these records, the Levites compiled Genesis and Exodus

- Adam was not created from dust from the ground, but from living cells
- Anunnaki left the planet in flying craft, as an enormous surge of water wiped out much of humanity
- Plato, Atlantis, Mu (Lemuria) and the Azores
- The Book of Job, which is believed to be an Arab work reveals great knowledge
- Psychiatrist and writer, Immanuel Velikovsky's theory was proven correct!
- Brian Desborough: The "White Martians" built the pyramids which have been recorded on Mars
- "White Martians" became the white peoples of the Earth
- "White Martians" were the highly advanced race of the ancient world known as the Phoenicians or Aryans
- The Phoenicians were the 'brains' behind the Egyptian civilization
- The cataclysmic upheavals the Earth: Survival of extraterrestrials on Earth, the White Race and the Slave Race
- The Old Testament is a classic example of the religious recycling
- The human egg for the creation of the Lulu/Adam came from a female in Abzu, Africa
- The hybrid bloodlines became the British and European aristocracy and royal families
- The reptilian breeding program appears to have produced an Anunnaki-human hybrid (Adam?)
- Our genetic structure: 75% Anunnaki and 25% human.
- The most important gene is passed on by the female line
- The "Serpent King' bloodline: Iran, Kurdistan, Armenia, Turkey and the Caucasus Mountains
- Aryan: Reptile-Aryan or Reptile-Human (The White Race). A genetic manipulation of the Anunnaki
- The Arabs believed that it was Nimrod who built or rebuilt the amazing structure at Baalbek in the Lebanon
- A white 'Aryan' race introduced the ancient Sanskrit language to India
- The Phoenicians brought civilization to Europe not the Greeks
- The Phoenicians created the civilization and culture of Minoan Crete, classic Greece and Roman Italy
- The Sicilians are the direct descendants of the Phoenicians

*** *** ***

The Real Truth of How Humanity Began!

David Icke is always stimulating. And his theories are unmatched. Mr. Icke has his own version of the creation of our world. And of course, the extraterrestrials are always the primordial part of the story. So here it is, punches unpulled. And right after this essay, you will find a similar article in content, context and complete sentences, with minor variations. I founded it on "news4you." How this article was reproduced there, and who is the claimant or ghost author? I have no clues. It is a carbon copy of what you will read in the first part of this chapter. However, it remains puzzling and equally informative.

A race of interbreeding bloodlines, a race within a race in fact, were centered in the Middle and Near East

In summary, a race of interbreeding bloodlines, a race within a race in fact, were centered in the Middle and Near East in the ancient world and, over the thousands of years since, have expanded their power across the globe.

A crucial aspect of this has been to create a network of mystery schools and secret societies to covertly introduce their agenda while, at the same time, creating institutions like religions to mentally and emotionally imprison the masses and set them at war with each other. The hierarchy of this tribe of bloodlines is not exclusively male and some of its key positions are held by women. But in terms of numbers it is overwhelmingly male and I will therefore refer to this group as the Brotherhood.

Importance of ancient Babylon and the "Brotherhood Agenda".

Even more accurately, given the importance of ancient Babylon to this story, I will also call it the Babylonian Brotherhood. The plan they term their 'Creat Work of Ages', I will call the Brotherhood Agenda. The present magnitude of Brotherhood control did not happen in a few years, even a few decades or centuries: It can be traced back thousands of years.

The structures of today's institutions in government, banking, business, military and the media have not been infiltrated by this force, they were created by them from the start. The Brotherhood Agenda is, in truth, the Agenda of many Millennia. It is the unfolding of a plan, piece by piece, for the centralized control of the planet.

The bloodline hierarchy at the top of the human pyramid of control and suppression passes the baton across the generations, mostly sons following fathers. The children of these family lines who are chosen to inherit the baton are brought up from birth to understand the Agenda and the methods of manipulating the 'Great Work' into reality.

Advancing the Agenda becomes their indoctrinated mission from very early in their lives. By the time their turn comes to join the Brotherhood hierarchy and carry the baton into the next generation, their upbringing has moulded them into highly imbalanced people.

They are intellectually very sharp, but with a compassion bypass and an arrogance that they have the right to rule the world and control the ignorant masses who they view as inferior. Any Brotherhood children who threaten to challenge or reject that mould are pushed aside or dealt with in other ways to ensure that only 'safe' people make it to the upper levels of the pyramid and the highly secret and advanced knowledge that is held there. Some of these bloodlines can be named.

The British House of Windsor is one of them, so are the Rothschilds, the European royalty and aristocracy, the Rockefellers, and the rest of the so-called Eastern Establishment of the United States which produces the American presidents, business leaders, bankers and administrators.

The cabal which controls the human race operates from the shadows outside the public domain

But at the very top, the cabal which controls the human race operates from the shadows outside the public domain.

Any group which is so imbalanced as to covet the complete control of the planet will be warring within itself as different factions seek the ultimate control. This is certainly true of the Brotherhood. There is tremendous internal strife, conflict and competition. One researcher described them as a gang of bank robbers who all agree on the job, but then argue over how the spoils will be divided.

That is an excellent description and through history different factions have gone to war with each other for dominance. In the end, however, they are united in their desire to see the plan implemented and at the key moments they overwhelmingly join forces to advance the Agenda when it comes under challenge.

The origin of the bloodlines and the plan for the takeover of the Earth began thousands of years with the extraterrestrials

You will probably have to go back hundreds of thousands of years to find the starting point of this story of human manipulation and of the family lines which orchestrate the Great Work. The more I have researched this over the years, the more obvious it has become to me that the origin of the bloodlines and the plan for the takeover of the Earth goes off planet to a race or races from other spheres or dimensions of evolution. Extraterrestrial as we call them. If you doubt the existence of extraterrestrial life then consider this for a moment. Our Sun is only one of some 100 billion stars in this galaxy alone.

Sir Francis Crick, the Nobel laureate: There are at least one million planets in our galaxy that could support life as we know it.

Sir Francis Crick, the Nobel laureate, says there are an estimated 100 billion galaxies in our universe and he believes there are at least one million planets in our galaxy that could support life as we know it.

Think of what the figure might be for the entire universe, even before we start looking at other dimensions of existence beyond the frequency range of our physical senses. If you travelled at the speed of light, 186,000 miles per second, it would take you 4.3 years to reach the nearest star to this solar system.

The idea is not to educate, but to indoctrinate

It says much for humanity's level of indoctrination that to speak of extraterrestrial life is to appear cranky, yet to dismiss it and suggest that life has only emerged on this one tiny planet is considered credible! You only have to consider the amazing structures that abounded in the ancient world to see that an advanced race existed then. We are told that only people primitive in comparison to modern humans lived in these times, but that is patently ludicrous.

Like most official 'thinking' the historical and archaeological establishment makes up its own stories, calls them proven facts, and simply ignores the overwhelming evidence that they are wrong. The idea is not to educate, but to indoctrinate.

Anyone who doesn't conform to the official line of history is isolated by their fellow historians and archaeologists who either know their jobs, reputations and funding are safer when they stick to the official version, or, frankly, they cannot see beyond the end of their noses.

The same can be said of most people in the teaching and 'intellectual' professions.

All over the planet are fantastic structures built thousands of years ago which could only have been created with technology as good as, often even better than, we have today. At Baalbek, north east of Beirut in the Lebanon, three massive chunks of stone, each weighing 900 tons, were moved at least a third of a mile and positioned high up in a wall.

This was done thousands of years BC! Another block nearby weighs 1,000 tons - the weight of three jumbo jets. How was this possible?

Official history does not wish to address such questions because of where it might lead.
Can you imagine ringing a builder today and asking him to do that?
You want me to do WHAT? He would say, You're crazy.
In Peru are the mysterious Nazca Lines. The ancients scored away the top surface of the land to reveal the white subsurface and through this method were created incredible depictions of animals, fish, insects and birds. Some of them are so large they can only be seen in their entirety from 1,000 feet in the air!
The knowledge which allowed wonders like Nazca, Baalbek, the Great Pyramid at Giza and other amazing creations to be built with such precision and scale, came from an advanced race who, in ancient times, lived among a far more primitive general population.

The Old Testament had many gods and their names were written in plural

This race is described as 'the gods' in the Old Testament texts and other works and in oral traditions of antiquity. I can hear followers of the Bible denying that their book speaks of 'the gods'. But it does. When the word 'God' is used in the Old Testament it is often translated from a word that means gods, plural - Elohim and Adonai are two examples.
You can easily understand that a race performing technological feats of such magnitude should be seen as 'gods' by a people unable to comprehend such abilities.

In the 1930s, American and Australian servicemen landed their planes in remote parts of New Guinea to drop supplies for their troops. The locals, who had never seen a plane, believed the servicemen were gods and they became a focus of religious beliefs.

This would have been even more extreme in the ancient world had their advanced race been beings from other planets, stars or dimensions, flying craft more advanced than anything flown (at least officially!) by today's military. An influx of knowledge from outside this planet or another source would explain so many of the 'mysteries' that official history greets with a deafening silence.
The incredible feats of building also become explainable and so does the mystery of why early civilizations like Egypt and Sumer (the land of Shinar in the Bible) began at the peak of their development and then fell into decay, when the normal course of evolution is to start at a lower level and slowly advance through learning and experience.
There was clearly an infusion of highly advanced knowledge that was later lost to most people. In every culture throughout the world are ancient stories and texts which describe the 'gods' who brought this advanced knowledge. This would again explain the mystery of how the ancients had a phenomenal understanding of astronomy. There are endless legends all over the world of a time they call the Golden Age, which was destroyed by cataclysm and the 'fall of Man'.

The ancient Greek poet, Hesiod, described the world before the 'fall':

> Man lived like Gods, without vices or passions, vexation or toil. In happy companionship with divine beings (extraterrestrials?), they passed their days in tranquility and joy, living together in perfect equality, united by mutual confidence and love. The Earth was more beautiful than now, and spontaneously yielded an abundant variety of fruits. Human beings and animals spoke the same language and conversed with each other (telepathy). Men were considered mere boys at a hundred years old. They had none of the infirmities of age to trouble them and when they passed to regions of superior life, it was in a gentle slumber.

Utopian as that may sound, there are countless stories from every ancient culture which describe the world in the distant past in those terms. We can recreate that vision again if only we change the way we think and feel. The most comprehensive accounts of an advanced race are contained in tens of thousands of clay tablets found in 1850 about 250 miles from Baghdad, Iraq, by an Englishman Sir Austen Henry Layard as he excavated the site of Nineveh, the capital of Assyria. This was located near the present Iraqi town of Mosul. Other finds have followed in this region which was once called Mesopotamia.

The Sumerian Texts are ignored because they demolish the official version of events and religions

The original source of this knowledge was not the Assyrians, but the Sumerians who lived in the same area from, it is estimated, 4,000 to 2,000 BC. I will refer to the clay tablets, therefore, as the Sumerian Texts or Tablets. They are one of the greatest historical finds imaginable and yet 150 years after they were discovered they are still ignored by conventional history and education.
Why?
Because they demolish the official version of events.
The most famous translator of these tablets is the scholar and author Zecharia Sitchin, who can read Sumerian, Aramaic, Hebrew and other Middle and Near Eastern languages. He has extensively researched and translated the Sumerian Tablets and has no doubt that they are describing extraterrestrials. Some researchers say that he used a later version of the Sumerian language to translate an earlier one and, therefore, some of his translations may not be 100% accurate. I think his themes are correct, indeed other accounts and evidence supports this, but I personally doubt some of the detail. I think that a number of Sitchin's interpretations are extremely questionable, while I agree with the overall thesis.
According to his translations (and others) the Texts say that the Sumerian civilization, from which many features of modern society derive, was a gift from the gods. Not mythical gods, but physical ones who lived among them.

The Tablets call these gods the AN.UNNAK.KI (Those who from Heaven to Earth came), and DIN.GIR (The Righteous Ones of the Blazing Rockets).

The name of Sumer itself was KI.EN.GIR (The Land of the Lord of the Blazing Rockets and also Land of the Watchers, according to Sitchin). The ancient text known as the Book of Enoch also calls the gods 'the Watchers', as did the Egyptians. The Egyptian name for their gods, the Neteru, literally translates as Watchers and they said that their gods came in heavenly boats.

Sitchin is mistaken in his Nibiru theory, though his main themes about the Anunnaki are correct.

According to Zecharia Sitchin, the tablets describe how the Anunnaki came from a planet called Nibiru (The Planet of the Crossing) which he believes has a 3,600 year elliptical orbit that takes it between Jupiter and Mars and then out into far space beyond Pluto. Modern science has identified a body it calls Planet X which has been located beyond Pluto and is believed to be part of this solar system. But an elliptical orbit would be incredibly unstable and difficult to sustain.

Scientists I trust believe that Sitchin is mistaken in his Nibiru theory, though his main themes about the Anunnaki are correct.

The Sumerians called Nibiru "TIAMAT"

The Sumerian Tablets, from Sitchin's translations, describe how, during the early formation of the solar system, Nibiru caused the near destruction of a planet that once existed between Jupiter and Mars. The Sumerians called it Tiamat, a planet they nicknamed The Watery Monster. They say that it was debris from Tiamat's collision with a Nibiru moon which created the Great Band Bracelet - the asteroid belt which is found between Mars and Jupiter. What remained of Tiamat was thrown into another orbit, the texts say, and eventually it became the Earth.

The Sumerian name for the Earth means the Cleaved One because a vast hole was created, they say, by the collision. Interestingly if you take away the water in the Pacific Ocean you will be left with a gigantic hole.

The Tablets are the written accounts of oral traditions that go back enormous amounts of time and you have to be careful that details have not been added or lost and that we don't take symbolism or parable as literal truth. I am sure that some confusion did occur in this way. I have doubts myself about the Nibiru-Tiamat scenario and its alleged timescale. But there is much truth in the Texts which can be proven, not least in their knowledge of astronomy.

The Tablets depict the solar system with the planets in their correct positions, orbits and relative sizes, and their accuracy has only been confirmed in the last 150 years since some of these planets have been found.

The Sumerian Tablets describe the nature and colour of Neptune and Uranus in ways that have only been confirmed in the last few years!

What's more, the modern 'experts' did not expect those planets to look as they did, yet the Sumerians knew thousands of years BC what our 'advanced' science has only just discovered.

Sumerian Tablets described the creation of Homo Sapiens

Most stunning about the Sumerian Tablets is the way they describe the creation of Homo Sapiens. Sitchin says the Anunnaki came to the Earth an estimated 450,000 years ago to mine gold in what is now Africa. The main mining centre was in today's Zimbabwe, an area the Sumerians called AB.ZU (deep deposit), he claims.

Studies by the Anglo-American Corporation have found extensive evidence of gold mining in Africa at least 60,000 years ago, probably 100,000. The gold mined by the Anunnaki was shipped back to their home planet from bases in the Middle East, Sitchin claims the Tablets say. I think there is much more to know about this 'gold mining' business, and I don't believe that was the main reason they came here, if indeed it was a reason at all. At first the gold mining was done by the Anunnaki version of their working classes, Sitchin says, but eventually there was a rebellion by the miners and the Anunnaki royal elite decided to create a new slave race to do the work.

The Tablets describe how the genes of the Anunnaki and those of the native humans were combined in a test tube to create the 'updated' human

The Tablets describe how the genes of the Anunnaki and those of the native humans were combined in a test tube to create the 'updated' human capable of doing the tasks the Anunnaki required. The idea of test tube babies would have sounded ridiculous when the tablets were found in 1850, but that is precisely what scientists are now able to do.

Humans were up grated some 200,000 years ago

Again and again modern research supports the themes of the Sumerian Tablets. For instance, there was a sudden and so far unexplained upgrade of the human physical form around 200,000 years ago. Official science is silent on the cause of this and mutters terms like 'the missing link'. But some unavoidable facts need to be addressed.

From Homo Erectus to Homo Sapiens to Modern Man

Suddenly the previous physical form known as Homo Erectus became what we now call Homo Sapiens. From the start the new Homo Sapiens had the ability to speak a complex language and the size of the human brain increased massively. Yet the biologist Thomas Huxley said that major changes like this can take tens of millions of years. This view is supported by the evidence of Homo Erectus which appears to have emerged in Africa about 1.5 million years ago.

For well in excess of a million years their physical form seems to have remained the same, but then, out of nowhere, came the dramatic change to Homo Sapiens. About 35,000 years ago came another sudden upgrade and the emergence of Homo Sapiens sapiens, the physical form we see today.

The Sumerian Tablets name the two people involved in the creation of the slave race: Enki and Ninkharsag

The Sumerian Tablets name the two people involved in the creation of the slave race. They were the chief scientist called Enki, Lord of the Earth (Ki=Earth) and Ninkharsag, also known as Ninti (Lady Life) because of her expertise in medicine. She was later referred to as Mammi, from which comes mama and mother. Ninkharsag is symbolized in Mesopotamian depictions by a tool used to cut the umbilical cord. It is shaped like a horseshoe and was used in ancient times. She also became the mother goddess of a stream of religions under names like Queen Semiramis, Isis, Barati, Diana, Mary and many others, which emerged from the legends of this all over the world. She is often depicted as a pregnant woman.

The texts say of the Anunnaki leadership:

They summoned and asked the goddess,
the midwife of the gods, the wise birthgiver (saying), To a creature give life, create workers!
Create a primitive worker, that he may bear the yoke!
Let him bear the yoke assigned by Enlil,
Let the worker carry the toil of the gods!

Enlil was commander of the Anunnaki and Enki was his half-brother. Enki and Ninkharsag had many failures as they sought the right genetic mix, the Tablets tell us.

There are accounts of how they created people with major defects and also human-animal hybrids. Horrible stuff, and exactly what is claimed to be happening today in the extraterrestrial-human underground bases around the world.

The story of Frankenstein, the man created in a laboratory, could be symbolic of these events.It was written by Mary Shelley, the wife of the famous poet. He and she were high initiates of the secret society network which has hoarded and suppressed this knowledge since ancient times.

The extraterrestrial Anunnaki found the right mix to create the Homo Sapiens and called him LU.LU (One who has been mixed, in Sumerian)

The Tablets say that Enki and Ninkharsag eventually found the right mix which became the first Homo Sapiens, a being the Sumerians called a LU.LU (One who has been mixed). This is the biblical 'Adam'. LU.LU was a genetic hybrid, the fusing of homo erectus with the genes of the 'gods' to create a slave, a human worker bee, some 200,000-300,000 years ago. A female version was also created. The Sumerian name for human was LU, the root meaning of which is worker or servant, and it was also used to imply domesticated animals.

This is what the human race has been ever since. The Anunnaki have been overtly and now covertly ruling the planet for thousands of years. The mistranslation of the Bible and symbolic language taken literally has devastated the original meaning and given us a fantasy story. Genesis and Exodus were written by the Hebrew priestly class, the Levites, after they were taken to Babylon from around 586 BC. Babylon was in the former lands of Sumer and so the Babylonians, and therefore the Levites, knew the Sumerian stories and accounts.

From these records, the Levites compiled Genesis and Exodus

It was from these records overwhelmingly, that the Levites compiled Genesis and Exodus. The source is obvious. The Sumerian tablets speak of E.DIN (The Abode of the Righteous Ones). This connects with the Sumerian name for their gods, DIN.GIR (the Righteous Ones of the Rockets). So the Sumerians spoke of Edin and Genesis speaks of the Garden of Eden.This was a centre for the gods, the Anunnaki. The Sumerian Tablets speak of King Sargon the Elder being found as a baby floating in a basket on the river and brought up by a royal family. Exodus speaks of Moses being found as a baby floating in a basket on the river by a royal princess and how he was brought up by the Egyptian royal family. The list of such 'coincidences' goes on and on.

> The Old Testament is a classic example of the religious recycling which has spawned all the religions. So when you are looking for the original meaning of Genesis and the story of Adam you have to go back to the Sumerian accounts to see how the story has been doctored.

Adam was not created from dust from the ground, but from living cells

Genesis says that 'God' (the gods) created the first man, Adam, out of 'dust from the ground' and then used a rib of Adam to create Eve, the first woman. Zecharia Sitchin points out that the translation of 'dust from the ground' comes from the Hebrew word tit (sorry mother) and this itself is derived from the Sumerian term, TI.IT, which means 'that which is with life'.

Adam was not created from dust from the ground, but from that which is with life - living cells. The Sumerian term, TI, means both rib and life and again the translators made the wrong choice. Eve (She Who Has Life) was not created from a rib, but from that which has life - living cells. The human egg for the creation of the Lulu/Adam came from a female in Abzu, Africa, according to the Sumerians, and modern fossil finds and anthropological research suggests that Homo Sapiens did indeed come out of Africa. In the 1980s, Douglas Wallace of Emory University in Georgia compared the DNA (the blueprint for physical life) of 800 women and concluded that it came from a single female ancestor.

- Wesley Brown of the University of Michigan said, after examining the DNA of 21 women of different genetic backgrounds from around the world, that they all originated from a single source who had lived in Africa between 180,000 and 300,000 years ago.
- Rebecca Cann of the University of California at Berkeley did the same with 147 women of diverse racial and geographical backgrounds and she said their common genetic inheritance came from a single ancestor between 150,000 and 300,000 years ago.
- Another study of 150 American women from genetic lines going back to Europe, Africa and the Middle East, together with Aborigines from Australia and New Guinea, concluded that they had the same female ancestor who lived in Africa between 140,000 and 290,000 years ago.

The human race was seeded by many sources

Personally I think the human race was seeded by many sources; not just the Anunnaki. The Sumerian Tablets and later Akkadian stories give the names and hierarchy of the Anunnaki. They call the 'Father' of the gods, AN, a word that means heaven.

Our Father in heaven?
AN, or Anu to the Akkadians, stayed mostly in heaven with his wife, Antu, and he made only rare visits to the planet they called E.RI.DU (Home in the faraway built), a word which evolved into Earth. Or at least that is the Zecharia Sitchin translation. The descriptions could also imply that Anu stayed mostly in the high mountains of the Near East where the 'Garden of Eden', the place of the gods, is reckoned on good evidence to have been, and he made only rare visits to the plains of Sumer. A Sumerian city was called Eridu. Anu sent two sons to develop and rule the Earth, the Tablets say. They were Enki, the guy they say created Homo Sapiens, and his half-brother Enlil. These two would later become great rivals for ultimate control of the planet. Enki, the first born of Anu, was subordinate to Enlil because of the Anunnaki's obsession with genetic purity. Enlil's mother was the half sister to Anu and this union passed on the male genes more efficiently than Enki's birth via another mother.
Later the Tablets describe how the Anunnaki created bloodlines to rule humanity on their behalf and these, I suggest, are the families still in control of the world to this day. The Sumerian Tablets describe how kingship was granted to humanity by the Anunnaki and it was originally known as Anuship after An or Anu, the ruler of the 'gods'. The Brotherhood families are obsessed with bloodlines and genetic inheritance and they interbreed without regard for love. The royal families (family!) and aristocracy of Europe and the so-called Eastern Establishment families in the United States are obvious examples of this.
They are of the same tribe and genetically related. This is why the Brotherhood families have always been obsessed with interbreeding, just as the Sumerian Tablets describe the Anunnaki. They are not interbreeding through snobbery, but to hold a genetic structure which gives them certain abilities, especially the ability to 'shape-shift' and manifest in other forms. I'll come to this in more detail shortly.
The Tablets describe how humans were given the ability to procreate by Enki and this led to an explosion in the human population which threatened to swamp the Anunnaki, who were never great in number. The Anunnaki had many internal conflicts and high-tech wars with each other, as the Enlil and Enki factions fought for control. It is generally accepted by researchers of the Anunnaki that Enki is on humanity's side, but it seems to me that both groups desire dominance over this planet, and that is their real motivation.
As Zecharia Sitchin documents in his translations, and readers of the Indian holy books, the Vedas, will confirm, there were many accounts of the 'gods' going to war with each other as they battled for supremacy. The Sumerian accounts describe how the sons of the Annunaki 'gods' were most involved in these wars.

These were the offspring of Enki and Enlil, the half-brothers who became fierce rivals, and their sons played out that battle in a high-tech conflict, the Tablets say. One battle they appeared to have been involved in was the biblical destruction of Sodom and Gomorrah.

These cities were probably located at the southern end of the Dead Sea where, today, radiation readings are much higher than normal. This was when, according to the Bible, Lot's wife looked back and was turned into a pillar of salt. After referring to the original Sumerian, Zecharia Sitchin says that the true translation of that passage should read that Lot's wife was turned into a pillar of vapour which, on balance, is rather more likely!

> ## Anunnaki left the planet in flying craft, as an enormous surge of water wiped out much of humanity

All over the world in every native culture you will find stories of a Great Flood and the Sumerian Tablets are no different. Sitchin says they tell how the Anunnaki left the planet in flying craft, as an enormous surge of water wiped out much of humanity.

There is no doubt that an unimaginable catastrophe, or more likely catastrophes, were visited upon the Earth between approximately 11,000 and 4,000 BC. The geological and biological evidence is overwhelming in its support of the countless stories and traditions which describe such events. They come from Europe, Scandinavia, Russia, Africa, throughout the American continent, Australia, New Zealand, Asia, China, Japan and the Middle East.

Everywhere. some speak of great heat which boiled the sea; of mountains breathing fire; the disappearance of the Sun and Moon and the darkness that followed; the raining down of blood, ice and rock; the Earth flipping over; the sky falling; the rising and sinking of land; the loss of a great continent; the coming of the ice; and virtually all of them describe a fantastic flood, a wall of water, which swept across the Earth. The tidal wave caused by the comet in the film, Deep Impact, gives you an idea of what it would have been like.

- **Old Chinese texts** describe how the pillars supporting the sky crumbled; of how the Sun, Moon and stars poured down in the north-west, where the sky became low; rivers, seas and oceans rushed to the south-east where the Earth sank and a great conflagration was quenched by a raging flood.
- **In America, the Pawnee Indians** tell the same story of a time when the north and south polar stars changed places and went to visit each other. North American traditions refer to great clouds appearing and a heat so powerful that the waters boiled.
- **The Greenland Eskimos** told early missionaries that long ago the Earth turned over.
- **Peruvian legend** says that the Andes were split apart when the sky made war with the Earth.

- **Brazilian myth** describes how the heavens burst and fragments fell down killing everything and everyone as heaven and Earth changed places.
- **The Hopi Indians** of North America record that the Earth was rent in great chasms, and water covered everything except one narrow ridge of mud.

*** *** ***

Plato, Atlantis, Mu (Lemuria) and the Azores

All of this closely correlates with the legends of Atlantis and Mu or Lemuria: Two vast continents, one in the Atlantic and the other in the Pacific, which many people believe were ruled by highly advanced races. The continents are said to have disappeared under the sea in the circumstances described above, leaving only islands like the Azores as remnants of their former scale and glory. Atlantis was described by Plato (427-347 BC), the ancient Greek philosopher and high initiate of the secret society-mystery school network.

To this day this secret network has passed on much knowledge to the chosen few while denying that privilege to the mass of the people. Official history dismisses Plato's contention that such a continent existed and there are apparent historical discrepancies in his accounts, but there is geological support for his basic theme. The Azores, which some believe were part of Atlantis, lie on the Mid-Atlantic Ridge which is connected to a fracture line that encircles the planet.

This line continues for a distance of 40,000 miles. The Mid-Atlantic Ridge is one of the foremost areas for earthquakes and volcanoes. Four vast tectonic plates, the Eurasian, African, North American and Caribbean, all meet and collide in this region making it very unstable geologically.

Both the Azores and the Canary Islands (named after dogs 'canine' and not canaries!), were subject to widespread volcanic activity in the time period Plato suggested for the end of Atlantis. Tachylite lava disintegrates in sea water within 15,000 years and yet it is still found on the sea bed around the Azores, confirming geologically-recent upheavals.

Other evidence, including beach sand gathered from depths of 10,500-18,440 feet, reveals that the seabed in this region must have been, again geologically-recently, above sea level. The oceanographer, Maurice Ewing, wrote in National Geographic magazine that: Either the land must have sunk two or three miles, or the sea must once have been two or three miles lower than now. Either conclusion is startling.

The Mid-Atlantic Ridge, the centre of earthquake and volcanic activity in the area of the Atlantic Ocean where Plato apparently placed Atlantis.

The geological and biological evidence also suggests that the widespread volcanic activity which caused the sinking of the land in the region of the Azores, happened at the same time as the break up and sinking of the land mass known as Appalachia which connected what we now call Europe, North America, Iceland and Greenland.

Even their degree of submergence appear closely related. Similar evidence can be produced to support the view that the continent known as Mu or Lemuria now rests on the bed of the Pacific. The so-called Bermuda Triangle between Bermuda, southern Florida, and a point near the Antilles, has long been associated with Atlantis. It is also an area steeped in legends of disappearing ships and aircraft. Submerged buildings, walls, roads and stone circles like Stonehenge, even what appear to be pyramids, have been located near Bimini, under the waters of the Bahamas Banks and within the 'triangle'. So have walls or roads creating intersecting lines.

Some other facts that most people don't know: the Himalayas, the Alps and the Andes, only reached anything like their present height around 11,000 years ago.17 Lake Titicaca on the Peru-Bolivia border is today the highest navigable lake in the world at some 12,500 feet. Around 11,000 years ago, much of that region was at sea level!

Why are so many fish and other ocean fossils found high up in mountain ranges? Because those mountains were once at sea level.

Recently so in geological terms, too. There is increasing acceptance that the Earth has suffered some colossal geological upheavals. The debate (and often hostility) comes with the questions of when and why. These upheavals have obviously involved the solar system as a whole because every planet shows evidence of some cataclysmic events which have affected either its surface, atmosphere, speed and angle of orbit or rotation.

I think the themes of the Sumerian Tablets are correct, but I doubt some of their detail, not least because of the vast period that passed between 450,000 years ago when the Anunnaki are said to have arrived, and the time, only a few thousand years ago, when these accounts were written down.

There was certainly an enormous cataclysm on the Earth around 11,000 BC which destroyed the advanced civilizations of the high-tech Golden Age and that date of 13,000 years ago is highly significant and very relevant to the time we are living through now. Just as the planets of the solar system revolve around the Sun, so the solar system revolves around the centre of the galaxy, or this part of it at least.

This 'central sun' or galactic sun, is sometimes referred to as the Black Sun. It takes about 26,000 years for the solar system to complete a circuit of the galactic centre and this is known in the Indian culture as a yuga. For half of that 26,000 years the Earth is tilted towards the Black Sun, the light source, and for the second 13,000 years it is tilted away, some researchers believe. These cycles are therefore very different as the planet is bathed in positive light for 13,000 years and then moves into the 'darkness' for the next 13,000.

This fundamentally affects the energy in which we all live. Interestingly, it was 13,000 years ago that the Golden Age would appear to have concluded in cataclysm and conflict, and today, with the 13,000 year cycle of 'darkness' reaching its conclusion, there is a rapid global spiritual awakening and incredible events await us in the next few years. We are entering the light again. So there was a fantastic cataclysm around 13,000 years ago which brought an end to the high-tech civilizations of the Golden Age. But was it the only one? The evidence suggests not.

A friend of mine in California, Brian Desborough, is a researcher and scientist I have great respect for. He has been involved in aerospace research and has been employed in this and other scientific research by many companies. Brian is a feet-on-the-ground guy who looks at all the evidence and goes where it, rather than convention, takes him. He has compiled some highly detailed and compelling information about the ancient world and its connection to the Brotherhood manipulation of today.

While he worked for a major United States corporation in the 1960s, their physicists completed their own independent studies which suggested that about 4,800 BC a huge body, which we now know as Jupiter, careered into our solar system.

The outer planets were thrown into disarray and Jupiter eventually crashed into a planet which orbited between the present Jupiter and Mars. The physicists said the remains of this planet became the asteroid belt and that part of Jupiter broke away to become what we now call Venus. As Venus, then a vast chunk of matter, was projected into space, it destroyed the atmosphere and life of Mars before it was caught by the Earth's gravitational field, the study claimed. Venus made several orbits of the Earth before its momentum hurled it into its current position in the solar system. It was those orbits, the physicists said, that brought devastation and a tidal wave about 4,800 BC.

They believed, as Brian Desborough does, that before this time Mars orbited where the Earth is now and the Earth was much closer to the Sun. The brilliant light of Venus as it passed close to the Earth may have led to the idea of Lucifer, the 'light bringer'. The most ancient Mesopotamian and Central American records do not include Venus in their planetary accounts, only later does it appear. There was an obsession with Venus in many cultures, with human sacrifices being made to it.

The unofficial study by the physicists has never been published, but let us consider the evidence for some of its claims. When you sprinkle particles on a vibrating plate you can recreate the planetary orbits of the solar system. When vibratory waves moving outward from the plate's centre meet waves moving in the other direction, a so-called standing wave is formed as the two collide. This causes the particles to build up and create a series of concentric circles.

These will be equally spaced if single frequencies collide with each other, but if, as with the solar system, a spectrum of frequencies are involved, the circles will be unequally spaced in accordance with the vibrational pressures. Place an object on these vibrating circles of particles and it will begin to orbit the centre of the plate, carried by the energy flow caused by the vibrational interactions. Heavier objects placed anywhere on the plate will be drawn to one of these concentric circles and these objects will themselves form wave patterns around themselves which will attract lighter objects to them. In our solar system, the most powerful waves are being emitted from the centre by the Sun, obviously, because that represents 99% of the matter in the solar system.

These waves from the Sun interact with other cosmic waves, so forming a series of standing waves which, in turn, form concentric circles or vibrational fields orbiting the Sun. The heaviest bodies, the planets, are caught in these circles and thus orbit the Sun.

The planets also create less powerful wave circles around themselves and these can attract lighter bodies which orbit them. The Moon orbiting the Earth is an example of this. So anything that would disturb this harmony of vibrational interaction would affect these concentric circles of energy and, if this was powerful enough, change the orbit of planets. What the physicists say happened with Jupiter and Venus would certainly be powerful enough to do this.

These circles of standing waves exist around the Sun in relation to the vibrational pressures involved and they do not need a planet to exist. They exist anyway and a planetary body merely locks into them. Therefore there are many more of these vibrational 'roadways' in the solar system than there are planets, and if a planet or body is ejected from its orbit it will eventually lock into another wave, another orbit, when its momentum slows enough to be captured. This, Desborough believes, is what happened when the fantastic vibrational pressures of the Venus 'comet' passed close to Mars and the Earth and hurled them into different orbits.

Venus would have been an ice-coated 'comet', Desborough says, and the ice would have disintegrated when Venus approached the Earth and reached a point known as the Roche Limit.

This is a vibrational safety device, if you like. When two bodies are on collision course, the one with the smallest mass starts to disintegrate at the Roche Limit. In this case, the ice would have been projected from Venus's surface towards the Earth.

Also, as it entered the so-called Van Allen Belt, which absorbs much of the dangerous radiation from the Sun, the ice would have been ionized - magnetized - and therefore attracted to the Earth's magnetic poles.

Billions of tons of ice, cooled to -273 degrees centigrade, would have fallen on the polar regions, flash-freezing everything in little more than an instant.[20]

This, at last, would explain the mystery of the mammoths found frozen where they stood. The mammoth, contrary to belief, was not a cold region animal, but one which lived in temperate grasslands.

Somehow those temperate regions were frozen in a moment. Some mammoths have been found frozen in the middle of eating! There you are munching away and the next thing you know you're an ice lolly. If this ionized ice did rain down from Venus, the biggest build up would have been nearest to the magnetic poles because they would have had the most powerful attraction. Again, that is the case. The ice mass in the polar regions is greater at the poles than at the periphery and yet there is less snow and rain at the poles to create such a build up.

The Book of Job, which is believed to be an Arab work reveals great knowledge

The Venus scenario explains this. In the Book of Job, which is believed to be an Arab work much older than the rest of the Bible, the question is asked: Whence cometh the ice? I would say we could have the answer. This further explains how the ancients could have had maps of what the north and south poles looked like before the ice was there.

The poles were ice-free until about 7,000 years ago. There was no ice age as officially suggested. It's another illusion. When you look at the 'evidence' that official science presents to support the conventional idea of an ice age and the way this 'evidence' is fundamentally contradicted by the provable facts, it is astonishing how such nonsense could become conventional 'truth' in the first place.

Before this incredible cataclysm, and/or one of the others, the Earth had a uniform tropical climate, as fossilized plants have shown. This would have been changed not only by the arrival of the ice on the surface, but also by the destruction of a canopy of water vapour around the Earth, as described in Genesis and other ancient texts. This canopy would have ensured a uniform tropical climate everywhere, but suddenly it was gone.

The dramatic change in temperature at the poles would have collided with the warm air and caused devastating winds, exactly as described by Chinese folklore. The physicists said that the pressures created by the orbits of 'Venus' around the Earth would have produced a 10,000 foot tidal wave in the oceans and this again fits with the evidence that agriculture began at altitudes of 10,000 feet and higher.

Plato wrote in his work "Laws", that agriculture began at high elevations after a gigantic flood covered all the lowlands. The botanist, Nikolai Ivanovitch Vavilov, studied more than 50,000 wild plants collected around the world and found that they originated in only eight different areas - all of them mountain terrain. The tidal wave would have produced pressures on the Earth's surface of two tons per square inch, creating new mountain ranges, and fossilizing everything within hours.

Artificial stone today is created by pressures of this magnitude. Intact trees have been found fossilized and that would be impossible unless it happened in an instant because the tree would normally have disintegrated before it could be fossilized over a long period of time. In fact, fossils of this kind are not forming today. They are the result of the cataclysmic events here described, Desborough says.

Psychiatrist and writer, Immanuel Velikovsky's theory was proven correct!

The Russian-Jewish psychiatrist and writer, Immanuel Velikovsky, caused outrage among the scientific establishment in the 1950s by suggesting that the Earth had been through enormous upheavals when Venus which was then, he said, a comet, careered through this part of the solar system before settling into its present orbit. When Venus was photographed by the Mariner 10 mission, many of Velikovsky's descriptions proved correct, including what appeared to be the remnants of a comet-like tail. The Mariner 9 pictures of Mars also supported some of Velikovsky's theories. He said that the 'comet' Venus had collided with Mars as it careered through the solar system. Velikovsky's time for these events was about 1,500 BC. Different researchers dismiss each other's findings because they suggest very different periods for major upheavals when in truth there were almost certainly a number of cataclysms in that window of 11,000 to 1,500 BC, and even more recently.

The study by the physicists also said that Mars was devastated by these events involving Venus. They felt Mars was thrown out of orbit and followed a highly unstable elliptical orbit which took it between the Earth and the Moon every 56 years. The last of these passes appears to have been about 1,500 BC when the great volcano exploded on the Greek island of Santorini and the Minoan civilization on Crete passed into history. In this same period of 1,600-1,500 BC, ocean levels dropped about 20 per cent, glacial lakes formed in California, and this was most likely the time when the vast lake in the fertile Sahara was emptied and the desert we see today began to be formed. Eventually, Mars settled into its present orbit, but by then life on its surface had been obliterated. Yet again the evidence on Mars supports all this. The Mars Pathfinder mission found that Martian rocks lack sufficient erosion to have been on the surface for more than 10,000 years. Brian Desborough believes, like the physicists he knew and worked with, that the Earth was once much nearer the Sun than it is today and that Mars orbited where the Earth now resides. If, as is claimed, the deep canyons on Mars surface were caused by massive torrents of water, there had to have been a warmer climate on Mars, because today it is so cold that water would freeze instantly and the near-vacuum atmosphere would make the water instantly vaporise. Desborough says that the Earth's closer proximity to the Sun demanded that the first Earth humans were the black races with the pigmentation to cope with the much fiercer rays of the Sun.

Brian Desborough: The "White Martians" built the pyramids which have been recorded on Mars

Ancient skeletons found near Stonehenge in England and along the west coast of France display the nasal and spinal characteristics of many female Africans. Desborough says that Mars, then with a climate very much like ours, had a white race before the Venus cataclysm. His research has convinced him that the white Martians built the pyramids which have been recorded on Mars and they went to war with an advanced black race to conquer the Earth. These wars, he says, are the wars of the 'gods' described in endless ancient texts, not least the Hindu Vedas.

The "White Martians" became the white peoples of the Earth

Desborough adds that after the cataclysm, the white Martians who had settled on Earth were stranded here without their technology and with their home planet devastated. These white Martians, he says, became the white peoples of the Earth. Fascinatingly, some scientists claim that when white people are immersed in sensory deprivation tanks for long periods, their circadian rhythm has a frequency of 24 hours 40 minutes, which corresponds not to the rotational period of the Earth, but of Mars! This is not the case with non-white races who are in tune with the Earth's rotation.

The "White Martians" were the highly advanced race of the ancient world known as the Phoenicians or Aryans

Desborough believes that these white Martians were the highly advanced race of the ancient world known as the Phoenicians or Aryans and they began the long process of returning to their former technological power after the upheavals which destroyed the surface of their own planet and devastated this one.

My own research supports this basic theme, although, like everyone seeking the truth of what happened, I have many questions.

The Phoenicians were the 'brains' behind the Egyptian civilization

A white race, known as the Phoenicians and other names, was certainly the 'brains' behind the Egyptian civilization, at least from the period around 3,000 BC, and the Giza Plateau, where the Great Pyramid was built, was formerly known as El-Kahira, a name which derived from the Arabic noun, El-Kahir, their name for Mars. Ancient texts reveal that the measurement of time was much related to Mars, and March 15th, the Ides of March (Mars), was a key date in their Mars-related calendar, as was October 26th. The first marked the start of Spring and the second was the end of the year in the Celtic calendar. The Holy Grail stories of King Arthur connect with this theme, also. Camelot apparently means Martian City or City of Mars.

The cataclysmic upheavals the Earth: Survival of extraterrestrials on Earth, the White Race and the Slave Race

I think there is truth in all the views summarized in this chapter of the cataclysmic upheavals the Earth has suffered in the period between 11,000 and 1,500 BC. The first one ended the Golden Age and obliterated the high-tech civilizations that had existed before then. The extraterrestrial races either left the planet beforehand or survived at high altitudes or by going deep within the Earth. The same with the later cataclysm. Many of the extraterrestrials, and most Earth humans, did not survive these events. Those that did were left with the job of starting all over again without, at least at first, the technology available before. The survivors fell into two main categories, those of mostly extraterrestrial origin who retained the advanced knowledge, and humans, the slave race in general, who did not. The former also fell into two camps. There were those who wished to use their knowledge positively and communicate their information to humanity, and those who sought to hoard the knowledge and use it to manipulate and control. The struggle between those two groups over the use of the same knowledge continues to this very day. As societies recovered from those upheavals of 11,000 BC, the other cataclysms brought more devastation over the thousands of years that followed and humanity was faced with many new beginnings. One common theme throughout, however, has been the manipulation of humanity by an intellectually, though not spiritually, advanced race or races of extraterrestrial origin. On that subject, I must now introduce an added dimension to this story which will stretch your credulity to breaking point.

SOURCES:
1 - T. W. Doane, Bible Myths, And Their Parallels In Other Religions (Health Research, P0 Box 850, Pomeroy, WA, USA 99347, first published 1882), p 10.
2 - The information about the Anunnaki and the Sumerian Tablets comes from the Zecharia Sitchin series of books collectively known as The Earth Chronicles. Individually they are called The 12th Planet, The Stairway To Heaven, The Wars Of Gods And Men, The Lost Realms, and When Time Began. Another Sitchin work is Genesis Revisited. They are published by Avon Books, 1350 Avenue of the Americas, NY
3 - Genesis Revisited, p 22.
4 - Ibid, p 161.
5 - Ibid, p 198.
6 - Ibid, p 199.
7 - Ibid.
8 - Ibid, p 200.
9 - For a comprehensive documentation of these global legends and the scientific support for them, see the excellent book by D. S. Allen and J. B. Delair called When The Earth Nearly Died (Gateway Books, Wellow, Bath, England, 1995).
10 - Ibid, p 31.
11 - Ibid, p32.
12 - Maurice Ewing,   New Discoveries On The Mid-Atlantic Ridge, National Geographic magazine, November 1949, pp 614, 616.
13 - When The Earth Nearly Died, pp 32, 33.
14 - Ibid, p 34.
15 - Charles Berlitz, Atlantis, The Eighth Continent, (Fawcett Books, New York, 1984), pp 96-101.
16 - Ibid.
17 - When The Earth Nearly Died, pp 25-28.
18 - Brian Desborough, The Great Pyramid Mystery, Tomb, Occult Initiation Center, Or What? A document supplied to the author and also published in the The California Sun newspaper, Los Angeles.
19 - Ibid.
20 - Ibid.
21 - Ibid.
22 - When The Earth Nearly Died has some impressive documentation to show that the Ice Age is a myth.
23 - The Great Pyramid Mystery.
24 - Ibid.
25 - Ibid.
26 - Ibid.
27 - Ibid.
28 - Ibid.
29 - Ibid.
30 - Ibid.
31 - Ibid.
32 - Ibid.
33 - Ibid.
34 - Preston B. Nichols and Peter Moon, Pyramids Of Montauk, (Sky Books, New York, 1995), p 125.
35 - Ibid, p 129.
Note: On the next page is the Mirror Article I referred to at the beginning of the chapter. Please compare both versions.

The Old Testament is a classic example of the religious recycling

Our Sun is only one of some 100 billion stars in this galaxy alone. Sir Francis Crick, the Nobel laureate, says there are an estimated 100 billion galaxies in our universe and he believes there are at least one million planets in our galaxy that could support life as we know it. Think of what the figure might be for the entire universe, even before we start looking at other dimensionsof existence beyond the frequency range of our physical senses. Genesis and Exodus were written by the Hebrew priestly class, the Levites, after they were taken to Babylon from around 586 BC. Babylon was in the former lands of Sumer and so the Babylonians, and therefore the Levites, knew the Sumerian stories and accounts. It was from these records overwhelmingly, that the Levites compiled Genesis and Exodus. The source is obvious. The Sumerian tablets speak of E.DIN (The Abode of the Righteous Ones). This connects with the Sumerian name for their gods, DIN.GIR (the Righteous Ones of the Rockets). So the Sumerians spoke of Edin and Genesis speaks of the Garden of Eden.

The Old Testament is a classic example of the religious recycling which has spawned all the religions. So when you are looking for the original meaning of Genesis and the story of Adam you have to go back to the Sumerian accounts to see how the story has been doctored.

The human egg for the creation of the Lulu/Adam came from a female in Abzu, Africa

The human egg for the creation of the Lulu/Adam came from a female in Abzu, Africa, according to the Sumerians, and modern fossil finds and anthropological research suggests that Homo Sapiens did indeed come out of Africa. In the 1980s, Douglas Wallace of Emory University in Georgia compared the DNA (the blueprint for physical life) of 800 women and concluded that it came from a single female ancestor. Wesley Brown of the University of Michigan said, after examining the DNA of 21 women of different genetic backgrounds from around the world, that they all originated from a single source who had lived in Africa between 180,000 and 300,000 years ago. Rebecca Cann of the University of California at Berkeley did the same with 147 women of diverse racial and geographical backgrounds and she said their common genetic inheritance came from a single ancestor between 150,000 and 300,000 years ago.

The Sumerian Tablets and later Akkadian stories give the names and hierarchy of the Anunnaki. They call the 'Father' of the gods, AN, a word that means heaven. AN, or Anu to the Akkadians, stayed mostly in heaven with his wife, Antu, and he made only rare visits to the planet they called E.RI.DU (Home in the faraway built), a word which evolved into Earth. Or at least that is the Zecharia Sitchin translation.

The descriptions could also imply that Anu stayed mostly in the high mountains of the Near East where the 'Garden of Eden', the place of the gods, is reckoned on good evidence to have been, and he made only rare visits to the plains of Sumer. A Sumerian city was called Eridu. Anu sent two sons to develop and rule the Earth, the Tablets say. They were Enki, the guy they say created Homo Sapiens, and his half-brother Enlil. These two would later become great rivals for ultimate control of the planet.

The hybrid bloodlines became the British and European aristocracy and royal families

These hybrid bloodlines became the British and European aristocracy and royal families and, thanks to the 'Great' British Empire, they were exported across the world to rule the Americas, Africa, Asia, Australia, New Zealand and so on. These genetic lines are manipulated into the positions of political, military, media, banking and business power and thus these positions are held by lower fourth dimensional reptilians hiding behind a human form or by mindpuppets of the these same creatures. They operate through all races, but predominantly the white one. As is well acknowledged, there is an area of the human brain to this day known as the reptile brain. Within the brain is the original segment to which all other parts are additions.

And, according to the neuroanatomist, Paul MacLean, this ancient area of the brain is driven by another prehistoric segment which some neuroanatomists call the Rcomplex. 22 R is short for reptilian because we share this with reptiles.

The reptilian breeding program appears to have produced an Anunnaki-human hybrid (Adam?)

The reptilian breeding programme appears to have produced an Anunnaki-human hybrid (Adam?) around 200,000-300,000 years ago. There were already reptile-Aryan bloodlines among the Martians when they came to Earth. One of the main locations for the Anunnaki and the Martians or Aryans, particularly during and after the Venus cataclysm of around 4,800 BC, were the mountains of Turkey, Iran and Kurdistan, and it was from here that they and their hybrids re-emerged when the waters receded.

It was they who created the 'instant' advanced civilisations in the low lands of Sumer, Egypt, Babylon and the Indus Valley. A particular centre for the Anunnaki reptilians would seem to have been the Caucasus Mountains and this is an area that will appear again and again in this story. I feel there was a major breeding programme in this region, probably underground, which produced a very large number of hybrid reptile-human crossbreeds. One area of research that is highly relevant to this region are the number of people with Rh negative or rhesus negative blood. Often rhesus negative babies turn blue immediately after birth. This is the origin of the term 'blue bloods' for royal bloodlines and other terms like 'true blue'. It is speculated that the 'blue' bloodlines could be of Martian decent and from wherever the Martian bloodlines came from before that. Far more white people are Rh negative than blacks or Asians.

The Anunnaki-human crossbreed elite was described by the Sumerians and there are many other accounts of the interbreeding of extraterrestrials and humans, or the 'gods' and 'sky people' interbreeding with humanity. This is most famously noted in Genesis where it says "When men began to increase in number on the earth and daughters were born to them, the sons of God saw that the daughters of men were beautiful, and they married any of them they chose...The Nefilim were on the earth in those days -and also afterwards - when the sons of God went to the daughters of men and had children by them They were the heroes of old, men of renown." Genesis 6:1-4. The early offspring of these genetic encounters were the giants of legend and there are many records of such hybrids being born. The Hopi, you will recall, speak of originating within the Earth. The Ethiopian text, the Kebra Nagast (Nagas were Indian shape-shifting 'serpent gods'), is thousands of years old, and it refers to the enormous size of the babies produced from the sexual or genetic unions of humans and the 'gods'. It tells how: "...the daughters of Cain with whom the angels (extraterres-trials) had conceived...were unable to bring forth their children, and they died." It describes how some of these giant babies were delivered by caesarean section:...having split open the bellies of their mothers they came forth by their navels." Over the thousands of years since these royal reptile-human hybrid bloodlines were created, they have become more integrated into the general populafion and less physically obvious, but the basic genetic structure remains and the Brotherhood maintains very detailed genetic records of who has it and who doesn't.

Our Genetic Structure: 75% Anunnaki and 25% human

Christian and Barbara O'Brien say in "Genius Of The Few", that if the Annunaki had interbred with humanity hundreds of thousands of years ago and then interbred with them again about 30,000 years ago, the result of the second interbreeding would be a genetic structure that was 75% Anunnaki and 25% human. I think there was another breeding programme far more recently, after the Venus flood of about 7,000 years ago. These later bloodlines would have been even more Anunnaki than previous versions, of course. These are the reptilian crossbreeds who run the world today and it this profusion of reptilian genes which allows such people to shape-shift into reptilians and back into an apparently human form.

The most important gene is passed on by the female line

These bloodlines also have the ability to produce an extremely powerful hypnotic stare, just like a snake hypnotising its prey, and this is the origin of the term 'giving someone the evil eye'. All this is the real reason for the obsession with blood and the interbreeding of the 'blue blood' families and their offshoots.

217

The "Serpent King' bloodline: Iran, Kurdistan, Armenia, Turkey and the Caucasus Mountains

This is why since the earliest times of known history, the blue blood heirs married their half-sisters and cousins, just as the Anunnaki did according to the Sumerian Tablets. The most important gene in this succession is passed on by the female line, so the choice of female sexual partner has been vital to them. It is highly significant that the 'serpent king' bloodline should originate from Iran because it is from this region of Iran, Kurdistan, Armenia, Turkey and the Caucasus Mountains, that these reptile-human bloodlines emerged to take over the world. A Brotherhood insider, a Russian, said there was a massive vortex, an interdimensional gateway, in the Caucasus Mountains where the extraterrestrials entered this dimension. That would explain a great deal. The name Iran comes from the earlier Airy-ana or Airan, which means Land of the Aryas or Aryans. Still today there are two distinct races in Kurdistan, the olive skinned of medium height with dark eyes, and the much taller, white skinned people, often with blue eyes. You will note that these traits were considered the 'Master Race' by the Nazis and this was because the Nazis knew the history and the connection with the reptilians. Andrew Collins in his book, "From The Ashes Of Angels", presents compelling evidence that the biblical Garden of Eden was high up in this region of Iran-Kurdistan and, of course, the theme of the serpent is at the heart of the Eden story. In neighbour-mg Media, the kings were known by the Iranians as Mâr which means snake in Persian.

Aryan: Reptile-Aryan or Reptile-Human (The White Race)
A genetic manipulation of the Anunnaki

As the flood waters receded after the Venus cataclysm the survivors came down from the mountains and up from within the Earth. They settled on the lowlands and plains and began to rebuild. This was when Sumer, Egypt and the civilisation in the Indus Valley suddenly appeared at a very high level of tech ological advancement, although they had existed before and were now restored after the upheavals. The Sumerian society began at the peak of its development because of this sudden infusion of knowledge and the white Aryan race, originally from Mars, expanded out from the Caucasus Mountains and the Near East down into Sumer, Egypt and the Indus Valley where, as even conventional history agrees, highly advanced societies spontaneously emerged. However within this white race, and others also, was a genetic stream I will call reptile-Aryan or reptile-human. Whenever I use the term Aryan I am referring to the white race. These were the crossbreed bloodlines created from the genetic manipulation of the Anunnaki.

218

The major centre for the reptile-Aryan bloodlines, in the ancient world after the flood waters receded, was Babylon in the south of the Sumer region alongside the River Euphrates. A closer look at the evidence appears to date the foundation of Babylon far earlier than previously believed and it was one of the first cities of the post-flood era. It was here that the mystery schools and secret societies were formed which were to span the globe in the thousands of years that followed. The Brotherhood which controls the world today is the modern expression of the Babylonian Brotherhood of reptile-Aryan priests and 'royalty' which came together there after the flood. It was in Babylon in this post-flood period from around 6,000 years ago that the foundation beliefs - manipulated beliefs - of today's world religions were established to control and rule the people. The founder of Babylon according to ancient texts legend was Nimrod who reigned with his wife, Queen Semiramis. Nimrod was described as a 'mighty tyrant' and one of the 'giants'.

*** *** ***

The Arabs believed that it was Nimrod who built or rebuilt the amazing structure at Baalbek in the Lebanon

The Arabs believed that after the flood it was Nimrod who built or rebuilt the amazing structure at Baalbek in the Lebanon with its three stones weighing 800 tons each. It was said that he ruled the region that is now Lebanon and, according to Genesis, the first centres of Nimrod's kingdom were Babylon, Akkad and others in the land of Shinar (Sumer). Later he expanded further into Assyria to build cities like Nineveh where many of the Sumerian Tablets were found. But this mountainous region around the Caucasus and down to the plains of Sumer and Egypt is a key to the true history of humankind over the last seven thousand years.

A white 'Aryan' race introduced the ancient Sanskrit language to India

The Caucasus Mountains came up again and again in my research and how appropriate that in North America white people are known as 'Caucasian'. Even according to official history it was a white 'Aryan' race from the Caucasus Mountains region which moved into the Indus Valley of India about 1550 BC and created what is today known as the Hindu religion. It was this same Aryan race (they called themselves 'Arya') which introduced the ancient Sanskrit language to India and the stories and myths contained in the Hindu holy books, the Vedas. L. A. Waddell, in his outstanding research into this Aryan race, established that the father of the first historical Aryan king of India (recorded in the Maha-Barata epic and Indian Buddhist history) was the last historical king of the Hittites in Asia Minor. The Indian Aryans worshipped the Sun as the Father-god Indra, and the Hittite-Phoenicians called their Father-god Bel by the name, Indara.

Under many names this same Aryan people also settled in Sumer, Babylon, Egypt and Asia Minor, now Turkey, and other Near Eastern countries, taking with them the same stories, myths, and religion. This Aryan expansion began as far back as 3,000 BC, probably earlier, with their seafaring branch, the Phoenicians.

The Phoenicians brought civilization to Europe not the Greeks

They were a technologically advanced people who have been marginalised by official history and this has obscured their true identity.

They are fundamental to understanding where we have come from and where we are now. It was they who brought both their genetic lines and their knowledge to Europe, Scandinavia and the Americas, thousands of years BC. Their story is told by L. A. Waddell in his book, "The Phoenician Origin Of Britons, Scots And Anglo-Saxons." Waddell was a fellow of the Royal Anthropological Institute and spent a lifetime researching the evidence. He shows that the Phoenicians were not a Semitic race as previously believed, but a white Aryan race. Examination of Phoenician tombs reveals that they were a long-headed Aryan race and of a totally different racial type to the Semites. The Phoenicians of the ancient world travelled by sea from their bases in Asia Minor, Syria and Egypt to settle in the islands of the Mediterranean like Crete and Cyprus and also Greece and Italy.

The Phoenicians created the civilization and culture of Minoan Crete, classic Greece and Roman Italy
The Sicilians are their direct descendants

It was the Phoenicians who carried the knowledge which later emerged as the civilization of Minoan Crete, classic Greece and Roman Italy. The Phoenicians were not confined to the Mediterranean and the Middle East. They landed in Britain around 3,000 BC and unmistakable Phoenician civilizat have been found in Brazil, as well as possible Egyptian remains in the Grand Canyon in America. The Phoenicians landed in the Americas thousands of years before the manufactured 'photo opportunity' better known as the journey of Christopher Columbus. The reason that the native legends of the Americas speak of tall 'white gods' coming from the sea bringing advanced knowledge is because that is precisely what happened, if you forget the gods bit. They were the Aryan race and the reptile-Aryans from the east landing in the Americas thousands of years ago, the same Aryan race or 'gods' who the Sumerians said gifted them their civilization after the flood.

*** *** ***

CHAPTER 7

THE ORIGINS AND BEGINNING OF THE HUMAN RACES FROM THE ANUNNAKI TO THE PRESENT

- Betty Rhodes: There had to be at least four distinct origins to the major races of people on the planet
- The beginning and origins of the human races
- Caucasoid, or the white races
- African or Negroid, the black races,
- Asiatic or Mongoloid, the so-called yellow
- Brown or red races
- The original creation
- The original evolved creatures of the Earth, first known as Homo-Erectus
- The original created hybrid ADAMS – the father of all brown-skinned [RED-skinned]
- The original created Eves – the first hybrid woman, was the mother of all black-skinned peoples of Africa.
- The Nefilim created Mongoloid and Asiatic peoples.
- The Elohiym royal godhead: Their descendants became the twelve/thirteen tribes of Israel
- The white races of people are descendants of the Anunnaki
- Mixed races – are a result of intermarrying amongst all races of people: The people of India, the Aborigines of Australia, the Blackfoot of North America, and the Polynesians
- Esau's descendants
- Cain's descendants – Assyrians>>>Babylonians>>>Romans
- Ishmael's descendants – the Arabs
- Jacob's descendants; Elohiym descendants.

- Mitochondria DNA: African races have more genetic diversity than any other human groups
- Neanderthals did not contribute DNA to modern Europeans
- The Elohiym family of "gods", originally created the "black-haired" people

*** *** ***

The Origin Of the Human Races
From The Anunnaki To The Present

Betty Rhodes: There had to be at least four distinct origins to the major races of people on the planet

Betty Rhodes on the various races of humanity, ranging from the velvety black-skinned people, to the lily white skinned peoples; and with hair coloring and consistency ranging from course, thick, curly, and black, to the finest light blonde shades of thin, straight hair - and all the shades and variations in between.

Consider the wide range of facial features, such as the shape and sizes of lips, eyes, noses, and heads - not to mention the difference in body build. It does not take the wisdom of Solomon to see that there had to be at least four distinct origins to the major races of people on the planet. It is to the origin of each of these races where the dilemma and controversy exists. Some folks just do not care, and some folks assume that `God' merely made many races of people for variety, and let it go at that. However, there are those who are serious truth-seekers and want the answers to everything, and then there are scholars who know why there are various races of humankind, and so far none has dared come forward with the scientific facts, fearing justifiably, the loss of public funding.

During the early years, when `political correctness' was first being orchestrated [1950 – 1970], the United Nation's Educational, Scientific, and Cultural Organization, called UNESCO, made a series of official statements regarding the race controversy. In these statements, UNESCO put forth a goal of eliminating racism around the world by declaring race classification, unfounded and damaging to society. In other words, being `politically correct, at all costs', originated with the organization known as, UNESCO, and they so much as, declared that scientific facts, were `to be kept hidden', from the general public. Finally, [from "Keeper of the Celtic Secrets"], knowledge about the origins of the major races, who call the Earth home, is being shared with others. You must keep an open mind - stay out of your cave now, or you won't be able to grasp the wisdom being presented here. Yes, Virginia, there really were E.T.'s, who do you think provided the wisdom to build the pyramids, give us mathematical equations, science and astronomy? Are you ready for some real wisdom? OK - Good.

THE BEGINNING AND ORIGINS OF THE HUMAN RACES

The origins of the human races are as follows:

As per old family journals containing knowledge from ancient Ireland, the origins of races are as follows:

1) Caucasoid, or the WHITE RACES, descend from:

- The Anunnaki,
- Elohiym godhead. The ancient Israelites, are actually descendants of the Elohiym royal family.

2) African or Negroid, the BLACK races, descend from:

- The evolved Homosapiens,
- The hybrid created Adams; they are the EVES.

3) Asiatic or Mongoloid, the so-called YELLOW skinned people, descend from:

- The Nefilim, the ousted royal party from Hibiru - notice I say Hibiru NOT Nibiru - Hibiru/Hebrew - are you still with me here? The Nefilim 'giants' were the reigning godhead until the Elohiym family ousted them, casting them to the Earth;.

4) BROWN or RED races: Indigenous or Native peoples of the land, descend from:

- The evolved Homo Sapiens,
- The Anunnaki - some not authorized by the Elohiym, but boys will be boys, and they made a good working stock of slaves. These people were the ADAMS.

*** *** ***

THE ORIGINAL CREATION

A)-**The original evolved creatures of the Earth, first known as Homo-Erectus,** who evolved to Homo sapiens, i.e., the Neanderthal – eventually this species became extinct due to the Ice Age, the Great Flood, famines, diseases, natural disasters, etc. This race was black skinned with coarse black hair, large features, and type O Rh-positive blood.

B)-**The original created hybrid ADAMS – the father of all brown-skinned [RED-skinned],** indigenous, `native' peoples of the world. The `Adams' were one-half

Anunnaki and one-half Earth evolved people. Descendants of the Adam's inhabited all continents and islands of the world. Note: the Adam's were of lighter skin tones than were the hybrids known as the Woman - `Eve'. The Adams and the Eves all naturally have Rh-positive blood, connecting them to the Earth.

C)-The original created Eves – the first hybrid woman, was the mother of all black-skinned peoples of Africa. The Eves, a.k.a. `the woman', was/is made up of one-half Adam's [DNA], and one-half Neanderthal, making her one-fourth Anunnaki, less black than the original Homo sapiens, but nevertheless, black-skinned. `Eve's' bloodline was created to preserve the race of natural Earth-Evolved creatures, who were becoming extinct. All black-skinned races of Africa are from `Eve'.

D)-The Nefilim created Mongoloid and Asiatic peoples. A race that once lived and reigned politically on planet Hibiru, but were eventually ousted and sent to Earth – they were the `fallen giants' in Biblical accounts, as well as in the St. John family journals. The Nefilim make up the Mongoloid and Asiatic peoples of the world, and originally had type B blood – RH negative – not of this Earth.

E) The Elohiym royal godhead: Their descendants became the twelve-thirteen tribes of Israel, i.e. the multitudes of Hebrew people - a white race descending primarily from EL, and his brother, Enki's, bloodline. The bloodline of the Israelites makes up the multitudes of Celtic, Irish, Scottish, Welsh, Anglo-Saxon, true Jews who aren't from the brown races, and most western white races. Note: The genetics of this group is probably the same as 'F' [below] – as both groups descend from the Anunnaki race, but 'E' represents the 'godhead', i.e. the reigning royal family. The original blood type of these descendants was RH negative, i.e. not of the Earth. Science today has no explanation as to where the Rh negative factor originates - well, it originates with the Elohiym family godhead. The royal godhead were not permitted to marry, and bear children, to any other than their own blood type. This is also the reason that the Israelites were held for 40 years in the Sinai - giving them time to 'cleanse' their bloodline by marrying only within their own race.

F) The WHITE races of people are descendants of the Anunnaki. Some from the white race are descendants of the Elohiym - which simply implies the royal family godhead who were/are in political power on Hibiru. However, some from the white race do not have a bloodline from the royal family of Elohiym, but are in fact, descendants of Anunnaki citizens. Their blood types were originally the same as above, but due to intermarrying with the BROWNS, as well as other created races, both groups now have large amounts of Rh-positive blood types. Rh positive is more dominant that is Rh negative, an Rh negative mother may have ten children from an Rh positive father, but may have only one Rh negative baby out of ten.

G) Mixed races – are a result of intermarrying amongst all races of people – producing various shades of skin tones, facial features, hair color and consistency, and blood types. Examples might be the people of India, the Aborigines of Australia, the Blackfoot of North America, and the Polynesians.

H) Esau's descendants – Turkey, Pakistan, Afghanistan, etc

I) **Cain's descendants – Assyrians>>>Babylonians>>>Romans**

J) **Ishmael's descendants – the Arabs**

K) **Jacob's descendants [Elohiym descendants.** We must not forget too, that the master scientist/physician, Enki, did many experiments with DNA manipulation and cloning in his laboratories here on Earth, accounting for many different and varied features amongst the races of people, which could have resulted in blonde-haired Aborigines in Australia, and the fine-featured black-skinned peoples of India.

*** *** ***

Mitochondria DNA: African races have more genetic diversity than any other human groups

There is an "out of Africa" hypothesis that was first proposed based on genetic studies of a type of DNA analysis known as mitochondria DNA, which is inherited through the maternal line; and the Y chromosome, which is inherited through the paternal line. These particular studies show that the African races have more genetic diversity than any other human groups, and that this diversity has been accumulating for perhaps 100,000 to 200,000 years. This finding implies that all modern humans are descended from a small population of Homo Sapiens that originally lived in Africa some 100,000 to 200,000 years ago.

Neanderthals did not contribute DNA to modern Europeans

However, analysis of mitochondria DNA, from a Neanderthal fossil found in Germany, also suggests that the Neanderthals did not contribute DNA to modern Europeans. Thus, evidence has been accumulating that modern Europeans are not descended from Neanderthals of Africa. (Source: paraphrased from Microsoft Encarta Encyclopedia – 2002)
Nobody will dispute the fact that black haired, ruddy [brown] skinned peoples, have occupied every continent and island on the face of the Earth since the `Adams' were first created.

The Elohiym family of "gods", originally created the "black-haired" people

The Elohiym family of "gods" originally created the "black-haired" people, in part because the Anunnaki hated to do manual labor, such as, mining gold, diamonds, and other precious metals.

Therefore, the creation of black-haired, ruddy-skinned peoples was initially to provide manual workers for the extraterrestrials, a.k.a., the Anunnaki people.

The descendants of the Anunnaki are the white races of peoples, who were originally a light-skinned race, with either red, blonde, or light-colored hair, and brightly colored eyes, such as blue, green, light gray, or hazel. Many white-skinned peoples still resemble the ancient space travelers who came to Earth thousands of years ago.

While the Israelites are descendants of the Elohiym godhead, and Enki and Enlil's family, not all white races descend from this politcal family. Nevertheless, Enki knew that the population on Hibiru was in trouble, so to preserve the Elohiym royal family line; many Elohiym descendants remained behind on Earth in order to preserve their race. Other Anunnaki descendants also inhabit the Earth today, but Enki and Enlil's descendants are identified as being Israelites.

NOTE: All the WHITE and ORIENTAL races would actually be HEBREW - having their origins from the planet by the same name, HIBIRU [aka Nibiru].

In summary, what the St. John family journals say regarding the various races is as follows:

1) A brown or red race of black-haired, ruddy-skinned people who are half-Anunnaki and half Homo-Sapien.

2) A black race that is one-half Homo-Sapien and one-half hybrid Adam;

3) A white race of people who are descendants of the Anunnaki;

4) An Oriental race of people who are the descendants of the Nefilim.

CHAPTER 8
EXTRATERRESTRIALS, HUMANS AND THEIR GENES/DNA CLOSE RELATIONSHIP

- Zecharia Sitchin's theories
- Extraterrestrial Genes and DNA
- "Junk Human DNA" was created by some kind of "extraterrestrial programmer"
- The big code
- Extraterrestrials' rush to create humans resulted in creating cancer
- The Human Genome Project
- Discovery implications associated with "Human-looking Extraterrestrials"
- "Star seeds", "star children" or "star people"
- Benevolent extraterrestrial races
- Representations concerning 'Ancient astronauts'
- Representation by academics from "Exopolitics" groups
- Human extraterrestrial races can easily integrate with human society
- Alleged Human ET efforts to promote the unity of humanity through religious spirituality
- Many groups allege Jesus was a "Human ET"
- ETs who allegedly contacted Alex Collier stipulate that *Jesus* did in fact live

*** *** ***

Extraterrestrials, Humans and their Genes/DNA Close Relationship

Zecharia Sitchin's theories

Dr. Zecharia Sitchin stated: "Ancient history and legend around the world, as well as the Bible, attest to the fact that there were once giants in the earth; men of awesome dimensions, bulk and height. In Genesis 6:1-4 we read: "And it came to pass, when men began to multiply on the face of the earth, and daughters were born unto them, that the sons of God saw the daughters of men that they were fair; and they took them wives of all which they chose...There were giants in the earth in those days; and also after that, when the sons of God came in unto the daughters of men, that they bare children to them, the same became mighty men which were of old, men of renown". The Book of Enoch, an ancient text discovered in Ethiopia in 1773 (and because of references to it in ancient Hebrew writings considered to be among the oldest manuscripts in existence) speaks about 200 angels who came down to earth to mate with the "daughters of man". Led by a high angel named Azazyel, the angels produced giant men.

During this strange occupation, Enoch writes that humans were taught to make swords, knives, shields, breastplates, mirrors, jewelry, paints and dyes, make cosmetics, and use valuable stones. The people also learned sorcery, use of roots and plants for medicine, astronomy, astrology and other "signs", and the importance of the motion of the celestial bodies

Extraterrestrial Genes and DNA

John Stokes stated that a group of researchers working at the Human Genome Project indicate that they made an astonishing scientific discovery: They believe so-called 97% non-coding sequences in human DNA is no less than genetic code of extraterrestrial life forms.

The non-coding sequences are common to all living organisms on Earth, from moulds to fish to humans. In human DNA, they constitute larger part of the total genome, says Prof. Sam Chang, the group leader. Non-coding sequences, originally known as "*junk DNA*", were discovered years ago, and their function remained a mystery. The overwhelming majority of Human DNA is "Off-world" in origin.

The apparent "extraterrestrial junk genes" merely "enjoy the ride" with hard working active genes, passed from generation to generation.

"Junk Human DNA" was created by some kind of "extraterrestrial programmer"

After comprehensive analysis with the assistance of other scientists, computer programmers, mathematicians, and other learned scholars, Professor Chang had wondered if the apparently "junk Human DNA" was created by some kind of "extraterrestrial programmer". The alien chunks within Human DNA, Professor Chang further observes, "have its own veins, arteries, and its own immune system that vigorously resists all our anti-cancer drugs."

Professor Chang further stipulates that, "Our hypothesis is that a higher extraterrestrial life form was engaged in creating new life and planting it on various planets. Earth is just one of them. Perhaps, after programming, our creators grow us the same way we grow bacteria in Petri dishes. We can't know their motives - whether it was a scientific experiment, or a way of preparing new planets for colonization, or is it long time ongoing business of seedling life in the universe."

The big code

Professor Chang further indicates that, "If we think about it in our human terms, the apparent "extraterrestrial programmers" were most probably working on "one big code" consisting of several projects, and the projects should have produced various life forms for various planets. They have been also trying various solutions. They wrote "the big code", executed it, did not like some function, changed them or added new one, executed again, made more improvements, tried again and again."

Professor Chang's team of researchers furthermore concludes that, "The apparent "extraterrestrial programmers" may have been ordered to cut all their idealistic plans for the future when they concentrated on the "Earth project" to meet the pressing deadline.

Very likely in an apparent rush, the "extraterrestrial programmers" may have cut down drastically on big code and delivered basic program intended for Earth."

Professor Chang is only one of many scientists and other researchers who have discovered extraterrestrial origins to humanity.

Extraterrestrials' rush to create humans resulted in creating cancer

> Professor Chang and his research colleagues show that apparent, "extraterrestrial programming' gaps in DNA sequencing precipitated by a hypothesized rush to create human life on Earth presented humankind with illogical growth of mass of cells we know as *cancer*."

Professor Chang further indicates that, "What we see in our DNA is a program consisting of two versions, a big code and basic code." Mr. Chang then affirms that the "First fact is, the complete 'program' was positively not written on Earth; that is now a verified fact.

The second fact is, that genes by themselves are not enough to explain evolution; there must be something more in 'the game'. Soon or later", Professor Chang says "we have to come to grips with the unbelievable notion that every life on Earth carries genetic code for his extraterrestrial cousin and that evolution is not what we think it is."

*** *** ***

The Human Genome Project
Discovery implications associated with "Human-looking Extraterrestrials"

"Star seeds", "star children" or "star people"

> The implications of these scientific finds would reinforce claims by other scientists and observers of having contact with 'off-world' human looking extraterrestrials. The 'off-world' human looking extraterrestrial have been claimed to have provided some of the genetic material for human evolution, and that many of these extraterrestrials have allowed some of their personnel to incarnate as 'star seeds' on Earth in human families.
>
> These "star seeds", "star children" or "star people" are described by Brad and Francie Steiger as individuals whose 'souls' were formally incarnated on the worlds of other star systems and then traveled to Earth and decided to incarnate here in order to "boost" the spiritual evolutionary development of humanity.

Benevolent extraterrestrial races

Most of humanity would consider this group of extraterrestrials to be 'benevolent' as described by 'contactees' such as George Adamski, Orfeo Angelucci, George Van Tassell,

Howard Menger, Paul Villa, Billy Meier and Alex Collier who each explain the nature of their voluntary interactions with these human looking extraterrestrials.

These "contactees" often provide physical evidence in the form of photographs, film and/or witnesses of their contacts with extraterrestrial races. The most extensively documented and researched contactee is Eduard 'Billy' Meier who provided much physical evidence for investigators.

Representations concerning 'Ancient astronauts'

Indeed, 'ancient astronaut' writers believe that a race of intelligent extraterrestrial beings visited and/or colonized Earth in the remote past, whereupon they upgraded the primitive hominid Homo erectus by means of genetic engineering to create the human race as we know it: Homo sapiens. Evidence for this idea is found,
(a) in the improbability of Homo sapiens emerging so suddenly, according to the principles of orthodox Darwinism
(b) in the myths of ancient civilizations which describe human-like gods coming down from the heavens and creating mankind 'in their own image'
Homo sapiens is thus regarded as a hybrid being, incorporating a mix of terrestrial genes from Homo erectus and extraterrestrial genes from an ascribed "race of the gods".
Prior to the modern age of space travel and genetics, this theory for the origins of humankind could not have been conceived. And even now, in the 21st century, there are many people who would regard it as science fiction. However, in the light of the problems with the orthodox theory of human evolution, the idea of a genetic intervention by an intelligent human-like species (who themselves evolved on another planet over a more credible time frame) does require to be taken seriously as a potential solution to the mystery. The most famous exponents of the ancient astronaut intervention are the Swiss writer Erich von Daniken and the American writer Zecharia Sitchin. The latter, in particular, has argued the case in great detail.

Representation by academics from "Exopolitics" groups

Dr. Michael E. Salla is one of the founders of an Exopolitics movement which seeks an open and informed dialogue on, and with, Extraterrestrials, toward the affirmation of "global democracy" and the quality-of-living of humankind as socially responsible beings in the Universe.

Dr. Salla indicates that "There are an extensive number of extraterrestrial races known [by various research institutions and agencies] to be currently interacting with Earth and the human population."
Dr. Salla, is also the author of Exopolitics: Political Implications of the Extraterrestrial Presence (Dandelion Books, 2004.) He has

held full time academic appointments at the Australian National University, and American University, Washington DC. He has a Ph.D. in Government from the University of Queensland, Australia.

During his professional academic career, he was best known for organizing a series of citizen diplomacy initiatives for the East Timor conflict funded by U.S. Institute of Peace and the Ford Foundation. He is also the Founder of the Exopolitics Institute; and Chief Editor of the 'Exopolitics Journal' and Convener of the "Extraterrestrial Civilizations and World Peace Conference."

In a 1998 interview, Clifford Stone, a retired U.S. army Sergeant who served in the U.S. Army for 22 years and allegedly participated in operations to retrieve crashed extraterrestrial ships and extraterrestrial biological entities (EBE's), revealed there were a variety of extraterrestrial races known [by various institutions and agencies].

Dr. Salla further elaborates that, "The most compelling testimonies on the different extraterrestrial races comes from 'whistleblowers' such as Sergeant Stone; and also 'contactees' who have had direct physical contact with extraterrestrials and communicated with them." Dr. Salla further notes that Master Sergeant Bob Dean had a twenty seven year distinguished career in very senior areas of the military indicates that among the know extraterrestrials one group, "looked so much like us they could sit next to you on a plane or in a restaurant and you'd never know the difference."

Human extraterrestrial races can easily integrate with human society

Apparently "Human extraterrestrial races can easily integrate with human society in the manner described by Dean and others where they can be indistinguishable from the rest of humanity." Dr. Salla corroborates.

According to Alex Collier who claims to be a contactee, "a variety of extraterrestrial races have provided genetic material for the human experiment." Alex Collier indicates that "Earth humans" are, "a product of extraterrestrial genetic manipulation, and are possessors of a vast gene pool consisting of many different racial memory banks, also consisting of at least 22 different races."

Alleged Human ET efforts to promote the unity of humanity through religious spirituality

Alex Collier further claims that constituents of "Human ETs" seek to "ensure that global humanity evolves in a responsible way without endangering both itself and the greater galactic community of which it is part. "

234

Exopolitics groups and independent contactees also indicate that constituents of "Human ETs" seek to "uplift human consciousness and to promote the unity of religion."

Alex Colliers alleged contact with ETs suggest that fundamentalist messages in from Christianity to Judaism to Islam, and other institutionalized religions, as well as outright apparent 'cult' groups, have been specifically placed by "hostile elements" to manipulate and control humankind.

Many groups allege Jesus was a "Human ET"

Jesus, who many groups allege was "Human ET" sought to inspire the social consciousness of humankind toward unity, and not to create a "Christian religion", with its *sexually repressive* as well as *homophobic undertones*, which also have been used for the execution of racism, and to legitimate atrocities like the 'slave trade'.

ETs who allegedly contacted Alex Collier stipulate that *Jesus* did in fact live

ETs who allegedly contacted Alex Collier, also further allegedly stipulate that *Jesus* did in fact live; and lived out the rest of his life in Massada; and that *Jesus* was only *crucified* through the religious doctrine, and myth-making associated with 'the palms'.

As far as the "saviour scenario" is concerned, for example, Alex Collier was allegedly told by ETs that it has been put into our belief systems to "disempower us."

The *saviour scenario* within the dogma of institutionalized religions legitimate the creation of an elite driven oppressive power structure who appoint themselves as "judgers of morality".

These religious elites have historically used their self-appointed roles to execute a comprehensive system of social controls that complement their joint pursuit of greed-oriented self-aggrandizement with other elites from government to business enterprises.

The alleged efforts of socially progressive Human ETs to inspire the affirmation of the quality-of-living of 'Earth Humans' through spiritual and other "emissaries", have been undermined by the efforts of "capitalists" to exploit such alleged initiatives in the pursuit of an oppressive agenda of greed and fascistic power.

Constituents of Human ETs allegedly seek to "help humanity find freedom from oppressive structures through education and consciousness raising."

*** *** ***

CHAPTER 9
THE ANUNNAKI'S SUPER PHYSICS, SCIENCE AND GENETIC ENGINEERING

- The Anunnaki knew of a process to change the gold to a monoatomic form
- Enki the chief science officer and Ninhursag the top medical officer experimented with mixing various animal genes with the primitive primates without much success.
- The elite Anunnaki who took human women as wives and had children by them infuriated the Anunnaki's High Council
- The double helix of the DNA molecule appear in the records of the Sumerians
- Did Darwin get it wrong? In the Atlantium continuum the answer is YES
- The Anunaki super tech
- The Anunaki organized the primitive Homo Erectus humans as gold miners
- Science calls it "Terra-forming"
- Homo Erectus proved to be very difficult to manage
- The Anunnaki used their own blood to create the Homo Sapiens
- Earth was the 7th planet for the Anunaki because they came from beyond Pluto
- Anunaki lived very long lives, tens of thousands of years and they could sleep for 5 or 6 years.
- Ancient DNA research
- The ancient Sumer believed that their creators the Anunaki literally designed them in a laboratory.
- Modern science: Humans are extremely closely related to every thing on earth
- Study: Human genome was concluded and determined that a Mitochondrial Eve in fact existed Anunaki Android helpers...Grays?
- When the Anunaki first came to earth they found man in a very primitive state
- After numerous generations man was re-engineered into the current Homo Sapiens model
- Anunnaki, gray aliens and abduction
- Are the Helpers still involved in the on going evolution of mankind?

The Anunnaki's Super Physics, Science And Genetic Engineering

The Anunnaki knew of a process to change the gold to a monoatomic form
Advanced physics proves its existence

> Was the genetic engineering, the only super science the Anunnaki developed to create and control the human race?
> How much did they know about DNA?
> Did they discover anti gravity properties?
> How important the monoatomic form was to the Anunnaki?
> Did they forsee the Deluge?
> Did the Anunnaki blend animal genes with the primitive man?
> Did the Anunnaki use their own blood to create thye Homo Sapiens?

Here are the answers in the thesis of Roc Hatfield. The detailed creation story told by the Sumerians sounds like a science fiction novel written by a top author today. The Sumer claimed that an advanced vanguard of gods from a distant planet named Nibiru landed near the Persian Gulf over 400,000 years ago. The Anunnaki were in search of gold. Apparently they knew of a process to change the gold to a monoatomic form which has anti gravity properties. This idea was rediscovered by modern science in the last few years. No one has figured out how to make the monoatomic gold but advanced physics proves its existence. The Anunnaki enlisted the local Homo-Erectus population to work as slaves in the gold mines but were unhappy with their abilities.

> **Enki the chief science officer and Ninhursag the top medical officer experimented with mixing various animal genes with the primitive primates without much success.**

Enki the chief science officer and Ninhursag the top medical officer experimented with mixing various animal genes with the primitive primates without much success. Finally they tried mixing Anunnaki genes with early man and eureka, a stable mining worker was created. The newly minted Homo-sapien was just the ticket. Soon the humans began to populate the planet and became a well adapted creature that overwhelmed the Anunnaki.

The elite Anunnaki who took human women as wives and had children by them infuriated the Anunnaki's High Council

The elite Anunnaki took human women as wives and had children by them. This was considered an outrage to the high council of the Anunnaki. It was by an order at the highest levels that the hybrid Anunnaki-Human be destroyed. The experiment was a complete failure all of the human hybrids must be eliminated.

The Anunnaki were aware that an impending natural catastrophe was near and that they would allow it to kill all the hybrids. Enki, the top Anunnaki official that had overseen the hybrid project was sympathetic to the humans he had genetically engineered and saved them from a worldwide flood.

The Sumerian records describe in great detail how these genetically engineered hybrids lived and worked as slaves, warriors and mates to the Anunnaki.

The double helix of the DNA molecule appear in the records of the Sumerians

Clay tablet images resembling the double helix of the DNA molecule appear in the records of the Sumerians.

Could these images be a commemoration of the Anunnaki-Human hybrid experiment?

How could these ancient people living at the dawn of human history create such an amazing story?

Drawings of the Anunnaki in their lab brewing up hybrids have been found and add weight to this startling story. 2000 years after the Sumerians recorded this information the Hebrew Patriarch Moses wrote in Genesis 6:1-4,"And it came to pass, when men began to multiply on the face of the earth, and daughters were born unto them, That the sons of God saw the daughters of men that they were fair; and they took them wives of all which they chose...There were nephilim in the earth in those days; and also after that, when the sons of God came in unto the daughters of men, and they bore children to them, the same became mighty men which were of old, men of renown."

Did Darwin get it wrong?

Are we the descendants of the Anunnaki Human Hybrids?
Did Darwin get it wrong?
In the Atlantium continuum the answer is YES. It is evident that every culture from the beginning of recorded time recalls this same story over and over again. It is possible that the Sumerians have found the missing link and it is not an evolutionary link but the result of ancient biotech.

The Anunaki Super Tech

The Anunaki organized the primitive Homo Erectus humans as gold miners

The 6500 year old writings of the Sumerians and later the carvings of the Babylonians and Assyrians focus on a super tech race known to them as the Anunaki. These creatures described as gods that came to earth from heaven are credited with among many other things the actual creation of the first man. One Sumerian creation myth tells of a time before modern man when the Anunaki came to Earth in search of gold. The Anunaki organized the primitive Homo Erectus humans as gold miners.

It seems that the Annunaki are from a planet called Nibiru which is the 10th planet in our solar system.

Nibiru sails around an elliptical orbit that takes it out beyond Pluto and every 3600 years it comes back into our neck of the woods.

Science calls it "Terra-forming"

The planet is warmed internally by friction and is dark most of the time due to its vast distance from the sun. According to the Sumerians the Annunaki wanted to vaporize the gold that was mined here on earth and introduce it into their planets' atmosphere in order to create a global insulation blanket. Trapping the heat coming from the planets' surface and preventing it from escaping into space. We call this Terra-forming today, the idea that a planet can be made livable by generating an atmosphere and ecosystems on a global scale. This idea is at best 75 years old but the Sumerains thought of it 6500 years ago.

Homo Erectus proved to be very difficult to manage
The Anunnaki used their own blood to create the Homo Sapiens

Homo Erectus proved to be very difficult to manage and gold production was inadequate. The top two Anunaki leaders established an R&D project to see if various animal genes could be blended with the primitive man in an effort to produce a better more productive worker. Apparently many bazaar creatures were developed but none met the needs of the Annunaki. Finally Anunaki blood was used in the experiment and the result was a success, Homo Sapiens were born. This new and improved human was just what was needed to fit the bill.

The Earth was the 7th planet for the Anunaki because they were coming here from beyond Pluto

The story of the Anunaki and his relationship with his creation continues for thousands of years up until the time of the Sumerian culture. These ideas are easy to shrug off as just fantasy myths and grand story telling. We are immersed in many of these ideas today due to books, movies and television, but the Sumerian stories are ancient going back to the very beginning of recorded history. When these stories are coupled with the many visual images that have been left a very solid platform begins to emerge. A base that science can build on by looking at these ancient stories in a whole new way. One panel left by the Sumerians clearly depicts seven planets and the sun. The Earth was the 7th planet for the Anunaki because they were coming here from beyond Pluto and they considered Nibiru to be the 10th planet.

Anunaki lived very long lives, tens of thousands of years and they could sleep for 5 or 6 years

The Anunaki are always pictured as beings that could fly, many flying vehicles are apparent in many of the ancient Sumerian and Babylonian carvings.

They typically are wearing what could be a watch or personal information device. One relief reveals two Annunaki swimming under water with fish nearby with what looks like Scuba gear.

One daunting feature that is always present in the depiction of the Anunaki is a very large calf muscle. This could be the result of living on a larger planet with greater gravity than Earth. Many images of the Anunaki seem to include industrial strength sun glasses. They hail from a very dim world and the Earths' sunlight could be damaging or at least painful to there sensitive eyes.

The Anunaki were revered and worshiped as gods by the Sumerians, Babylonians and the Assyrians.

An overwhelming amount of information has been found over the last 200 years about these super advanced beings and now we are starting to see these records in a new and exciting light. According to the Sumerians the Anunaki lived very long lives, tens of thousands of years and they could sleep for 5 or 6 years. They were very slow to make changes taking centuries to make decisions and alter plans. Everything for them was on a grand scale even their planet took 3600 years to go around the sun once. Are the Anunaki just the stars in an ancient creation myth?

Are the thousands of writings and carvings just an ancient form of comic book?

In the Atlantium continuum the answer is "NO". It is plausible to piece together a story that holds up to scientific scrutiny from the writings of the Sumerians. We haven't found a 10th planet as yet but Pluto wasn't discovered until 1930.

The real question is how mankind would handle the idea that their origins could lie in the need for a good slave?

Ancient DNA research

Craig Venter the world famous and tediously controversial DNA researcher stunned the science community with his announcement that he had created a complex synthetic chromosome. Venter and his team of scientist stitched together laboratory chemicals to create a gene that is 381 genes long and contains 581,000 base pairs of genetic code.

The synthetic life form is then placed in the cell work of a bacterium known as Mycoplasma genetailia. Once inserted the DNA takes over the workings of the cell and becomes an entirely new form of life. The new bacterium has been dubbed Mycoplasma Labortorium.

Designer lifeforms could provide completely new ways of solving problems in many areas from energy to medicine. No doubt these new genetically engineered creatures will open up new unseen uses, but are we just relearning ancient knowledge?

The ancient Sumer built super cities and lived in very modern like conditions over 6500 years ago. The existence of this civilization has only been known since the 1800's and researchers have only begun to scratch the surface of the many artifacts that have been discovered. The Sumerians were excellent record keepers and invented a way to engrave metal and stone cylinders to make clay seal panels. The panels still completely intact today offer some insight into the pantheon of the Sumer society. Their beliefs regarding man's creation are very well documented in the seals and tablets that they generated. One image that stands out is the double helix of the entwined snakes.

This image has been used ever since as the symbol for medicine.

The medical establishment today still prominently uses this ancient image as its mascot.

The ancient Sumer believed that their creators the Anunaki literally designed them in a laboratory.

The ancient Sumer believed that their creators the Anunaki literally designed them in a laboratory. In one clay panel, the Anunnaki are depicted sitting among what appear to be flask jars and vases while presenting a human infant, the tree of life a symbol used in many Sumer panels is standing in the room representing creation. The tree of life and the entwined snakes have appeared frequently in Sumer clay panels. The Anunaki came down from heaven and created man and woman.

The Anunaki made man in his own image by using his own blood to make man. These detailed creation myths have been reinterpreted by modern researchers like Zecheria Sitchin to read like a Sci-Fi novel. Sitchin's research has lead him to believe that the Anunaki were a space fairing race that came to Earth 400,000 years ago to mine for gold and other valuable minerals. While here they took indigenous primates and other animals and experimented with their DNA, finally breeding Homo-Sapiens some 150,000 years ago.

Interestingly, the Hebrew Bible written some 3000 years after the Sumer wrote their creation story asserts that the "Elohim" said; "Let us make man in our own image". The Elohim are the same individuals as described by the Sumer as the Annunaki. The name Anunaki means "Those who came to earth from heaven". Zecheria Sitchin and others firmly believe that the Anunaki were a very advanced race from a distant planet called Nibiru. The Anunaki were skilled in all the sciences we are familiar with today.

*** *** ***

Modern Science: Humans are extremely closely related to every other thing on earth

It seems that they may have been a few hundred years ahead of where we are currently. Of course there is no way to know how advanced they really were. But 500-800 years into our future could be amazing. After all Columbus could have never imagined our world today only 500 years ago. His little wooden ships state of the art at the time took months to cross the Atlantic.

Today thousands of people cross the oceans everyday in hours. Our modern DNA research has mapped the human genome and discovered that humans are extremely closely related to every other thing on earth.

We share 50-60 percent of the genes of plants and bacteria, and 99 percent of the same genes as other primates like chimps. It is clear that man is the most complex being on the planet and a product of the evolution and improvement of the lower species.

Man has evolved from the successes of all the lower creatures that have come before. It turns out that there are 223 genes in the human genome that don't show up anywhere in any of our predecessors.

In other words there is a milk man somewhere in our past. 223 genes is almost 1% of our total 30,000 gene instruction package.

Where did these unrelated genes come from?

Study: Human genome was concluded and determined that a Mitochondrial Eve in fact existed

The Anunaki were said to have used their own blood to make mankind more like them, to improve them physically and mentally.

These unique genes show up in man at the same time as the Anunaki reigned in Sumer, our modern day Iraq.

A recent study of the Human genome was concluded and determined that a Mitochondrial Eve in fact existed.

Eve would have lived 140,000 years ago in the north of Africa near southern Iraq where the Sumer settled.

Was ancient man genetically altered by an advanced race of beings from a distant planet?

Is the missing link the result of altered DNA? In the Atlantium continuum the answer is "YES". The Sumer, Hebrews, Egyptians and others have been telling us this fact about ourselves for Millennia. It is very difficult to come to the realization that we may be hybrid beings. As races here on earth we mix together frequently and this should stand as an example of how blending can be good.

Anunaki Android Helpers...Grays?

On a cool autumn night two star struck lovers drive their vehicle down a secluded country road searching for a location to park. Suddenly, bright headlights shine in their eyes from a car coming down the road just ahead of them. The young lady cautions her beau to pull over and let the fast moving car pass. The lights now extremely bright prompt our alarmed passengers to flash their high beams to indicate their presence in the road. The entire area where their car is setting is engulfed in a blindingly bright light so intense you can almost touch it. Then as fast as the light appeared it disappears just like it was turned off by switch. A light breeze rustles the leaves on the nearby trees and a million stars shine bright in the crystal clear night sky. Once the excitement of the event subsides our drivers notice that the dashboard clock has jumped ahead 2 hours. This story or a variation of it has been reported to authorities hundreds of times over the last 50-60 years. The story elements vary, but the perpetrators remain consistent. Short gray men with big almond shaped eyes.6500 years ago the ancient Sumer wrote about their gods the Anunaki and a creation myth that has recently opened a new train of thought about our species true origins. The Sumer articulated endlessly about many aspects of the lives of the Anunaki. The Annunaki are described as a race of highly technologically advanced individuals with space fairing capabilities.

When the Anunaki first came to earth they found man in a very primitive state

When the Annunaki first came to earth from their home world Nibiru they found man in a very primitive state. Between 450-150 thousand years ago they began modifying man with genetic engineering in an effort to bring him up to a standard more suitable for servitude. The Annunaki were unable to come here in great numbers and would need the help of the locals to mine minerals, build pyramids and fight wars as proxy armies over the earth's natural resources.

After numerous generations man was re-engineered into the current Homo Sapiens model

After numerous generations man was re-engineered into the current Homo Sapien model.

Most of the Sumerian record was left to us from the time after the deluge and records revel how this global cataclysm was foreseen by the Annunaki.

Perhaps more incredibly the Sumer refer to beings called the "Helpers" a term used to describe creatures that assisted the Anunaki in every aspect of their lives.

These Helpers were created by the Anunaki and were alive but not living. This statement could be describing an android. The creatures assisted their creators by flying the vessels that the Annunaki traveled in.

The Helpers remained in the orbiting ships in space and came down to the Earth on shuttle flights. Artifacts of the Helpers left by the Sumer depict a creature that is very familiar with what we now call the Grays.

Anunnaki, Gray Aliens and Abduction

Thousands of individuals have come forward in the last 30-40 years with stories of being abducted by small aliens with big heads and large almond shaped eyes.

The stories told by these varied victims all center around these Grays sedating them and then subjecting them to a cadre of medical experiments that seem focused on reproduction.

The Sumer believed that the Helpers assisted the Anunaki in the creation of man and took part in the engineering process. Curiously 6500 years later people claim to have been experimented on by creatures that look very much like ancient Sumerian artifacts of Helpers.

Critics of the abduction phenomenon say that the subjects are suffering from a common type of sleep sickness that allows the brain to be awake but leaves the body paralyzed. Sleep Paralysis is a well known and documented disorder.

This how experts explain the wave of abduction reports. This disorder can cause vivid out of body type experiences. There is a mass epidemic of sleep paralysis making its way around the world, be sure it doesn't happen to you.

Images of the Grays have appeared down through history on cave walls and Egyptian temples. The modern Grays according to the lore are very interested in human reproduction usually taking sperm samples and eggs from abducted humans. Some women have cited being shown human-alien offspring that they claim are their children. Many of the victims tell of being abducted on many occasions since childhood. A tracking device is implanted under their skin so that they can be located easily. Today scientists perform all of these tasks to keep track of endangered species and assist in helping them reproduce.

Are the Annunaki Helper artifacts accurate records made in clay?

Are the Helpers still involved in the on going evolution of mankind?

In the Atlantium continuum the answer is "YES". The Sumer recorded a number of unique aspects of the Helpers that are in every way similar to the folk myth of the modern Grays. If the Anunaki were involved in the development of the human race they may still be monitoring us with the assistance of their android Helpers. The ability to use such a sophisticated robot to fly to a distant planet and carry out complex observations is mind boggling at a minimum.

It would be completely essential for a hyper advanced civilization to use androids to reach out to distant planets to monitor long running experiments.

The Mars Rover would have seemed as amazing to us 500 years ago as the idea of the Anunaki Helpers do to us today. -Roc Hatfield.

*** *** ***

CHAPTER 10
ADAM AND HUMAN LONGEVITY
AND
THE ANUNNAKI DNA

- Possible explanation: A Genetic component was involved
- It's all in the diet? What kind?
- Was it star fire, elixir of life, powder of gold, soul food, Manna, or Anunnaki DNA?
- There is definite distinction between Star Fire of the Goddess and an ORME

*** *** ***

Adam's Family Tree and Human Longevity and Anunnaki DNA

Geneticists, biblical scholars and scientists always wondered about the legendary longevity of the biblical patriarchs. It is unconceivable, even incomprehensible to many who have studied the Old Testament that such longevity could be possible. Others questioned its religious importance and purpose. Most certainly, to the Gnostics, skeptics and atheists, it is simply a fairy tale. However, it was historically recorded by eminent historians of the ancient world such as Hestiaeus, Hieronymus, Josephus, Hecataeus, Hellanicus, Hesiod, Ephorus to name a few. Same longevity story was told and embellished in Phoenician tales and the records of Sumerian kings. Dan Ward said: In addition, the "Sumerian King Lists" tell the same story, and furthermore, note a profound discontinuity of lifetimes before and after the Great Flood/Deluge." In addition to his convincing comments, Ward demonstrated the strangeness of the Adam's Family Tree in a chronological tables illustrated below, where the far left column is dated from the birth of Adam, the number under each name is that person's age when his son was born (e.g. Seth was 105, when Enos was born), and the underlined numbers are age of the patriarch at his death. (The years are taken from the King James version of the Bible.)

From Adam to Noah											
000	Adam										
130	130	Seth									
235		105	Enos								
325			90	Cainan							
395				70	Mahalaleel						
460					65	Jared					
622						162	Enoch				
687							65	Methuselah			
874								187	Lamech		
930	930										
987							365				
1042		912									
1056									182	Noah	
1140			905								
1235				910							
1290					895						
1422						962					
1556										500	Shem
1651									777		
1656	--------	--------	--- The	Flood	---------	---------	---------	969		600	100
2006										950	
2156											600

248

Ward's first table shows that when Noah was born he had six generations of his family still living, with Enoch having "ascended to heaven" rather than dying. Inheritances were obviously few and far between in those days! Meanwhile, Noah's father, Lamech, could have set on his great, great, great, great, great, great grandfather's knee, while Methuselah apparently survived the Great Flood/Deluge!

As Ward stated, the average age of the pre-flood patriarchs (not counting the special case of Enoch) is 913. This is in sharp contrast to the line from Shem to Abraham -- even though Shem was born before the Flood. The Sumerian King Lists show a similar sharp change in the longevity of their kings immediately following the Flood.

From Noah to Abraham (Abram)											
000	Noah										
500	500	Shem									
602		102	Arphaxad								
637			35	Salah							
667				30	Eber						
701					34	Peleg					
731						30	Reu	(the day!?)			
763							32	Serug			
793								30	Nahor		
822									29	Terah	
892										70	Abram
940						239					
941									148		
950	950										
970							239				
993								230			
1027	-	-								205	
1040	-	-	438								
1067	-	-									175
1070	-			433							
1100	-	600									
1134					468						

From the second table, there is even more intrigue. On the one hand, fathers were having their sons at a relatively early age (31.4 average) for seven of the generations (as compared to an average of 150 in all of the previous generations).

Curious fact. Meanwhile, Noah did quite well for himself in terms of longevity (in line with all of his previous generations), while Shem didn't quite make it to the end of "middle age" (i.e. less than 2/3rds of Noah). The next three generations averaged 446 years (about half of the Adam to Noah clan). And then yet another drop in the following six generations to an average of 206 years! This led to the weird situation (there's no other name for it), whereby Noah's son, Shem, outlived all but one member of the next *eight* generations! Shem and the three generations behind him, far outlived the following five generations. After growing up with ancestors from *ten* generations still hanging around, Abraham must have felt incredibly unlucky, when he died prior to his great, great, great, great grandfather, his great, great, great, great, great grandfather, and his great, great, great, great, great, great, great grandfather! After Abraham, everything went even further downhill, i.e. at the time of their death:

Isaac was 180	Amaram was 137
Jacob was 147	Moses was 120
Job was 140	Joshua was 110
Levi was 137	Eli was 98
Kohath was 133	David was 70

How can this strangeness be explained?

Possible explanation: A Genetic component was involved

Ward explains: If we assume that Adam and Eve were born of a genetic DNA combination of Anunnaki and Homo Erectus blood, and that the Anunnaki were extremely long-lived compared to humans (i.e. on the order of 500,000 years), then the long lives of the pre-flood patriarchs are not that much of a surprise.
There is easily a clearly genetic component involved. But DNA alone doesn't suffice to explain the step-wise decrease in longevity from the time of Noah to that of David. There is a huge gap between Noah (950) and his son, Shem (600), another gap between Shem and the next three generations (446), and yet another huge gap before the following six generations (222), and then a gap and slow decrease over the next ten generations (down to 70). A slow degradation of the genetics might explain a part, but not why the pre-flood patriarchs showed no signs of decreasing longevity, nor why the subsequent decreases came in steps.This leaves environmental causes as a possible answer. Theories have been suggested in this regard, but a change in the environment doesn't explain the step-wise progression either.
Environmental processes typically don't show a series of discontinuities. But perhaps, the change is more obvious -- perhaps it's something they ate, or didn't eat!

Was the long-term mortality of Adam's Family due to the something in their diet that provided an extended mortality, and that the step-wise removal of this key ingredient was responsible for the quantum reductions in longevity? As opposed to a serious aversion to inheritance taxes?

It's all in the diet? What kind?

Was it Star Fire, elixir of life, powder of gold, soul food, Manna, or Anunnaki DNA?

In other words, the simplest explanation is pretty much a version of the modern day explanation for living long: It's all in the diet?

The key ingredient appears to have been the ORME (aka Star Fire, elixir of life, "white powder of gold," Ma-Na or Manna). This is the literal version of "soul food", which feeds the soul and thereby allows for substantially prolonged life times.

Consider the following scenario: During the pre-flood days, everything was progressing pretty much in accordance with the establishment's (i.e. Anunnaki's) agenda, and thus the kings and patriarchs who were given their charge by the so-called Gods and Goddesses were provided ready access to the ORME (in any of its versions and by any of its names).

After the flood, however, there was a sea change (pardon the pun) in how things were going. There is, after all, nothing like having the vast majority of civilized man wiped out to cause a certain lack of confidence by men in their gods. There is also the distinct possibility that the gods themselves (the Anunnaki) had decided that perhaps it was not in their best interests to have their human middle managers (aka kings) hang around so long. (This is a problem that many modern day CEO's can appreciate.)

There is definite distinction between Star Fire of the Goddess and an ORME

Accordingly, and with the exception of Noah, things started to change. There is definite distinction between, for example, Star Fire of the Goddess and an ORME "supplement". By the time of Moses, for example, the Exodus hero was totally dependent upon the ORME, which he attempted to manufacture in his furnace atop Mount Sinai (aka Mount Horeb). Laurence Gardner has noted that "it was from the milk of Hathor [the Egyptian Mother Goddess, and an aspect of Isis the Great Mother] that the pharaohs were said to gain their divinity, becoming gods in their own right." [1] Gardner also noted that "In more ancient Sumerian times, during the days of the original Star Fire ritual, the bloodline kings who were fed with the hormone-rich lunar essence of the Anunnaki goddesses were also said to have been nourished with their own milk -- notably that of Ishtar."

This Star Fire was actually the divine menstruum, which supposedly "constituted the purest and most potent life force." The "white powder of gold" (the ORME), which was manufactured as a substitute for the Goddess Star Fire, may have had other potential uses, but it was simply not as potent as the original. The bottom line is the Goddess Star Fire was undoubtedly fully available to the pre-flood patriarchs, but less so to the post-flood gang.

There is also the possibility that it may have been replaced in incremental steps by the ORME, and/or other substitutes as time passed, and as the middle managers came and went. While the ORME might have been used for generations by the Anunnaki as the key to their longevity (which over time would have made major DNA changes), for the humans (kings, et al) the Star Fire may have been a combination of ORME and the benefits of Anunnaki-style "mother's milk".

Finally, just as supplements don't really replace healthy organically grown foods, the ORME simply wouldn't have the carrying power of Star Fire. But even with the ORME, Star Fire, elixir of life, or what-have-you, there is also the need to approach its consumption with the right attitude, or for lack of a better term, a sense of righteousness. It's all about where the food is from, how it's obtained, and importantly, how it's consumed.

References: [1] Laurence Gardner, *Genesis of the Grail Kings*, Bantam Press, NY, 1999.

*** *** ***

CHAPTER 11
EXTRATERRESTRIALS
EXTRATERRESTRIALS AMONG US

- Allegations of "Human ET" encounters on Earth
- Contact testimonies of 'Extraterrestrials Among Us'
- Extraterrestrials have spent years living on earth, learning the language, getting jobs and mixing with the human population
- Representation on earth humans relative to "non-earthbound" humans
- Advanced human ETs view earth humans as barbarians and savages, and as a threat to themselves
- Star visitors living among us on earth
- The "Tall Whites": An alien race from a location near but behind the Arcturus star system
- The "Tall Whites" look quite human
- Description of the spaceships of the "Tall Whites" aliens
- The "Tall Whites" in their interactions with humans often carry stun devices for protection
- Earth serves as a handy mid-way rest to aliens
- Aliens have a base at Dog Bone Lake, 25 miles east of French Peak on the Nellis Air Force Range, Nevada.
- The Tall Whites have made arrangements with the U.S. government at the highest levels
- Visitors from other star system to come and study the English language and American culture.
- A Zeta-human hybrid teenage girl lives as a college student at Lost River College in California
- "Four Corners" base is a U.S. Government-run Star Visitor Reception Area and Ambassadorial Interface Facility for representatives from the Intergallactic Council.
- Tall White Alien passing for human with disguise

- The main housing area for the Tall Whites was located underground
- Female alien disguised as a human woman, DownTown Las Vegas outside the Hotel Fremont and Casino.
- Tall White aliens' nervous system is roughly 2 to 2-and-a-half times faster than the human nervous system operates
- Humanoid Star Visitor race (Sammi People "Norwegians") live above the Arctic Circle in Norway, Finland, Sweden and a northwestern peninsula of Russia
- They have their own distinctive language, and traditionally survived by herding reindeer.
- Former U.S. Air Force Airman Charles Hall: "I personally and frequently observed on many separate occasions the tall white scout craft and the Tall Whites…"
- The deep space craft always arrived from space and departed back into space by using Dog Bone [Dry] Lake as their landing…
- Former U.S. Air Force Airman Charles Hall: "I personally witnessed the Tall Whites, using their scout craft, with small groups of high ranking American generals on board apparently taking short tours of the Moon."
- There are five areas of "gravity anomaly" on the moon
- United States has a base on the moon
- Another Star Visitor race (Laplanders) that has been resident on earth for some time
- An Air Force Colonel reveals the existence of United States government undisclosed Nevada base for Visitors from various star systems around the galaxy
- A United States Air Force Colonel adopts a Zeta-human hybrid daughter
- Anunnaki Also Landed in Ancient Africa. They're Still There
- The tale of Credo Mutwa, a Zulu shaman: Alien abduction and reptilians
- The Chitauli came to Earth in terrible vessels which flew through the air, shaped like great bowls
- The Chitauli gave human beings the power of speech
- When the Chitauli gets sick this way, a young girl, a virgin, is usually kidnapped

*** *** ***

Extraterrestrials Among Us

Allegations of "Human ET" encounters on Earth

In Dr. Salla's article "Extraterrestrials Among Us" published in October 2006, he alleges that, "There is startling evidence from a number of independent sources that 'human looking' extraterrestrial visitors have integrated with and lived in major population centres up until recently, and this is known by a select number of institutions."

Aside from whistleblower testimonies, like Sergeant Major Robert Dean, a number of private individuals claim to have encountered extraterrestrials posing as ordinary citizens in major cities around the planet.

George Adamski was the first to write about extraterrestrials secretly living among the human population.

In his second non-fiction book describing his extraterrestrial contact experiences, "Inside the Flying Saucers", George Adamski discussed how human looking extraterrestrials had established a presence among the human population.

"They apparently looked so much like us", Dr. Salla notes "that they could get jobs, lived in neighbourhoods, drove cars, and could blend in easily with the human population."

Dr. Salla further notes that, "Adamski wrote about how they contacted him to set up meetings that led to his famous flights aboard extraterrestrial vehicles."

But as Dr. Salla explains "While controversy over Adamski's contact experiences and his credibility continues, Adamski's UFO sightings and contacts with extraterrestrials were supported by an impressive collection of witnesses, photographs and films that a number of independent investigators concluded were not hoaxes."

Dr. Salla additionally stipulates that, "Adamski's testimony offers important insights into how extraterrestrials may be living incognito among the human population."

After discussing the Adamski case and the strongest evidence supporting it, Dr. Salla in that article further discusses other contactees similarly claiming to have encountered extraterrestrials acting like ordinary citizens. Finally, Dr. Salla in "Extraterrestrials Among Us" examines the official testimony of a number of whistleblowers concerning knowledge that extraterrestrials live among ordinary Earth-bound individuals.

Contact Testimonies of 'Extraterrestrials Among Us'

Adamski's famous *"Desert Center"* meeting with an extraterrestrial emerging from a 'scout ship' on November 20, 1952 was apparently seen by six witnesses who signed affidavits confirming Adamski's version of events in his subsequent book, *The Flying Saucers have Landed* (1953).

In fact, four of the witnesses immediately reported what had happened to a nearby newspaper, the *Phoenix Gazette* that published a story on November 24 featuring photos and sketches. The *Desert Center* encounter was among those of Adamski's claims regarding extraterrestrial contact that, according to UFO researcher Timothy Good, were "accurately reported," and "sensible and verifiable", as footnotes by Dr. Salla.

Given the clear supporting evidence supporting Adamski's first meeting with an extraterrestrial traveling in a scout craft, it is worth examining closely his alleged subsequent meetings with extraterrestrials living on Earth.

In the first chapter of *Inside the Flying Saucers*, Dr. Salla re-visits Adamski's testimony of his meeting with two extraterrestrials while he was sitting in the lobby of a Los Angeles Hotel on February 18, 1953.

"I looked at my wrist watch and saw that it said ten-thirty. The lateness of the hour, with still nothing of extraordinary significance having taken place, sent a wave of disappointment through me. And just at this moment of depression, two men approached, one of whom addressed me by name.

Both were complete strangers, but there was no hesitancy in their manner as they came forward, and nothing in their appearance to indicate that they were other than average young businessmen... I noted that both men were well proportioned. One was slightly over six feet and looked to be in his early thirties. His complexion was ruddy, his eyes dark brown, with the kind of sparkle that suggests great enjoyment of life. His gaze was extraordinarily penetrating.

His black hair waved and was cut according to our style. He wore a dark brown business suit but no hat. The shorter man looked younger and I judged his height to be about five feet, nine inches. He had a round boyish face, a fair complexion and eyes of grayish blue. His hair, also wavy and worn in our style, was sandy in color. He was dressed in a gray suit and was also hatless. He smiled as he addressed me by name. As I acknowledged the greeting, the speaker extended his hand and when it touched mine a great joy filled me. The signal was the same as had been given by the man I had met on the desert on that memorable November 20, 1952." (Described in the book Flying Saucers Have Landed). Significant in Adamski's description is how the two extraterrestrials could pass off as businessmen. Aside from a penetrating stare, nothing struck him as unusual in their appearance.

Adamski goes on to explain how he went with them in their car to travel to a remote desert location:

"Together we left the lobby, I walking between them. About a block north of the hotel, they turned into a parking lot where they had a car waiting. They had not spoken during this short time, yet inwardly I knew that these men were true friends. I felt no urge to ask where they proposed to take me, nor did it seem odd that they had volunteered no information. An attendant brought the car around, and the younger man slid into the driver's seat, motioning me to get in beside him.

Our other companion also sat with us on the front seat. The car was a four-door black Pontiac sedan. The man who had taken the wheel seemed to know exactly where he was going and drove skillfully. I am not familiar with all the new highways leading out of Los Angeles, so I had no idea in which direction we were headed. We rode in silence and I remained entirely content to wait for my companions to identify themselves and explain the reason for our meeting."

"What's significant here is that the two extraterrestrials possessed a car and knew how to navigate on the newly completed Los Angeles highway system. This is no mean feat and suggests that the extraterrestrials had taken the time to learn the road traffic rules and how to navigate through Los Angeles."

Dr. Salla indicates in "Extraterrestrials Among Us", that Adamski further reveals: "Lights and dwellings thinned as we left the outskirts of the city. The taller man spoke for the first time... His voice was soft and pleasant and his English perfect. I had noticed that the younger man also spoke softly, although his voice was pitched higher. I found myself wondering how and where they had learned to speak our language so well. We are what you on Earth might call 'Contact men.' We live and work here, because, as you know, it is necessary on Earth to earn money with which to buy clothing, food, and the many things that people must have. We have lived on your planet now for several years.

At first we did have a slight accent. But that has been overcome and, as you can see, we are unrecognized as other than Earth men. At our work and in our leisure time we mingle with people here on Earth, never betraying the secret that we are inhabitants of other worlds. That would be dangerous, as you well know. We understand you people better than most of you know yourselves and can plainly see the reasons for many of the unhappy conditions that surround you."

257

> **Extraterrestrials have spent years living on Earth, learning the language, getting jobs and mixing with the human population**

Dr. Salla indicates also that, "This passage [previous] is significant since it describes how the extraterrestrials have spent years living on Earth, learning the language, getting jobs and mixing with the human population. Furthermore, it appears as though extraterrestrials living among the human population may work in pairs, a kind of buddy system that would make sense in terms of ensuring safety and communications with the home world if an emergency ever occurred. If Adamski is accurate in his recollections and the extraterrestrials are telling the truth, then it would appear that there could be a significant number of extraterrestrials who are living incognito among the normal population in many if not most major cities on the planet. Upon examining other contactee cases and the testimonies of whistleblowers, it does appear as though this is indeed the case."

Exopolitics groups furthermore provide additional representation that Adamski was not the only one of the contactees who are making representation that the extraterrestrials were blending in with the human population. Howard Menger, for example, also claimed to have been contacted by extraterrestrials posing as ordinary human citizens. In one case, the extraterrestrial was posing as a real estate salesperson and asked Menger to accompany him in one of the extraterrestrial's vehicle. In addition to seeking to learn about human values and civilization, it appears that "Human ET" visitors were conducting a low key education effort to promote awareness of their presence to a limited number of individual 'contactees'.

These "Human extraterrestrial visitors" have been represented has often having as very attractive physical characteristics, with "Human extraterrestrial females" being described as among the most beautiful women that male observers have witnessed.

The "Human extraterrestrials visitors" furthermore have been represented as going to great trouble in learning the indigenous language of the culture they are immersed in, learning how to drive and navigate on highways systems, and taking innocuous jobs over several years.

"Extraterrestrials Living Among Us" appear to be operating in a manner similar to a "celestial peace corps" where they try to blend in. They presumably wish to learn about Earth culture and behaviour; and to, perhaps, assist in passing on information to selected individuals.

Representation on Earth Humans relative to "non-Earthbound" humans

Advanced Human ETs view Earth Humans as barbarians and savages, and as a threat to themselves

Alex Collier alleges that ETs revealed to his that there are over 135 other billion human beings in the 8 galaxies closest to ours.

Alex Collier alleges that, "The first time I walked on to one of their ships [Human ETs] , a bunch of their children started to run away from me.

They knew that I was from Earth. We have a very bad reputation," Alex Collier indicates, "because we are the only human race in the galaxy that kills itself, that turns on itself. We are the only race [human] that allows itself to live in poverty. We are the only ones who allow members of our race to starve. We are the only ones that allow members of the race to be homeless. We are the only race that would sell itself into slavery. I don't like the reflection they give me of us. It's not that they are judging. They just don't understand why we do it. If anyone's got an answer for it, I'm open. Yes, we've been manipulated by belief systems, but why do we believe these belief systems?"

According to testimony by Alex Collier in associated with alleged ET contacts, Earth Humans "are the only race of human beings which oppresses and kills itself."

If Human ETs do exist, as scholarly and other representation suggests, the saving of Humanity from its current apparent course of self-destruction, including on-going catastrophic Global Warming, may very well vitally rely on human governance systems placing its greed-driven bigotries aside, toward a constructive dialogue.

Star Visitors Living Among Us on Earth

"I am struck with the synchronicity of the emergence of the book, "Raechel's Eyes" revealing what went on at Area 51 decades ago about ambassadorial hospitality offered various visiting Star Beings and Zeta hybrids, at about the same time that Charles James Hall was Weather Range Officer at Indian Wells Auxiliary Air Force Station about 95 miles south of Area 51, also at the Nellis Air Force Range. Hall tells of his contacts with Tall White humanoid Star Visitors on the IWAAFS ranges, in his book, "Millenial Hospitality". Is this the government's Public Acclimation Program allowing private authors to actually publish tell-all books that actually see the light of day in public view?" - *Richard Boylan, Ph.D.*

The "Tall Whites": An alien race from a location near but behind the Arcturus star system

Dr. Boylan stated that recent communication exchange with former USAF Airman Charles J. Hall, author of the "Millennial Hospitality" trilogy, coupled with content revealed in his books, brings forth the following interesting revelations.

There exists an extraterrestrial race whom Mr. Hall has called the Tall Whites. This race originates from a location near but behind the Arcturus star system. These Tall Whites are in adulthood around six feet in height and have generally humanoid features.

They have blond hair, generally worn short, and the women tend to wear their hair in a feminine form of short cut. They are blue-eyed, and have larger-than-human eyes which wrap part-way around the side of their head.

The Tall Whites look quite human

The Tall Whites otherwise look quite human, except that their skin is a chalky-white in color. They have hands with four fingers, which do not end in finger nails but rather in harder, two-inch-long claw-like appendages. The typical clothing of the Tall Whites is an aluminized, chalk-white jump suit of canvas-looking fabric. They also wear gloves of the same material, and an open, white, motorcycle-like helmet. Both the suit and the helmet emit a three-inch-out field of soft-white flourescent light. The intensity of this emitted light can be varied from soft to too bright to look at without strain.

These Tall Whites have very high intelligence and an information-processing speed which Mr. Hall estimates at 3-1/2 times faster than bright humans. The Tall Whites's technology is advanced. One element of their technology is a transporter suit which they put on which provides personal antigravity levitation and above-ground movement, as well as force-field protection against attacks, e.g., would slow a bullet to where it would fall to the ground.

Description of the Spaceships of the "Tall Whites" Aliens

Another element of their technology is their spacecraft. They operate smaller scout ships which can transport a limited number of individuals. And then they have deep-space vessels than can travel between star systems. Their scout craft are white in color, ellipsoidal or egg-shaped, with a molded flat bottom. It has a row of large windows on each side, sort of like an airplane. Its size is comparable to that of a passenger train's diesel engine, and has two windows in front like such a train diesel engine. The range of these scout craft permit travel as far as the Moon or even Mars.

But not deep space. Their deep space vessels are very large, sleek, black antigravity craft, 70 feet high, 300 feet wide, and 500 feet long. These vessels also have pilot windows, as well as have regularly-spaced running lights along their edges. Their range extends out many light years into space. Their top speed exceeds the speed of light by a considerable margin. Yes, Einstein was wrong about that.

The "Tall Whites" in their interactions with humans often carry stun devices for protection

The Tall Whites in their interactions with humans often carry stun devices for protection, eight-inch-long white tubes which can emit a microwave beam that can excite the sodium atoms in the nervous system of a threatening human and render the human unconscious for a limited period of time.

A contingent of Tall Whites have been resident in the Indian Springs Valley region of central Nevada since before the first Euro-American settlers moved west. These Tall Whites have found Earth to be a convenient way-station in their travels within this sector of the galaxy.

As Charles Hall explains it, Earth's sun is located in the middle of a very large, 10-light-year-diameter almost-empty section of the galaxy.

Most stars occur in groups, with another star within two light-months distance.

Earth serves as a handy mid-way rest

Thus, for civilizations living on star systems near this near-empty space "bubble", Earth serves as a handy mid-way rest, supply and repair station. The Tall Whites have established a residential location within French Peak, about 25 miles north-northwest of Indian Springs Auxiliary Air Force Station, Nevada.

Aliens have a base at Dog Bone Lake, 25 miles east of French Peak on the Nellis Air Force Range, Nevada.

They also have a main base and space vehicle repair facility which is also built into the side of a hill at the north end of Indian Springs Valley, not too many miles from their residential location.

When Tall Whites deep-space vessels approach Earth from space, they make an initial landing at Dog Bone Lake, 25 miles east of French Peak on the Nellis Air Force Range, Nevada. Then they make a lateral transition to the main hanger, where huge doors part to admit the vessel, then re-close.

Presidents (including LBJ), select top Senators and Congressmembers, and select Generals and Admirals are aware of, and have actually met Tall Whites, either at carefully arranged events in Washington, DC, or on the Nellis Air Force Base Range, Nevada.

The Tall Whites have made arrangements with the U.S. government at the highest levels

The Tall Whites have made arrangements with the U.S. government at the highest levels to have their central-Nevada facilities undisturbed. In exchange they provide advanced scientific and technological information which has permitted rapid advances in science and technology on Earth. Some of their scientists work as technical consultants at advanced laboratory installations, including northern California, Nevada, and elsewhere.

Visitors from other star system to come and study the English language and American culture.

The Tall Whites facilities in central Nevada serve as locale for Visitors from other star system to come and study the English language and American culture. These Visitors aree intensely curious about life and customs on Earth.

A Zeta-human hybrid teenage girl lives as a college student at Lost River College in California

Helen Littrell, along with co-author Jean Bilodeaux, provides parallel and corroborative information in her new book, "Raechel's Eyes". This book tells the gripping story of how a compassionate Air Force officer on a Perimeter Security Team befriended a Zeta Reticulan survivor, who happened to be a Zeta-human hybrid teenage girl. The Zeta Reticuli star system is seen from Earth's southern hemisphere, and is about 39 light-years distant. The book chronicles his subsequent daring experiment, authorized by the National Security Council through the Air Force's Aerospace Technical Information Command, to adopt this hybrid, now dubbed "Raechel", and let her try out living a normal life as a college student at Lost River College in California, while living as a roommate with the author's daughter, Marisa.

Her adoptive Colonel "father" was stationed at an Air Force Base near his adoptive daughter's college.

"Raechel's Eyes" also provides an accurate picture, minus the usual disinformation in such matters, as to what really goes on below the surface of the heretofore undisclosed "Four Corners" base, which is sister to and apparently north of the better-known Area 51 Complex in the central Nevada desert.

"Four Corners" base is a U.S. Government-run Star Visitor Reception Area and Ambassadorial Interface Facility for representatives from the Intergallactic Council.

"Four Corners", (which is misleadingly not anywhere near the real U.S. Southwest Four Corners area), is actually a U.S. Government-run Star Visitor Reception Area and Ambassadorial Interface Facility for representatives from the Intergallactic Council. And it also serves as a cultural integration and tutoring place for those Star Visitors who want to fit in and be able to walk around and observe Earth while passing for human. This latter effort is called the Humanization Project. "Raechel's Eyes" closely parallels information about the underground activity at Area 51, leaked by Army Command Sergeant-Major Robert Dean, the NSC's Dr. Michael Wolf, former [Area 51] Site S-4 physicist Robert Lazar, and USAF "Project Pounce" head, Colonel Steve Wilson.

I believe that all Star Kids and Star Seeds will find the day-to-day struggle of hybrid Raechel, and of the Tall Whites residing at Indian Wells Valley, to try to get accepted in the human world to be an Nth-degree case of the basic struggle so many Star Kids (and Star Seed adults) experience in trying to define themselves, and be openly who they are without the rejection, ridicule and avoidance too many humans dish out to someone who is different.

Tall White Alien passing for human with disguise

And different can be Zeta-human hybrid, Tall White passing for human with disguise, or a human Star Kid or Star Seed whose advanced abilities "just aren't normal". As "regular" humans learn to accept their own children, the Star Kids, perhaps this will accelerate the day when the public is ready to accept the Zeta-human hybrid "Raechels" and Tall White "Harry's" of the galaxy as just other people here to visit.

The Tall Whites have established a residential location within French Peak, about 25 miles north-northwest of Indian Springs Auxiliary Air Force Station, Nevada.

Charles Hall wrote me concerning this: "I do believe that in the 1965 - 1967 time frame, the Tall Whites did have an additional scout craft hanger and rest area located near the top of French Peak, because I frequently saw them in their scout craft entering and leaving the valley below French Peak and entering Indian Springs valley."

Also the range maintainence men told me on many occasions that the Tall Whites had such a hanger and they frequently observed them when they were up on the mountain.

"Remember, as described in book II, the Tall Whites had several such scout craft hangers and rest areas located in the northern portion of the Indian Springs valley, in addition to their base and main hanger. "

The main housing area for the Tall Whites was located underground

However, I, myself, never actually saw the Tall Whites up on French Peak, partly because I very very seldom went over to that valley, and the mountain was not visible from Range #3. "The French Peak site, however, in 1965-1967 was not their main housing area. The mountains at the north end of Indian Springs Valley have two main peaks. The main housing area for the Tall Whites was located underground where I have indicated it on the maps. That peak was the peak located immediately north-north-west of the peak that contained the main hanger.

"Remember that there still exists a significant number of my personal experiences that I have not yet captured on paper or verbally described, for various reasons."For example the UASF captain and pilot of the twin engine Cessina plane that came out from the Pentagon at the end of every month, did not stop at French Peak.

He did not stop at Area 51 or at Groom Lake. He landed on the short runways located in the valley north of the main Tall White hanger and landed again at the short runway located at the base of the alien housing area. "He also made a third langing up in that vicinity, before returning to Indian Springs to refuel.

"I have no idea what the status of French Peak or the Indian Springs facilities are today.

However, in the 1965-1967 time frame, the Tall White facilities and their locations were so excellent, allowing their deep space craft to arrive using Dog Bone Lake as an arrival/landing area, I wouldn't think that they would easily agree to any changes. [Regarding the Tall Whites Star Visitors' hand and fingers], about which I (Richard Boylan) had asked whether they have hands with four fingers, and whether they end not in finger nails but rather in harder, two-inch-long claw-like appendages?

Charles Hall replies: "The claws were probably artifical and worn for self defense. I was never sure. "One night when I was out at Range #3, I saw the Teacher standing with her arms crossed with her hands resting on her upper arms. On that evening, she was certainly wearing 2-inch long claws.

> **Female alien disguised as a human woman, DownTown Las Vegas outside the Hotel Fremont and Casino.**

On a different evening, I saw her in DownTown Las Vegas outside the Hotel Fremont and Casino. On that evening she was disguised as a human woman, and she was definitely not wearing claws.

"The Tall Whites are quite frail by human standards. Their arms and hands do not have anywhere near the strength that human arms and hands have. The wearing of artifical sharp claws would provide them with a set of weapons with which they could defend themselves against bees, hornets, snakes, etc. Such artifical claws would also be quite useful as tools when outside in a Nevada desert environment.

"Incidentally I do not have any problem with the statement, 'Mr. Hall estimates at 3-1/2 times faster than bright humans,' because the best I could do was only to form a rough estimate. However, in Book #1, in the chapter entitled "Olympic Tryouts", I carefully timed Range Four Harry when he was running northwest from the corner of my barracks out into the open desert, and he was running at approximately 35 mph.

Tall White aliens' nervous system is roughly 2 to 2-and-a-half times faster than the human nervous system operates

"Since the Olympic world record for humans for the mile run is only 15 miles per hour, that would mean the the Tall White alien known as Range Four Harry had a nervous system that was operating at approximately 35/15 = roughly 2 to 2-and-a-half times faster than the human nervous system operates.

"Of course, when I timed myself, the fastest that I could run was just barely 7 miles per hour. So Range Four Harry's nervous system might have been running 35/7 = 5 time faster than mine. I can only guess..."For example, I do not know where the home planet of the Tall Whites is located, but I feel certain that they arrive here on earth from the direction of the star Arcturus (book 2, chapter "Olympic Dreams").

I guessed at the time that their home planet orbited a star located approximately 105 light years from earth, whereas Arcturus is located at 36 light years from earth. However, that was only my best guess based on my personal observations at the time. The Tall Whites, themselves, would never say. "The Teacher stated that Pamela had never been back to their home planet, and that Pamela had been born in Indian Springs Valley when James Madison was President, (i.e. approximately the year 1812), (book III, Chapter "The End of the Innocence.")

*** *** ***

Humanoid Star Visitor race (Sammi People "Norwegians") live above the Arctic Circle in Norway, Finland, Sweden and a northwestern peninsula of Russia

I (Richard Boylan) think it should be emphasized that Charles Hall does not claim that the Tall Whites come from Arcturus, but rather from a location/star system many light years far "behind" Arcturus (from Earth's point-of-view). And that is his conjecture based on comments from the Tall Whites. Thus, I think one should be hesitant to call the Tall Whites "Arcturians".

I am enclosing below an excerpt from Chief Golden Eagle/Standing Elk's 1996 Star Knowledge Conference, because a Speaker there, former Acting Surgeon-General of Finland, Dr. Rauni Kilde, MD, spoke about the Sammi people. This is apropos of Airman Charles Hall's mention of not only the Tall Whites Star Visitors having a resident contingent on Earth, but also that he knew of another humanoid Star Visitor race that he dubbed the "Norwegians" (actually, Laplanders or Sammi people). These Sammi people live above the Arctic Circle in Norway, Finland, Sweden and a northwestern peninsula of Russia.

They have their own distinctive language, and traditionally survived by herding reindeer.

They have their own distinctive language, and traditionally survived by herding reindeer. They have only 24 teeth instead of the usual 32 found in "regular" humans. Further the Sammi have another set of reserve teeth below the gum-line ready to grow into place if an adult tooth falls out. Their teeth also have much shorter roots than the "regular" human tooth. But Dr. Rauni herself has not been involved in any diagnosis of hypodontia among the Sammi people that she lived among.

Hall heard of some of these "Norwegian" Sammi who emigrated to the United States immigrants, and generally settled in northern-tier states like Wisconsin.

It is fascinating, I think, to learn that a race from the stars who look so much like us that they "pass" undetected, and who calmly reside among us, while Carl Sagan & the SETI Project had been desperately sending radio signals out into space to see if there is any intelligent life out there.

[Star Knowledge Conference - 1996 extract:] "Finnish physician Rauni-Leena Kilde spoke of her extraterrestrial experiences among the Sammi (Laplander) people she was raised with above the Arctic Circle and in Scandinavia. Her first remembered contact was when she was in a severe car crash. As she laid there mortally injured, a small Star Visitor (not a Sammi) was at her side working on healing her injured liver. Later the hospital staff could not understand how she survived the crash. Later she remembered Star Visitor contacts as a child living among the Sammi. She reported that there is a change of attitude in Scandinavia and the European Union about cosmic contacts. She hears positive reactions to Star Visitor encounters. In Scandinavia the so-called "Grey" aliens are rare. Most common there are the small, short, wrinkled "Dwarf" Star Visitors. [The Gnomes?] Her country borders Russia, whose cosmonauts were threatened with death if they talked openly about UFO encounters."

Former U.S. Air Force Airman Charles Hall: "I personally and frequently observed on many separate occasions the tall white scout craft and the Tall Whites..."

Former U.S. Air Force Airman Charles Hall, author of the "Millennial Hospitality" trilogy, has more to reveal about what he learned while serving at Nellis Air Force Base Range proximate to the locations of the resident Tall Whites Star Visitors. In personal email to me, Charles stated: "During the two and a half years that I spent at Nellis AFB and at Indian Springs, Nevada, I had a significant number of personal experiences that are not related in my three books for various reasons."

There are at least two groups of such experiences that you will probably wish to discuss with me in person, since I am not able to properly relate them in this short email. "The first group of experiences is centered on the location of the Tall White facilities located near the peak of French Peak.

In the 1965-1967 time frame, I personally and frequently observed on many separate occasions the tall white scout craft and the Tall Whites entering and leaving the valley just below French Peak.

Several of the range maintaince men at that time informed me that the Tall Whites had at least a scout craft base dug in toward the top of French Peak in addition to their main base at the north end of Indian Springs Valley.

*** *** ***

The deep space craft always arrived from space and departed back into space by using Dog Bone [Dry] Lake as their landing...

"However, the deep space craft always arrived from space and departed back into space by using Dog Bone [Dry] Lake as their landing, and their deep space approach area. Once the deep space had arrived (or landed) by hovering out over Dog Bone Lake, the Tall Whites seemed to greatly prefer to bring the deep space directly and immediately to a landing out in front of the main hanger on the mountains where the hanger was located.

The deep space craft were not very maneuverable once they had arrived here on earth, and the Tall Whites greatly preferred to park it in the main hanger as quickly as they could."

*** *** ***

"I personally witnessed the Tall Whites, using their scout craft, with small groups of high ranking American generals on board apparently taking short tours of the Moon."

"No matter where their various facilities are located, I would expect that they would still be using Dog Bone Lake as their landing area. The second group of experiences are centered on several times that I personnally witnessed the Tall Whites, using their scout craft, with small groups of high ranking American generals on board apparently taking short tours of the Moon. They would do so when the Moon was just a few days past the fourth quarter.

They would take off just after sunrise from Indian Springs Valley, head straight towards the sunlight side of the Moon (which would be directly overhead at the time), and return to Indian Springs Valley just before noon. "When the American Generals got off the craft they would be laughing like children who were just returning from Disneyland. I feel certain that they had been to the Moon and back. "I have always believed that the Americans have a base on the Moon possibly located in the crater Ar[i]starchus (? spell) For that reason, I believe it is entirely possible that high resolution pictures of that area of the Moon also show building, hangers, and other structures which could well be American-Made. "

I met with Charles Hall and his gracious wife, Marie Therese, Monday night, December 6, 2004 in San Francisco, where he was attending the Oracle computer convention. (Mr. Hall is a computer consultant now, in addition to having a Master's degree in nuclear physics. He currently holds a Secret Clearance, and in the past has held a Top Secret Clearance as well as a Department of Energy Q Clearance.

We discussed the various matters relating to his experience with the Tall Whites and related matters. Interestingly, he states that "None of my work at Indian Springs [Auxiliary Air Force Station, Nevada Test Range] was ever classified, although my orders were very highly classified."

In our conversation, Mr. Hall explained that the reason his orders assigning him to Indian Springs AAFS were so "very highly classified" is because the interview he had at Nellis Air Force Base before getting assigned to Indian Springs AAFS included Tall Whites Star Visitors as well as Air Force officials as members of the interview team.

The Tall Whites Star Visitors wore disguise, but Mr. Hall in retrospect recognized who they were after his exposure to the Tall Whites on the Indian Springs AAFS Ranges.

Mr. Hall indicated he was aware of sensitive installations at Area 51 (Groom Dry Lake Base) and Area 52 (Papoose Dry Lake satellite Base, aka S-4) as well as several other Areas on the Nellis Air Force Base Range. In these latter Areas, the Tall Whites were also present.

There are five areas of "gravity anomaly" on the Moon

Mr. Hall never went to the Area 51 facilities nor the S-4 Papoose Lake facilities, because all he would be able to see where the above-ground buildings and entrance doors to within-mountain facilities, which were of minimal interest. And there was always the possibility of a mix-up and getting accosted or worse by guards who were unaware of his special permission to roam the entire NAFB Range (surface). As regards Air Force generals being taken on one-day round-trip rides to the Moon and back by Tall Whites in the Tall Whites' space vehicles in the time-frame 1965-67, it certainly boggles the mind to know that at that very same time, Air Force Public Information Officers were publicly stoutly discrediting any civilian reports of flying saucers.

United States has a base on the Moon

Mr. White indicated that there are some things he is not free to talk about, but that he is aware that there are five areas of "gravity anomaly" on the Moon, and strongly hinted that these were related to Star Visitor installations there.

He also stated his belief that the United States has a base on the Moon, and that his personal inclination is that it is located in Crater Aristarchus. (Parenthetically, I note that NSC consultant Dr. Michael Wolf also told me that the U.S. had a base on the Moon, and a tiny station on Mars.)

(Also, parenthetically, I can now better understand why the Powers That Be threw a royal hissie fit when the UK television documentary, "Alternative Three" came out years ago touting a get-away base on Mars. Though subsequently disowned as "a prank", the documentary came too close to the truth, it would seem.)

Another Star Visitor race (Laplanders) that has been resident on earth for some time

Mr. Hall and I also discussed another Star Visitor race that has been resident on Earth for some time, and is represented among the Sammi (Laplanders) people of the northern region of Norway (and adjacent states) above the Arctic Circle. These special "Norwegians" are noted for their having 24 teeth instead of the normal human count of 32. Charles repeated his anecdote about some of these Sammi Star Visitors becoming stranded here after their craft was damaged during the 20 light-year voyage from their home world (perhaps Barnard's Star), and that they could not return, and so settled in a lightly-populated sector of the polar regions, which has a climate similar to their home world.

An Air Force Colonel reveals the existence of United States government undisclosed Nevada base for Visitors from various star systems around the galaxy.

I told Charles Hall of my finding clinical reports of a high prevalency of hypodontia (fewer-than-normal teeth) among young Sammi adults studied in Scandinavia even despite some amount of intermarriage between the Sammi and European people in Scandinavia.

When I asked Mr. White if he had ever been approached by the equivalent of the Men-In-Black or any other government agents and been told to keep quiet about his experiences, he said he had not. Thus, I am left to conclude that his being allowed to publish his experiences is another step in the Public Acclimation Program's effort to acquaint and acclimate the American public to not only UFO reality, but also the presence of resident Star Visitors among us. And these "Resident Aliens" do not have Green Cards. :-) (And to avoid any misunderstanding, I do not think that Charles Hall is consciously a participant in the Public Acclimation Program.)

A United States Air Force Colonel adopts a Zeta-human hybrid daughter

The government's Public Acclimation Program, in passively "allowing" Helen Littrell to come out publicly with her account of her daughter's having been roommates with a Zeta-human hybrid, Raechel, as fellow junior college students, and Raechel's adoptive father, an Air Force Colonel revealing to Helen that the government maintains an undisclosed Nevada base, "Four Corners", at which contingents of Visitors from various star systems around the galaxy are welcomed and provided hospitality, orientation, and education in Earth language and customs; and in "allowing" Charles Hall to tell of almost-daily contacts with the Tall Whites on the Nellis Air Force Base Range, as well as his knowledge of Sammi Star Visitors immigrating to the United States from Norway many decades ago, has *substantially* raised the bar on what the public is allowed to be aware of.

We have come far from faltering admissions by former Air Force officers that certain UFO photos are authentic. The well-informed members of today's public can now know that U.S. Air Force generals have been engaging in junkets to the Moon aboard Star Visitor-manned space craft since almost forty years ago.

The well-informed public is now allowed also to know from a retired military serviceman that the Star Visitors are not only visiting, but some of them are in residence here, and some of these Visitors have been resident on Western American soil since before the white man came.

The Sci-Fi movie poster says, "We are among you."

Only it isn't science fiction. And just think: no War of the Worlds has happened!

Can interstellar peaceful coexistence be in our future?

Why not?

It has already been going on for centuries.

- Richard Boylan, Ph.D.

Anunnaki Also Landed in Ancient Africa. They're Still There

> ### The Tale of Credo Mutwa, a Zulu shaman

Sometimes, you can read or hear something and the sincerity of the narration is unmistakeable. This man, Credo Mutwa, a Zulu shaman, had a tale to tell...and what a tale it is. Below, is an unedited excerpt:

From Credo Mutwa on alien abduction and Reptilians

Our people believe, sir, that we, the people of this Earth, are not masters of our own lives, really, although we are made to think that we are. Our people say, that is, Black people of all tribes, all of the initiated ones, all of the shamans everywhere in Africa, when they get to trust you and share their deepest secrets with you, they say that [with] the Imanujela, there is Imbulu. And there is another name by which these creatures are known. This name is Chitauli. Now, the word Chitauli means "the dictators, the ones who tell us the law". In other words, "they who tell us, secretly, what we are to do."

(BG: in Sumerian SITA UL I = "Beings of splendor/ancients, who dominate, dictators" This lends support to the evidence that there was knowledge of the same Anunnaki "gods" in Africa as well as in ancient Sumer.)

Now, it is said that these Chitauli did a number of things to us when they came to this planet. Please forgive me, but I must share this story with you. It is one of the strangest stories that you find everywhere in Africa in shamanic secret societies and other places where the remnant of our ancient knowledge and wisdom are still preserved. It is that, originally, the Earth was covered by a very thick blanket of fog or mist. That people could not actually see the Sun in the sky, except as a nimble of light. And they also saw the Moon at night as a gentle claw of light in the sky, because there was this heavy mist. And the rain was always falling in a steady drizzle. There was no thunder, however. There were no storms.

BG: This is an exact description of the condition of the Earth during the time of Atlantis.

Mutwa: The world was thickly covered with great forests, great jungles, and people lived in peace on Earth at that time. People were happy and it is said, at that time, we human beings did not have the power of speech. We only made funny sounds like happy monkeys and baboons, but we did not have speech as we now have it. And in those centuries, people spoke to each other through their mind.

272

A man could call his wife thinking about her, thinking about the shape of her face, the smell of her body, and the feel of hair as a woman. That a hunter would go out into the bush and call out for animals to come, and the animals would select one of their number which was old and tired, and this animal would offer itself to the hunter so that he may kill it quickly and take it as meat to his cave.

There was no violence against animals. There was no violence against Nature by human beings at that time. Man used to ask for food from Nature. He used to come to a tree and think about fruit, and the tree would allow some of its fruit to fall to the ground, and man would take it.

The Chitauli came to Earth in terrible vessels which flew through the air, shaped like great bowls

And then it is said, however, that when the Chitauli came to Earth, they arrived in terrible vessels which flew through the air, vessels which were shaped like great bowls and which made a terrible noise and a terrible fire in the sky. And the Chitauli told human beings, whom they gathered together by force with whips of lightning, that they were great gods from the sky and that from now on they would receive a number of great gifts from the god. These so-called gods, who were like human beings, but very tall, with a long tail, and with terrible burning eyes, some of them had two eyes-yellow, bright eyes-some had three eyes, the red, round eye being in the center of their forehead (BG: These are known as "Kingu"). These creatures then took away the great powers that human beings had:
- the power of speaking through the mind only
- the power of moving objects with their mind only
- the power of seeing into the future and into their past
- the power to travel, spiritually, to different worlds

The Chitauli gave human beings the power of speech

All of these great powers the Chitauli took away from human beings and they gave human beings a new power, now, the power of speech. But, human beings found, to their horror, that the power of speech divided human beings, instead of uniting them, because the Chitauli cunningly created different languages, and they caused a great quarrel between people.

Also, the Chitauli did something which has never been done before: they gave human beings people to rule over them, and they said, "These are your kings, these are your chiefs. They have our blood in them. They are our children, and you must listen to these people because they will speak on our behalf. If you don't, we are going punish you very terribly."

Before the coming of the Chitauli, before the coming of the Imbulu creatures, human beings were spiritually one. But when the Chitauli came, human beings became divided, both spiritually as well as by language.

273

When the Chitauli gets sick this way, a young girl, a virgin, is usually kidnapped

Now, there is another thing, sir: It is that one of the things that the Chitauli like to do in their underground caves, where many fires are always kept ablaze, we are told, is that when a Chitauli gets sick and starts to lose a large area of skin on his body, it is said that there is a disease that the Chitauli suffer from which causes them to lose large areas of their skin, leaving only raw flesh [BG: certain species of the reptilian Anunna do "molt", or shed their skin periodically.)

When the Chitauli gets sick this way, a young girl, a virgin, is usually kidnapped by the servant of the Chitauli and is brought to the underground place. There the girl is bound, hand and foot, and wrapped in a golden blanket, and is forced to lie next to the Chitauli, the sick Chitauli, week after week, being well fed and well cared for, but kept bound hand and foot, and only released at certain times to relieve herself. It is said that after the sick Chitauli shows signs of getting better, then the human girl is manipulated into trying to escape. She is given a chance to escape, a chance which is really not a chance. Then, when the girl escapes, she runs, but she is pursued over a long distance underground by flying creatures which are made of metal, and she is recaptured when she reaches the height of fear and exhaustion.

Then she is laid on an altar, usually a rough rock, flat on top. Then, she is cruelly sacrificed, sir, and her blood is drunk by the sick Chitauli, which then recovers. But, the girl must not be sacrificed until she is very, very, very frightened, because if she is not frightened, it is said that her blood will not save the sick Chitauli. It must be the blood of a very frightened human being, indeed.

Now, this habit of chasing a victim was also practiced by ordinary African cannibals, sir. In Zulu-land, in the last century, there were cannibals who used to eat people, and their descendants, even today, will tell you, if they trust you, that the flesh of the human being who has been frightened and made to run over a great distance, while trying to escape, tastes far better than the flesh of someone who was simply killed. (Source: ThothWeb)

*** *** ***

CHAPTER 12
REMNANTS
OF
THE ANUNNAKI AMONG US
WHY ARE THEY HERE?

- The Aliens have manipulated and/or ruled the human race through various secret societies, religion, magic
- The Anunnaki created humanity in order to exploit it as a slave race
- Dr. Courtney Brown: Remnants of Anunnaki are hidden on earth
- Clandestine government agencies are aware of the Anunnaki remnants on Earth
- The "Helper Perspective"
- According to this perspective, the 'helper ETs' are here to assist humanity
- Helper ETs pass down knowledge of advanced technologies and alternative energy
- Dr. Richard Boylan: B2 stealth bomber uses anti-gravity technology not fuel as the general public believes
- Captain Robert Salas: 16 nuclear-armed missiles were disarmed by UFOs hovering over NORAD
- The helper ETs describe the Milky Way galaxy, as being populated by numerous advanced civilizations
- Advanced universe civilizations exist in other dimensions parallel to our own
- The "Watcher Perspective"
- The Mayan calendar
- The Watcher ETs are here to learn how humanity deals with the energy shifts
- ETs decided to sponsor a hybrid race that would comprise the diverse genetic pools
- Earth is the third of 3 grand experiments in polarity integration

*** *** ***

Remnants of the Anunnaki Among Us
___WHY ARE THEY HERE?___

Dr. Michael Salla in his outstanding essay on the "Manipulator Perspective", stated that this perspective covers conspiracy theories suggesting that an advanced race of ETs with enhanced psychic abilities and superior technology, has been either overtly controlling or covertly manipulating humanity ever since the first human presence on the planet.

The Aliens have manipulated and/or ruled the human race through various secret societies, religion, magic

Elaborating on this theme of ET 'manipulation', Bill Cooper writes: "[t]hroughout our history, the Aliens have manipulated and/or ruled the human race through various secret societies, religion, magic, witchcraft, and the occult."[60] It is claimed that these ETs played a direct role in creating the human species as a sources of slave labor, and therefore feel entitled and even responsible for guiding-controlling the human race either overtly by direct control or covertly through human proxies. According to the William Bramley...the human race was once a source of labor for an extraterrestrial civilization and still remains a possession today. To keep control over its possession and to maintain Earth as something of a prison, that other civilizatation ("Custodians") has bred never-ending conflict between human beings, has promoted human spiritual decay, and has erected on Earth conditions of unremitting physical hardship. This situation has lasted for thousands of years and it continues today.[61]

The Anunnaki created humanity in order to exploit it as a slave race

One of the most widely cited scholarly sources for conspiracy theorists falling into this perspective is the Sumerian scholar Zechariah Sitchin.[62] In his translations of thousands of Sumerian cuneiform texts, Sitchin describes how an ancient ET race, described by the Sumerians as the Anunnaki or as the Nephilim in the Old Testament, created humanity by genetic engineering. Mixing their own DNA with that of the primates then existing on Earth, the Anunnaki created humanity in order to exploit it as a slave race and a natural resource for the Anunnaki.

There were, however, violent disputes between different factions of the Anunnaki that resulted in much regional destruction and decimation of the captive human population.

Sitchin claimed that these are the same beings variously described in the Book of Genesis and the Book of Enoch; and that biblical stories of the Elohim, rebel angels and the Serpent, referred to the conflict between different factions of the Anunnaki over how to manage humanity.[63] There were apparently two distinct races among the Anunnaki, one a humanoid race of giants, while the second was a non-human race that was 'serpent-like' in appearance which has given rise to the more popular term for this race, 'Reptilian'. The author, R.A. Boulay, has extensively analyzed a variety of historic sources and argued that there is sufficient evidence to support the conclusion that an ancient ET race of Reptilians inhabited the Earth and played a role in the creation of humanity.[64] Sitchin describes these ET races as having overt control of the human population for millennia, but then largely disappearing from the scene approximately 4000 years ago after an intense factional battle between them. Presumably, the bulk of the Anunnaki left the scene believing it was no longer necessary to exercise direct rule over a humanity that was ready for self-rule.

However, a rebel cohort that disagreed, remained behind intent on secretly monitoring and influencing human affairs from deep underground ET bases to demonstrate how unfit humanity was to exercise stewardship over the planet Earth. References to 'serpents' in biblical books suggest that elements of the Reptilian race stayed behind.

Such a scenario is consistent with the chronology used by the Egyptian historian Manetho who claimed that prior to the 30 dynasties of human kings that ruled Egypt, there was direct rule by the Gods and the demigods.[65]

*** *** ***

Dr. Courtney Brown: Remnants of Anunnaki are hidden on earth

The view that remnant Anunnaki ETs are hidden on Earth is supported by Dr Courtney Brown and others who have conducted extensive remote viewing sessions on the presence of ET races on and off the planet.[66] Brown has concluded that a rebel faction of Anunnaki, who he and others describe as Reptilians, is concealed on Earth and it is estranged from the larger body of their race.

According to Stewart Swerdlow, who claims to have participated in clandestine government projects located at the Montauk Air force/Naval facility;[67] the investigative journalist, Jim Marrs;[68] and the controversial British author, David Icke;[69] this remaining band of Anunnaki on Earth, has influenced humanity through human proxies derived from ET/human interbreeding that eventually became the aristocratic 'blue bloods' of Europe and other nations.

According to Icke, a race of interbreeding['royal' reptile-human hybrid] bloodlines...were centered in the Middle East and Near East in the ancient world and, over the thousands of years since, have expanded their power across the globe...creating institutions like religions to mentally and emotionally imprison the masses and set them at war with each other.[70]

These human elites maintained certain esoteric traditions by which they could maintain contact with those Anunnaki rebels concealed in different locations on Earth. Brown, Marrs, Bramley, Icke and others claim that this advanced race covertly influences humanity in order to produce resources that sustain these hidden ETs.[71]

The author/channeler Alex Collier, claims that the small number of Anunnaki beings at the moment concealed on Earth eagerly await the return of the Anunnaki elite, who they hope will end the secrecy of the Anunnaki history and presence, and reestablish overt Anunnaki control and end the need to rule covertly through unreliable human proxies.[72] Brown describes the Anunnaki remnants as often being in conflict with the ET intruders, the Grays.[73]

*** *** ***

Clandestine government agencies are aware of the Anunnaki remnants on Earth

In the *Stargate Conspiracy,* Lynne Pickett and Clive Prince describe the process by which this advanced race of ETs established religion as a control instrument for humanity.[74]

They argue that clandestine government agencies are aware of the Anunnaki remnants on Earth and are divided over how to respond to the anticipated return of the Anunnaki elites in the immediate future that may attempt to reestablish overt control over the planet.

Brown, Picknett and Prince claim that clandestine government programs are using 'exotic' technologies such as psychotronic weapons activated by thought, enhanced psychic abilities, 'star gates', and even time travel, to militarily prepare for the return of the Anunnaki who possess a technology supposed to be superior to anything reverse engineered from downed Gray space craft.[75]

A number of individuals who claim to have participated in clandestine military programs with ET races have also reported interacting with or witnessing a large Reptilian species that presumably are associated with the historic Anunnaki presence on the planet.

Andy Pero, who claims to have been recruited as a super soldier by a clandestine government organization, gave testimony of such an encounter: On one occasion I was introduced to a Reptilian being while in an underground base sometime in 1989-90. At first I saw a 7-foot tall human Aryan looking man. He walks towards me and I notice that his image phases out as if something interfered with an energy field.

He does something to a device on his belt and tells me, "OK, I'll show you." He then pushes some button and then I see his image change into a 7-foot tall lizard like creature who looked like he weighed over 400 lb.[76]

According to other participants including Michael Relfe, Al Bielak and Preston Nichols, Reptilian beings are involved with time/interdimensional travel technology, mind control, psychotronics and other exotic weapons.[77]

Conspiracy theories falling into this perspective suggest that humanity needs to counter subversive efforts of the concealed Anunnaki remnants, and prepare for the potential threat posed by the returning Anunnaki who may attempt to deprive humanity of their sovereignty by reestablishing overt control on the basis of global mismanagement by human elites.

This perspective suggests those Anunnaki remnants concealed on Earth continue to manipulate international events through human proxies to create the right international environment to influence the decision of their superiors. War, poverty, and environmental collapse are presumed to constitute the favorable climate for the return of the Anunnaki elites who would present themselves as saviors of humanity who would solve these problems and 'punish' human elites responsible for them. The moral categories used to describe the Anunnaki presence, in contrast to the Gray ET presence, clearly fall into the malevolent end of the moral spectrum. There are few morally redemptive features of the ET presence concealed on Earth, and suspicion over the intentions of the larger body of Anunnaki presumed to be returning. In contrast to the intruder perspective that focused on a clandestine government conspiracy not to reveal the ET presence, this perspective focuses on an ET conspiracy to subvert and control humanity through human proxies.

The primary information sources for conspiracy theories in this perspective are drawn, in order, from the last three categories of Remote Viewing, Independent Archeology, and Channeling. While these sources have weak to moderate evidentiary strength, the small number of 'whistleblowers' who have come forward to support the manipulator perspective suggests ranking this category at the upper end of moderate evidentiary support.

The "Helper Perspective":

According to conspiracy theories that fall into this perspective, ETs are here to help humanity deal with a myriad of political, socioeconomic and environmental problems, but this is not disclosed to the general public by clandestine government agencies. The ETs in this category are described as humanoid in appearance, with a height of 8 feet or more, and often having the physical characteristics of Northern Europeans and typically called Nordics or Semites.[78]

Dr. Michael Wolfe claims to have worked with these humanoid races in secret military facilities in the US, and claims that the "The Semitics and Nordics [ETs] come from Altair 4 and 5 and from the Pleiades [star systems]."[79] A more controversial description of these helper ETs is Billy Meiers who claimed to have been visited by beings from the Pleiades who allowed him to photograph their ships and to have extended communication with him.[80] Meier quickly attained celebrity status and people were coming from around the world to hear his story and the secret history of the ET-Earth connection, and the esoteric ET philosophy.

Some of the principal supporters of the helper perspective include Dr. Steven Greer who has personally interviewed and analyzed hundreds of whistleblower testimonies on the ET presence; Dr. Richard Boylan who has interviewed a range of 'contactees' and military/intelligence 'insiders' with knowledge of the ET presence; and Alfred Webre a former Science adviser to the Carter White House now based at the Stanford Research Institute who is a pioneer in advanced communication techniques with ET races.[81] There are numerous 'channellers' of ET races who also support the perspective of an advanced race of ETs quietly assisting humanity evolve.[82]

*** *** ***

Why Are They Here?

According to this perspective, the 'helper ETs' are here to assist humanity
---

According to this perspective, the 'helper ETs' are here to assist humanity in a number of interrelated ways. First, the helper ETs assist humanity in empowering itself by developing more advanced levels of consciousness whereby humans use a greater proportion of their inherent psychic capacity and spiritual potential. The theme of self-empowerment through transformational activities such as prayer, meditation and connecting with the energy field of the planet is a recurring theme in descriptions of what the Helper ETs are attempting to teach global humanity.[83] This was the theme promoted by Meiers in his account of the philosophy taught to him by ETs from the Pleiades who were apparently concerned that self-destruction had occurred when earlier human civilizations that had integrated Pleiadian technology before self-destruction.

According to Meiers: "Semjase and the Pleiadians who had chose to return again to Earth were descendants of a peaceful Lyrian [star system Lyra] faction that now felt responsible for guiding Earth in its spiritual evolution, so the Earth humans could avoid the setbacks long ago experienced by their Pleiadian ancestors."[84] Courtney Brown argues that his remote viewing sessions consistently turn up evidence of a Galactic Federation of races that assists humanity in its evolution.[85]

Helper ETs pass down knowledge of advanced technologies and alternative energy

A second way in which helper ETs assist humanity is to pass down knowledge of advanced technologies and alternative energy sources that are more harmonious with the biosphere which they regard as a living organism which needs to be protected. The early twentieth century inventor, Nikola Tesla, is often cited as one assisted by ETs to develop and disseminate these environmentally friendly technologies.[86] According to the statements from witnesses in the Disclosure Project, a number of 'free energy technologies' are possessed and used by the government, but are not disclosed to the general population.[87] Paul Czysz, who has worked for 38 years either with the US Air force or the exotic technologies department of the military contractor, McDonnell-Douglas, explains why these technologies are withheld as follows:

The people that have access to [these advanced energy technologies] don't know how to let go of it, because they're afraid of who's going to get their hands on it. Even though there would be a tremendous benefit to mankind, they're also worried that somebody could take that same energy source and do the equivalent of what they did with the USS Cole – instead of blowing a hole in the side, they could just obliterate the whole ship.[88]

*** *** ***

Dr. Richard Boylan: B2 stealth bomber uses anti-gravity technology not fuel as the general public believes

According to interviews of 'government insiders', Richard Boylan claims that the B2 stealth bomber operates largely using anti-gravity technology for its propulsion system but this is not disclosed to the general public who believe it relies on conventional fuel sources.[89]

A third way helper ETs assist humanity is to encourage humanity to achieve peaceful resolution of international conflict, and prevent nuclear proliferation and the use of other destructive weapons. A number of former government and military officials have provided testimonies that support this perspective of ETs as helpers. ETs have displayed significant concern for nuclear weapons and even, in some instances, disarmed nuclear weapons.

Captain Robert Salas: 16 nuclear-armed missiles were disarmed by UFOs hovering over NORAD

According to Captain Robert Salas in testimony given in December 2000 as part of the Disclosure Project, 16 nuclear-armed missiles were simultaneously disarmed in two separate launch facilities after guards reported UFO's hovering over 2 NORAD facilities in March 1967.[90] Other sources report that during the early years of the Eisenhower administration, a group of ETs secretly met with US government officials appointed to deal with the ET question, and offered to assist with a number of environmental, technological, political and socioeconomic problems, with the sole condition that the US dismantle its nuclear arsenal.[91] When the government officials declined, this group of ETs subsequently withdrew and played no role in the government's clandestine program to reverse engineer ET technology for advanced weaponry. It is claimed that these 'helper ETs' would subsequently concentrate their efforts with consciousness raising of the general public; warning of the hazards of nuclear and 'exotic' weapon systems reverse engineered from ET technology; limiting the environmental impact of clandestine projects; encouraging the development of alternatives to using fossil fuel as an energy source; and preparing the general populace for eventual disclosure of the ET presence.

The helper ETs describe the Milky Way galaxy, as being populated by numerous advanced civilizations

Finally, the helper ETs describe the Milky Way galaxy, and indeed the universe, as being populated by numerous advanced civilizations.[92] By understanding more about ET races and interstellar politics, the helper ETs believe this will help the evolution of humanity. Alfred Webre, who briefly headed a 1977 Special Study on Communications with Extraterrestrials initiated by President Carter, has written a book based on the politics of ET races and their interaction with Earth:

Earth appears to be an isolated planet in the midst of a populated Universe. Universe society consists of highly organized and consciously evolving, advanced civilizations. Universe civilizations function within our own interstellar Universe, as well as within other dimensions in the Universe at large.

Advanced Universe civilizations exist in other dimensions parallel to our own

They access our own planet, galaxy, and all of interstellar space. Life-bearing planets such as Earth are part of a collective Universe whole, operating under Universal law. Think of Earth as part of a Universe commons. Life is implanted and cultivated here under the tutelage of more advanced societies, in accordance with the over-all principles of Universe ecology.

Where necessary, Universal law applies restrictive measures to a planet that endangers the collective whole. Universe government can remove a planet from open circulation within Universe society. This fate appears to have happened to Earth in our distant past.

Earth has suffered for eons as an exopolitical outcast among the community of Universe civilizations.

Earth is isolated because it is under intentional quarantine by a structured, rational Universe society. There are signs around us of a Universe initiative to reintegrate Earth into interplanetary society. It is possible that Earth may be permitted to rejoin Universe society, under certain conditions, or at a future time certain.[93]

The rapidly growing information of these helper ETs comes from an extensive range of sources. Former military and government 'whistle blowers' have revealed the activities of clandestine government agencies and interests opposed to incorporating ET technology into the public arena.[94] An extensive number of witnesses of these Helper ETs continue to make reports about being physically visited by helper ETs and communicating with them either by both verbal and/or telepathic means, that are collected and closely analyzed by a number of highly credentialed individuals and organizations.[95]

Further sources of information are participants in scientific remote viewing projects either conducted under governmental supervision or private organizations; and individuals who claim to be in telepathic communication with these helper ETs and often become popular 'channels' of insights for the general public. In sum, the Helper ET perspective depicts the ET presence as being clearly benevolent in their moral orientation, and that their intentions and activities aim to assist humanity deal with a range of global issues, including rogue ET elements intent on destabilizing global institutions, the biosphere or abducting the human population for genetic experiments.

The conspiracy theories that stem from the helper perspective focus on the efforts of clandestine governmental organizations to suppress information of the presence of the ET helpers, and even contrive a military conflict with ETs in general in order to maintain the status quo. The primary information sources for conspiracy theories in this perspective are drawn from all the categories with the exception of the abduction category. The most persuasive is from the Whistle blower category. This suggests strong evidentiary support for this perspective

*** *** ***

The "Watcher Perspective":

The fourth perspective can be distinguished from the first three insofar as it relies exclusively on the last two categories of sources - individuals claiming to be in telepathic contact with ETs ('channels') and independent archeologists.[96] The main idea advocated by these authors is that many ETs are primarily here to simply observe how humanity resolves its numerous societal and global conflicts at a time when cosmic energy surges in the solar system and the galaxy adds to the intensity of these conflicts. According to the Watcher perspective, humanity represents an elaborate galactic experiment designed by ETs who wish to observe how humanity responds to the galaxy wide energy surges.

According to this perspective, the entire universe is comprised of vibrating energy fields that wax and wane in long historical cycles that have their origin in the cosmic and galactic energies that emanate from the cores of galaxies, and elsewhere in the universe. At different points in these cycles, energy fields will be intensified by cosmic and galactic energies that have a cycle similar to that of our sun which every 11 years experiences an increase in the emission of Solar Flares, Coronal Mass Expulsions, and the various electromagnetic energies that make up the Solar Wind. These energy shifts prove to be very profound in terms of their impact and the future of planetary civilizations, according to this perspective, is determined by how well they respond to these energy shifts. While it may appear strange at first to believe that reality is nothing but energy, quantum physics has indeed shown that sub-atomic particles are made up of rapidly vibrating energy fields rather than discrete particles that was earlier thought to be the ultimate substratum of reality. According to Robert Becker in his best selling, *The Body Electric,* the human body is nothing but concentrated electrical and magnetic energy fields that respond constantly to the energy fields of the larger environment.[97]

*** *** ***

The Mayan Calendar

According, to this perspective, the contemporary era corresponds to the end of a number of important celestial cycles revealed by the Mayan Calendar. One is the end of a Mayan cycle of 5,200 years, another is the end of a solar cycle of 25,920 years corresponding to the precession of the equinoxes. [98] Some argue that cycles up to as long as 225,000,000 years also come to completion at this time.[99] According to John Major Jenkins, the solar cycle corresponds with the time it takes for the plane of our solar system (the ecliptic) to realign itself with the 'galactic core' where cosmic and other energies from the center of the galaxy dramatically influence consciousness all around the planet.[100] These historic shifts in consciousness, according to Jenkins, are described in the Mayan, Vedic and Egyptian traditions and explain the dramatic rise and falls of different civilizations throughout the ages.

The profound consciousness shift occurs due to the cyclic transitions and realignment with the galactic core changing the intensity of all the 'energies' – electromagnetic, solar, gravitational, cosmic, etc. - that influence life throughout the solar system. This means, for example, that all the thoughts, feelings and actions which all combine to influence an individual's reality are either magnified or diminished. In the case of a magnification, this has two polarized outcomes. One is that human civilization implodes due to the intensification of all the latent conflicts and dysfunctional energies that come to the surface of human collective life, in a kind of 'planetary spring cleaning', and prove to be unmanageable.

An analogy to help understand this is that of psychological process of 'projection' wherein unbalanced individuals project onto others their own unresolved psychological issues. If this were to occur to an extreme degree with large numbers of individuals, such a society could implode in a violent cathartic release of repressed negative emotions. The second outcome of a magnification of energies influencing human consciousness is that the energy surges make it possible for a jump in evolution from the 'dimensional reality' that a particular civilization finds itself in, to a higher dimension where more refined powers of creation are possible. According to a number of authors, human civilization currently occupies a 'third density level' and is preparing to make the transition to the 'fifth density level' at the end of the current 5000-year cycle of the Mayan Calendar in December 2012.[101]

This philosophy of differing density levels that can also be described as making up a 'multidimensional reality' can be understood by the metaphor of water molecules at different temperatures. At temperatures below 0 degrees centigrade, water freezes into ice crystals. The degree of difficulty or energy used in manipulating these water molecules when in ice form in terms of movement, storage, shapes, etc., is a metaphor for the difficulties encountered by beings who live in a low density level such as the third density which human civilization reportedly occupies. At temperatures between 0 and 100 degrees centigrade, water is in liquid form wherein the molecules are much easier to move, store, and place in different shapes. This is a metaphor for the ease with which civilizations are able to shape their external reality according to the energy used. Finally, water at temperatures above 100 degrees centigrade, becomes a gas where it is easiest to manipulate the water molecules in terms of movement, storage and shape. Again, this is a metaphor for the ease with which civilizations are able to shape their external reality according to the energy used.

*** *** ***

The Watcher ETs are here to learn how humanity deals with the energy shifts

According to this perspective, the Watcher ETs are here to learn how humanity deals with the energy shifts that intensify the latent conflicts and dysfunctional energies from human history. They desire to observe whether human civilization implodes, or is successful in making the transition from a third density environment, into fourth and then fifth density environments. While it may appear odd at first to hear that advanced ET civilizations are here to observe and possibly learn from humanity, it may not be so strange if 'galactic history' is explained from the perspective of a number of authors claiming to be in telepathic communication with ETs.[102] According to these authors, the Milky Way galaxy has witnessed intense armed conflict between large alliances of ET races divided by competing philosophies, histories and genetic heritages.

In its most simple terms, these conflicts have been polarized around two competing visions about how the galaxy is best organized, and took place primarily in the constellation of Orion. [103] One vision is that all ET races should have an equal role and voice in galactic decision making, while the other is that the oldest and most technologically advanced race, rightfully has a privileged position.

According to this perspective, the most powerful elites from the two sides many millennia ago, realized that the coming cyclic energetic changes, what can be termed the 'Great Shift', would in most likelihood lead to another galactic war due to the intensification of all the issues that were never completely resolved in previous conflicts and which lay dormant.[104] This would be disastrous since this would mean great devastation and loss for those ET civilizations not able to make the transition to a higher density. Only a comprehensive galactic unity would guarantee that these latent conflicts would not result in a new Galactic War, and that most civilizations could successfully move up in density levels during the 'Great Shift'. However, these elites from the respective ET races recognized that the intense divisions between them in terms of history, genetics and philosophy, would in most likelihood not be overcome in time for a comprehensive galactic union to be reached, thereby making another galactic war inevitable.

ETs decided to sponsor a hybrid race that would comprise the diverse genetic pools

In order to overcome this problem and avert future disaster, the ET elites decided to sponsor a hybrid race that would comprise the diverse genetic pools found in the galaxy. As a result of genetics, and interventions by differing ET races at appointed times, this race of beings would experience a history that closely mirrored that of the galaxy. If this hybrid race could resolve its internal differences by the time of the Great Shift to achieve a comprehensive political unity, then this would provide an example for the rest of the Galaxy for how they could in turn deal with the Great Shift.

Thus the human race was born as a 'Great Galactic Experiment' whose true purpose was known only among a few of the elite of the most powerful ET races.[105]

While these few elites from the oldest and most advanced ET civilizations presumably knew that only a galactic union would avert future disaster, this was not widely accepted among the bulk of the ET races that believed that their favored viewpoint would prevail in a future galactic conflict. These is analogous to human conflict where hard line military leaders strongly believe that they will militarily prevail in another confrontation and disagree with more prudent calls for dialogue and negotiation.

Those few ET elites that could prophesy such a future galactic calamity sponsored the evolution of humanity throughout the varied ET interventions in history, both benevolent and malignant, in order to demonstrate to the rest of the Galaxy how to handle the Great Shift. One of the principal advocates of the Watcher perspective is Barbara Marciniak whose writings have become a seminal source in the channeling community. Marciniak, channeling a group of ETs from the Pleiades describes this 'Great Galactic Experiment' as follows:

Much of existence is focused on you at this time, although that is not to say everyone has their telescopes pointed at Earth. However, there are legends in the cosmos, just as there are legends on Earth, and cosmic legends speak of this time of change and refer to you as a gem of a genetic library tucked away, an experiment made for a 'just-in-case' time. And this experiment has been fought over and discounted, recognized and forgotten, valued and given away; you have experienced all these events in the collective of your consciousness, in the cells of who you are...You are the Gods' secret tucked away in time, and they wait to see if you can change from one form of being into another in a nanosecond – in their terms; in yours, perhaps it takes a lifetime, a lifetime enriched and extraordinary, above and beyond ordinary existence. You have an exquisite opportunity to create a completely unique kind of power and to bring purposefulness and meaning to Earth. Cosmic legends are full of this tale about you humans. Just as your legends on Earth are filled with tales of magicians, at this juncture in time you are looked upon in the Book of Earth as magicians yourselves, the whole lot of you, not simply a few. The heavens hold the rich imprint of electromagnetic aliveness, and as you move through space, your planet, solar system, and galaxy all traverse new territory. This territory has been planned for you to encounter, one that will recode your DNA in this lifetime to connect you to the multidimensional intelligence that exists beyond your biology, and is your inheritance.[106]

Earth is the third of 3 Grand Experiments in Polarity Integration

According to the Watcher perspective, recent human experience in terms of two World Wars in the first half of the twentieth century, and fears of a third World War either in the latter part of the twentieth or early twenty first century, mirrored the history of earlier galactic conflicts. In so far as humanity has been able to avert a third world war, the human experiment has thus far been a great success story. Humanity has shown how a civilization can overcome a long history of racial and cultural differences, political and economic conflict, and environmental degradation at the same time as the Great Shift intensifies all the aspects of these differences.

This viewpoint is clearly outlined by the popular author Jeleila Starr who claims to channel a higher dimensional ET race associated with the seeding of planet Earth: Earth is the third of 3 Grand Experiments in Polarity Integration.

This means that she is a special planet set aside from all others and populated with every species in the known universe for the specific purpose of integration. In this melting pot of species, and with the aid of highly evolved incarnated souls and their angels/guides, it is hoped that full integration of the Light and Dark can be achieved. If this occurs, peace will reign in the galaxy and universe.

Why? Each species will have the blueprint, created in the Grand Experiment by their star-seeded children, to resolve any conflict no matter how ancient. It is these painful, ancient irresolvable conflicts between races and species that have resulted in numerous galactic wars that have brought about the necessity of this experiment. If Earth fails to achieve full integration, the galaxies will be destroyed because there won't be any way to resolve the conflicts. If Earth succeeds and peace is established, the Polarity Game will end and all souls who achieved integration will have the opportunity to move on to other realms and create new universes and games through which they can continue to learn and grow.[107] The planet Earth, Humanity and the galaxy, it is claimed, has a deadline to prepare for this transition to a higher dimensional or 'density' level at the end of the current 5200 year cycle of the Mayan Calendar in December 2012.[108]

In sum, the Watcher perspective suggests that a galactic/cosmic conspiracy exists where humanity has been set up to create a solution to a galactic problem not of humanity's own making. The Watcher ETs are represented as merely observing how humanity integrates its diverse heritage and resolves the historic conflicts expected to emerge over the next decade. Rather than directly intervening in human affairs, the ET Watchers are portrayed primarily as observers who over the course of millennia are somehow able to influence or decide which other ET races are allowed to intervene in human affairs. The ET Watchers are depicted as being able to calculate the effects of such interventions in a way that predisposes humanity to arriving at a uniquely human solution to a complex galactic problem. The moral dimension of this perspective is primarily neutral due to the observational nature of the ETs described, and the long-term effort involved in promoting and learning from the 'human experiment'. The primary information sources for this perspective are drawn overwhelmingly from Category E, Channels. Additional evidence comes from independent archaeology and remote viewing but these lack the clarity and coherence of channeled information. The reliance on channeled information suggests weak evidentiary support for this perspective.

Despite its weak evidentiary support base, an interesting aspect of this perspective is that it integrates the earlier perspectives into what appears to be a coherent conspiracy framework integrating all the other conspiracy theories concerning the ET presence.

Furthermore, those advocating this perspective, write with clarity of purpose, coherence and persuasiveness that wins many converts who desire to know the 'big picture' about the ET presence and human history. One might view this perspective as the 'mother of all conspiracies', where this grand galactic conspiracy by higher dimensional ET races, lays the foundations and rules for all other conspiracies involving ET races and human elites.

References:

[60]. Milton Wiliam Cooper, "The Secret Government: The Origin, Identity, and Purpose of MJ-12" (Huntington Beach, CA: Manuscript copyright, 1989). Website: www.abovetopsecret.com/pages/mj12.html

[61] William Bramley, *Gods of Eden* (Avon, 1989) 37. Also cited in Jim Marrs, *Rule By Secrecy, The Hidden History That Connects the Trilateral Commission, the Freemasons, and the Great Pyramids* (Harper Collins, 2000) 406.

[62]. Zecharia Sitchin, *The Earth Chronicles*, Books 1-6.

[63]. The Book of Enoch describes in great detail this conflict. An online version can be found at http://wesley.nnu.edu/noncanon/ot/pseudo/enoch.htm

[64] R. A. Boulay, *Flying Serpents and Dragons: The Story of Mankind's Reptillian Past* (Book Tree, 1999).

[65]. Manetho,, *Manetho,* tr.,W.G. Waddell (Harvard University Press, 1940).

[66]. Courtney Brown, *Cosmic Explorers.*

[67] Stewart Swerdlow, *Blue Blood, True Blood: Conflict & Creation* (Expansions Publishing Co., 2002).

[68]. Jim Marrs, *Rule By Secrecy* (New York: Perennial, 2000).

[69]. David Icke, *The Biggest Secret,* 2nd Ed. (Bridge of Love Publications, 1999). For online information on Icke and his most recent work, go to http://www.davidicke.com

[70] Cited by Jim Marrs, *Rule By Secrecy,* 406. Source: David Icke, *The Biggest Secret,* 1.

[71]. Rather than mining for material resources such as gold and other precious metals that Sitchin describes as being the initial reason the Annunaki established humanity, Icke claims that this race uses humans as a basic resource supplying hormones derived from emotions such as fear and anger, and using humans as a food source. *The Biggest Secret.*

[72]. Alex Collier, *Defending Sacred Ground: The Andromedan Compendium,* Edited by Val Valerian, January 1997, Revised July 1998. Website: www.lettersfromandromeda.com/

[73]. Grays captured and/or influenced by the Annunaki remnants, supposedly perform subversive tasks such as cattle mutilation, extraction of human hormones and genetic experimentation, confrontation with the US and other military forces, and sowing fear in the human population. *Cosmic Explorers,* 159-221

[74]. Lynn Picknett & Clive Prince, *The Stargate Conspiracy* (New York: Berkley Books, 1999).

[75]. The term `exotic weapons systems' has been defined to include weapons designed to damage space or natural ecosystems (such as the ionosphere and upper atmosphere) or climate, weather, and tectonic systems with the purpose of inducing damage or destruction upon a target population or region on earth or in space. Space Preservation Act of 2001 (Introduced in the House), HR 2977 IH, 107th CONGRESS, 1st Session, H. R. 2977. Website: www.fas.org/sgp/congress/2001/hr2977.html

[76] See Interview with Andy Pero, "Project Superman," available at: http://www.hostileinvader.com/

[77] For two ebooks detailing Michael Relfe's memories of his encounters with Reptilians, see *The Mars Records,* published online at: http://www.themarsrecords.com/ See also Preston Nichols & Peter Moon, *Pryamids of Montauk: Explorations in Conciouness* (Sky Books 1995); and "Interview with Al Bielek," *Connecting Link* (Issue 19, Oct 1993); available online at:
http://psychicspy.com/montauk1.html

[78]. For a detailed description of the Nordic ETs, see Richard Boylan, "The Various Kinds of Star Visitors," http://www.drboylan.com/etraces.html.

[79] Quoted by Richard Boylan, "Extraterrestrial Base On Earth, Sanctioned By Officials Since 1954, Now Revealed. Also Disclosed: Secret U.S.-USSR Manned Space Station, Positioned In Orbit For Past 30+

Years," in Boylan and Boylan, *Labored Journey To The Stars.* Available online at: http://drboylan.com/basespst2.html

[80] Kal K. Korff, *Spaceships of the Pleiades: The Billy Meier Story* (Prometheus Books, 1995).

[81]. Steven M. Greer, *Extraterrestrial Contact: The Evidence and Implications* (Crossing Point Publications, 1999). Richard Boylan, *Labored Journey to The Stars: An anthology on human responses, governmental, civilian and Native, to extraterrestrial visitation,* Rev., 2002. Alfred Lambremont Webre, *Exopolitics: A Decade of Contact* (Universe Books, 1999). His book is available online at http://www.universebooks.com/

[82] These include Barbara Marciniak, *Family of Light*, (Bear and Co., 1999); Lyssa Royal & Keith Priest, Preparing for Contact: A Metamorphosis of Consciousness (Royal Priest Research, 1993); & Sheldan Nidle, *First Contact* (Vancouver: Blue Lodge Press, 2000).

[83]. See Marciniak, *Family of Light*, and Nidle, *First Contact.* Two self help themes are, first, the ETs are here to help humanity develop their inherent capacity to shape their external environment by focusing their conscious intent on whatever it is they wish to change or create. The helper ETs believe humans have surrendered their inherent power to create through conscious intent as a result of self-limiting belief systems propogated by political and religious institutions, the media and the education system. For example, the belief that one must work in unsatisfying jobs in order to survive, according to the helper ETs, is a self-limiting belief system that prevents humans from following their passion which is the key ingredient for their inherent ability to create through conscious intent. The helper ET philosophy is that if humans realize their inherent power to shape reality through focusing their conscious intent, many social, political, economic and environmental problems on the planet would quickly disappear. Second, the helper ETs promote the view that the external reality of an individual or community is a mirror of the internal consciousness of individuals/communities. Repressed emotions such as fear or anger, are said to generate energies that draw into the environment of individuals and groups, conditions which mirror these emotions. For example, an individual who unconsciously fears failure will repeatedly draw into his/her environment, cases of failure until they overcome their fear of failure. The helper ETs stress the importance of cultivating positive emotions such as compassion and unity in order to generate positive external events. They claim that this is especially important when it comes to meeting advanced ET cultures since these repressed emotions can influence the nature of the interaction. For example, the reported failure of the helper ETs to negotiate an agreement with US government representatives stemmed from the latter's fear that sacrifising the US nuclear arsenal would make the US vulnerable in any future conflict with the ETs. This fear then creates an opportunity for more aggressive ET races to exploit such fears through technology transfers with US government representatives that ultimately increase the level of fear and suspicion, and in the end make it more likely for a conflict to occur.

[84] Cited in Marrs, Alien Agenda, 303. Original source: Gary Kinder, *Light Years* (Pocket Books, 1987) 98-99.

[85] Brown, *Cosmic Explorers.*

[86] For information of the connection between Tesla and ETs, see Tim Swartz, Timothy Beckley, *The Lost Journals of Nikola Tesla : Haarp - Chemtrails and Secret of Alternative 4* (Global Communications, 2000).

[87]. See testimonies in section 5, Greer, ed., *Disclosure,* 489-559. Dr Greer further claims that these efforts have been stymied by vested interests opposed to alternative energy sources.

[88] Testimony of Paul Czysz, *Disclosure,* ed., Greer, 519

[89]. Boylan, "B-2 Stealth bomber as antigravity craft" in Boylan and Boylan, *Labored Journey To The Stars.* Available online at: Website: www.drboylan.com/waregrv2.html

[90]. See "Testimony of Captain Robert Salas, US Air force," in Disclosure, Greer, 167-71. See also *Executive Summary of the Disclosure Project Briefing Document*, 49; available online at http://www.disclosureproject.com

[91]. See Michael Wolf, *Catchers of Heaven*; and Bill Cooper, *Beyond a Pale Horse*. In a website article, Cooper wrote: [A] race of human-looking aliens contacted the U.S. Government. This alien group warned us against the aliens that were orbiting the Equator and offered to help us with our spiritual development. They demanded that we dismantle and destroy our nuclear weapons as the major condition. They refused to exchange technology citing that we were spiritually unable to handle the technology which we then possessed. They believed that we would use any new technology to destroy each other. This race stated that we were on a path of self-destruction and we must stop killing each other, stop polluting the earth, stop raping the Earth's natural resources, and learn to live in harmony. These terms were met with extreme suspicion especially the major condition of nuclear disarmament. It was believed that meeting that condition would leave us helpless in the face of an obvious alien threat. We also had nothing in history to help with the decision. Nuclear disarmament was not considered to be within the best interest of the United States. The overtures were rejected.
Website: http://www.abovetopsecret.com/pages/mj12.html

[92]. See Nidle, *First Contact*. In something resembling the prime directive of the popular series Star Trek, the alliance of advanced ET races that the helper ETs belong to, often described as the 'Galactic Federation', does not interfere in less developed planetary societies unless either directly requested to by the population, or in the case that the developing planetary society poses a threat to the biosphere and/or other planetary civilizations by the use of destructive technology such as nuclear and 'exotic' weapon systems. The helper ETs report that they have been historically in conflict with aggressive ET civilizations primarily based in the constellation of Orion, referred by some as the Orion Alliance that does not adhere to the non-interference directive. The races mentioned earlier the intruder and manipulator perspectives both reportedly have their origin in the star systems of Orion.

[93] Alfred Lambremont Webre, JD, Med, *Exopolitics: A Decade of Contact* (2000) an ebook published online at http://www.universebooks.com/exoone.html

[94]. See Steven M. Greer, *Extraterrestrial Contact: The Evidence and Implications* (Crossing Point Publications, 1999).

[95]. See for example, Richard Boylan and Lee K. Boylan, *Close Extraterrestrial Encounters: Positive Experiences With Mysterious Visitors* (Wildflower, 1994). Website: www.drboylan.com

[96]. The most popular 'channels' advocating this perspective include Barbara Marciniak, *Family of Light;* Robert Shapiro, *Shining the Light*, Vols 1-6 (Light Technology Publications); Jelaila Starr, *We Are the Nibiruans: Return of the 12th Planet* (New Leaf Distributing Co., 1999)*,* and Drunvalo Melchizedek, *The Ancient Secret of the Flower of Life,* Vol 2 (Light Technology Publications, 2000).

[97] Robert Becker and Gary Seldon, *The Body Electric: Electromagnetism and the Foundation of Life,* New York: Quill, 1985.

[98]. John Major Jenkins, *Maya Cosmogenesis 2012*, Santa Fe: Bear and Co., 1998. According to this perspective, the entire universe is comprised of vibrating energy fields that wax and wane in long historical cycles that have their origin in the cosmic and galactic energies that emanate from the cores of galaxies, and elsewhere in the universe. At different points in these cycles, energy fields will be intensified by cosmic and galactic energies that have a cycle analogous to that of our sun which every 11 years experiences an increase in the emission of Solar Flares, Coronal Mass Expulsions, and the various electromagnetic energies that make up the Solar Wind. These energy shifts prove to be very profound in terms of their impact throughout the galaxy and the future of planetary civilizations is determined by how well they respond to these energy surges.

[99] Barbara Hand Clow, *The Pleiadian Agenda: A New Cosmology for the Age of Light* (Bear and Co., 1995) 49.

[100] John Major Jenkins, *Galactic Alignment: The Transformation of Consciousness According to Mayan, Egyptian, and Vedic Traditions* (Inner Traditions International, 2002).

[101]. The most well known author advocating this timeline is Jose Arguelles, *The Mayan Factor,* Santa Fe: Bear and Company, 1987. For discussion of different dimensions/densities, see Lyssa Royal & Keith Priest, *The Prism of Lyra: An Exploration of Human Galactic Heritage*, Rev ed. (Royal Priest Research, 1993) 1-9.

[102]. Some of the popular sources for Galactic history include, Royal & Priest, *The Prism of Lyra*; Sheldan Nidle, *First Contact*, and Barbara Marciniak., *Family of Light;* and Fred Stirling, *Kirael: The Great Shift,* Oughten House Publication, 1998.

[103] For the conflict in Orion, see Royal and Priest, *The Prism of Lyra,* 39-46.

[104]. The term 'Great Shift' is used by Fred Stirling, *Kirael: The Great Shift. Website:* www.kirael.com

[105] The idea that humanity is a hybrid race comprising various ET genetic strands is promoted by Zecharia Sitchin, *Earth Chronicles* (Bks 1-6). For discussion of the galactic politics surrounding the genetic make up of human races and the ET involvement, see Royal and Priest, *The Prism of Lyra,* 67-74.

[106] Marciniak, *Family of Light,* 186-87. For a similar perspective see Royal and Priest, *The Prism of Lyra,* 67-74.

[107]. Jelaila Star, January 3, 2003, website update. Website:http://www.nibiruancouncil.com/html

[108]. The most well known author advocating this timeline is Jose Arguelles, *The Mayan Factor,* (Santa Fe: Bear and Company, 1987). See also Jenkins, *Cosmogenesis.*The idea of differing energy densities can be understood by the example of water molecules. At temperatures below 0 degrees centigrade, water freezes into ice crystals. The degree of difficulty or energy used in manipulating these water molecules when in ice form in terms of movement, storage, shapes, etc., is a metaphor for the difficulties encountered by beings who live in a low density level such as the third density which human civilization reportedly occupies. At temperatures between 0 and 100 degrees centigrade, water is in liquid form wherein the molecules are much easier to move, store, and place in different shapes. This is a metaphor for the ease with which civilizations are able to shape their external reality according to the energy used. Finally, water at temperatures above 100 degrees centigrade, becomes a gas where it is easiest to manipulate the water molecules in terms of movement, storage and shape. Again, this is a metaphor for the ease with which civilizations are able to shape their external reality according to the energy used.

*** *** ***

CHAPTER 13
THE STAR PEOPLE
Races, Categories And Intent

- The future intent of the Star People
- The Star People will be speaking with the People in a stepped-up program of mass contact
- Dr. Boylan: The Star Visitors are saying that the individuals known as Jesus and Mother Mary will return along with "other Great Teachers
- Dr. Boylan thesis
- The various kinds of star visitors
- Star Visitors' variations in size and details of appearance may represent origins on different planets
- The "Grays" are stereotyped by uninformed or careless writers
- Different categories and variants of the "Grays"
- Another source of variation is clothing
- The "Praying Mantis type" race
- The "Reptilians", or "Reptoids"
- The "Jawas"; another group of Star Visitors
- "Screen memory": Star Visitor-imposed mental visualization in the mind of the experiencer
- The "Dwarf" Star Visitors
- The "Bird People" race
- The" light and energy" beings

*** *** ***

293

The Star People: Races, Categories and Intent

> Dr. Boylan is the Director of the Star Kids Project and Star Visitor researcher who has made a huge impact on worldwide acceptance of "extraterrestrial" contact, including visiting Monsignor Balducci in the Vatican and obtaining from him the Catholic Church's position that star visitors have in fact been coming to Earth since biblical times.

The Star People will be speaking with the People in a stepped-up program of mass contact

Now, Dr. Boylan has issued a new proclamation concerning the future intent of the Star People. In a nutshell, the message is that our governments have failed us, and that from now on the Star People will be speaking with the People in a stepped-up program of mass contact.

Dr. Boylan makes the basic points below:

- The Visitors, a federation of races who are in contact with Earth, are displeased that the major seven governments of our developed countries continue to cover up Star Visitor contact, and have given up trying to convince our governments to end the cover-up.
- The Visitors feel that civilized people do not bomb others and wage war, and they feel the need to do something about our population's continued belief in these behaviors.
- Because the 2012 date that ends our current time cycle is almost upon us, the Visitors have concluded that their program of close encounters with individuals is going too slowly. At the apex of this cycle, Dr. Boylan reports, Earth people will need to be "retrieved" until the new cycle can begin, and at the current rate of education, not enough people will be psychologically or socially prepared for this experience. Therefore...
- The Star Visitors are intending soon (no later than 2006) to begin making appearances to large groups of civilians in such a way that no one will be able to deny or forget what happened (the example Dr. Boylan gave was the Visitors appearing to all the people in a shopping mall).

- The Star Visitors are aware that many people will interpret them as angels or saints. They also are saying that the individuals known as Jesus and Mother Mary will return along with "other Great Teachers," at which point the churches' distortions of the original message they were supposed to give to the People will be addressed.
- The Visitors also intend to work directly with religious leaders of all faiths and with indigenous peoples worldwide.
- The message of "Love Your Neighbor" will be basic to our experiences of the Star Visitors in the future, so that, Dr. Boylan says, these encounters will be experienced in the context of a "family reunion."

*** *** ***

The Various Kinds of Star Visitors

Dr. Richard Boylan said that "Race" distinguishes various Star Visitors of decidedly different appearances. More research into exo-biology, (the science of Star Visitor life's physical structure and processes), will help us understand better how many races of intelligent species we are dealing. So would the declassifying of the Government's already considerable covert research on Star Visitor ("exo-") biology, (such as is going on at NASA's Ames Research Center, Sunnyvale, CA, and at Los Alamos National Laboratories, NM.

Dr. Boylan's Thesis

Here is the thesis of Dr. Boylan in his own words: For convenience I shall use the term "race" to distinguish Star Visitors of significantly different anatomical features.

Star Visitors' variations in size and details of appearance may represent origins on different planets

The most common Star Visitor race encountered has a number of variants. These variations in size and details of appearance may represent origins on different planets. This race is popularly, and rather imprecisely, called the "Grays".

The "Grays" are stereotyped by uninformed or careless writers

The "Grays" are stereotyped, by uninformed or careless writers, as: short, upright, two-legged beings, three-and-a-half feet tall, with grayish- white skin, large, hairless, fetal-shaped heads, with huge, all-black, sloping, almond-shaped eyes without pupils or eyelids, whose eyes wrap around partially towards the temple-area sides of the head, a narrow jaw tapering to almost a V, small nostril holes but no nose, a small, thin, lip-less, horizontal slit for a mouth, thin torsos with no ribs and no genitals evident, long, spindly, but surprisingly strong arms reaching to the knees, similarly long, very thin legs, and hands with three long, non-tapering, joint-less fingers, which end in claws instead of fingernails, but no thumb.

Different categories and variants of the "Grays"

To be sure, there is such a race of beings; or at least a race, of which this is one variant. However, there are also:

- five-foot tall "Grays",
- seven-foot tall "Grays",
- "Grays" with mushroom-white skin,
- "Grays" with brown skin,
- "Grays" with black skin,
- "Grays" whose large eyes have a thin nictating membrane which can extend across the eye,
- "Grays" with midnight-blue eyes,
- "Grays" with wispy fine small amounts of hair on their heads,
- "Grays" with four fingers,
- "Grays" with three or four fingers and another finger positioned where the human thumb would be,
- "Grays" whose fingers end with suction-cup-like tips.

There have also been Star Visitors reported who have a large process of folds along the back of their heads, a series of deep creases or crevices along the top of the head, sloping down forward towards the front, and with a strongly-pronounced brow- ridge above the eyes.Are these twelve different races; or variants based on evolving in different climactic zones on one planet?

*** *** ***

- Does this represent racial variation within inhabited planets in one star system?
- Or are these variations which occur within one cluster of star systems?
- Or does the "Gray" genotype tend to appear in many different star systems, on some planets, along with other races, on other planets, within those same star systems?

The truth is, we do not know. Or at least that information has not been released to the public. Thus, we are still at the stage of gathering information on the various different types of intelligent lifeforms visiting our planet.

Another source of variation is clothing

Another source of variation even within what is apparently one race is clothing.
- Many experiencers report that their "Gray" visitors wore no clothes.
- Others have seen "Grays" wearing long robes and hoods over their heads.
- Others have seen crews where both versions of attire, as well as close-fitting jumpsuits, were in evidence.

Yet Grays are not the only ones wearing robes. Another race of Star Visitors is the 4-to-5 1/2-foot tall Being, with a somewhat large head (by comparison with the human head) but not as proportionally large as the "Grays", and who has somewhat large (but smaller than the "Grays") dark oval eyes, spindly frame and limbs, and a hand with three long, cartilaginous, bone-less fingers, which end with neither claw nor suction-cup, but rather "ordinary" fingertip shape, except that their fingers do not taper.

The "Praying Mantis type" race

A more distinctive kind of Star Visitor is the "Praying Mantis type" race. These Beings have long, narrow faces, with long, narrow, large eyes, sharply slanted upward and outward in an almost narrow-V position, given an almost insect-like appearance. This comparison is heightened by the Praying-Mantis types' extremely thin, long torsos, long, extremely-thin arms which are usually crooked into a sharp bend at the mid-joint, with the hand and fingers/mitten sloping almost vertically downward from the "wrist", and legs also bent at an almost right-angle at the mid-joint, creating a crouched pose.

The overall effect is the characteristic "Praying Mantis" look.

It should be noted that experiencers feel that this type is no insect, but rather an intelligent, gentle-spirited, but somewhat "hyper" and jerky-moving, human-like lifeform.

There are both males and females.

The "Reptilians" or "Reptoids"

Another race is the so-called "Reptilians", or "Reptoids", although I note again that there is no implication in these descriptors of anything other than of intelligent, communicative persons.

What distinguishes these "Reptilian" Star Visitors is their skin, which has small, fine scales, rather than smooth, their face, which has larger-than- human yellowish-green eyes with a "starburst"-shaped pupil, the eyes often oval, and an almost snout-like blunt process in the area of the nose and mouth, giving this type an almost dragon-like humanoid appearance.

The "Jawas"; another group of Star Visitors

Another group of Star Visitors for convenience, I call the "Jawas", after their resemblance to the creatures in the film, Star Wars. This group is distinguished by their clothing.

- They wear hoods and robes, are generally short (three to four-and-a-half feet tall)
- Their faces are concealed by the shadows thrown by their hoods.
- Sometimes there is a much taller hooded and robed one on board the UFO, who often stands to the Experiencer's left as s/he lies on the Visitor medical examining table. This Tall One appears to direct the procedures, and often is the one who telepathically communicates with the Experiencer.
- A few Experiencers have noted glowing eyes under the "Jawas'" hoods.
- Other Experiencers have reported that when they got a glimpse of the Being whose face was shadowed by the hood, it was a type of "Gray".
- Still others saw neither glowing eyes nor "Grays" under the hoods, but rather never could distinguish the features in the shadows of the hoods.
- There are often mixed- race crews on the UFO's. In such cases there could be "Jawas" or "Praying Mantis" types or "Reptoids" or "Grays", joining in a coordinated effort in carrying out scientific or medical tasks.
- A few Experiencers have noted robot-like figures, whose movements and "vibes" (or rather lack thereof) strongly suggest that these are robots sent remotely by the Star Visitors to observe, reconnoiter, and possibly retrieve objects. However, I have not encountered any reports of robots actually interfacing with humans to accomplish communication, or to remove the human to their craft for scientific examination.
- The robot-like figures appear to be relegated to the more impersonal tasks of information-gathering and stealthy surveillance, without the risk to the Star Visitors that they would otherwise run of possibly encountering hostile human

responses. My research has also come up with a goodly number of reports of "Humanoids", "Blondes", or "Nordics", Star Visitors almost indistinguishable from humans. Indeed, Native American and other indigenous people's traditions point to their origin from the worlds of these human-looking Visitors in the Pleiades, Sirius, Orion and other star systems. If you were to place a pair of sunglasses on one of these "Nordic" Visitors, they would be indistinguishable from a Scandinavian-American citizen.

"Screen memory": Star Visitor-imposed mental visualization in the mind of the experiencer

I have also encountered reports where the Experiencer believed that the Star Visitor s/he was dealing with appeared to be a human. However, in some cases, this turned out to be a Star Visitor-imposed mental visualization in the mind of the experiencer, the so-called "screen memory".

Upon closer looking, the experiencer was able to see the actual nonhuman face of the Star Visitor behind the mentally-imposed "human" mask. My favorite variation of this mental cloaking experience occurred to one experiencer who believed she was encountering a human "spaceman".

I invited the Experiencer to look closely and carefully at the face of the "human spaceman". When she did so, she suddenly was startled. "Oh, my", she said," It's not a human after all. It's one of those Grays."

Other details made me suspect we were still not done. I suggested she study closely the face of her "Gray" visitor. Startled, she could see that it was a "Reptoid" who had previously cloaked himself mentally as a "Gray".

The "Dwarf" Star Visitors

Another Star Visitor racial type described are the short, chubby "Dwarf" Star Visitors, with round pudgy faces. They seem to be relegated to doing the menial chores during a contact.

The "Bird People" race

Yet another race is what could be dubbed the Bird People. This group's most pronounced feature is a broad, downward-sloping proboscis, somewhat like an oversize broad bird beak or flexible dolphin beak, with the mouth underneath the beak. These Visitors have graceful ovoid heads, and long thin necks. They have thin, horizontal, slit-like eyes with dark pupils. They are telepathic, kind-hearted, and powerful healers and teachers.

The light and energy beings

Then there are:
- The light beings,
- The energy beings,
- The pure, disembodied consciousnesses.

The light and energy beings do not have a solid, three-dimensional body, but rather there presence is marked by the presence of a structured orb or an ill-defined mass of light or other energy. In the case of the pure consciousnesses, the only signal of their presence is the onset of telepathic contact, and, occasionally, their influence on something in the local environment.

Undoubtedly, many more races could be described. We as humans are challenged by intelligent life that looks so different from us, a challenge which can be disturbing. But it can also remind us that the Source of All is myriad in its expression of lifeforms, including intelligent lifeforms, across the vast Universe. Only the most anthropocentric would be offended by the Supreme Source's creation of intelligence in other anatomical packages.

And, indeed, Star Visitor messages tell us that we are that special variant mix of intelligent life: part-Earth primate, part-Star Visitor intelligent lifeform. Thus, when any of us has an encounter with a Star Visitor, we truly are meeting our "distant cousins".

*** *** ***

CHAPTER 14
ANUNNAKI'S DESCENDANTS AND REMNANTS AMONG US, AND ALIENS BEHIND WORLD GOVERNMENT

- The plan for the New World Order did not originate on Earth – it is a system devised by aliens
- Basis and agenda of the New World Order
- The vast majority of the ruling elite of the world are descendants of Anunnaki remnants among us
- The New World Order appears to be under the control of the "Vulturites", an elite group of Anunnaki remnants among us
- The Reptilian Anunnaki remnants who were previously residing in human bodies in the United States are now in China
- Anunnaki Remnants' agenda
- Already, humans are being secretly micro-chipped with physical implants
- The minds of people are currently being altered
- The highest echelon on Earth are following orders from a "controller" who is not in a physical body
- The Anunnaki have set up and facilitated all popular religions on the planet
- The Anunnaki "controller" has an "elite guard" of fighters who are called the "Rumblers"
- The earth is one of the final hiding places for the Anunnaki
- The Anunnaki remnants intend to clone the human mind and insert it into artificial life forms.
- John Adams, James Madison, John Marshall and Alexander Hamilton were Anunnaki-sponsored participants
- Thomas Paine, Thomas Jefferson, and Benjamin Franklin are Attas consciousness
- Albert Einstein was an Anunnaki scientist

Anunnaki's Descendants And Remnants Among Us, And Aliens Behind World Government

The plan for the New World Order did not originate on Earth – it is a system devised by aliens.

D.M.'s theory goes like this: The concept of the New World Order is based upon an old Anunnaki system which has been employed in other galaxies a long, long time ago. This system is now being pushed for implementation on Earth by the Anunnaki Remnants who remain on Earth. The Anunnaki Remnants are the ones that were left behind on Earth by the Anunnaki Elite when they escaped this world.

Basis and Agenda of the New World Order

The New World Order is based upon the premise that there is to be a supreme commander who oversees the affairs of the world. During transition into a global government smaller and weaker nations are being forced or lured into accepting self-appointed stronger nations to act as their police force.

Later, the police force will expand and become an international police force under a single master. At first, this will appear to be a plan for a peaceful co-existence amongst nations which will benefit all nations.

However, it is a plan to eliminate all nation states, freedom, civil rights and to control the people of the world under a single ideology in the name of one global community.

The New World Order is a One World Order with a hidden agenda to rule by fear, control, exploitation and bullying.

The ruling elite of the world's wealthy, powerful and influential have been pushing for a New World Order with a One World Government under the pretence of establishing world peace while they are in fact imposing their will upon every nation.

They call themselves the "peacemakers" but in truth they are an international police force which organized "war crimes" tribunals, supposedly to give the "political criminals" a fair trial before persecuting them.

*** *** ***

The vast majority of the ruling elite of the world are descendants of Anunnaki remnants among us

The vast majority of the ruling elite of the world are either descendants of Anunnaki remnants or their supporters. A trait of the Anunnaki is to rule by instigating people to remain in a state of perpetual conflict. Peace is not even a consideration of the Anunnaki, who are a warmongering, bloodthirsty, lustful, perverted, deceptive, brutal race of beings who have controlled the Earth for a long time.

At present, the fragmentation, conflict, hate, jealousy, suspicion, mistrust, intolerance, biasness amongst nations, cultures and those of diverse religions etc. appear to be obstacles to the realisation of One World Order.

However, each of those traits was introduced by the Anunnaki as part of their plan to rule by segregation and division. The rule by fragmentation was only a transitional phase in a very long-range plan to bring about a One World Government by claiming that such a government can bring about world peace. In fact, the One World Government is a tool for the establishment of an absolute dictatorship over the entire world – a tyranny. Once the plan is in its final stages, it will be forced upon everyone. The people of the world will have no choice but to toe the line and follow the dictates of the One World Order or face severe consequences.

For a New World Order where diverse nations are drawn together under supposedly one common cause, humanity becomes enslaved to its One World Order sovereignty. The New World Order will not happen overnight. The idea was seeded a long, long time ago, and slowly but certainly it is weaving its way unsuspectedly through the monetary, political, religious, cultural, educational, scientific etc. systems. It started to gain momentum in the last 10 years.

The speed of its emergence has taken a quickened stride in the last three years, with one planned event after another taking place in various parts of the world in order to test and exercise the power of the would-be New World Order under the leadership of self-proclaimed, "high" moral standing personnel with the backing of a powerful dictatorial government.

The New World Order appears to be under the control of the "Vulturites", an elite group of Anunnaki remnants among us

At present, while the current push for a New World Order appears to be under the control of an elite group of Anunnaki Remnants which I call the "Vulturites", the real control is under the more cunning group of Anunnaki Remnants, which have been called the "Reptilians". These two groups of Anunnaki Remnants are in perpetual conflict with one another.

303

However, for the time being, the Reptilians are purposely backing off to trick the Vulturites into doing the dirty job of setting up the New World Order before taking it over from them when they feel the time is right.

The Reptilian Anunnaki Remnants who were previously residing in human bodies in the United States are now in China

As I have stated a long time ago, most of the consciousnesses of the Reptilian Anunnaki Remnants who were previously residing in human bodies predominantly in the United States and some parts of Europe have now shifted their locations to China. Consciousnesses of the Vulturite Anunnaki Remnants have now taken over most of those bodies previously occupied by the Reptilian Anunnaki Remnants.

The process towards the One World Order was implemented long ago on Earth.

Recent aspects of the move are seen in the evolution of credit card systems, identification systems, smart card systems, social security systems, taxation systems, health care cards etc. – these are just some of the recent systems introduced to control, condition, profile and keep tab of the whereabouts and activities of people. Yet superficially, these systems appear to be signs of advancement in technology and affluence so most people are not aware of the hidden agenda behind these schemes.

Anunnaki Remnants' Agenda

Already, humans are being secretly micro-chipped with physical implants

Already, humans are being secretly micro-chipped with physical implants for ease of identification and location of those chipped individuals – while also controlling their minds – by those working under the Anunnaki Remnants who have control of all facets of systems in this world, be they political, cultural, educational, commercial, pharmaceutical, monetary, military or otherwise. Every day when popular programmes are aired on radio, movie screens and especially on television, people are exposed to the risk of being programmed subliminally through the flashes of light, camera angles used, words uttered, musical accompaniment etc. to "think" as the Anunnaki Remnants want them to "think".

However, there is a small minority amongst the population in human bodies, especially those with alien ties, who have stronger will than most to resist such programming provided they do not give in to the ruling elite's threats, bribes etc.

The minds of people are currently being altered

The minority of the population on Earth who are resisting the "controller" are currently under surveillance. This minority group contains those who openly or quietly resist the so-called conventional and popular beliefs. They are not without the assistance of a Force which is fighting the Darkness of the "controller". Soon, this will become obvious. However, not everyone who is engaged in resisting the "controller" is of the Light.

Audible and inaudible sounds have also been released over the years to weaken human bodies and minds so as to control and poison their bodies, minds and actions. These sounds are also used to regulate various aspects of individual and collective human bodies and societal functions.

Ultimately, the aim of the ruling elite is to get rid of the majority of the human race before openly inhabiting and controlling the world that they now secretly control, and they have been doing so for a long time.

The highest echelon on earth are following orders from a "controller" who is not in a physical body

Many have considered how vast the conspiracy for a One World Order would have to be, and they have attempted to refute it by stating that certainly someone involved in such a massive project would have broken ranks and disclosed the conspiracy. This would be a valid argument, except only the highest echelon participants know of the agenda. However, none of the upper echelon have the entire picture – they are only aware of fragments of the plan.

The upper echelon cannot sort out the actual plan because it is built upon lies within lies within lies. Even the highest echelon on Earth are not the ultimate conspirators, they are merely following orders from their "controller" who is not in a physical body.

The minions unknowingly follow the plan to its inevitable conclusion because of programming and other factors.

Further, those of a dark essence will naturally gravitate towards compliance with the Anunnaki Remnants' agenda.

*** *** ***

305

The Anunnaki have set up and facilitated all popular religions on the planet

The public has little or no knowledge of what is occurring. Many of those who are resisting the One World Order have discussed at length the physical occurrences on the planet that point to the conspiracy and the New World Order.

Some of those have even addressed spiritual aspects of the plan to decimate and enslave the human race, however, most of those people are coming from a perspective of conventional religious backgrounds, and as I have discussed repeatedly, the Anunnaki have set up and facilitated all popular religions on the planet – including the New Age movement.

Unfortunately, there are always some good beings who get trapped in these movements.

Hence, those who promote a global community are really assisting the "controller's" plan, whether they are conscious of this or otherwise.

There are some humans who have already been chosen for survival by the ruling elite. These human survivors will be slaves to their masters.

Many have been chosen according to bloodlines, professions, ontological essences etc. to accommodate the needs of the Anunnaki Remnants' agendas.

The Anunnaki "controller" has an "elite guard" of fighters who are called the "Rumblers"

These Rumblers rarely left the "controller's" side in the past. They were only used in desperate situations. However recently, a few of them have arrived on the planet to try to block the Attas, (The Rescuers of the Light, The Amoebas) who are in combat with the "controller" and all its minions. Soon, the Rumblers will arrive on Earth in numbers. This will be a time when the battle between the forces of Light and Darkness will be in heightened conflict. The release of the Rumblers shows just how desperate the "controller" is becoming, especially since the "controller" is compromising its own protection by releasing its elite guard onto the planet.

The earth is one of the final hiding places for the Anunnaki

Contrary to popular belief, the Earth is not an important place –it is just one of the final hiding places for the Anunnaki – they have very few places to go to in these final stages of the Correction Process. The Attas are the targets of the Rumblers.

The average person could not withstand assaults by the Rumblers; however, the Rumblers are no match for the Attas. Many of these Attas have arrived as "walk-ins" on Earth in humble positions, in female and male human bodies.

There are many examples of mass mind control tests upon the population of Earth. One such example is the case of Diana Spencer. To the unaware, it appeared that her death had touched their hearts, but this was not the case. They were in fact programmed to respond with an enormous outpouring of emotions, grief and distorted views about the deceased. Most of these people did not even know her, nor did they have any ties to her. Little do the people suspect that emotional energy they spent was being sucked out of them and collected by the "controller" for its own selfish purposes and agendas. Imagine the vastness of the mind-control project necessary to condition so many millions into "spontaneously grieving" for the deceased.

On the other hand, when United States President John Kennedy was assassinated, there was an outpouring of grief and emotion, but some of the grievers were Light beings who sensed that they had lost a dear friend on this Earth. His death was felt by all the Attas parts in one way or another. However, his departure was expected by the Attas, and no attempt was made by the Light to try to prevent it for a very good reason. This was true grieving by many. The emotional mass programming by the ruling elite was only in its infancy at the time.

As another example of mass programming, the "controller" can now summon up millions of protestors to spout whatever slogans are desired to bring about a desired situation. And, yet, on the surface, it appears that the actions of the protestors occurred as an understandable and even reasonable reaction to a particular situation. In reality, the protestors are being programmed and used by the ruling elite to allow them to implement a particular plan.

In the near future, travel will become even more restricted than it is today; internet services could also be restricted. The time may come when internet services will be available only to certain ones using frequencies that will be unavailable to the population at large.

Wars, revolutions, famines, epidemics, recessions, depressions, catastrophes and casualties, bombings, murders, meaningless destruction and sometimes even natural disasters are planned by the "controller" for its own agenda.

There was a document released entitled The Report from Iron Mountain which was commissioned by President John Kennedy in August of 1963. Kennedy was overshadowed by an Attas consciousness (he had to play a double-game with many Anunnaki politicians in order to be accepted by them and be elected President of the United States), and while there were some reports about him that are not particularly complimentary, most of these are contrived or exaggerated by the ruling elite, who also sponsored many of the libels. This is much like what was done to Thomas Jefferson, another Attas consciousness.

Kennedy was assassinated three months after commissioning the report in which he was about to expose the warmongering mindsets of the people who are in control of the world.

The stated purpose of this report was to consider the problems involved in the contingency of a transition to a general condition of peace and to recommend procedures for dealing with this contingency.

This report, which was published three years after Kennedy's death, reveals the darkest recesses of demonic minds. It is filled with openly revolting revelations from many different political appointees about what is really on the minds of the ruling elite. In short, it is disgusting. Even though the report was leaked, it was never intended for public reading.

Many means of denial were employed to attempt to invalidate this document because the American government understandably wanted to distance itself from the report. Editors of newspapers were recruited and supposed authors came forward to claim they wrote it as a satire. It is hard to imagine that this document was intended as a satire, as it is devoid of humour – express or implied. Likewise, it is difficult to accept that a single author could be responsible for the extremely different styles and energies contained in the paper – not to mention the vast knowledge necessarily required to have written the document, which would not be available to a single person as even the higher echelon of the ruling elite have only fragments of the total plan.

This paper commences with the query of what would happen with a general détente amongst America, China and the Soviet Union, and asks the question: "Is the abolition of war, in the broad sense, really possible?"

In analysing the query, the paper states that stability of society is the common assumed objective of both peace and war.

Amongst other things, the paper dares to argue that were the war-making machines halted, all of the money saved would have to be rapidly consumed or else the people would have too much wealth, and become too cocky and difficult to control. Therefore, it was presented that in order to maintain stability it would be necessary to keep the people poor. The paper presented several wasteful programmes to dissipate any extra wealth that peace would bring to maintain economic control over the population.

Thus, it is learnt from the paper that since war is a system that has worked so effectively for so long it should be maintained. In a stark quote, the reader learns that: "Wars are not 'caused' by international conflicts of interest...war-making societies require – and thus bring about – such consuch conflicts." The report also concluded that: "The basic authority of a modern state over its people resides in its war powers."

When considering the report one begins to realise that since it is impracticable for everyone to be at real war, there are mini-wars throughout the society. Families are but microcosms of nation states with their miniature struggles for power and control. People within families use varying tactics for seizing power and control, whether it be done via manipulation or oppressive violence. Sports are another substitute for war, where the participants are actually putting less energy into the contests than the followers of the various sports.

In a sense, sports are the poor people's wars, where millions will buy a strong conflict instead of the billions or trillions necessary for all-out-nation-state wars.

And, to show the attitudes of the warmongering minds responsible for the report regarding the prospect of peace, consider this quote from the report: "In a broad social context, 'an eye for an eye' still characterizes the only acceptable attitude toward a presumed threat of aggression, despite contrary religious and moral precepts governing personal conduct."

This repulsive attitude continues today, and in fact has escalated with a huge percentage of the world's population being programmed to support the "eye for an eye" attitude. The ruling elite is worried that if there were no wars, they could lose power and control over the people. Hence, they believe that there must be a substitute for wars, otherwise, the people might not bow down to their leaders. This shows not only the warped minds of the people who thrive in this exploitative world, it clearly shows that for their own selfish gratification, they want to keep the evil system afloat at all costs.

The Anunnaki remnants intend to clone the human mind and insert it into artificial life forms.

As a part of the tyrannical plan, the Anunnaki Remnants intend to clone the human mind and insert it into artificial life forms. Worse still, they spread the untruthful propaganda that everyone is a "god" in the making, appealing to the egos and playing upon the ignorance of those receiving this nonsense.

There is even the promotion of biological immortality, supposedly under the guidance of the so-called "Ascended Masters". These Ascended Masters, by whatever name they usurp, are actually Anunnaki. What is actually happening by spreading such outrageous and dangerous untruths is that the people's thinking is being altered so greatly that the Anunnaki Remnants hope to capture the spirits of the victims and encapsulate those spirits in a "time capsule".

It is the distorted belief of the "controller" that if it could imprison these spirits and could clone artificial spirits, these would have no will of their own, but would be totally at the mercy of the "controller" and its hierarchy. While this sounds like science fiction, it is indeed the plan.

Many prominent figures in the world, in diverse roles, are not at all what they appear to be. Many have been placed into these positions because they do the bidding of the Anunnaki Remnants, whether they are conscious of this or not. This world has long been controlled by the Anunnaki and its Remnants, who rule by fear, brute force and deception.

Those who dare to go against the system are disadvantaged or removed from power. This can be seen by the assassinations of several of the American presidents.

Conversely, the British Prime Ministers do not share the same fate as their American counterparts because their positions were filled by Anunnaki Remnants or their representatives, such as Winston Churchill.

Having said this, it is imperative that we bear in mind the Anunnaki wear many disguises. They can appear to be a passionate proponent for peace, like Mahatma Ghandi, yet they are the very essence of deception of the Anunnaki. Contrarily, Indira Ghandi is a being of Light. Yet, both were assassinated.

John Adams, James Madison, John Marshall and Alexander Hamilton were Anunnaki-sponsored participants

Surrounding the American Revolutionary period, there were many Anunnaki Remnants and a few Light beings involved in playing prominent roles. For instance:

Anunnaki-sponsored participants:

- John Adams,
- James Madison,
- John Marshall,
- Alexander Hamilton

Were Anunnaki-sponsored participants. On the other hand:

Attas consciousness:

- Thomas Paine,
- Thomas Jefferson,
- Benjamin Franklin

Are all of Attas consciousness.

Elvis Presley, with his outward appearance of entrapment by glitter, glamour, fame, wealth and other issues, was not really trapped at all. He is an Attas who was here to do a specific job under the cover of a popular singer. His death took place, but not in the way the world believes it did. Like John Kennedy and Abraham Lincoln, Elvis too, was removed by the Dark Force, however, it was the time for each of them to go as they had completed their respective work.

It has recently been admitted by China that they execute at least 10,000 people each year, and it is easy to assume that the real figure is far greater.

310

China has always been an important battleground between Light and Darkness, even though Darkness seems to flourish there because China has always been a stronghold for the Anunnaki Remnants.

Since the Reptilian Anunnaki Remnants have shifted their consciousnesses to China, the increase in executions in that country is no surprise. Likewise, the increased interest in UFO activities amongst the people of China is to be expected.

Albert Einstein was an Anunnaki scientist

These days, there is a lot of talk about weapons of mass destruction. The real danger of weapons of mass destruction comes from the Anunnaki themselves. Many of these weapons were developed because of the work and theories of Anunnaki scientists such as Albert Einstein. These horrible weapons were developed so the Anunnaki in power can use them to threaten, coerce and enslave the people of the world.

This may sound like a very grim picture of the fate of humanity but this time the Attas are here with a whole host of reinforcements. They have come from the future and are amongst us today. As I have stated before, the Anunnaki Remnants are running out of time. Soon, they will be no more. In the meantime, each of us must consciously strengthen our WILL and never give it over to the oppressors.- This was the theory of D.M.

*** *** ***

CHAPTER 15
SEX WITH ALIENS

- Jazz singer tells of intense sex and orgasms with a reptilian alien.
- Pamela Stonebrooke: "I 'romped' with 6ft alien"
- Extra-terrestrial ... first visit was scary
- Sex on the astral, it is not physically localized
- Alien sex, voyeurism and hybrid-breeding: The Antonio Villas Boas account
- Almost from the start, sex and UFOs were inseparable bedfellows
- "A male protagonist having his genitals examined before sex with an alien female
- The female alien liquid had Viagra-like properties
- Marla, a beautiful alien blonde from space who claimed to be 500 years old
- Sex with Aura Rhanes, the captain of a flying saucer
- Elizabeth Klarer fell in love in Akon, an alien scientist
- Klarer said their "magnetic union" produced a perfect and highly intelligent son named Ayling
- Hybrid space babies
- 'Greys' were taking sperm and ova from human abductees.
- Raped by 6 humanoids
- Accounts of fairy and alien encounters
- Phantom pregnancies
- Aliens are confused by 'missing' fetuses
- Sex, surgery and space aliens
- Aliens repair a woman's faulty kidney
- Earth women would have sperm "injected into them."
- Fetuses mysteriously disappearing
- Women who report such genetic tampering are in the 35-40 age group
- Ridiculing alien sex
- The Centauri sex
- The Conehead sex

- The Tenctonese sex
- Victoria: Aliens don't have genital organs
- Victoria: Aliens do not practice sex. They reproduce in laboratories
- Aliens fertilize "each other" and keep the molecules in containers
- Alien babies are nourished by a "light conduit."

*** *** ***

SEX WITH ALIENS
Jazz Singer Tells of Intense Sex and Orgasms With "Reptilian" Alien

---

The story of Miss Pamela Stonebrooke is an astounding connection to humanity's ancient past. We all know the Biblical story of the angels who came to earth, were struck by the beauty of the daughters of man, married them and had children who were called Nefilim. The story of the Anunnaki, obviously a variant, tells of the same situation: extra terrestrials who come to earth, fall in love with Earth women, and have children with them. In the case of the Anunaki, much evidence exists that they really gave life to humanity as we know it.

Miss Stonebrooke tells us a story that is a replay of this scenario. She is abducted by an extraterrestrial, a stranger to her as the angels and the Anunnaki were strangers to the Earth women of old. To begin with, she is forced into a physical relationship with him, but eventually, she discovers the spiritual nature, the kindness, the intelligence of this being, and falls in love with him. It is not clear to me if the union gave birth to a child, but if it did, this is exactly the kind of hybrid that is described in the Nefilim and the Anunnaki stories. And even if a child was not born, it does not mean that the same story did not happen to many other abductees who did not have the courage to confess their love. The story may appear strange to many of us, but it rings true. History often repeats itself, and really, a few thousand years are insignificant in the life of the universe. The plan of creating the hybrids, and the love that can blossom between members of such diverse civilizations, is an old story – but perhaps it is constantly repeating itself. We do not know.

A few hours before I sent my book to the publisher, my friend Ben Zorab e-mailed me to let me know that he had written a relevant article about Miss Stonebrooke and her relationship with an alien. My staff had to reformat the book to fit it in, since it is an important revelation to our readers, and I did not want to miss such a fascinating revelation. Incidentally, Miss Stonebrooke is currently writing a book, telling the tale in her own words. It will be worth pursuing!

Ben Zorab's article.

Reproduced with a permission from the International News Agency (www.internationalnewsagency.org)

A 52-year-old jazz singer said: "I' romped with 6 ft alien and I enjoyed having sex with him…"My sources of information and data on divas' biographies and the history of entertainment's greats are Maximillien de Lafayette's books and encyclopedias on Jazz, cabaret and music; more precisely his 20 volumes of the "World Who's Who in Jazz, Cabaret, Music and Entertainment" and most recently his "Entertainment Greats from the 1800's to the Present." Until this month, when I learned about a Jazz singer by the name of Pamela Stonebrooke who claimed to have had sex with an extraterrestrial. Lafayette's academic books on Jazz did not even mention the name of Pamela Stonebrooke. But to my great astonishment I found something about her in a new kind of books written by Lafayette; books on UFOs! Would you believe it? Lafayette writing about aliens? Yes sir, he did, and he dashed out mind-boggling books on UFOs and aliens' abduction.

In two of his most recent books "The Anunnaki's Genetic Creation of the Human Race" and "Zeta Reticuli and Anunnaki Descendants Among Us", Lafayette wrote extensively on Stonebrooke. So, any statement or article about Stonebrooke by Maximillien de Lafayette, an authority on jazz, entertainment and extraterrestrials, would trigger my curiosity. So, I began my quest and search for Pamela Stonebrooke. And Lord! I did find a vast literature and so many articles about her. They are everywhere. Even in England, major newspapers interviewed her, and TV channels both in the US and Europe aired shows and documentaries about Stonebrooke.

In the Sun, Louise Compton wrote: "Few people can claim to have experienced? out of this world' sex - but Pamela Stonebrooke is a woman who can.

The 52-year-old jazz singer says she enjoyed mind-blowing alien romps with a six-foot reptilian for three years. Her story is among a number featured in World's Strangest UFO Stories which premieres this Sunday on the Discovery Channel. Speaking exclusively to The Sun Online, Pamela revealed: My first sexual encounter with an alien was unlike any love-making I've experienced before.

"It was so intense and enjoyable and, without wanting to get too graphic, he was so much larger than most men. I remember exactly how I felt when I saw him for the first time. I awoke from my sleep to find myself making love to what appeared to be a Greek god. At first I assumed it was an exceptionally lucid dream.

But the sex was very intense and as I closed my eyes I was overwhelmed by how comfortable I felt with this unknown being. The next time I opened my eyes he had transformed into a reptilian entity with scaley, snake-like skin. It was then I realized I was making love to a shape-shifting alien. Sensing I was scared, the reptile whispered: "We've always been together, we love each other.' The orgasms were intense. When I tell men about my reptilian experience, they find it difficult."

Pamela Stonebrooke: "I 'romped' with 6ft alien"

Let's start with the very beginning of this fascinating story with what the UFO International Congress stated about Pamela Stonebrook: "Pamela Stonebrooke is a recording artist, singer and songwriter from Los Angeles, who had no interest in UFOs or aliens until she was forced to confront the phenomena when she awoke inside a spacecraft surrounded by Greys. For the next year and a half, she went through a dark night of the soul as she dealt with the trauma of emerging memories of other abductions, as well as the alienation from friends and family who could not accept her experiences. She finally went public 2 years ago, and is currently writing a book about her life and her encounters entitled "Experiencer". Pamela talks about her encounters with her four Grey hybrid daughters, and openly discusses her intimate interactions with the renegade 'bad boys of alienology", the Reptilians. From terror and denial to awakening and expansion, she proposes a metaphysical perspective of the abduction phenomenon. She also discusses the interdimensional and transformational aspects of her experiences and shares some tools for making the encounters more than manageable."

Pamela Stonebrooke: "Let me just say that one of the most frustrating things about coming forward with this information is the constant third-hand misinterpretation from a misquoted, misrepresented article...picked up and rehashed and sensationalized for yet another article...ad nauseam. Add to that, the judgmental belief systems that this misquoted information is filtered through...and then paraphrased...and added to...and then further distorted and again disseminated. I could spend every waking moment attempting to clarify something for which most people have no frame of reference."

Pamela Stonebrooke, a professional jazz singer residing in Los Angeles, California, says she will tell her own incredible story of alien encounter in a forthcoming book to be published by Ballantine Books, a division of Random House. According to a June 3, 1998 report in the New York Post newspaper, Ballantine outbid at least two other major publishers for Stonebrooke's story. The Post left little doubt about why the book attracted so much attention. Stonebrooke's own book proposal says she engaged in sex with a "reptilian" alien. "She recounts this act of interspecies intercourse in a graphic, no-holds-barred, tour de force description, unique in UFO literature, replete with precise physical and emotional detail, sensational without being sensationalistic," the Post said, quoting from the book proposal. But Stonebrooke told CNI News that the Post article "seriously misrepresented the true nature" of her ET encounters. The real point of her story, she says, is not the lurid sex, but that she succeeded in not becoming a "victim" in a potentially overpowering situation. "The book will tell about my reptilian encounters, a subject that very few women are prepared to speak openly about," Stonebrooke wrote in a June 8, 1998 "open letter" to UFO researchers. But, she said, "I'll be examining and exploring my contact experiences in light of their transformative aspects, recognizing that the phenomenon is, and can be, an incredible catalyst for expanded self-awareness. Reptilians are not a politically correct species in the UFO community, and to admit to having sex with one -- much less enjoying it -- is beyond the pale as far as the more conservative members of that community are concerned... But I know I am not unique in reporting this kind of experience," Stonebrooke wrote in her open letter.

CNI News editor Michael Lindemann interviewed Pamela Stonebrooke on June 21, 1998. Stonebrooke says she has been a professional singer since she put her first band together at the age of 14. She's played jazz clubs in Europe, England and Japan, and now works mostly in her home town of Los Angeles. She's played with the best musicians in the business, she says, and she writes most of her own music. Like many people who claim to have what Temple University professor David Jacobs terms a "secret life" as an alien abductee, Pamela Stonebrooke seems to be a successful, self-confident, rational person. She's smart, articulate, and often funny. Apparently she did not need the notoriety of a tell-all book to earn her 15 minutes of fame. "To even come forward with this has really put me in a tenuous spot," she says. "I'm actually reluctant to be famous...I have a deep reverence for my artistry and my life, in terms of it being peaceful. I now wonder if I've shattered that possibility." Her strange experiences didn't seem "alien" at first, she says. Years ago, she took an interest in so-called out-of-body experiences and paranormal phenomena.

Pamela Stonebrooke: I've been digging into the paranormal for quite some time. I astral projected about thirteen or fourteen years ago. I had an out of the body experience. I had no idea what was happening.

Michael Lindemann: You weren't trying to do it?

PS: No. But it was such an incredible experience that I wanted to find out what it was and see if I could do it again. So I really set out to become a skilled astral projector. I read every book I could find...I went to other planets. I went to places that scared the living daylights out of me, but I thought it was all in my imagination. I was fine when I came back. So I was really having a ball.

ML: Do you continue to do this today?

PS: Absolutely. It's one of my greatest adventures.

ML: How does this relate to the ET encounters you say you've had?

PS: When I had this [alien encounter] experience, it had the flavor of an out of body experience. The thing that freaked me out about my first encounter was that I awoke aboard what I think is a spacecraft -- I was in a metallic room, oddly shaped...

ML: When was this?

PS: This was five years ago.

ML: Was this again an unexpected, spontaneous event?

PS: Yes, it was.

Stonebrooke says she awoke to find herself surrounded by strange "gray" beings with huge black eyes, the kind of alien that is most often reported by abductees. She says she had no idea who these beings were, because up to this time she had never paid any attention to UFO lore.

PS: I had not paid much attention to this whole thing. I was into metaphysics and channeling and opening my chakras. I had never read any accounts, never been to a UFO conference. I wasn't really interested in that stuff.

ML: How did you feel when you first saw these beings?

PS: I was panicked. They were filing into the room and standing around me, and I was literally shaking in a corner. I was in a fetal position, going "No, no, where am I? What is going on?" And this being that I perceived as a female came over to me, put her hand on my shoulder and said, "Don't be afraid. All you have to do is be here. Come with me." She took me into a room. It's still very vivid to me. On this metallic table that was a couple of feet from the floor were these four little girls, ages about 8, 9, 10 and 11 -- something like that -- and they came running over to me, calling me "Mommy." I was literally paralyzed against the wall. They were grabbing the bottom of my arms. I was trying to pull my arms away, and they were grabbing me.

ML: How did you react to these little girls calling you "Mommy"?

PS: I was panicked, because I had never wanted to be a mother. I had always made sure that I had never been pregnant. However, putting pieces together now, I remember years ago having four false pregnancies which I couldn't explain at the time. I didn't worry about them then, because I hadn't been with anyone.

ML: You're saying that you can recall, in the "normal" part of your life years ago, that you had four unexplained false pregnancies?

PS: Yes. At the time, I was really busy, partying a lot and living the lifestyle of a musician. So I had excuses for why I was hemorrhaging, or why I had weird symptoms or morning sickness. I had other reasons. I was heavily into the music scene, so I made excuses for all that stuff and really didn't worry about it.

ML: Did the four little girls look like normal human children?

PS: They didn't look human, but human-like. They really looked like a mixture. I was afraid of them because, first of all, I couldn't imagine me being a mother, and secondly, I couldn't imagine being the mother of something I didn't fully recognize as human. In retrospect, I've dealt with the guilt I felt for not being able to embrace them and accept them.

ML: When you woke up the next morning, was all of this clear in your memory?

PS: Yes, vivid. And I knew that something about it was different than an astral projection. Because, literally, I have astral projected to places where there were half-animal, half-human beings tearing at me, and have awakened in the morning and said, "Oh man, I'm glad that was only a projection." So now we have little girls grabbing my arm, and I'm totally panic-stricken. It doesn't make sense.

319

ML: Was there something in particular the next day that convinced you that this had been more physicially real than an out-of-body experience?

PS: Yes. I had my kimono on, and I noticed that my arms were sore at the bottom. So I pulled my kimono sleeve up, and I saw little bruise marks on my arm, from my elbow down to my wrist. The minute I saw them, it was a confirmation to me that something really physical had happened.

ML: How did you feel about that?

PS: For the next year and a half, I was pretty much a mess. I was trying to share with friends, and with my minister at Science of Mind church. And I was really unhappy at not being taken seriously -- in fact, looked at like I was crazy. My friends stopped calling me because I wasn't fun any more. All I wanted to talk about was this...

Feeling increasingly frustrated and anxious, Stonebrooke says, she went to a well-known local channeler named Darryl Anka, seeking advice. Anka gave her a recently published book by a woman named Kim Calrsberg, called "Beyond My Wildest Dreams." In the book, Carlsberg describes her own struggle to come to terms with alien abduction.

PS: Darryl gave me Kim Carlsberg's book, and I think I must have sobbed all the way through it. It was somehow healing. It helped me start processing stuff. I still have a real hard time talking about some of the medical procedures that I remember from incidents after that. In fact, that's the only thing that I can't really talk about without having the trauma come back in my face.

ML: Do you mean to say that you've recalled other abductions where you experienced medical procedures?

PS: Yes, I started to remember other encounters, and they were very disturbing to me. Most of the stuff that scared me was the medical stuff, because of the coldness and the detachment that I felt from the beings, not to mention the physical symptoms.

ML: Judging from hints you've previously given about your forthcoming book, you seem to feel very differently about your encounters with so-called "reptilian" aliens. You've even suggested that you enjoyed your sexual encounters with these beings.

PS: I've said that the connection we had, and the sex, was better than anything I had experienced. But it wasn't so much the physical act of sex as the whole experience of ecstatic mental, spiritual, emotional and physical -- a combination of experience -- that made it so amazing to me.

ML: When did you first have an encounter with a being you call a reptilian? How did that come about?

PS: I was really getting through my "gray stuff" pretty well. I had managed to finally apply my metaphysics, one of the fundamentals of which is that our spirit -- the part of us that is a spark of the infinite -- signs us up for some lessons to be learned in this life. We basically pick our script, make our contract, come here, do it the best we can, and if we're lucky, wake up to the fact that we can actually author this experience with our thoughts, beliefs and awareness. So I was able to apply my metaphysics and say, "If I signed up for everything else in my life, then I definitely signed up for this too.

320

Now, what can these experiences teach me?" Well, the first and most obvious thing is that it can make me face any fear. If I can get through the fear of something that I don't even have the vocabulary to explain, then there won't be much in this physical dimension that frightens me. So I said, if I signed up for this, I must be ready for it. And then I said, OK, I want to know more. What's really going on here? In my meditations, I said, Take me further...So, basically, the reptilian showed up. The first time, it shape-shifted from a gorgeous blond man to a reptilian being...

ML: When was this?

PS: That was about a year and a half after my gray stuff, when I really started to process it and feel comfortable. I was ready for anything.

ML: How is it that you wound up in bed with this gorgeous man? Was that intentional on your part, or a surprise?

PS: I woke up in my bed and he was making love to me. I was pretty sure that I was totally awake, that it wasn't a dream. And I said to myself, I don't know this person. I didn't bring him home last night. But I also felt like there was a mental connection. It didn't feel like a lucid dream, it didn't feel like out of the body. I didn't know what it was, but I felt pretty safe. And I was getting a telepathic communication: "You're safe with me. We have been together before."

ML: Then what happened?

PS: Basically, the entity shape-shifted into a reptilian being.

ML: When you say reptilian being, why do you say that? What features make this being reptilian to you?

PS: That's [how] I've come to identify it. It's humanoid, very sentient. I could tell there was an incredible intelligence and mental communication with this being. I felt in a lot of ways that I was looking at a part of myself once again, an aspect of myself, something very familiar to me. It did have almost like a snake's body -- if you rub it the way the scales flow -- firm but smooth. That's what it felt like to me.

ML: What kind of eyes did it have?

PS: The eyes were a bit larger than ours, and I was catching glimpses of colors: gold, speckles of red, and brown, with a vertical pupil.

ML: Vertical like a cat's eye?

PS: Yes. And very handsome, oddly enough. Maybe because, again, of the mental communication. I was shocked and frightened because of the appearance at first, and then I decided to participate.

ML: Are you saying that your lovemaking continued as this being became a reptile?

PS: That's correct.

ML: Did the being give you any indication why it revealed itself when it had been looking perfectly blond and normal to you?

PS: No. And in the other subsequent encounters I've had, there's been no shapeshifting involved. He just appears as a reptile.

ML: Is it clear to you that it's always the same one?

PS: My feeling is that it is, yes.

ML: Have you seen more than one?

PS: No, I haven't.

ML: Apart from your physical contact, apparently you have some sort of communication with this being. What's the nature of that communication, generally? Is he revealing secrets of the universe? Telling you he loves you? What does he say to you?

PS: Yes, love is expressed, but basically what I get -- and part of this is from hypnotic regression -- is an apocalyptic scenario that I would have to prepare for.

ML: Are you being shown an apocalyptic future?

PS: Possibly. That's the way I'm interpreting it. There may be something that I will see in my lifetime that I will have to deal with, and I'm being reminded of the amount of spiritual and emotional centeredness I must have to make whatever transition is necessary. Everything I say should be prefaced with, "It seems to me," because I have no answers to any of this stuff yet, and I may not, ever. I know I may have to make a friend of the unknown forever. But I want to make peace with this, because I don't want to live a life of desperation.

ML: Do you see a relationship between the various entities you've met -- grays and reptilians, for example -- or are these different types of entities operating separately?

PS: For me, they are somewhat separate. I think we're talking about many different factions within many different species, coming from the past, present and future as we know time. I think that there could be intelligent, benevolent, spiritually evolved reptilians. I think there could be warrior classes that are still raping and pillaging, like any invading force might do in a foreign land. One thing I want to stress is that it's really dangerous to generalize about any of these entities. I've come to realize [that] the more peace I make with these experiences, the more peaceful they are.

ML: You seem remarkably at ease, considering what you've been through. Is there any final thought you'd like to share with our readers?

PS: One of the most amazing things about this is that it really makes you look at your beliefs. I think that unless we all do that, we don't stand a chance of having the kind of life we're all entitled to -- one that's peaceful, that has a sense of unity and oneness. The truth is never going to be delivered in the package that we want it in. I think people are opening up to this. That's a really positive thing.

*** *** ***

The Sun online posted this: **Pamela Stonebrooke: Encounter...Pam says she enjoyed sex with an alien**

By Louise Compton

FEW people can claim to have experienced "out of this world" sex - but Pamela Stonebrooke is a woman who can. The 52-year-old jazz singer says she enjoyed mind-blowing alien romps with a six-foot reptilian for three years. Her story is among a number featured in World's Strangest UFO Stories which premieres this Sunday on the Discovery Channel. Speaking exclusively to The Sun Online, Pamela revealed: "My first sexual encounter with an alien was unlike any love-making I've experienced before. It was so intense and enjoyable and, without wanting to get too graphic, he was so much larger than most men. "I remember exactly how I felt when I saw him for the first time. I awoke from my sleep to find myself making love to what appeared to be a Greek god. At first I assumed it was an exceptionally lucid dream. But the sex was very intense and as I closed my eyes I was overwhelmed by how comfortable I felt with this unknown being. "The next time I opened my eyes he had transformed into a reptilian entity with scaley, snake-like skin. It was then I realised I was making love to a shape-shifting alien. Sensing I was scared, the reptile whispered, 'We've always been together, we love each other.' The orgasms were intense. When I tell men about my reptilian experience, they find it difficult."Pamela said her first alien bonk took place in 1998, more than a year after her first extra-terrestrial encounter. At the time, she was working as a high-powered celebrity agent in Houston, USA, and says she had no interest in the mysterious world of little green men. She told us: "My first conscious contact was in 1994. At the time I was working long hours so it was just a normal, busy day at the office. That night I went to sleep early and instead of waking up at the normal time and heading off to work, I awoke aboard what seemed to be a space craft. "I found myself huddled in the foetal position in a very dimly lit, metallic room, shaped like a truncated pyramid. ?I looked around nervously and a line of small, grey beings walked into the room looking at me. One of them, I think she was female, approached me and said: 'Don't be afraid, just come with me.' I followed her into another room and she shut the door behind us. As soon as it shut, it disappeared and there were three smaller female aliens looking at me and calling me 'Mummy'. All my fears hit me at once. I was absolutely terrified. Then the next thing I knew I was back in my bed again. It left me feeling incredibly frightened because the experience was so real.

Extraterrestria'sl first visit was scary

"I got up to splash my face with water and as I did so, I rolled up the sleeves of my kimono and noticed a number of little bruise marks on my arms. When I saw them it brought everything back. And I remembered them grabbing my arms which must have left the marks. I didn?t sleep well that night. In fact I didn't sleep well for nearly a year." Fascinated by her experience, Pamela arranged to be regressed via hypnosis to see if she could find out more about what happened to her. She told us: "It was fascinating and it brought back lots of memories which led me to believe I'd had more than one alien encounter. It was amazing because I had always found the extra-terrestrial world pretty ludicrous. But I began to see things differently. I even asked an artist to draw my impressions of the reptilian visitor and started a support group for people who have experienced similar things. It was initially difficult to tell family and friends about, but I overcame the embarrassment factor pretty quickly. I honestly don?t care if people laugh at my story because I would have been the same prior to my mind-expanding encounters." Pamela's story is among a number featured in World's Strangest UFO Stories which premieres this Sunday on Discovery Channel.-End of the article.

SEX ON THE ASTRAL, IT IS NOT PHYSICALLY LOCALIZED

Pamela Stonebrooke: "I do not teach people to get out of their bodies to have sex with Reptilians... As for sex on the astral, it is not physically localized."

Pamela explains her experiences, astral projection and sexual affair with an alien. She stated (Verbatim): "I would simply like to share that astral projection is one of the most powerful tools for the exploration of consciousness that I have found to date, and believe me, I have walked down many paths in the quest for my spirit.

I do not teach people to get out of their bodies to have sex with Reptilians. I have been astral projecting for nearly two decades, and for over a year now I have been able to consciously control and direct my experiences to unravel and confront "many" life issues. We have access to those interdimensional realms and they are within our reach to explore.

I believe it is the cutting edge of experiential consciousness exploration.

I have met loved ones who have transitioned, gone to past lives, and what I perceive to be future lives. I have seen other entities that I cannot/will not even begin to label, much less, discuss on the internet. These experiences are sacred to me and I'm learning not to offer them up to an onslaught of viciousness and ridicule. I will, however, tell you that in the astral state, I have had healings, and have floated in a sea of knowingness that is beyond thought...overwhelmed with love, acceptance and forgiveness...as close to the "source" as I have ever felt. I must admit that it is my primary target when I consciously get out. This skill is the same as a near death experience but it is controllable, repeatable and not trauma based. Many NDEers have stated, it is life altering. Imagine doing it at will, without it being trauma induced, and controlling your destination. It is a thought responsive realm in which your focused/directed thought/intention will immediately manifest the experience of your choice. My goal is to be "awake" 24 hours a day. Let me further add that I have been able to target/direct my exploration to see my four hybrid daughters. I had suffered much guilt at having rejected them and in that interaction (meeting them on the astral) I was able to tell them how sorry I was and express my love. It was as healing and cathartic as lifetimes of therapy. I have also targeted the Reptilians and I feel that they are a soul group of mine, as are the Greys. I can't go into the many experiences I've had that suggest this to me, but that is my feeling.

324

> **As for sex on the astral, it is not physically localized.** Nor is it the religiously orchestrated, guilt-ridden, pornographic act that we have relegated the sexual union to...allowing it to be bastardized on this plane of existence. Sex on the astral is a complete merging of energy and spirit...a communion and knowingness that goes beyond so-called rational thought, into a realm of pure being.

The astounding experience of the higher astral planes are perceived as somewhat orgasmic only because that is the only way we have of describing that incredibly profoundly ecstatic state of being. We keep trying to ascribe our moral values, attitudes and definitions to other worldly experiences where they simply do not apply.

As John Mack says "You can't get there from here." It would be helpful if we could start looking beyond our dualistic views, judgments and limited perceptions. My feeling is that the entities that we come in contact with are soul groups that we have had incarnations with. It's like an expanded understanding of reincarnation that goes beyond our physical/human lifetimes. Perhaps through the hybridization program we are creating a species that our spirits will one day inhabit? Please understand that these are my impressions and I fully understand that these concepts will be beyond the pale for those who cannot embrace these ideas.

One of the reasons I teach people consciously controlled out of the body is that I'm very aware that you cannot convince anyone that "any" experiences are real, much less, paranormal ones. But, when we are able to have our own personal and experiential validation of the multidimensional beings that we are, we gain an unprecedented and expanded view of the nature of reality. We can switch on that dormant DNA and accelerate our spiritual evolution, often beyond our capacity to articulate it. Homo Noeticus...the next leap in our evolution. We are awesome and creative beings capable of much more than we can ever "fully" know...it's simply a matter of how much "more" you "want" to know. Personally, it is an insatiable passion.

Victimization and fear (and certainly "hard" science) will never solve this mystery....but paranormal pioneers might stand a chance of piercing the veil. I believe that to know yourself as an inter/multidimensional being can put you on equal ground with any entity that you come in contact with. I know, from my own experience and several other people, that OOB exploration can be a powerful tool for experiencers in terms of processing these interactions.

An open letter from Pamela Stonebrooke to the members of the UFO community

I'm writing this in response to the news item that appeared in a recent issue of The New York Post about my forthcoming book, Experiencer: A Jazz Singer's True Account of Extraterrestrial Contact. Since the article unfortunately conveyed the impression that the book would be sensationalistic, it seems appropriate that I share some thoughts with you, and set the record straight about the book I am writing. I know that The New York Post piece seriously misrepresented the true nature of the book. The book is multi-faceted, and treats the abduction phenomenon, in all of its complexity, with the sensitivity, respect and seriousness it deserves, presenting not only my own experiences, but those of other experiencers as well.

I'll be examining and exploring my contact experiences in light of their transformative aspects, recognizing that the phenomenon is, and can be, an incredible catalyst for expanded self-awareness.

Interaction with extraterrestrial intelligence has many aspects, of course, but the transformational aspect is fundamental to me. The book will tell about my reptilian encounters, a subject that very few women are prepared to go public with or speak openly about. I praise the courage of the few that already have - and endured public ridicule as a result. Reptilians are not a politically correct species in the UFO community, and to admit to having sex with one - much less enjoying it - is beyond the pale as far as the more conservative members of that community are concerned.

But I know from my extensive reading and research, and from talking personally to dozens of other women (and men) that I am not unique in reporting this kind of experience. I am the first to admit that this is a vastly complex subject, a kind of hall of mirrors, where dimensional realities are constantly shifting and changing. Certainly, the reptilians use sex to control people in various ways.

They have the ability to shape-shift and to control the mind of the experiencer, as well as to give tremendous pleasure through their mental powers. I have wrestled with all of these implications and the various levels of meaning and possibilities represented by my encounter experiences.

I will say, however, as I have said before, that I feel a deep respect for the reptilian entity with whom I interacted, and a profound connection with this being.

In a past life regression I did recently, I went to a very remote period in earth's history (perhaps hundreds of thousands of years ago), and saw myself as one of a brotherhood of reptilian warriors facing a catastrophic event in which we perished together (it was possibly nuclear in nature, since I saw a red cloud and felt tremendous heat).

I believe that on one level, I may be meeting these entities again, perhaps fellow warriors from the past warning us of an impending, self-inflicted doom - or perhaps they are different aspects of myself. I don't really know; I'm just trying to unravel this puzzle like everyone else.

Following my initial Art Bell interview, I received hundreds of letters and e-mails, many from people describing similar encounters to mine. I know that there are people out there who are suffering in isolation and silence, thinking they are going crazy.

I have been able to give some of these people strength and courage, so that they can move through their fear and come out the other side, empowered and still able to celebrate life as the incredible adventure that it truly is.

I know that when I was processing my Grey experiences, if it had not been for people like John Mack, Budd Hopkins, Kim Carlsberg, Whitley Strieber, John Carpenter, and other researchers and experiencers who have been courageous enough to come forward, putting their lives and reputations on the line, I would have stayed in fear a lot longer, cowering in a corner, my self-esteem and identity shattered.

Thanks to them and to the wonderful members of my support group, I am still standing, intact and whole.

I believe that the alien abduction experience is profoundly linked to the momentous shift in consciousness that is occurring as we enter the new millennium. We are witnesses to and participants in the most fantastic era in human history. And contrary to the mood of pessimism from some individuals regarding the way mainstream media treats the UFO phenomenon, and the trepidation that is felt regarding its ultimate impact on the human race, I am unashamedly a "Positive."

Everywhere I turn, I find much greater public acceptance of the alien abduction/UFO phenomenon, and active curiosity from enormous numbers of people. I am also encouraged by the fact that many more experiencers are coming forward, no longer hiding behind the cloak of anonymity. I believe that within ten years the reality of alien abduction will be accepted as a fact by the majority of people on this planet, and ridicule of the subject by the media or anyone else will be regarded as naive and irresponsible.

I think the problem that exists between UFOlogy and the media stems from the fact that the UFO community has been so sadly wounded in the past fifty years by rejection and ridicule that it has been somewhat demoralized as a movement. It has been a long, uphill battle, with many martyrs shedding their blood along the way, but I believe that we are winning the battle for public acceptance and are closer than ever before to solving the mystery of the alien presence itself. I am looking forward to appearing on major TV talk-shows, and to bringing the message directly to the public about this phenomenon. This is a subject that must - and will - be taken seriously, even, eventually, by the likes of Leno and Letterman. I was amazed, I might add, by the number of editors in the New York publishing community who are "believers," and I predict that within the next few years, UFO and abduction books will routinely top the bestseller lists as the public hungers to learn more about what our encounters mean, and their implications for the human race.

If my book is successful, everyone in the UFO community will benefit.

The floodgates are about to open, and when they do, all experiencers, UFO investigators, writers and researchers will find wider acceptance for their work. The days and years ahead are going to be full of challenges and opportunities, but we need to change ourselves in order to change the world. We need to work together harmoniously with mutual understanding and respect.

I want to thank everyone who is willing to cut me some slack with regard to the article in The New York Post. I'm sure it won't be the last test of my strength or your discernment.

Please keep those stones in hand until you read my book. I am confident that if and when you do, you will be able to recommend it to experiencers and non-experiencers alike.

I would also like to thank everyone in the UFO community who has assisted me on my journey to awareness these past five years.

*** *** ***

327

Alien Sex, Voyeurism and Hybrid-breeding: The Antonio Villas Boas Account

> Almost from the start, sex and UFOs were inseparable bedfellows
> "A male protagonist having his genitals examined before sex with an alien female."

Nigel Watson told fascinating stories about humans, males and females who had sex with extraterrestrials, and romantic affairs with aliens who became so attached to the human flesh. I included Watson's stories in this chapter.

One particularly unusual story is the affair of Brazilian manwith a beautiful, fair-haired woman. It is the strange tale of "a male protagonist having his genitals examined before sex with an alien female."It goes like this:

Almost from the start, sex and UFOs were inseparable bedfellows. The adventure of 23-year-old Antonio Villas Boas on 16 October 1957 in Brazil is probably the most famous case of interstellar intercourse. Antonio was ploughing a field on the family farm when the engine of his tractor cut out; at the same time, an object with purple lights descended from the sky. Humanoids in spacesuits emerged from the object and took him into their craft, subjecting him to what seemed like a medical examination. They stripped him, spread a strange liquid over him and took a sample of his blood. He was left alone in a room for what seemed a long time, until a beautiful, fair-haired woman arrived.

The female alien liquid had Viagra-like properties

She was naked and Antonio was instantly attracted to her. Without speaking or kissing, they had sex, during which she growled like a dog. Despite his strange circumstances or perhaps because the female alien liquid had Viagra-like properties Antonio was soon ready for a second helping. Interviewed later, he said: "Before leaving she turned to me, pointed to her belly, and smilingly pointed to the sky." Before letting him go, his captors gave Antonio a guided tour of the spaceship. Antonio went on to become a successful lawyer and still stood by his story over 30 years later.

Marla, a beautiful alien blonde from space who claimed to be 500 years old

Equally lurid stories of sexual liaisons with UFO occupants came from the world-famous contactees of the 1950s. Howard Menger, for one, had regular meetings with Marla, a beautiful alien blonde from space who claimed to be 500 years old. She projected "warmth, love and physical attraction," which he found irresistible. Menger divorced his wife to marry Marla (aka Connie Weber).

Sex with Aura Rhanes, the captain of a flying saucer

From July 1952, Truman Bethurum had many meetings with Aura Rhanes, the captain of a flying saucer, whom he found to be "tops in shapeliness and beauty".

Bethurum's wife wasn't so impressed with this "queen of women" and cited Rhanes in her divorce petition. From the late Forties to the early Sixties, female contactees in contrast to today's female abductees are few and far between.

Elizabeth Klarer fell in love in Akon, an alien scientist

This is more than made up for by the astonishing story of Elizabeth Klarer, who in 1956 fell in love with Akon, a scientist who took her to his home planet, Meton. There, he seduced her, saying: "Only a few are chosen for breeding purposes from beyond this solar system to infuse new blood into our ancient race." This smooth talk worked; "I surrendered in ecstacy to the magic of his lovemaking," she wrote later.

Klarer said their "magnetic union" produced a perfect and highly intelligent son named Ayling

She was sent back to South Africa alone and died in 1994; as far as we know her starman and son live on somewhere beyond Alpha Centauri. Rather ordinary tales of 'contact' are thus transformed into heroic fantasies of youthful virility.
Antonio Villas Boas claimed to have done what any healthy young man would have done in the same situation; he and Elizabeth Klarer delivered the goods, helping to save an alien race from extinction. Scientific ufologists, more interested in 'hard' evidence (like radar traces, photographs and forensic samples) condemn this 'wet' material as too subjective, relegating claims of sexual assault and abduction to the fields of psychology and folklore (which they likewise distrust). The early contactee literature provides a rich variety of such stories and, whatever their validity, it is a pity they have been largely neglected or ridiculed. When ufologist John Keel visited college communities in Northeast America during the mid-1960s, several young women told him they had been raped by aliens, and young men confessed that aliens had extracted their semen.

Hybrid space babies

By the 1970s, the idea of hybrid 'space babies' was more widely known but taken seriously only by UFO cultists who, said Keel, feared, that "the flying saucer fiends are engaged in a massive biological experiment creating a hybrid race which will eventually take over the Earth."
A decade later, these notions were part of mainstream ufology.

'Greys' were taking sperm and ova from human abductees.

Serious researchers some of them academics, like John E. Mack and David Jacobs openly declared their belief that the 'Greys' were taking sperm and ova from human abductees.

It was common to hear female abductees tell of being impregnated, of the ftus taken from their wombs, and of later being shown their hybrid babies in a nursery on a flying saucer.
Historically, pregnancy and abortion have been surrounded by a constellation of myths and old wives' tales and it is, perhaps, no surprise to find unidentified flying saucers' mythology being used to explain unexpected pregnancies, 'mysterious' discharges and missing or malformed babies.

Raped by 6 humanoids

In the 1970s, a 19-year-old Californian girl attributed the birth of a blue-skinned, web-footed baby to being gang raped by six blue-skinned web-footed humanoids who attacked her after she watched their spaceship land on a beach.

Similar stories of lusty mermen (the ocean has some affinity with space) can be found in folklore and are usually given as explanation for the birth of deformed babies with reptilian or fish-like characteristics.

Some researchers are aware of intriguing similarities between the lore of witches and fairies and modern abduction reports, and nocturnal sexual encounters with supernatural beings of all types can be found in most cultures to the present day. In the past, hundreds of men and women confessed (not always under torture) to sexual intercourse with demons.

Some shapeshifting demons were said to lie with a man (as a succubus) to obtain sperm and then (as an incubus) impregnate a woman with it.

Accounts of fairy and alien encounters

Ufologists, in particular, have been aware of the structural similarities between accounts of fairy and alien encounters. A recent study by James Pontolillo compared 1517th century accounts of sexual relations with demons to 20th century encounters with aliens and concluded that both traditions expressed a fundamental fear of female sexuality but today the male body and mind are just as likely to be under attack.

"Communion" author Whitley Strieber famously described being sodomised by a narrow, 1ft (0.3m)-long alien probe.

He felt that, while inside him, it seemed alive and was surprised, on its removal, to find it was a mechanical device. In my own research I have interviewed 'Martin Bolton' who had visions of, and telepathic communications with, three young space women. On behalf of these entities, he window-shopped for female attire and watched porn films. They were the 'goodies'; the 'baddies' beamed pain to his brain and for a three-year period stretched his penis during the night.

Phantom pregnancies

On several occasions they afflicted him with phantom pregnancies. Ridley Scott's movie Alien (1979) dramatised the nature of the alien sexual assaults; the proof of their inhumanity is that they don't always differentiate between the sexes or even between species.

Historian David Jacobs who offers accounts, in his book, of abductees compelled to have sex with fellow victims while aliens watched speaks for many who believe that the apparently spontaneous experience of abduction by so many different people implies the phenomenon really exists as an objective threat. Yet Rogerson has demonstrated that most of the elements of the abduction narrative appeared together as early as 1967 in "The Terror Above Us" by Malcolm Kent.

This science fiction novel anticipated such ufological themes as the 'Oz factor' (the sensation of being transported to a different reality), the supernatural cold, the doorway amnesia (the informant cannot remember what went on inside a room after entering), the alien in disguise, and impersonal scientists experimenting on humans.

For good measure, the story also includes a male protagonist having his genitals examined before sex with an alien female.

Another critic of the hybrid-breeding idea is British ufologist Peter Brookesmith, who compared the described activities of the alien 'doctors' with the procedures used by terrestrial fertility specialists.

Aliens are confused by 'missing' fetuses

He found that the alien inseminators singularly fail to take their subjects at the premium time for egg removal, namely within 48 hours of ovulation. And the aliens are just as likely to be confused by 'missing' fetuses as are humans, given the general difficulty of diagnosing pregnancy within the first eight weeks. For all their cosmic superiority, the alien inseminators can make pretty elementary, and farcical, errors.

Aliens inserted a long needle into Betty Andreasson's navel. They said their purpose had to do with creation and were puzzled to find 'something' missing. Andreasson had to explain to them that she'd had a hysterectomy. Whatever the genesis of such reports, we have to consider that folk have reported sexual contact with all manner of supernatural beings throughout history. Either the aliens have been conducting their beastly experiments for millennia, or such stories meet some deep-seated socio-psychological need. Until any solid medical evidence is provided, the latter hypothesis seems the more likely.

SEX, SURGERY AND SPACE ALIENS

Reprinted from an article appearing in The Weekly Newsmagazine, British Columbian Report, May 27, 1991, Volume 2 Number 39. Barbara Tandory

Last week researcher Chris Rutkowski, of Winnipeg revealed that British Columbians reported 114, or 49% of the 232 UFO sightings in Canada in 1990. For some the survey was confirmation of a long-held belief that B.C. is home to more than its share of those on the lunatic fringe. But for those who claim to have encountered beings from outer space, the survey was a confidence-builder. They could take comfort in the knowledge that more and more of their neighbours are willing to risk being classified as crazies [sic], by speaking of encounters with extra-terrestrials.

Aliens repair a woman's faulty kidney

Alvena Scott, a 41-year old Vancouver receptionist, is one of those finding security in numbers. Miss Scott claims she has been about as close as anyone can get to a space alien. Indeed she is one of about 20 people in the Vancouver area who say they have been abducted by extra-terrestrials. Apparently some of the aliens were nice enough to operate on her to repair a faulty kidney.

Others, however, were only interested in her reproductive capacity. She says the latter group impregnated her during a March 1990 abduction. Three months later, despite the fact she had been celibate for years, she experienced a miscarriage.

Miss Scott says that in the summer of 1985 she was experiencing excruciating pain in the area of her left kidney. Doctors told her the kidney would have to be removed but she feared surgery and would not consent to an operation. She explains that during this period she began nightly meditations and it was after one of these sessions that the first alien showed up in her bedroom. The next thing she knew she was in a circular room surrounded by seven-foot-tall, blue-eyed, human- like creatures. She awoke in her bed the next morning to find blood on her sheets and on her torso. But her kidney problem was gone.

Earth women would have sperm "injected into them."

Miss Scott says that five years after her encounter with the beneficent, tall, blue-eyed beings she had a bad experience with some small, insect-featured extra-terrestrials. She claims that in March of 1990 she was "forcibly taken" in the middle of the night to a spaceship. Apart from going through a series of tunnels she remembers nothing of the journey to the spaceship but she has vivid recollections of her experiences aboard the aliens' craft. She was one of about 20 "earth people," of both sexes, on the ship.

After communicating with the aliens by telepathy she learned the earth women would have sperm "injected into them." She received sperm but was not told who or what provided it. Three months later she had a miscarriage.

Fetuses mysteriously disappearing

A tissue sample from the miscarriage has allegedly been given to Lorne Goldfader, director of the Vancouver-based UFO Research Institute of Canada (UFORIC). Mr. Goldfader says other UFO researchers have had evidence of fetuses mysteriously disappearing. To reduce the risk of theft he's not disclosing where the tissue is being stored. The 41-year-old Vancouver postal worker says the sample, which "appears to be in the first stage of a foetus [sic]," will be examined by a pathologist in due course. However, as of last week, despite a year-long search, Mr. Goldfader had been unable to find a lab willing to perform the analysis.

Another UFO researcher, Graham Conway from Delta, says that based on his knowledge of the case and the phenomenon, the sample tissue "does indeed look to be what he (Mr. Goldfader) claims it is." Mr. Conway, 64, described the material as a tiny but "perfectly human (-looking) foetus [sic] with a tiny umbilical chord attached to it." The former high school teacher says he has no doubts about Miss Scott's "sincerity" in the matter.

And after 44 years in the (UFO research) field, he thinks this might well be the long-awaited breakthrough in abduction research.

His experience in the field leads him to believe that accounts like those of Miss Scott are becoming too numerous to ignore. "If it's a figment of the imagination, it is happening to a lot of imaginations. I believe that there's inference with birth."

Women who report such genetic tampering are in the 35-40 age group

In another case he investigated, a B.C. woman reported being taken aboard a spacecraft and introduced to a boy she was told was her son. He says most of the women who report such genetic tampering are in the 35-40 age group. He adds that a significant number of "abducted" women have been sexually abused in their earth lives.

For her part Miss Scott says the alien encounters not only cured her kidney problems but also gave her a whole new outlook on life and made her "a much more spiritual person." Still, she confesses that there has been a negative side-effect. "My relatives think I'm nuts."

RIDICULING ALIEN SEX

Several sitcoms, sci-fi series and cartoons ridiculed men and women who claimed to have had sex with aliens. Some are funny, while many others are grotesque and silly. But almost all of them made money. Only in America! Let me give you some examples:

The Centauri Sex - On the sci-fi series BABYLON 5/SYN/1994-98, the Centauri race, though humanoid in appearance, possessed quite a different sexual package below the waist. Male Centauri have six "tentesticles" which extend from the sides of the body and fold in over the solar plexus when not in use. Their female counterparts have six orifices on the base of their spine (three on either side) just above the hips. Their levels of sexual pleasure are heightened by the number of tentesticles used. It can take hours of manipulation to obtain ultimate ecstasy. As if to advertise, their well-endowed sexual organs, all the male dolls sold on Centauri are anatomically correct. Because the Centauri sexual organs are positioned over a larger area in the front of their bodies, they have developed an unarmed fighting style called "Tronno" that concentrates on kicking moves to protect their exposed upper regions where the male genitals rest. The rival race of Narns, a reptilian biped species, use the Vopa Ka'Chur, a sexual manual akin to the Earth's Kama Sutra to help improve their sexual relationships.

The Conehead Sex - The primary sexual activity of the Coneheads (aliens from the planet Remulak as seen on the NBCs SATURDAY NIGHT LIVE) is the touching of the "cone," (i.e.,"their pointy heads"). When a Conehead wants to hone (have sex) they first engage in pre-hone activity (foreplay). To achieve sexual arousal, Senso-Rings (furry hoops) are tossed/slid on and off their cones. Because foreplay is so enjoyable, Immediate Progenitors (parental units) often worry about their Young Ones getting into trouble for Flairndepping (uninvited groping of the Cone with intent to hone). When a Remulakan gets married it is called Geneto-bonding.

These Geneto-mates (husband or wife) will make love in a Guzz Chamber (bedroom or lovemaking room) and sleep on a slar pad (upright bed). The Guzz Chamber is equipped with a Pleasure Spool, a sphere charged with magnoelectricity that induced a satisfying tingling sensation to each partner's cones as they floated inside the charged orb. On their Guzz trip, (honeymoon) they share the intimate secrets of the Plarg (male genitalia); the Sard (Butt-the Coneheads have no butt crack); their Gorelks (Two handle like growths protruding from the small of the back that resemble the horns of a giraffe); and their tongues (an adult Conehead tongue is nearly two feet long).

If the mating process is successful, the female egg's (they have seven eggs-four female, three male) will be fertilized and within four Earth months, the female can be heard shouting "Pluvarb" (as in "My water has broken").

Although most Coneheads practice monogamy, additional sexual gratification can be obtained by going to a Flarthag (prostitute) or by keeping the company of Frenetomates (concubine or mistress). The High Master (the Ruler of Remulak) may have up to six Frenetomates as well as his genetomate. For additional information on the planet Remulak read: *Coneheads: The Life and Times of Beldar Conehead by Tom Davis and Dan Aykroyd - as told to Gorman Seedling, INS Commissioner, Retired* (Hyperion, 1993).

The Tenctonese Sex - On the sci-fi series ALIEN NATION/FOX/1989-91, a race of alien beings from the planet Tencton (a.k.a. "The Newcomers") were stranded on Earth and settled into Little Tencton, an area of Los Angeles. One of the first things the aliens discovered was that vibrations from the high-pitch tone of the emergency broadcast signal regularly transmitted on TV and radio sexually aroused the Tenctonese women. Their method of procreation was also quite unique.

For the Newcomers to conceive, a third person known as a "binnaum," a Tenctonese male capable of preparing the female for fertilization, was required. (There are two kinds of Newcomer males, gannaum and binnaum.

Fertilization of the female's egg requires both types of male). Only a few hundred out of every 135,000 aliens could fertilize the female eggs (one binnaum for every

600-700 females). These individuals formed a brotherhood and each of them service hundreds of females a year.

The ceremony of fertilization is shared by close friends. While holding burning candles, those in attendance discretely turned their backs on the female as the binnaum prepared her for her spouse. The binnaum "prepares the channel with the catalyzing emission," and the gannaum (the father) provides the sperm. The binnaum does not contribute genetically to the offspring, however. Another strange fact about the alien sex behavior-the male, not the female gave birth. The pod is initially carried by the female then given to the male to incubate and finally deliver. Det. George Francisco (Eric Pierpoint) delivered his child while on duty with the assistance of his human partner Matthew Sikes (Gary Graham) who himself had fallen for a pretty Newcomer neighbor, a biochemist named Cathy Frankel (Terri Treas). They shared their first kiss in May 1990.

Victoria: Aliens don't have genital organs

Victoria, the wife of an Anunnaki told me that extraterrestrials do not have genital organs. But she was quick to point out that a lower level of aliens who inhabit the lowest interdimensional zone do! So?

What could we conclude from Victoria's revelation?

Perhaps, we should ask this question: What to make out of the claims of so many women and men who insist that indeed they had sexual relations with aliens?

I have no intelligent answer to this question.

Yet, many scientists and gynecologists who pushed aside their medical career to devote themselves - full time – to ufology strongly believe that sexual relationships with an alien race could and would occur. And apparently, they have all the medical data to prove it.

Mainstream scientists (who are still practicing their scientific profession) laugh at these stories. They claim that it is absolutely impossible for two different races (alien and human) to have a normal intercourse and "produce babies".

Yet, one of the most brilliant gynecologists in Canada assured me that this could happen, and that indeed, it did happen twice in Toronto!

*** *** ***

Aliens do not practice sex. They reproduce in laboratories. Alien babies are nourished by a "light conduit."

Victoria assured me that the stories of the abductees who claim to have had sex with aliens are to be disregarded. Those stories are pure fiction.

335

Aliens fertilize "each other

Victoria told to me the following:

- 1-Aliens reproduce in laboratories.
- 2-Aliens do not practice sex at all.
- 3-Aliens fertilize "each other" and keep the molecules (not eggs or sperms, or mixed liquids from males and females) in containers at a very specific temperature and following well-defined fertilization-reproduction specs.
- 4-Alien babies are retrieved from the containers after 6 months.
- 5-The following month, the mother begins to assume her duty as a mother.
- Alien mothers do not breast-feed their babies, because they do not have breast, nor do they produce milk to feed their babies.
- 6-Alien babies are nourished by a "light conduit."
- 7-Human sperm or eggs are useless to extraterrestrials of the higher dimension.
- 8-Extraterrestrials are extremely advanced in technology and medicine. Consequently, they do NOT need any part, organ, liquid or cell from the human body to create their own babies. However, there are aliens who live in lower dimensions and zones who did operate on abductees for other reasons – multiple reasons and purposes – some are genetic, others pure experimental.

Note: Victoria provided more explanations and revelations that I have included in my book "Revelation of an Anunnaki's Wife: Christianity, The White House and Victoria's Hybrid Congressman Son." Please refer to.

*** *** ***

CHAPTER 16
PROJECT SERPO

- Zeta Reticuli, aliens, and the United States government
- In the beginning, the project was named "Crystal Knight".
- How Project SERPO started
- US military man: "The live entity established communications with us and provided us with a location of his home planet."
- Year 1965: The US military chose 12 individuals, 10 men and 2 women, for an extreme psychological and physical training to prepare them for the mission to Zeta Reticuli.
- The trip to Zeta Reticuli
- It took 9 months to reach the planet
- Description of the Planet SERPO
- SERPO has an atmosphere was similar to Earth's and contained the elements of Carbon, Hydrogen, Oxygen, Nitrogen.
- Description of the EBE civilization: Country and people
- Only a minor part of the EBEs knew English
- Two alien crafts crashed at Roswell
- Four dead aliens, the account goes on, were found at the Corona site, and six at the Datil site.
- The alien said that he was from a planet in the constellation Zeta Reticuli, about 40 light years from earth
- Los Alamos scientists figured out how to use the device correctly to communicate with the extraterrestrial race
- Ten men and two women, plus four alternates, were chosen by the USAF to go to SERPO
- All the team members were "sheep-dipped," i.e., all identification records were purged

- Four of the team members who were pilots were taught to fly an Eben craft back to earth
- The 1964 rendezvous with extraterrestrials at Holloman Air Force Base
- 16 senior U.S. government officials greeted the extraterrestrials
- The trip to SERPO took ten months
- The team was able to communicate with earth HQ at Kirtland AFB, using the alien device, for the entire trip.
- The American team landed in SERPO
- Description of the landscape of SERPO
- The alien doctor at SERPO used the dead body of an American astronaut to create a type of cloned human being
- On SERPO, bodies from other planets being grown and maintained in tubs
- No guns or weapons of any type were seen on SERPO
- Kepler's Law of planetary motion did not apply to SERPO
- Carl Sagan: Laws of physics do not necessarily apply out of this solar system
- Key elements of the story of SERPO
- Project SERPO: Fact or Fiction?
- The notorious "Anonymous", the UFOS' mailing lists and 3000 page secret report
- Victor Martinez' position
- Richard Doty's statement
- Mr. Anonymous and the "real" Roswell incident: Two crash sites
- The bodies of the aliens were taken to Los Alamos
- The live entity established communication with the U.S. military
- An exchange program was set up between our two races.
- Background of United States government's involvement with the extraterrestrials biological entities
- An exchange program between an alien race and twelve U.S. military personnel from 1965 to 1978
- Colonel Casey: In 1965, twelve U.S. military men were placed on an extraterrestrial spacecraft and flew to an alien planet some 40 light years away
- Major points and perspectives by Bill Ryan
- From the Jerry Pippin website
- Anonymous is actually a composite of three (3) people
- The Mission Team took cameras, 16 (sixteen) different types of cameras and drawing/drafting equipment.
- Bill Ryan's website posted a sample of Eben written language received from Anonymous, and the real portrait of EBE-1
- The American Chronicle published this article about U.S. military team to another planet

*** *** ***

PROJECT SERPO
ZETA RETICULI, ALIENS, AND THE UNITED STATES GOVERNMENT

Project SERPO is the name of an alleged American top secret exchange program, between the late 1940s and the mid-1960s, in which a selected, trained US military team was sent to Zeta Reticuli star system, home of a friendly race of Extraterrestrial Biological Entities (EBEs).

Michele Bugliaro Goggia tells and explains the whole scenario: Project SERPO is the name of an alleged American top secret exchange program, between the late 1940s and the mid-1960s, in which a selected, trained US military team was sent to Zeta Reticuli star system, home of a friendly race of Extraterrestrial Biological Entities (EBEs), aboard one of the star visitors' spacecraft. SERPO is how the team called the planet on which they stayed.

In the beginning, the project was named "Crystal Knight".

The Serpo case has been started on November 2, 2005 by a retired senior official within the US Defense Intelligence Agency (DIA) who calls himself "Anonymous". Up to this day, no one knows his real identity. Anonymous has written that he is not acting individually and is part of a group of six DIA personnel working together as an alliance: Three current and three former employees. He is their chief spokesman.

Until December 21, 2005 all informations regarding Project SERPO were released through a mailing list moderated by Victor Martinez. No more information was transmitted until January 24, 2006, convincing most that the anonymous source had gone away.

Bill Ryan, webmaster of serpo.org website, started receiving further communications from "Anonymous". Ryan has posted all the information on his website.

How Project SERPO started

Following "Anonymous", everything started from two UFO crashes, one occurring at Corona in 1947. One EBE was found alive, hiding behind a rock. As other investigators have already reported, the crash site was later cleaned and all evidence removed. "Anonymous" claims the bodies were taken to Los Alamos National Laboratory, because they had a freezing system that allowed the bodies to remain frozen for research.

The craft was taken to Roswell and then onto Wright Field, Ohio.

US military man: "The live entity established communications with us and provided us with a location of his home planet."

It is nonetheless legitimate to think the US military tried to gather informations from the EBE. In fact, the anonymous source has written that: "The live entity established communications with us and provided us with a location of his home planet. The entity remained alive until 1952, when he died. But before his death, he provided us with a full explanation of the items found inside the two crafts. One item was a communication device. The entity was allowed to make contact with his planet." Source: serpo.org

*** *** ***

Year 1965: The US military chose 12 individuals, 10 men and 2 women, for an extreme psychological and physical training to prepare them for the mission to Zeta Reticuli.

The EBE who recovered from the crash had a communication device that allowed him to communicate with his people on Serpo. Communication between the EBE and the military never was easy: The US military didn't know the EBE language, while the EBEs didn't know English. Only further efforts brought some common ground between the two sides. Thanks to these public relations, in the end, *an exchange program* was possible.

The year is 1965. The US military chose 12 individuals, 10 men and 2 women, for an extreme psychological and physical training to prepare them for the mission to Zeta Reticuli.

It was planned for the team to stay 10 years on the alien planet, until 1975. Indeed, 8 returned in 1978: 2 died during the mission and 2 chose to stay on Zeta Reticuli. Once returned on Earth, The *Air Force Office of Special Investigation* (AFOSI) was responsible for their security and safety. AFOSI also conducted debriefing sessions with the returnees.

The trip to Zeta Reticuli

Thanks to a written diary and audio records made by the team during the whole mission (no one saw nor heard any), details about the whole trip and stay on Serpo are abundant. "Anonymous" has therefore been able to recall the team's trip aboard the EBE spacecraft as difficult: "During the trip, each team member was frequently dizzy, disoriented and suffered headaches. The craft did not go through any weightlessness during the trip. The craft was very large and allowed the team to exercise." (Source: serpo.org.)

It took 9 months to reach the planet.
Description of the Planet SERPO

In spite of the obvious problems related with human-EBE communication, the EBEs were kind and helpful, reports the anonymous source.

It took 9 months to reach the planet. The anonymous source has described in detail the planet Serpo: It was estimated to be about three billion years old. The two suns were about five billion years old, but only by estimation. There was a period of darkness, but not total darkness. The alien planet is located within a solar system of the Zeta Recticular Star System.

The planet had two suns, but their angles were small and allowed some darkness on the planet depending on one's location. Furthermore, the planet was tilted, which allowed the northern part of the planet to be cooler. The planet was a little less than Earth's size.

SERPO has an atmosphere was similar to Earth's and contained the elements of Carbon, Hydrogen, Oxygen, Nitrogen.

The atmosphere was similar to Earth's and contained the elements of Carbon, Hydrogen, Oxygen, Nitrogen. Considering how the long trip caused physical problems, the arrival on Serpo wasn't less difficult. Following "Anonymous", the team required many months to adapt to the new conditions. The days being longer, perception of time wasn't the same. The brighter suns, in particular, seemed to be a problem for them. Not only: radiation levels were a bit higher than the Earth levels.

For these reasons, the team later moved north to a cooler area of Serpo. Food represented also quite a challenge, since their military rations eventually finished and the team had to switch to native Serpo food. The exchange team, appearently, was able to gather datas about Serpo, even collecting soil, plant samples (no one ever saw them, anyway).

Description of the EBE Civilization: Country and People

"Anonymous" doesn't avoid details on the alien culture. EBEs are what we call Grays. The alien civilization was estimated to be about 10.000 years old. They evolved from another planet, not on Serpo. Their original home planet was threatened with extreme volcanic activity, so they had to relocate to Serpo in order to survive. This occurred some 5.000 years ago.

- The friendly EBEs possess a well structured, somehow centralized society.
- Each birth is planned, each alien builds whatever he needs.
- There are scientists and industries.
- There is a quick mention about a clone named "J-ROD".
- The EBEs have one education centre and a kind of council that governs each aspect of their lives.
- Their chief looked like different: "The leader of the Ebens is a larger creature than the others. He seems to be more aggressive than the other Ebens. When I write aggressive, I don't mean in a hostile way. He seems to be the boss, similar to me, as the team commander. His voice, although after all this time, I still can't understand any words, is harsh and with a tone that is different from the rest." (Source: serpo.org)

Only a minor part of the EBEs knew English

As already stated, communication with the aliens was an issue. Only a minor part of the EBEs knew English, yet they could not understand everything. A female EBE, nicknamed "EBE2", demonstrated enough English skills to become the "trait d'union" between the team and the rest of the aliens. Nonetheless, a misunderstanding about the use of a team member's dead body nearly lead to a diplomatic incident.

Is it true?
Of course, the big question is: Is the story true?
"Anonymous" claims how the team encountered difficulties in adapting to the spaceship and to the planet. This is plausible but, unfortunately, nothing more than that.

The rest is pure fiction: The science contained in Project Serpo cannot stand up. Other versions of an exchange program have surfaced as well. Even a famous movie ended with a team being sent aboard a spacecraft. A believer may argue that the story is essentially true, but that the details are not. A story that doesn't receive solid confirmations remains just a story, which doesn't help.

One more: the planet Serpo is located in the Zeta Reticuli star system, suggesting there is life. Unfortunately, astronomy tells us there is no Earth-like planet near the binary yellow dwarfs of Zeta Reticuli. John Dreher, Ph. D., of the SETI Institute, has stated very clearly: "On the astronomy front, Zet 1 Ret (HD 20766) and Zet 2 Ret (HD 20807) are a wide binary system in the southern skies. Each component is a G star much like the Sun. The binary orbit period is long enough that planetary systems could be stable around these stars; however, to the best of my knowledge, no one has detected any planets so far. They are 36 lightyears from Earth." (Source: madsci.org)

In the end, it's honest to say there is no evidence to support it. The source remains anonymous, which is useless to the research. Furthermore, no UFO researcher will ever find the files related to Project SERPO, if the project ever existed and if the project is secret. A sceptical source even claims that "Anonymous" is Richard C. Doty, the one involved in the mental breakout of Paul Bennewitz .

*** *** ***

Len Kasten stated that in the movie "Close Encounters of the Third Kind," written and directed by Steven Spielberg and released in 1977, an alien spaceship lands, by prearrangement with the U.S. government, on a high mesa called The Devil's Tower in a remote corner of Wyoming and an ambassadorial exchange takes place. A single alien disembarks and is escorted away, presumably to a secret site. Then, twelve American astronauts in orange jumpsuits and industrial strength sunglasses, with duffel bags slung over their shoulders, ten men and two women, march into the spacecraft to be whisked away to the alien home planet. In the previous scene, they are blessed by a clergyman, who refers to them as "pilgrims."

Was this just some inventive touch conceived by Spielberg, or did he base it on something real?

Since it is now widely believed in UFO circles that a pre-arranged alien landing did take place at or near Holloman Air Force Base in New Mexico in April of 1964, it seems not unreasonable, to true believers, to suspect that Spielberg may have had an inside track on classified information, and that the ambassadorial exchange with an alien race may also have been a real event.

Now, in what could be an unprecedented break with government secrecy policy, a few former military insiders have come forward to say that the exchange was indeed real, and actually took place almost exactly as depicted in the movie.

Under the auspices of a Defense Intelligence Agency program referred to as Operation Crystal Knight, or what is now being called "Project Serpo."

It has been claimed that twelve astronauts left the earth in July of 1965, and were taken to the planet Serpo in the constellation Zeta Reticuli aboard an alien spaceship, as part of an exchange program. The bulk of the information about this program is said to have been dribbled out to the world via 21 e-mails from an individual referred to only as "Anonymous" to a closed circle of high-level UFO insiders beginning on November 2, 2005. Anonymous says that he was formerly a senior officer of the Defense Intelligence Agency, and is now the official spokesman for a group of six DIA personnel, three retired and three still currently employed there.

It was decided by the group, and agreed to by Anonymous, that a web site should be created to publish all the e-mails on the Internet.

One of the researchers in the group, Bill Ryan from England, volunteered for the job, and so began www.serpo.org, what has now developed into the official source for all Serpo-related information, including updates from Ryan, a link to a public forum, and supporting e-mails from other insiders who had knowledge of the Serpo project.

For the UFO community at least, the site has become something of a sensation. For what it's worth this is the story offered on the site.

Two alien crafts crashed at Roswell

The tale told by Anonymous is indeed amazing. If it is true, then, at a minimum, the entire history of the government pretense of ignorance about UFOs and extraterrestrials is completely blown away. Not surprisingly, it all begins with Roswell.

Anonymous says that the Roswell crash did occur, but that it involved two alien crafts.

The first was found relatively intact, embedded into a hillside southwest of Corona, New Mexico on July 5, 1947 by a university archaeology team.

This site is about 75 miles northwest of Roswell, and is famously referred to as the "Roswell crash" because all the remnants of the crash were brought to the Roswell Army Air Force base, where the military took control of the information.

The second crash site wasn't discovered until August, 1949. Another downed craft, it is said, was found almost completely intact at a remote place outside of Datil, New Mexico by two ranchers.

Evidently, the two spacecraft had collided somewhere near the Brazel ranch, thus accounting for the debris field, but the second craft, before hitting the ground itself, had limped on to the vicinity of Datil, about 80 miles west of Corona.

*** *** ***

Four dead aliens, the account goes on, were found at the Corona site, and six at the Datil site.

The alien said that he was from a planet in the constellation Zeta Reticuli, about 40 light years from earth

However, one alien survived the Corona crash and was found hiding behind a rock. He was taken to Los Alamos, and became known as EBE #1 (Extraterrestrial Biological Entity #1). Although he "spoke" in tonal variations, just as in *Close Encounters*, the scientists at Los Alamos found a way to communicate with him, and he informed them that he was from a planet in the constellation Zeta Reticuli, about 40 light years from earth. The constellation was also referenced in the famous 1966 UFO abduction account of Betty and Barney Hill.

EBE #1 also provided researchers with a complete explanation of all the devices found in the crashed spacecraft, one of which was a piece of equipment for communicating with his home planet that survived the impact. However, the Los Alamos scientists could not get it to work until they discovered how to hook it up to the energy source on the crashed Corona disc. That was in the early summer of 1952. However EBE#1 died later that summer after sending six unanswered messages to his planet.

Los Alamos scientists figured out how to use the device correctly to communicate with the extraterrestrial race

After the death of EBE#1, says Anonymous, the Los Alamos scientists figured out how to use the device correctly to communicate with the extraterrestrial race they had now named the "Ebens," and they received the first reply around December, 1952. Eventually, they were able to converse in rough English. Over the next nine years, the communications wrinkles were slowly ironed out, mostly by trial and error. Finally, in 1962, it was arranged that the Ebens would send another mission to earth in April of 1964, and that we would meet the craft at Holloman Air Force Base near Alamogordo, New Mexico. By this time President Kennedy was in office. Then, according to Anonymous, "Several months into the planning process, President Kennedy decided to approve a plan to exchange a special military team. The USAF was tasked as the lead agency. The USAF officials picked special civilian scientists to assist in planning and crew selection." It was arranged that we would send twelve astronauts to Serpo, and they would leave one Eben here in the custody of the U.S. government.

Ten men and two women, plus four alternates, were chosen by the USAF to go to SERPO

As might be imagined, the selection and training of the twelve astronaut-ambassadors was an extraordinary undertaking. After months of discussion it was ultimately decided that they be career military, single with no children and preferably orphans themselves, and with multiple special skills. Originally, about 56,000 files were screened of which 158 were picked by the selection committee. The final twelve, ten men and two women, plus four alternates, were chosen based on complex psychological, medical and other tests.

All the team members were "sheep-dipped," i.e., all identification records were purged

This included social security, IRS, medical, military et al, and they were all listed as "missing" and discharged, so that no connection with their former identities remained. They were then assigned three digit numbers as new identities. They went through very difficult training for six months, mostly at Camp Perry in Virginia. Anonymous says, "Each team member had to endure extreme psychological and physical training. In one training test, each team member was locked inside a 5' x 7' box buried seven feet underground for five days, with just food and water, no contact with anyone else and in total darkness."

Four of the team members who were pilots were taught to fly an Eben craft back to earth

The team members used for training the space ship recovered in 1949, in case it was necessary to escape from Serpo. In addition to the four pilots, the team consisted of two linguists, one biologist, two scientists, two doctors, and one security man. They were all given suicide pills and the team was assigned four 45 Colt revolvers and eight M2 carbine rifles.

THE 1964 RENDEZVOUS WITH ALIENS AT HOLLOMAN AIR FORCE
16 senior U.S. government officials greeted the extraterrestrials

The 1964 rendezvous occurred almost exactly as planned. Two Eben craft entered our atmosphere during the afternoon of April 24, 1964. After an initial mix-up, one landed just west of Holloman Air Force Base near the southern entrance to the White Sands Army Base, precisely at the designated location. The alien visitors were greeted by 16 senior U.S. government officials. It is not known whether or not President Johnson was among them. The Ebens brought electronic translating devices with them to facilitate communications. The remains of the eleven dead aliens were taken on board.

Anonymous does not give the agenda of the meeting, but it is believed they presented us with the "Yellow Book," a complete history of planet earth.

The twelve astronauts were ready to board at that meeting and waited on a bus, but the aliens decided then that the exchange should wait until 1965. Then, in July, 1965, an alien craft returned, this time to the Nevada Atomic Test Site. Very much like the scene in Close Encounters, this was a simple, unceremonious, working meeting.

The twelve courageous astronauts boarded the Eben craft along with 40 tons of supplies, for an intended stay of ten years. Four of them would never see Mother Earth again. Two would die, and two would choose to remain on Serpo. The others would not return until thirteen years later.

The trip to Serpo took ten months
"We See Two Suns"

The trip to Serpo took ten months, during which the astronauts experienced considerable discomfort. They were offered Eben food, but all agreed that it tasted like paper, and they stuck with the C-Rations they had brought along. The diary of the team commander recounts the second day on board: "We sat in the chairs and a clear container was placed over us and the chair. We were isolated in this bubble or sphere.

We could breath (sic) OK and could see out, but we really felt dizzy and confused. I think I fell asleep or fainted. I think this is another day, but my watch says one hour since we sat." They used small metal containers for elimination, which the Ebens emptied for them. Eventually, they were able and allowed to wander freely around the enormous ship.

The team was able to communicate with earth HQ at Kirtland AFB, using the alien device, for the entire trip
The American team landed in SERPO

Prior to reaching Serpo, the team member known as 308 had some sort of accident and died of a pulmonary embolism. The Ebens were respectful of the funerary rites of the astronauts, but they took possession of the body.

The team commander's account of the landing is vivid. "We see the planet for the first time. We walk down the ramp. Large number of Ebens waiting for us. We see a large Eben, largest one we have seen yet...I guess this guy is the leader. About one foot taller than the others.

The leader tells us we are welcome to planet...we are lead (sic) to an open arena. Looks like a parade field.

Description of the landscape of SERPO

The ground is dirt. Looking up, I see blue skies. The sky is very clear. We see two suns. One brighter than the other. The landscape looks like a desert, Arizona or New Mexico. No vegetation that we can see. There are rolling hills but nothing but dirt...The brightness is almost too much for our eyes without sunglasses. What a planet."

They were quartered in four huts that appeared to be adobe-like, and all their gear was stored in an underground facility. The temperature was 107.
The buildings all had lights and electricity generated by a small box.
They were able to plug their electrical devices into the box, and they all worked.

The alien doctor at SERPO used the dead body of an American astronaut to create a type of cloned human being

The one they called Ebe2 was a female and spoke English well. The team commander asked her for the body of 308. They were taken to a large building where they met an Eben doctor who spoke English. The commander's diary describes the confrontation: "This doctor told us that 308's body was not inside the container. The Ebens have done experiments with 308's body because they considered it an honor to have such a specimen to work with. The doctor told us they have used 308's body to create a type of cloned human being. I stopped the doctor at this point. I told the doctor that the body of my teammate was the property of the United States of America, planet Earth. The body did not belong to the Ebens. I did not authorized (sic) any experiments on the body of 308."

It was a tense situation. The Ebens were upset with the team's reaction, and Ebe2 told them that "everyone should be nice," and repeated it several times. The astronauts had to back off to prevent a major escalation of the incident.

On SERPO, bodies from other planets being grown and maintained in tubs

The commander and the scientists (700 and 754) were given permission to view what was left of the body of 308. This brought them into a building where biological experiments were being carried out. They were shocked by what they saw. The commander says they viewed "Strange looking bodies. Not human bodies, at least not all of them" from other planets being grown and maintained in tubs.

348

The Eben doctor tried to explain the science behind their work, but the earthlings didn't comprehend because they didn't really understand DNA bio-technology in 1965. The team commander concluded that it was all evil stuff. He says, "I saw the dark side of this civilization."

The population of Serpo is about 650,000. Anonymous says that the Eben civilization is about 10,000 years old originating on another planet which they were forced to leave 5,000 years ago due to volcanic destruction.

*** *** ***

No guns or weapons of any type were seen on SERPO

The Ebens fought a devastating interplanetary war about 3,000 years ago, and wiped out their enemies using particle beam weapons. The war lasted about 100 years. The Ebens have a "Council of Governors," which is in complete control of the population, with membership for life. The astronauts observed no crime, but there is an army, which also acts as a police force. But no guns or weapons of any type were seen by the team. There is one large community, which is the center of the civilization. All the industry is concentrated there. The Ebens do not use any type of currency—they are all issued whatever they need from central distribution centers. All adult Ebens do some type of work.

Kepler's Law of planetary motion did not apply to Serpo
Carl Sagan: Laws of physics do not necessarily apply out of this solar system

Timekeeping was a problem for the astronauts, since the batteries controlling the timepieces brought by the team eventually ran out. This meant they could not keep track of the calendar, so they eventually relied on Serpo time, which was governed by the movement of their suns. So they lost track of earth time and ended up staying thirteen years instead of ten. It was determined by earth scientists that Kepler's Law of planetary motion did not apply to Serpo. Carl Sagan was consulted on this, and wrote about 60 pages of opinion on the subject, but ultimately had to acknowledge that earthly laws of physics do not necessarily apply out of this solar system.
The eight astronauts returned in 1978, and were debriefed for a solid year by the Air Force Office of Special Investigations, which resulted in a 3,000-page book. Anonymous claims to have a copy of this book. They were then released into civilian life. The last survivor of this brave and historic band of pioneers passed away in 2002. They had all absorbed large doses of radiation while on Serpo, and it is believed that this shortened their lives. In retrospect, it seems a shame that President Kennedy didn't live to see his initiative become a reality.

He was assassinated only five months before the first landing. Would he have used the occasion to reveal the extraterrestrial connection, perhaps with worldwide TV coverage? Could that have been his plan from the beginning? Perhaps some powerful insiders didn't want that to happen. In any case, thanks to Steven Spielberg, maybe we got to see it after all.

*** *** ***

Key elements of the story of SERPO

William Burns wrote: Among the more exciting threads that have surfaced on UFO email lists over the past couple of months is the story of Project Serpo, which in previous incarnations, is not a new story. Many in the UFO community have heard versions of this tale before. Among the key elements of this particular story are the following:

1. The Roswell crash didn't take place in Roswell, actually, but in Corona and near Datil, New Mexico.
2. The surviving ET or EBE, according to the MJ-12 briefing documents, was from the Zeta-Reticuli system, the same system that was home to the alien abductors of Betty and Barney Hill.
3. This EBE made contact with its home planet and in the ensuing negotiations between the U.S. government and the EBEs the parties agreed to set up an exchange program under which U.S. military personnel with different professional specialties would be taken to the EBE's home planet, Serpo, for an extended reconnaissance mission.
4. The basis of this story made its way to Steven Spielberg and was part of the background for his 1977 movie Close Encounters of the Third Kind.
5. Some members of this mission to Serpo returned to earth. They have since died but have passed their story along to others.
6. Those others, still fearful of releasing classified information, do want to tell the story and are looking for ways to release the information without any criminal sanctions, or worse.
7. There is a Red Book that contains the debriefing information and history of the mission.
8. The journals of some of the mission members are still extant.
9. Photographs of the mission may or may not be released.
10. This story has been above top secret for decades even though some folks in the intelligence inner circle know all about it.

*** *** ***

There are many more aspects to this story, each of which is as exciting as the next. However, only those who either read the files and know the files are true and not disinformation or those who actually went on the mission know if this story is true. However, it does make for exciting speculation, regardless of whether it is true or false.

If we give those who are telling the story the benefit of the doubt-and why not-we can claim that we are keeping thoroughly open minds. Unlike the Burisch story, which is aggressive in its exclusivity and virulently antagonistic to all who dare dispute a story of an alleged PhD holder who can't produce his PhD diploma, the narrators of this story openly seem to encourage questions, criticisms, challenges, and the like.

So, for the time being, we should keep our minds open even though this story is utterly fantastic and raises more questions than it answers. Besides, doing so is just plain fun in a sometimes funless world.

One attorney who has been following this story posted his opinion that, because the Serpo report was ostensibly completed in 1980, it might be conceivable that there are aspects of declassification of previously classified material that could corroborate parts of this story.

What if, because there is a group of former high-ranking intelligence officers that have decided to release selective facts of one of the most secret United States military intelligence operations in history, that the National Security Council has decided to go along with the release?

After all, who can really be hurt after 40 years? And what if, rather than having the EBEs themselves show up on the White House lawn, the powers-that-be have all agreed that the story should be allowed to come out on its own?

If so, a disclosure on a quiet UFO email list is probably the best way to let it get out. After all, would you want to be the POTUS who stands up before a news conference to talk about UFOs, ETs, secret missions to a distant planet, and why we kept that secret for so long?

On the other hand, what a better way to ensure your legacy than to be the disclosure president? We'll leave those question for others to answer.

Ufologists will have their own criticisms and comments about the Serpo story. Those who comment will also have their own thoughts and criticisms about other commentators. That, too, is part of the fun of the Serpo story.

My own questions concern the way the story relates to the different presidents under whose tenure the UFO incidents first began. For example, we now have the private ruminations of presidents who never intended their ruminations to become public.

Notwithstanding the infamous Richard Nixon tapes, there exist the Lyndon B. Johnson tapes released to the public by Lady Bird Johnson, the John F. Kennedy tapes, and the Harry S. Truman diary.

The Truman diary entries for the latter half of 1947-and these were very private diaries-make absolutely no mention of anything having to do with UFOs, even though President Truman reveals that he thinks he sees or feels Abraham Lincoln's ghost making its presence known in the White House.

It seems that Eisenhower has left no private record of anything having to do with a decision to send U.S. military personnel to a distant planet. No one has said that JFK revealed anything about the Serpo mission in his Oval Office tapes.

And, a careful review of the excellent Michael Beschloss book, Taking Charge: The Johnson White House Tapes, 1963-1964 (Simon & Schuster, 1997), containing the transcripts of LBJ's Oval Office tapes indicates no commentary about Serpo.

Maybe the Serpo references were redacted by Lady Bird herself. Maybe. But why would the former First Lady take out references to a space mission when she did not take out a piece of incredible evidence inculpating her husband and former FBI Director J. Edgar Hoover in a conspiracy to conceal information of a murder conspiracy, specifically the JFK assassination, from the very commission LBJ assembled to investigate the crime?

In one of the released transcripts, Hoover reveals to LBJ that the FBI has discovered that there was another Lee Harvey Oswald. This Lee Harvey Oswald was an CIA plant, not the real Oswald. Thus, there is a CIA conspiracy afoot. LBJ and Hoover agree to keep the secret to themselves and not to tell former CIA Director Dulles that they know. Now it's a double conspiracy. Yet, astoundingly, this conversation appears in the LBJ tapes. But nothing about Serpo.

We have it on very good authority directly from Jackie Gleason himself that Richard Nixon took him to Holmstead Air Force Base in Florida where The Great One saw ET bodies with his very own eyes. Yet, no mention from Nixon that the U.S. had an ongoing military exploration mission to Serpo. Wouldn't Nixon, who clearly wanted to satisfy Jackie Gleason's curiosity, have revealed the truth about this? Maybe he did, and Jackie simply did not tell the person who told it to me.

President Jimmy Carter, despite his subsequent denials over the ensuing years, did seem to know something about our government's involvement with extraterrestrials. He even asked DCI George H. W. Bush for the inside information, but was promptly turned down. Reagan seemed to know something because he certainly referred to extraterrestrials enough times during his administration and even admitted to following a UFO across the California desert.

And, finally, Anonymous reveals that President Clinton tried to get the Serpo mission re-started but was dissuaded from that by members of his administration. An astounding story, indeed, especially in light of another piece of information from the same person who told me that Jackie Gleason had revealed his Holmstead Air Force Base experience to him personally.

I am told that this person asked Bill Clinton shortly before his inauguration whether he planned to find out what the government knew about UFOs. Reportedly, Clinton told him that "they" would not let him get near it. After his inauguration, did the president finally learn the truth, and was he so astounded that he wanted the mission to continue? Is this something that President Clinton is inclined to talk about?

*** *** ***

Project Serpo: Fact or Fiction?

Tim Swartz wrote: "First let me introduce myself. I am a retired employee of the U.S. government. I won't go into any great details about my past, but I was involved in a special program." This was the opening statement sent by an anonymous source in November, 2005, to a UFO email discussion group, coordinated by former U.S. government employee Victor Martinez. The emails revealed the existence of Project Serpo, an alleged exchange program between the U.S. government and extraterrestrials from Serpo, a planet in the Zeta Reticuli star system.

The origins of the program supposedly started after two UFOs crashed in Roswell and Corona, NM in 1947. The one surviving extraterrestrial recovered from the Corona crash supposedly assisted the U.S. military in establishing contact with the Ebens, his fellow beings on Serpo. This communication eventually led to a 1965 exchange program, where 12 specially trained U.S. military personnel went to Serpo aboard one of the Eben's spacecraft as part of a 12-year mission to learn more about Serpo's geology and biology, as well as learning more about the Ebens.

During the mission, it was learned that Serpo is approximately 37 light years away from Earth, has two suns, is slightly smaller than Earth, and has a similar atmosphere. However, the radiation levels on Serpo were higher than on Eart, so the team had to keep their bodies covered at all times. The Ebens had leaders but no real form of government and they lived in small communities with one large city which acted as the central point of the civilization. The total population on the planet was around 650,000.

The 12-man team remained on Serpo until 1978, when seven men and one woman returned to Earth. Two team members died on Serpo while two others decided to remain behind. Upon returning to Earth, the team was isolated until 1984 for debriefing. Of the eight who returned, all have since passed away of illnesses caused by the excess radiation from Serpo's dual suns. Nothing is known about the four who remained behind on Serpo.

These reports originated from a highly placed anonymous source that reportedly had access to audio tapes of the debriefing of the returning Project Serpo crew (the written form comprises the 3,000-page Project Serpo report, of which portions can be read at www.serpo.org

It is a good story, a tale that seems to have a ring of truth to it, and one that has been circulating among UFO researchers for more than 20 years. But knowing what we do about past UFO hoaxes, can we accept Project Serpo at face value?

An Old Story Made New

Author and filmmaker Linda Moulton-Howe was first told about an Earth/alien exchange program in 1983, when doing research for UFOs: The ET Factor, a documentary for HBO.

At the time, she was approached by Air Force Sergeant Richard C. Doty who said that he had been given approval to allow her to air secret Air Force information and video footage in her documentary. Some of this information he said involved an alleged exchange program of humans who left Holloman Air Force Base in 1964, for Zeta Reticuli. Howe was told that three humans went but one died on the alien planet; one went insane (but there was no information on his fate); and one returned to Earth and was then living in a U.S. government safe house on an undisclosed island.

Doty promised to supply Howe with material that would confirm the existence of an extraterrestrial race, including official government and military documents, film, and photographs. However, he continued to string Howe along until he finally told her that his superiors had decided against releasing any further information. Without Doty's evidence, HBO gave up on the documentary in 1984.

Since that time, Doty's name has surfaced in connection with other alleged UFO/government secrets, such as the MJ-12 papers, so it is no surprise to find out that Doty (now a civilian) is also connected with the release of the Project Serpo story. And this fact alone makes the story suspect. Other UFO researchers over the years have also been told similar stories about a secret exchange program between the U.S. and an alien race, but the recent Serpo revelations contain more information than has been released to date.

As to why earlier stories vary considerably on details (such as the number of team members sent to Serpo), it has been suggested that information has been deliberately leaked out in bits and pieces by those on the inside who feel that such secrets should not be kept from the public, and that errors were intentionally inserted in order to disguise the identities of the whistleblowers.

There has been talk of the eventual release of photographs taken on Serpo by the exchange team, but so far, nothing has emerged to lend credence to this baffling story.

Until the time when actual, physical evidence about Project Serpo is released, this story unfortunately has to be treated as just another unverifiable UFO tale, albeit an intriguing one.

The notorious "Anonymous", the UFOS' mailing lists and 3000 page secret report

According to Mark Pilkington, Rumours of an ET-human exchange program in the 1960s have set the Internet's UFO community aflame. Is it a hoax, a reality, or something in between?

Pilkington said: "First let me introduce myself. My name is Request Anonymous. I am a retired employee of the U.S. Government. I won't go into any great details about my past, but I was involved in a special program..." So began the email received on 1 November 2005 by Victor Martinez, a substitute teacher on America's West Coast who runs what must be one of the most remarkable mailing lists in our Solar System. Its 200 or so members make up a veritable Who's Who of scientists, military personnel and intelligence officers known to have had an interest, or more often than not, a direct involvement in the UFO phenomenon over the past 30 years. Here you'll find one-time and current US government remote viewers, disinformation agents, employees of the CIA, DIA and NSA, 'free energy' researchers, theoretical physicists and venture capitalists, plus a healthy smattering of mystics, witches, hoaxers, contactees, abductees and, of course, representatives of the media.

Then there's Request Anonymous - henceforth to be known simply as Anonymous. According to Martinez, Anonymous had been monitoring the list for about six months before dropping his bombshell. As yet, nobody knows who Anonymous is, though several educated guesses have been mooted by the list's insiders. Martinez hasn't tried too hard to find out, remaining pragmatic on the identity issue: "If word ever got back to [Anonymous] that I was trying to ID him, he would simply have packed up his bags and found another UFO list moderator to release his incredible story through." And incredible is the right word to describe Anonymous's account, which, between November 2005 and February 2006, currently spans 15 emails and over 20,000 words. Anonymous claims to be drawing his information from a 3,000-page report compiled in the late 1970s. Where this hefty tome currently resides we don't know, but it's not at your local library.

The salient facts are as follows:

The 1947 crash of not one but two ET spacecraft in New Mexico - the event known since the late 1970s as the Roswell incident - left six ETs dead and one survivor. The remains of their craft were taken to Wright Patterson Air Force Base in Ohio, while the surviving ET, nicknamed EBE 1, was installed at Los Alamos Laboratories in New Mexico, where he lived until 1952. During this time he made contact with his home planet and preparations were made for a controlled landing of an ET craft, which took place on 24 April 1964 in the White Sands Missile Range - an event known in UFO history as the Holloman Landing (curiously dubbed Humanoid-Organisms-Allegedly-Extraterrestrial, or HOAEX, in one 1974 report).

About 18 months before the projected landing was due to occur, President Kennedy - who, some say, was killed before he could reveal the truth about UFOs - authorised a foreign exchange of cosmic proportions.

A team of 12 specially trained humans (there's some debate as to whether two of them were women) whose identities were subsequently erased, would return with the ETs to their home planet. In 1965, the Exchange Team took off while another ET, EBE 2, remained on Earth.

Named SERPO by the human visitors, the ETs' planet is 38 light years from Earth, in the Zeta Reticuli star system (famed in UFO lore since the 1962 Betty and Barney Hill alien abduction story). SERPO is a little smaller than Earth and has two suns. It is hot, flat and dry, harsh but habitable, especially in the cooler northern regions where the humans eventually made their home. The Team spent 13 years on SERPO where, despite a few misadventures, they were welcomed by the Ebens, as they are dubbed by Anonymous.

Further emails provided more details. There were about 650,000 Ebens on SERPO, living in about 100 small, autonomous communities around the planet.

There was no centralised government, though there was one large, central community that served as a hub for Eben industry and resources. All Ebens worked and were, in return, supplied with what they needed to live their Spartan but happy lives. Crime was non-existent in their quasi-socialist utopia, but war was not. 3,000 years ago, the Ebens had fought a vast, 100-year interplanetary conflict with the civilisation of another planet, which they had annihilated. Since then, the Ebens had been intergalactic drifters, visiting a number of other species and civilisations, including our own, before settling on their current home planet. Curiously, while we are provided with a wealth of detail about the Ebens' culture, their living habits, even their digestive systems, we're never given a description of what they look like, perhaps because the people reading the report already knew what they looked like - there was an Eben at Los Alamos after all.

The report includes a number of photographs, which Anonymous has promised to share with us, though none has yet emerged. By the time the human team returned to Earth in 1978, two of their number had died. Two chose to remain on SERPO, and stayed in contact with the Earth until 1988. It was discovered that those team members who did return had been exposed to relatively high doses of radiation on SERPO, and it was this that ultimately killed them - the last one in Florida in 2002.Rather than being greeted with incredulous laughter, Anonymous's first post was immediately verified by two members of Martinez's list- Paul McGovern and Gene Lakes (aka Loscowski)- who provided some significant extra background detail. McGovern has been identified as a former DIA security chief, stationed at Area 51. Lakes appears to be another DIA insider.Their credentials sound impressive, but have yet to be verified outside the confines of the online UFO community. Others on the Martinez list who verified the SERPO story included former Air Force Office Of Special investigations special agent Richard Doty, well known for his role in spreading disinformation within the UFO community during the early 1980s, though he insists that he has no role to play in this current arena.Further support for the SERPO exchange came from within the wider UFO community. On the Coast to Coast radio show, Communion author Whitley Strieber described meeting an old man at a UFO convention in the 1990s.

The man told Strieber he had been to another planet before muttering what Strieber thought was the word 'Serpico' (the name of a 1973 thriller starring Al Pacino, who is not currently suspected of playing a part in the UFO conspiracy).As excitement about the SERPO revelations began to spread, an English-Canadian management consultant and personal development trainer named Bill Ryan offered to set up a web site (www.serpo.org) as a clearinghouse for Anonymous's information. He also, bravely, and perhaps foolishly, took on the role of SERPO's front man. While no stranger to fringe beliefs and ideas - he admits to having dated a woman he believed to be an extraterrestrial - Ryan was a newcomer to the UFO scene.

SERPO has been his trial by fire, and he has since been accused of being a hoaxer, a government agent and a Scientologist. But he continues his work unbowed and remains convinced that SERPO is worth pursuing. "I think a simple hoax or a prank can absolutely be ruled out," he says.

"It's too complex for that, and there's too much circumstantial corroboration. Misinformation falls into the same category - that would mean it's all false. But it could be disinformation. That means part truth, part fiction. And the fiction part could be as little as five per cent for the entire story to be thrown off-kilter."

Indeed, even once you've got past the central plank of the story there are a number of problems with the material. Anonymous provided fairly detailed astronomical data about SERPO, allegedly assembled for the SERPO report by a reluctant Carl Sagan. Unfortunately, much of this data has been shown to be highly improbable. For example, the planet's alleged orbital period around one of its two suns contradicts Kepler's Laws for the motion of planets. SERPO's supporters say these wouldn't necessarily apply to planets in other solar systems, particularly those with two suns.

Rather than sensing a snake in the grass, Bill Ryan feels that such inconsistencies detract from the likelihood of this being a hoax for hoaxing's sake. He reasons that someone who would take the time to fashion such an elaborate tale wouldn't have to work that much harder to get their astronomical facts straight.

But focusing on such fine detail distracts - perhaps as a good disinformation programme should - from the larger question.

Is America in contact with an extraterrestrial race, and did it send some of its own to the ETs' planet?

The answer is that we simply don't know, though the possibility of such an exchange raises a number of rather obvious questions. If the SERPO exchange did take place, what exactly did the US get out of it? Why are we wasting our time fighting wars over obsolete fossil fuel technologies and building expensive space stations and telescopes?

While it's true that the revelation of a limitless, free energy source of some kind would be likely to bring the world's economy to its knees, it's hard to imagine that the revelation of an ET contact would be particularly devastating.

The US public has absorbed far more shocking incidents, like the US government's admission of its role in conducting radiation and mind-control experiments from the 1940s onwards.

UFO mythology

It simply doesn't make sense. Instead we have to approach the SERPO material as part of an ongoing narrative-that of the UFO mythology.

When we consider the SERPO story, there's really very little there that isn't already present in UFO lore.

The Roswell material needs no introduction, even if the details are slightly different from those usually touted in the literature. Likewise the Holloman AFB landing features in any good overview of the subject, though the given dates vary depending what source you read: Sometimes 1964, sometimes 1971. The name given to the planet, SERPO, can be drawn from this same event.

According to some sources, the large-nosed, humanoid aliens who landed on that occasion sported jumpsuits bearing insignia made up of three lines and a winged serpent.

This symbol led the late conspiracy theorist William Cooper to connect them to the international think tank the Trilateral Commission; the winged serpent could also be the Mesoamerican god Quetzalcoatl, but that's another story. Elsewhere in the SERPO material we get references to the Ebens being keen dancers - Whitley Strieber's aliens also enjoyed the occasional shuffle - and singing like Tibetan monks.

This refers to the often ridiculed statement made on an infamous 1989 US TV show, UFO Coverup Live, possibly by Richard Doty himself, that the ET living at Los Alamos enjoyed listening to recordings of Tibetan chanting.

He was also partial to strawberry ice cream.

There is no mention of such treats on SERPO, though the Ebens apparently ate sweet fruits, as well as numerous vegetables and something like bread.

Other details in the SERPO report previously surfaced in material from the late 1980s and early 1990s, disseminated by the likes of Bill Cooper, Richard Doty, Bob Lazar; John Lear, 'Branton', OH Krill (thought to be John Lear and an accomplice) and others. A key element is the Ebens' own involvement in developing humankind here on Earth, both through genetic seeding and 'teachers' who visited our planet, notably one who dropped by some 2,000 years ago.

This extraterrestrial re-weaving of religious myth dates back to the very earliest days of ufology, but was also revived in the early 1980s. It is a key theme of 'The Yellow Book', an ET history of the Earth, contained in a holographic device allegedly seen by Richard Doty, Bob Lazar and others; it also figures prominently in the SERPO material.

But the clearest precedent for the story is Steven Spielberg's 1977 film Close Encounters of the Third Kind, which climaxes with a number of military personnel entering the ET craft, along with the Richard Dreyfuss character, at a secret landing site.

Leaving aside the Jesus-like pose Dreyfuss takes on as he is carried, arms outstretched, into the giant disco ball spacecraft, SERPO watchers have wondered aloud whether the timing of the film's release, just one year before the

Exchange Team returned from the Eben planet, was more than coincidence. Since its release, the film has been surrounded by rumours that it was based on real events and, like the Day the Earth Stood Still in 1951, was part of an ongoing programme to acclimatise us to the reality of extraterrestrial contact.

So is the SERPO story the bigger picture that all these previous insider releases of information have been leading towards, or is it just cunning weave of pre-existing lore into an alluring new package? One can argue the finer points until the Ebens come home, and people have done so on various online message boards.

Is the story a straightforward hoax? An online marketing campaign that grew out of control? Was it concocted by a cabal of ufologists to inject new life into a field that has suffered badly since the glory days of the mid 1990s? Every few years, a new 'insider' story emerges from the UFO underground: we've had J-Rod, the ET living at Los Alamos Labs; the alleged Area 51 microbiologist Dab Burisch and his somewhat dismal, sub-X-Files tales of alien genetic tampering; and further releases of MJ12 papers detailing the activities of the US government's ET liaison wing. All these tales incorporate elements from earlier UFO folklore, but none has caught the ufological imagination like SERPO, perhaps because all ufologists secretly harbour dreams of one day travelling to an alien planet.

That SERPO is part of a disinformation campaign is another tempting proposition. It certainly wouldn't be the first time that ETs and UFOs have served as a handy cover for secretive military projects: in his impressive recent book Body Snatchers in the Desert, Nick Redfern suggests that the Roswell incident actually involved test flights of experimental aircraft using mentally and physically handicapped human beings. It's as plausible an explanation as any we've yet heard from the US Air Force - or, for that matter, the ufologists.

It's interesting to consider how the Internet has changed the way that sensitive information - whether genuine or bogus - might be released into the underground. Back in the early 1980s, the MJ12 papers were delivered on a roll of film through TV producer Jamie Shandera's letterbox. They were later published by Timothy Good in his groundbreaking book Above Top Secret and made their way out into the world. The process of properly examining them took years, by which time the suggestion that they were either a hoax or disinformation made little impact. The trenches of belief had been dug, and the documents are still accepted as real by much of the UFO community.

These days, things are very different - the Internet allows the material to get to its targets instantaneously, and spread, virus-like, to thousands, if not millions, of interested parties.

But releasing the material into the UFO world doesn't guarantee that it will break out into the mainstream media, as happened with MJ12.

Instead of taking years for the sceptics to dissect the SERPO story, it happened almost instantaneously as the material appeared. Discrepancies and problems were highlighted, suspicions aired and the red flag was raised within weeks of its appearance.

We can speculate further, without the need for UFOs or ETs that this could be a sociological or psychological research project being carried out by one or other intelligence agency, or a university, perhaps by a member of Martinez's list. Think of it as memetic tracking: tracing the paths that information follows might be a very useful exercise in our data-saturated age. Like attaching a transmitter to a whale, or following barium radio-isotopes through a hospital patient's digestive system, it can teach us a lot about both the object being followed and the territory it's travelling through. Certainly with all the intelligence and military personnel monitoring Martinez's list, it's easy to imagine it as a vivarium for living information.

One interesting idea raised online, then swiftly shot down, was that Anonymous had actually stumbled Upon genuine government documents, but ones that had originally been created in order to fool somebody else - perhaps the Russians, or even the ufologists. One could see the Ebens' blissful communal existence appearing to the Russian political machine of the 1960s or '70s as a utopian version of their own world. One contributor to the Above Top Secret UFO forum suggested that the SERPO material was the work of Alice Bradley Sheldon. Sheldon worked for US Air Force Intelligence in the 1940s and as a CIA operative in the 1950s, before being celebrated as a New Wave science fiction writer under the pseudonym James Tiptree Jr. Curiously, this same poster then claimed to have been feeding false SERPO information to the Martinez list as part of a university sociology project, before vanishing forever into the digital void.

At the time of writing, the SERPO story is ongoing, though Anonymous himself (or themselves) has been less forthcoming with information of late. A much-promised series of photographs from SERPO, including one of the Ebens playing football, has failed to materialise. One plan diagram of an Eben spacecraft turned out, suspiciously, to be composed of drawing templates for toilet and bathroom equipment.

What the purpose of such a campaign might be - whether to bamboozle Russian agents, prepare us for the shocking truth about our ET contacts or, more simply, to make a mockery of the Internet UFO community, we can't know. What we do know is that SERPO has struck ufological gold, pushing the grand narrative a step forward for the first time in a decade. Whether the material will enter the UFO Hall of Fame, or end up alongside other nonstarters on the Wall of Shame remains to be seen.

For now however, the excitement has died down. Bill Ryan soldiers on, having weathered his ufological trial by fire with grace and good humour. Victor Martinez's email list continues, and somewhere out there, Anonymous is watching...

Victor Martinez' position

Victor Martinez said that here are two issues I'll address here. Here is his statement verbatim:

First, I've been asked to comment on whether I believe the postings from a high-ranking U.S. government source from the Defense Intelligence Agency who has taken the name Anonymous are authentic or are part of some incredibly complex hoax; and second, what is the best method for releasing this information? Should it be through a small but highly specialized email group's moderator or through a more credible, traditional source like CNN or Fox News?

With respect to the authenticity of the emailed postings to me from Anonymous, I believe they are true and correct in terms of the basic or core story: In 1965 twelve very carefully screened and selected individuals were sent to an alien home world called Serpo approximately 38.42 light years away in the Zeta Reticuli binary star system. They resided there until 1978, when eight of them returned. Two died on the foreign planet, and two decided to remain there.

Their story, their journal entries, their photographs, and the samples they brought back were all memorialized in a final 3,000-plus page report entitled Project Serpo, which was finalized in 1980 with two supplementary reports to which the late Dr. Carl Sagan contributed and grudgingly but finally signed off on regarding the astronomical and math anomalies that did not add up.

Many have found themselves bogged down in the minutiae of whether it was ten men and two women or twelve men, or how could Anonymous make a mistake over the amount of equipment taken?

Was it 9,100 pounds or 91,000 pounds? So what! Let's concentrate on the core story-the overall big picture-that twelve of our citizens from the United States of America embarked on a 13-year mission to live on another world. That's where the focus should be-not on all of these petty, nit-picky details! That's what everyone should be in awe of.

What BS!

Little wonder ufology finds itself progressing ever so slowly over the years. It constantly shoots itself with all its inhouse pettiness and fighting; it finds itself hardly any further along after a major disclosure is made in the UFO field. The evidence we have that such a human-alien exchange program did take place is backed up by several high-ranking former government officials: Retired USAF colonel Ed Doty, ex-AFOSI special agent Richard Doty, Paul McGovern, Gene Loscowski, and USAF Colonel Jack Casey. In addition, author Whitley Strieber claims to have met a surviving team member of Project Serpo in Florida. Anonymous later confirmed Whitley's story to me-that, in fact, Whitley ran into this team member on three separate occasions.

A retired USAF colonel actually oversaw the project and commented privately to an acquaintance of Bill Ryan, amazed that details were now being released; this incident is recounted in the comments section of the website of serpo.org

I know his name from Anonymous, as confirmed by Bill, but I will withhold it since he has chosen not to go public at this time. Next, there is the former high-ranking government official who is actually coordinating this programmed release between the former DIA officials who worked on and oversaw the project and the three DIA officials who allow them access to the secure reading room where they can transcribe this material to be released to the general public through me. His name would be known to 99.99 percent of the readers of this magazine and my UFO email list because the readers and subscribers to these two forums follow such intelligence and black-world matters more closely than the general public. For obvious reasons I'm not going to disclose his name because many UFO investigators, kooks, and freaks would soon be beating down his door asking him if it were true, and he would say, "No, it isn't true!" and then make it so. He'd order it stopped. And last but not least, former high-ranking government official Paul McGovern had lunch at an Arlington, Virginia restaurant on December 8, 2005 with another former high-ranking intelligence official now retired and working as a consultant. Paul gave me a brief summation of his conversation with this official under several administrations and the official said he was never briefed on the specific details but was aware of the project's existence and its overall big picture. I was going to provide his name for this article, but after careful reflective thought, I've decided not to for the same reasons I cited above: I don't want him harassed by anyone reading this article and the zillions of self-styled investigators in this field called ufology.

This former official believes in disclosure, but he feels that some of the information should be kept from public view, and I totally agree now that I've been made privy to much of it via the postings from Anonymous. Much of it which will never see the light of day. Besides, for the UFO field enough never seems to be enough. I could have provided twelve names who have gone on record that such a program did in fact take place while stating that I had another twelve names that I was keeping to myself, and people would still want those other twelve names; the twelve they got just wouldn't be good enough. It never is with the kooky, mental whack-job ufologists. And now on to the second issue-the method of disclosure-which I'll briefly address to my highly regarded and respected colleague in all of this, Richard C. Doty. In Sergeant Doty's piece, he suggests that while there was really nothing wrong with Anonymous making his stunning revelations through me, it would have carried more credibility had it been done through a more open source like CNN or Fox News.

Again: BS! More credible than li'l ol' me? Absolutely! I agree with Rick, but the real question is: Would those more credible, mainstream open sources have ever run with it and published the material from Anonymous? Absolutely not.

CNN, CBS, NBC, ABC, 60 Minutes, Dateline, 20/20, and others would have demanded that the story be verified by the White House itself, meaning either Bush, Cheney, or one of their subordinates, with their implicit knowledge and permission, would have signed off on such a disclosure before being made public.

Now does Doty or anyone reading this article really believe that the single most secretive presidential administration of the past 50 years or so would sign off on verifying such a highly classified project? Does anyone in their right mind imagine the White House spokeshole as saying to one of these major news media outlets: "Oh, yeah, wow, so you found out; someone leaked it to you guys. OK, the cat's out of the bag, so yes, it's all true. Go ahead and run with it; President Bush is fine with it!"

Yeah, right. And my mother's the Queen of England! In fact, look at what's happened in fewer than 60 days with postings 1-11, November 2-December 21, 2005 coming through me: It's sparked a worldwide phenomenon and has caused people to really, seriously consider that a mind-boggling human-ET exchange program actually occurred during that time period.

At this point, I won't elaborate on how postings to my small but highly influential UFO email list, ironically loaded with former and current government insiders, really got the word out much more effectively than a mainstream news media outlet would ever have, except to refer the readers of this article and magazine to the absolutely brilliant summation written by my learned, scholarly, and erudite colleague Bill Ryan. He wrote an executive summary of sorts specifically for Anonymous on the tremendous reach, impact, scope, breadth, and sociological inroads Project Serpo has had thus far. Amazing! People are actually beginning to think outside of the box. Bottom line: Could approaching CNN or Fox have resulted in greater publicity for Project Serpo than the method chosen by Anonymous and his small group at the DIA?

That's right: We're not alone in the universe and our government, for its own paranoid, sick reasons has been keeping this-what ufology's cop-on-the-beat Stan Friedman calls the Cosmic Watergate-from us for umpteen years! And mind you, your tax dollars pay these government clowns to keep us in the dark. Does any of this really make sense?

Think about it: We pay these government kooks, spooks, and ne'er-do-wells high GS-grade salaries to keep us from learning what they've discovered over the years. That's the real outrage that the UFO community should be up in arms over, not about the gender makeup of our team members on Project Serpo nor the weight of the equipment taken on their 13-year journey. Gimme a break, mental patients! I respectfully disagree with Sergeant Doty, whose wise counsel and sage advice I have often sought with respect to intelligence matters, but I totally disagree with his assessment here. In all fairness to him, he is really out of his league.

Why the secrecy?

And when will it end with at least some major announcement regarding the UFO subject being made public?

The most troubling aspect of all this is that most people need an authority figure to come out and say this-and-that is so for reasons of credibility because most people can't think for themselves. In other words, they can't weigh and evaluate the evidence on its own merits and come to a definitive conclusion on their own; they need someone to do it for them.

Short of that, people are never going to buy this story-nor any other UFO-related story-short of a former director of Central Intelligence, secretary of Defense, or chairman of the Joint Chiefs coming out and saying: "Yes, Project Serpo occurred and I was apprised of its overall program, structure, makeup, and mission when I was the DCI during the XX administration." Keep dreamin'.

In closing, I'd like to cite a few choice passages from well-respected UFO author Timothy Good's 1996 ground-breaking book, Beyond Top Secret: The Worldwide UFO Cover-Up (William Morrow, 1988). Much has been made of the widely published comments that President Reagan made after a private White House screening of Close Encounters of the Third Kind, but what has been nearly forgotten were the following comments which appear in Good's book and which deserve equal consideration: Close encounters of the third kind-a reality

During a talk given to the Tulsa, Oklahoma Astronomy Club in 1982, former Air Force intelligence officer Steve Lewis revealed that the 12 years he spent investigating UFOs for the military both in the U.S. and abroad convinced him that intelligent extraterrestrial beings are visiting Earth. Apologizing for being unable to be more specific owing to strict orders from the Air Force not to divulge specific details about his UFO research from 1965-1977, Lewis stated that only a fraction of information accumulated by the military has been released. "That movie Close Encounters of the Third Kind is more realistic than you'd believe," he told the audience. "You can believe that or not." Pressed to reveal what had convinced him that UFOs are extraterrestrial spacecraft rather than top-secret military devices, Lewis commented: "The records, the information I saw while in my job. I no longer rule out what the possibilities might be." Next, we have this information, which includes a cryptic comment by former DCI and President George Bush: Nobody likes to look silly. Fear of ridicule is a very compelling reason for politicians to debunk the subject. British Air Minister George Ward explained [1954] that, if he admitted the existence of UFOs without evidence that the general public could actually touch, the public would consider that the Government had gone barmy.

Few politicians-in Britain, the United States and worldwide- have any inside knowledge of the subject of UFOs, which is why their repeated pronouncements debunking all the reports are so convincing. And those few who have troubled to study the matter, or who have been privy to top-secret information, may be so bewildered and even alarmed by the awesome complexity of the phenomenon that they would rather say nothing at all. "You don't know the half of it," was all former CIA Director George Bush could say when asked by a campaign committee member about UFO secrecy during his first presidential election campaign. Politicians, furthermore, are unlikely to speak out on such a controversial topic without a mandate from the electorate. Relatively few people write to their elected representatives about UFOs, although I am pleased to report than an increasing number are doing so." And continuing with these choice comments: In these respects, I am fully in sympathy with the current official policy. "From an intelligence point of view," remarks Dr James Harder, "the UFO phenomenon must be truly awesome - the worst of science fiction come to life.

However, over the years, the intelligence agencies must have come to the realization that the strangers from space are nothing exactly new - that evidence indicates that we are experiencing only an intensification of what may have been going on centuries. And continuing with this same line of thought, we have:

It has been suggested that those in the know are concerned about the reaction of the public and religious authorities to revelations regarding the link between the UFO phenomenon and religion (one hypothesis being that homo sapiens is genetically linked with extraterrestrials). And with one final notation on this same train of thought from Good's other book, Alien Base: The Evidence for Extraterrestrial Colonization of Earth (Harper Perennial, 1999): In addition to the visitors being responsible for genetically upgrading the human race on two occasions in our distant past, it was alleged that a few of our great spiritual leaders-including Jesus-were genetically "engineered" by a type of artificial insemination, in an attempt to instill Earth people with spiritual concepts. The reluctance of this particular group of extraterrestrials to communicate with humanity at large was due mainly to the fact that we simply are not psychologically nor spiritually ready for contact with a higher civilization, and it is necessary for us to evolve independently. Essentially, we are spiritual beings surviving beyond death.

And finally, these are author Timothy Good's personal, closing observations: It is my conviction that we are being visited by several groups of extraterrestrials, and that, while some may not be well-disposed towards us, others are benevolent. From my own investigations throughout the world, however, I am convinced that selective contacts have been made with possibly thousands of individuals.

The visitors have no need to establish open contact, nor do they want the majority of us to know what they are doing here. It is probably, in my view, that the cover-up is sustained to a certain extent by the aliens themselves.

And in closing, we have this choice snippet from former DCI Roscoe Hillenkoetter: One authority in a position to know facts- as known at the time-was former CIA Director Admiral Roscoe Hillenkoetter, who was unequivocal in his condemnation of official policy. "The public has a right to know," he declared in 1960. "It is time for the truth to be brought out in open Congressional hearings through official secrecy and ridicule, many citizens are led to believe the unknown flying objects are nonsense." Forty-six years later, we're still those mushrooms living under a canopy of darkness and ignorance somewhat like the infamous, ignorant inhabitants of Plato's Allegory of the Cave in Book VII of The Republic.

So, while the UFO community continues to wallow like swine in their petty jealousies and bicker, argue, and fight amongst themselves, this rather profound and awe-inspiring information will continue to be withheld from us. We berate the government insiders who withhold this information which rightfully belongs to us as losers. Believe me, they're not the only losers. Go look in the mirror and see who's staring back at you.

Richard Doty's Statement

My name is Richard Doty, retired special agent, Air Force Office of Special Investigation (AFOSI), and now a private citizen living in New Mexico. I've been an avid reader of UFO Magazine for the past several years. Recently Bill Birnes, the magazine's publisher, asked me to make some comments regarding the recent Serpo revelations. I told Bill I'd be very happy to write this article relating my personal analysis of the Serpo information, which describes an exchange program in 1965 between United States military personnel and extraterrestrials from the Planet Serpo in the Zeta Reticuli star system.

Before I go into the details of Project Serpo, let me explain that I've been a recipient of Victor Martinez's email listing for the past year. For those readers who don't know Victor, let me give a brief biographical review of him. Understanding the Project Serpo disclosure starts with understanding Victor's role.

Victor is a former U.S. government employee. He worked for a number of different Federal law enforcement agencies and now works in Los Angeles as a teacher. Victor has a longstanding personal interest in the subject of UFOs and maintains an email distribution list of well over a hundred recipients on the topic. In early November 2005 I learned from Victor that he'd been contacted by a person identifying himself as Anonymous who was telling an extraordinary story; moreover, it's one which I'd heard before.

Mr. Anonymous and the "real" Roswell incident: Two crash sites

Mr. Anonymous, as I like to call him, first introduced himself as a retired employee of the U.S. government and then went on to detail the "real" Roswell incident. He stated that the Roswell incident involved two crash sites: One southwest of Corona and the second site at Pelona Peak, south of Datil, New Mexico. The crash involved two extraterrestrial aircraft.

The Corona crash was found a day later by an archaeology team who reported the crash site to the Lincoln County Sheriff's department. A deputy arrived the next day and summoned a state police officer. One live alien being, an extraterrestrial biological entity (EBE), was found hiding behind a rock. The alien was given water but declined food, and was later transferred to Los Alamos National Laboratory in New Mexico.

The information eventually went to Roswell Army Air Field. The site was examined and all hard evidence was also removed to Roswell.

The bodies of the aliens were taken to Los Alamos

However, the bodies were taken to Los Alamos since they had a freezing system that allowed the bodies to remain frozen for research. The craft itself was taken to Roswell and then on to Wright Field, Ohio, later to be renamed Wright Patterson Air Force Base.

The second site was not discovered until August 1949 by two ranchers. They reported the findings several days later to the sheriff of Catron County, New Mexico. Because of the remote location, it took the sheriff several days to make his way to the crash site on horseback.

Once at the site, the sheriff took photographs and then returned to Datil. Sandia Army Base, later to become Kirtland Air Force Base, was notified. A recovery team took custody of all evidence, including six bodies. The bodies were initially taken to Sandia but were later transferred to Los Alamos.

The live entity established communication with the U.S. military.
An exchange program was set up between our two races.

The live entity established communication with the U.S. military and provided information about his planet and his race of extraterrestrials. Eventually, the U.S. Government made contact with the Ebens, as they were termed, and set up a meeting location, which turned out to be the well-known Holloman landing in 1964. Mr. Anonymous explained that the landing was near Holloman Air Force Base, not actually at Holloman itself.

During that meeting, an exchange program was set up between our two races. Our government selected twelve military personnel: ten men and two women. They were trained, vetted, and carefully removed from the military system, and in 1965 the twelve left on an Eben spacecraft to the planet Serpo.

That was the core story as presented by Mr. Anonymous in a sequence of eleven major releases of information to date, all so far via Victor Martinez. Readers can go to www.serpo.org and read the archive of the entire release, accompanied by further analysis from many different people. In this rest of this article, I'll offer my personal analysis of the initial contact made by Mr. Anonymous, and of the information released by him.

Background of United States government's involvement with the extraterrestrials biological entities

In early 1979, after arriving at Kirtland Air Force Base as a young special agent with AFOSI, I was assigned to the counterintelligence division of AFOSI District 17. I was briefed into a special compartmented program.

This program dealt with United States government involvement with extraterrestrial biological entities. During my initial briefing I was given the complete background of our government's involvement with EBEs.

This background included information on the Roswell incident, which did indeed state that two crash sites were found. The first crash site was located southeast of Corona and the second site was found south of Datil. Basically, this was exactly the same information that Mr. Anonymous released.

Other details about the location of the bodies and the site where the live entity was discovered were also mentioned. I learned these details in 1979 and can confirm that Mr. Anonymous did indeed state information that was previously unknown to the public. The fact that the bodies were taken to Los Alamos and that Sandia Base handled the second site were not known publicly in the past. This information is quite correct.

During a briefing in 1984 I read a document which mentioned an exchange program between an alien race and twelve U.S. military personnel.

The briefing did not mention any specific details of the exchange program, but it did refer to the program lasting from 1965 to 1978.

I tried to obtain more information during a Pentagon briefing in 1985, but I was told I didn't have the proper clearance for that information. I retired in 1988 and with one exception, I never learned anything further about the subject until very recently.

In 1991 during a retirement party for a AFOSI friend, I had a conversation with Colonel Jack Casey, retired Air Force Intelligence. I specifically asked Colonel Casey about the exchange program I'd heard about. With a look of surprise, Colonel Casey looked around as if to make sure no one was listening and then led me outside to a patio.

Colonel Casey: In 1965, twelve U.S. military men were placed on an extraterrestrial spacecraft and flew to an alien planet some 40 light years away

Colonel Casey then went on to give me a short briefing about the exchange program. He told me the following: In 1965, twelve U.S. military men were placed on an extraterrestrial spacecraft and flew to an alien planet some 40 light years away. The exchange program lasted until 1978 when the team returned. Some of the twelve died on the alien planet and by 1991, when I was given this information, some had died since. The final briefing of the returnees is still classified. Note: all the team members are now dead, the last surviving until 2002. Again, this was exactly what Mr. Anonymous has described. That was all the information Colonel Casey would or could provide. I did try over the years to obtain more information, but no one, not even the retired intelligence officers I knew, had any further data they possessed or were willing to share. Then in late 2005, 14 years later, Mr. Anonymous made the stunning release being discussed here.

Although much of the information correlates closely with what I've heard elsewhere, I do have a few concerns both regarding the method used by Mr. Anonymous in his initial release, and also regarding some of the information itself. First, I'd personally have preferred Mr. Anonymous to have chosen a different medium for his release; he could perhaps have used a more open source.

Although I have nothing but praise for Victor Martinez and his email forum, I think Mr. Anonymous could have chosen a widely recognized news medium, such as CNN, Fox, or the like, which would have given him more credibility and instant access to a much wider public.

If Mr. Anonymous wishes the information to be released broadly, then in my opinion what would work best would be for him to go to such an open source and make all the information available at one time. I don't actually know the exact reasons why he chose instead to release his information via Victor Martinez. Secondly, there are some apparent anomalies in the information that has been released to date. Many former intelligence officers have come forward after Mr. Anonymous made his initial release, and pointed out what they claimed were errors in some of the data. For instance, Mr. Anonymous stated that ten men and two women comprised the exchange team. However, both Paul McGovern, former security chief for the Defense Intelligence Agency, and Gene Loscowski (real name Gene Lakes), former director of security, Nevada Test Site, have come forward questioning this particular gender mix of the team. Three other former Air Force Intelligence officers have also questioned this information.

According to Mr. McGovern, twelve men were selected; no women. My other independent sources also confirmed that no women were sent on that mission. I'm not in any way wanting to upset female readers, but to understand how the military would have regarded this project, one must really look back to the U.S. military, not now-but way back in 1965.

During that time period women in the military were segregated. The USAF had women in the Air Force (WAFS), there were women in the Navy (WAVES), and the Army had women in the Army corps (WACS). Most military females were in medical, administrative, supply, or the personnel career field. Few women would have been qualified for such a long-duration mission. Female astronauts were not selected until the late 1970s. These are valid reasons to doubt Mr. Anonymous's particular statement that women were included on this particular mission.

Mr. Anonymous then detailed the training given to the twelve people selected for the mission. Two former Defense Intelligence Agency employees have come forward to state that the training actually fell in line with astronaut training and that the training lasted for one year and consisted of astronaut training rather then the intelligence and combat training detailed by Mr. Anonymous. If one stops and thinks about it, astronaut training would probably make a little more sense than the training described by Mr. Anonymous.

Mr. Anonymous also mentioned some items which were taken on the mission. According to his early reports, the team took 9,000 pounds of equipment with them.

However, Mr. Anonymous subsequently corrected this by saying 90,500 pounds of equipment was taken.

He then mentioned that liquid nitrogen canisters were taken as a fall-back weapon against the Ebens, who were sensitive to cold. But liquid nitrogen would not stay stable for an extended period of time and would last only a few weeks in a canister. Maybe Mr. Anonymous meant compressed air, which would last longer, or better yet, Freon, which would remain stable in a canister for a long period of time.

Finally, Mr. Anonymous mentioned handguns and rifles being taken as defense. I have mixed feelings regarding this. Since it was a military team, I could understand that some weapons would be taken as a routine measure. However, if you trusted the Ebens to the degree of allowing twelve United States military personnel to fly 40 light years for 12 or 13 years, why would anyone take weapons? What good would weapons be on a planet 40 light years away?

On the positive side of Mr. Anonymous's information, a number of insiders and researchers have reported hearing of such an exchange program before. These include such respected individuals as Linda Howe and Whitley Strieber, together with Colonel Casey and all the other former DIA officials mentioned above. Whitley Strieber's tantalizing and brief experience over 10 years ago was with a man he met at a convention who claimed to have been on the Serpo team before he left Strieber to consider what he had been told. This overall degree of corroboration seems highly significant, as I think readers will agree.

Some of the data provided by Mr. Anonymous seems off-beam-the orbital data and other scientific information-although he did state, intriguingly, that the laws of physics were not exactly the same on Serpo as they are here in our own solar system.

Nevertheless, there's a growing debate regarding the scientific information provided by Mr. Anonymous about the planet Serpo and that solar system. According to him, Serpo was a planet of a binary star system.

A binary star is a double star, each orbiting their common center of mass.

I'm not a math or science expert and will not state all the different figures or formulas, but it seems to me that there are legitimate arguments on both sides of this issue. But I have to say that I do feel that a simple hoaxer would have been sure to get the numbers right.

The purpose of a hoaxer, or even someone spreading disinformation, is-after all-to convince, not to lay himself open to criticism straight away.

To conclude, and aside from the broadly confirming testimony of my various colleagues, Mr. Anonymous is simply in my opinion not operating like a hoaxer would.

A hoaxer would have actually done a better job, so to speak, of researching information for his hoax.

Importantly, the apparent anomalies and absence of the promised photographs to date can all be accounted for if we suppose that the context under which Mr. Anonymous is operating is not exactly as it may first appear.

We must remember that Mr. Anonymous will hardly have the 3,000-page report in his living room just sitting there like a Sears catalog. The report will be guarded under the tightest conceivable security and the conditions of access are unknown by us. We can hypothesize that Mr. Anonymous may not even have access to the documents at all and may be relying on memory, someone else's memory, or someone else supplying him with the information maybe by phone or by tape under conditions over which he himself has no control.

As for the photographs, they may again be in a different location. Paradoxically, there is the factor of Mr. Anonymous having gone quiet since his last post on December 21 up to the time of my writing this on January 13 may be precisely because he has indeed met with difficulty caused by insider agents.

We know that there are different factions within the intelligence community regarding disclosure. Some may wish to obstruct a disclosure such as this while some others may be looking the other way, quietly supporting the disclosure by allowing it to happen. We just don't know at this point. These factors are not reasons in themselves to accept the story; however, they are persuasive reasons not to dismiss it without very careful thought indeed.

In conclusion, it seems to me that while there are some discrepancies in detail, there's a persuasively broad measure of agreement that such a project actually existed, and there are good reasons for us to suspend our disbelief. I earnestly hope that by the time this edition of the magazine is published we may have heard more from Mr. Anonymous, and that his important revelations will continue well into 2006.

Major points and perspectives by Bill Ryan

Bill Ryan said: To offer you my promised personal perspective on the enigmatic Serpo story, here are the major points and perspectives which I believe are worth dwelling on when analyzing the entire affair. For the most concise and also most recent overview of my own position in audio, there is an mp3 is available for download as a podcast for the Above Top Secret forum and was intended to be heard by a knowledgeable and reasonably sophisticated audience.

You can find it at www.podcast.abovetopsecret.com/atscpod_1232.mp3 .

Next, a summary of my reasons why I think the story should be taken seriously, and not dismissed without very careful thought. Some, but not all, of my points are covered on the website at www.serpo.org/consistencies.html .

The first compelling reason to believe this story is the accidental testimony of the retired Air Force colonel with 33 years in Intelligence. When he read the Serpo account in hard copy, he was visibly shocked and confirmed "Yes, [it's] all real." That full text is at www.serpo.org/ comments.html#1 and I recommend that it should be read carefully by any commentator.

In my view this is very important, and although it's circumstantial evidence, it seems to me to carry quite some weight. I have the name of the person who supplied me with the story, a very straight and intelligent man, a serving Air Force lieutenant colonel who checks out in every respect.

A number of insiders and researchers have reported hearing of such an exchange program before, including such respected individuals as Linda Howe, Paul McGovern, and Gene Loscowski, whose real name is Gene Lakes. All these people have gone on record as openly confirming the existence of the project; see Anonymous's website post #1 on www.serpo.org/information.html .

Rick Doty records a private conversation a number of years ago about Serpo with an individual whom he names, and he also confirms Anonymous's data about the Roswell incident. To my surprise, I don't think anyone has followed this up, an anomaly in itself considering how well researched Roswell is. If Anonymous's Roswell claims can be substantiated, this would lend some support to his other claims about Serpo, although the disinformation hypothesis is of course not ruled out by this.

Paul McGovern also clarified what the acronym DIM-an item on the equipment manifest-stood for. Anonymous didn't know.

McGovern explained it was the duty information manual. If this exchange was staged, with Anonymous saying he didn't know and McGovern supplying the answer, it was very clever and quite subtle; more so than the way the rest of the story seems to have been crafted, particularly in that the issue would have been totally overlooked if I had not drawn attention to it myself.

I'd jumped on the DIM question to draw attention to it and had thought I'd discovered what it meant. McGovern corrected me with a one-line email to myself and Victor Martinez. All that smelled very genuine to me. This is one of many indications, it must be said, that McGovern is privy to some, if not all, of the Project Serpo data.

Here's another incident that intrigues me: Whitley Strieber's tantalizing and brief encounter over 10 years ago with a man who, so it seemed, was claiming to have been on the Serpo team.

On the other hand, some of the data provided by Anonymous seems way off-beam, such as the information on orbital data, but a simple hoaxer would have been sure to get the numbers right. It's very easy to do. Doesn't a hoaxer want to convince? One can find accounts of believable worlds in the science fiction section of any bookstore. They are easy to research, craft, and create. Why would Anonymous, if intent on deception, have made himself so vulnerable by immediately presenting a world with some aspects that are actually quite hard to swallow?

Anonymous is not operating like a hoaxer or disinformationist. A hoaxer or disinformationist would actually have done a better job for himself. Many eventually proven UFO hoaxes have taken quite a bit of uncovering.

This story is too easy to dismiss as a hoax or disinfo without some serious thought, yet the factors above indicate that if it is a hoax or disinfo, it would have been much more sophisticated, for example, if it were choreographed by the DIA itself.

Yet Anonymous's releases are not sophisticated at all. Rather, they are naive, exactly like an elderly person telling a great story of what he did in his youth.

A bit of mental arithmetic can convince us that Anonymous is indeed elderly. Assuming he was involved with the project, directly or peripherally or is of the same military generation as those who were, he would be at least 70 and possibly in his 80s. Frustratingly for myself personally, there is no indication that Anonymous understands the requirements of effective public relations in the 21st century. But if we think of our own grandfather or great-uncle, maybe, why should we expect his generation to possess modern, sophisticated PR savvy? This seems to me to be a factor that a number of commentators have overlooked.

The apparent anomalies and absence of the photos to date can all be accounted for if we suppose that the context under which Anonymous is operating is not as it may first appear. Anonymous hardly has the 3,000 page report in his living room just sitting there like a Sears catalog. Such a report would be guarded under the tightest security and the conditions of access highly restricted.

We can hypothesise that Anonymous may not even have access to the document at all and may be relying on his memory, someone else's memory, or perhaps someone else is supplying him with the information maybe by phone or by tape under conditions over which he himself has no control.

It's worth remembering that it was not Anonymous who first mentioned the 3,000 page report. That was Paul McGovern. Anonymous subsequently quietly went along with that. Anonymous has never claimed to have access to the report; that has just been everyone's assumption.

As for the photos: They may again be in a different location, maybe not even in the U.S. Suppose Anonymous is receiving his information from a retired person who was involved in Project Serpo, who is, for example, now living in Thailand, Australia, or South Africa?

Anonymous could receive the voice transcripts by phone, which would explain the intermittent postings, the errors, and occasional later corrections, and the absence of hard data.

Maybe the photos are in a shoebox under his contact's bed.

This is, of course, just a picture painted to show that we still have no idea what is happening behind the scenes.

Paradoxically, Anonymous has gone quiet since December 21, and this may be precisely because he has indeed met with difficulties engineered by insider agents. He has stated to Victor Martinez that he's been experiencing significant problems from people "poking their noses in where they don't belong."

Why should we disbelieve this?

It's totally credible-even likely.

We know that there are different factions within the Intelligence community regarding disclosure.

Some, wishing to support disclosure, may be looking the other way, but some may be trying to stop Anonymous, or they might even have supplied him with false data after he started his disclosure.

Just about anything could be happening. These are not reasons to blindly accept the story, but they are persuasive reasons not to dismiss it without very careful thought.

Of course, it is absolutely possible that this is disinformation; even 10 percent injected fiction or altered data would account for all the factors in the story to which skeptics draw attention.

The point here is that if this story is 90 percent true-or even 10 percent true!-it's still the story of the last millennium. Some people cannot believe that twelve American astronauts could have made a trip to another planet nearly 40 light years away in 1965. It's just too much of a leap to believe.

But logically, if the visitors have come here, all that the twelve would be doing is catching the shuttle flight the other way. There's no illogic there. If the aliens can come here, we can also go there. It's just as easy. If we can accept the possibility of one, we must accept the possibility of the other. The reasons to reject that particular claim on the grounds of believability are purely emotional. The claims need to be believed or not only on the basis of evidence, which, despite all the above, we do not yet have.

There are a number of other minor factors which, if the story goes totally quiet-and it's too early yet to assume that it has died already-Victor Martinez and I can lay open to public view so everyone can pick over the tiniest bone. These factors all support the story, but all are circumstantial.

For instance, we believe that we know the names of some of the individuals involved at high levels and also the location of the 3,000 page report. We've also received an enigmatic threat described in general terms on the Above Top Secret podcast but which we cannot confirm was real. And even that incident has its own analysis: If it was real, then it further confirms the story, but if it was staged, then the nature of that deception was highly sophisticated, which Anonymous's releases have not been.

We have no source data apart from Anonymous's very first message to Victor Martinez on 1 November 2005, which he has archived. All the rest of the messages from Anonymous and everyone else have been deleted by Victor's Web TV system, which erases all messages after 96 hours by default. Victor has explained that he has cut and pasted some of the incoming information for presentational purposes and that sometimes that information has come from different sources.

Victor has explained that 85 percent of the information comes from one source, whom we have casually referred to Anonymous. But there is a second source contributing 13 percent of the information and a third source contributing 2 percent.

This third source sends information from a military address which cancels itself after sending and cannot be replied to. This is a standard military technique.

So the posts on the website, which are faithfully archived from Victor Martinez's postings, are not necessarily in Anonymous's words.

I should emphasise here that Victor's integrity is the highest and he has always done what he thinks is right and best in presenting this story to the public.

My own hypotheses: Anonymous is getting his information remotely, does not have personal access to the report or the photos, and it is not in his hands when and what kind of information he will relay to us. He's elderly and is doing his best.

He does not understand modern PR, is not a scientist, and does not understand the stringent requirements of proof or evidence.

He believes the story should stand on its own because he knows it's true himself, and he is both frustrated at the objections and at the increasingly level of obstruction, interference, and even harassment which he's been suffering privately.

He's in the twilight years of his life, and he could do without all this. He may pack up and go home if he feels others are ungrateful for his sincere efforts. He himself may wish that he'd never mentioned the photos, because he'd been given to understand at the time that they would be made available to him.

On the other hand, I could be convinced that there's an extremely clever disinformation campaign going on. It may even have started with a maverick self-starting individual, but insiders may have acted very quickly to add their own disinformational spin to the story while other insiders, favoring disclosure, may have been helping him as best they could.

Anonymous may not even be knowingly imparting disinformation, and the false-data percentage may not be high but inserted at critical junctures. You don't have to remove too many components from an engine to make it misfire. The project might even have existed, under a different name. Human astronauts may have indeed visited another planet, and why not?

The reason for this may be to ease the way for the real disclosure later or sooner; thus, the U.S. government gets to be the hero of the day. If the latter is the case, then I would predict that the photos will indeed be released, but they will eventually be shown conclusively to be fakes. Would not a disinformation campaign be sure to include impressive images or fabricated documents?

As many have argued, fabricated pictures of another world would be quite easy to create. We see them in every Star Wars movie.

So why have they not appeared?

Paradoxically, this suggests that if we see the photos then they may be fakes, and if they do not appear, then Anonymous may be fully genuine. But the problem is that once having promised them, their nonappearance will be a sure sign of chicanery. This is also theoretically possible, of course. The principal factor to consider here may be to ask oneself: If this were a disinformation campaign, how would it have been choreographed? Presumably great expense, together with hundreds if not thousands of man-days, would have gone into the planning and execution. How good would it be? What would it include? And would not the information offered by Anonymous be more sophisticated and convincing?

From the Jerry Pippin website

The Jerry Pippin website www.jerrypippin.com/UFO_Files_serpo_project.htm posted the following: In the following interview, Jerry talks with Bill Ryan, who less that two months ago, knew nothing about a remarkable, above top secret US government project, code named Serpo. Coincidentally, he was on an e-mail mailing list that had several Defense Department Officials, Black Project Managers and UFO Researchers which received a dispatch from "Anonymous".

This undisclosed person, who is still active in UFO related secret projects, wrote about the gradual release of confidential documents pertaining to a top secret exchange program between the Ebens, Extraterrestrial Entities (ETEs) from the planet Serpo, located in the Zeta Retuiculi star system and shown in the star catalogue image at left, which is some 39 light years from Earth.

Several Ebens and twelve US military personnel were involved in an exchange program between Earth and Serpo, between the years 1965-78. At the request of the recipient of this information, Victor Martinez, Ryan quickly set up a public service based website, www.serpo.org, to disseminate already provided and promised information, including photos of human beings associating with the inhabitants of the Planet Serpo.

In a wide ranging discussion, Ryan tells Jerry about the climate, flora and animals of this planet, as well as the history, culture and lifestyles of the intelligent beings, the Ebens, living on the planet.

Details never before revealed will astound you, the listener, with vivid descriptions given of encounters between American military personnel and the Ebens on their current home planet.

Project SERPO" UPDATE: Midnight, Eastern time, March 17, 2006 – Reliable sources have confirmed to us that the original ANONYMOUS ceased postings on "Project SERPO" on December 21, 2005.

These reports originated from a highly-placed source identified by our source, but not named for public consumption.

This source was highly-placed in a secret government operation and had access to audio tapes of the original narratives by the returning "Project SERPO" exchange crew who were debriefed in both audio and written form; the written form comprises the 3,000-page "Project SERPO" report.

For unknown reasons, this source stopped providing Victor Martinez information.

Bill Ryan, was then contacted by other anonymous sources none of whom have anything to do with the original one.

Anonymous is actually a composite of three (3) people

We believe upon information from trusted, but unidentified sources that this anonymous is actually a composite of three (3) people. These individuals were trained as part of the final pool of 16 for the original '65 "Project SERPO" mission, but did not go -- as they were alternates for the final 12 -- and their information to Ryan is based upon conversations with the other crew members who did return to Earth in '78.

The returning Team Members subsequently died of illnesses believed to have been caused by the excess radiation from the dual suns of the Zeta Reticuli planetary system where SERPO was the fourth planet.

Information has been received indicating some confirmations of the SERPO story came from top administrators in government departments charged with protecting official secrets, a name we would all recognize, but can't divulge because of promises to sources. It is expected that these three living witnesses -- who trained with the other 12 -- will be issuing further information to Ryan and his www.serpo.org website.

A producer for the Jerry Pippin show is currently in third party talks exploring the possibility of an interview with one of these three witnesses who underwent the same rigorous training for the mission, but was not chosen to be one of the 12 human-ET exchange program Team Members...

Also posted is the following: An email from Anonymous, forwarded by Victor Martinez on 3/28/06: E-mail message From: ANONYMOUS, Date: Mon, Mar 27, 2006, 11:01 p.m. (PST+3), POSTING 15a ADDENDUM. Subject: EXPLANATION OF ALIEN DRAWINGS aka 'EBEN OBJECTS'.

The Mission Team took cameras, 16 (sixteen) different types of cameras and drawing/drafting equipment.

VICTOR: Here is the explanation of the Alien Drawing or 'Eben Objects' as referred to on the www.serpo.org Web site posted by Bill [Ryan]. A great deal of planning went into the 10-year mission to SERPO [turned into 13 years]. Several teams of officials planned what equipment to take. These officials tried to imagine every conceivable situation where certain types of tools and other equipment might be needed.

One area was capturing the view and makeup of objects, artifacts and landscapes on Planet SERPO. The Mission Team took cameras, 16 (sixteen) different types of cameras and drawing/drafting equipment. Although no Team Member was trained in drafting, three (3) Team Members had drawing experience from their college days. Several different types of drafting templates were taken on the trip. The planning officials tried to envision every type of situation where a template might be needed.

The drawing ['Eben Object'], made by the Team Commander, depicts the base of the sundial [used globally by the Ebens on SERPO]. Each object meant a certain time of day to the Ebens. When the sun was directed -- through the sundial -- onto the object at the base of the sundial that meant a specific task [or change of] to the Ebens. For example, it might signal a change in work schedules, a time to rest, a time to eat, a time to celebrate, etc. After a few years, the Team learned each symbol and learned the meaning of each symbol. This drawing is a copy of the actual drawing made by the Team Commander in 1967.

The Team also took many photographs of the sundial symbols.

I know our detractors and skeptics will still harbor doubts about our message and incredible mission, but this will have to suffice for now short of the actual photographs which the debunkers would still find problems with.

Glad to be in touch with you and I'll be in contact again soon. – ANONYMOUS.

Ryan's website posted a sample of Eben written language received from Anonymous, and the real portrait of EBE-1

An email from Bill Ryan on 3/10/06: Many greetings to everyone. I have just updated the Serpo website. The latest installment of the Team Commander's log is now posted on the Serpo website. The information posted has been formally sanctioned by the group who is orchestrating the gradual disclosure. The public can make their own decision on the credibility of the material, all in the fullness of time, as more and more material is released.

Note: The website posted a sample of Eben written language received from Anonymous. [Re: the EBE-1 image, Robert Collins, author of *Exempt from Disclosure*, says the image above (as posted on Ryan's website), right is the real portrait of EBE-1, vouched for by Rick Doty.

Robert states: "It's a drawing of EBE-1. Rick Doty identified that drawing as EBE-1, taken from the files at LANL. Distribution was very limited." Larry Dicken agrees that the center image is more like a classic Grey. All the more reason to believe there may be some truth in this story, but the reality is not the story being currently presented.

More on this to come, but what if the origin of either the SERPO or Grey ETs was not Zeta Reticuli 2?

It is highly unlikely that all of these ET species have a home or operating base in the Zeta Reticuli system.] This is unconnected with Serpo, but may still be of considerable interest, and was received by e-mail from an ex-intelligence officer whose name is known to me. Both images are also attached here. Neither the script nor the EBE-1 image has been analyzed, and I offer them for your interest without further comment.

Please note that new website is being designed and will be launched quite shortly. There'll be some new material, but all the current information will be there in an easily accessible archive. Do stay tuned. I'm looking forward very much to all your comments and observations. With best wishes to all, Bill.

The American Chronicle published this article:
Alleged 'Project SERPO' sent U.S. military team to another planet?
By Steve Hammons

Steve Hammons is author of two novels about a secret joint-service U.S. Government research team investigating unusual phenomena: "Mission Into Light" and the sequel "Light's Hand" introduce readers to the ten women and men of the "Joint Reconnaissance Study Group" and their exciting adventures exploring the unknown. Both novels are available from the Barnes & Noble Web site, bn.com. Hammons also serves as a research analyst at the open source intelligence (OSINT) Web site IntelDesk.com.

In recent weeks, information has surfaced on the Web about an alleged U.S. Government military project called "Project SERPO." We've all heard about reports of unusual and unconventional secret government projects. Some of them seem so far out that you wonder if they are real or an "urban legend" floating around. Yet, many of us understand that people within our government and our military sometimes face unusual and strange phenomena in the course of their duties.

According to a mysterious source's comments on a recently-developed Web site, serpo.org, Project SERPO was an effort developed between the late 1940s and the mid-1960s. It was a joint project between the U.S. Government and a race of friendly beings from a planet in the Zeta Reticuli star system.

The source claims that diplomatic relations were established between the U.S. Government and these beings after their spacecraft crashed in New Mexico in 1947. Aw, give me a break, you may say.

What have these people been smoking – medical cannabis or something? We've heard and read about unconventional government projects before such as "remote viewing" intelligence-gathering methods, time-travel physics research, psychological studies on "magic mushrooms," unusual non-lethal weapons and similar efforts. But relations with visitors from another planet?

That's not all. Information on the SERPO Web site describes a project that selected and trained a joint-service U.S. military team to board a spacecraft of these visitors and go to their home planet for a planned ten-year stay.

And, that in the mid-60s, this was successfully accomplished. Most of the team members returned and were debriefed. Remember the movie "Close Encounters of the Third Kind?"

Remember when the government teams set up a landing zone for the "visitors" and how Army Special Forces personnel assisted with covert logistics?

Remember how 12 people in red jumpsuits were transported to the LZ for boarding? The entries on serpo.org allege that this is based on fact. In addition, the information posted there and elsewhere indicates that the government has been struggling since the 1940s to figure out how to break this kind of information to the general public without creating anxiety and negative disruption.

According to the information, various efforts have been underway over the decades to gradually prepare us for this reality.

Well, do you buy it?

It would make a good novel or movie, that's for sure. Is it possibly true or is it just someone's imagination and a bunch of warmed-over stories from movies, writings and UFO lore?

If there was some truth to it, how would Americans and the rest of humankind react? Would we have open minds and hearts toward friendly visitors?

Would we be afraid?

Would we feel intimidated if they had more advanced technology and knowledge? Would we hate them because they look different and have different beliefs? Undoubtedly, it would add more complexity to our view of things. Not only do we have trouble getting along with other countries and other people who are different, now we would really need to be tolerant and open-minded.

And, are their other kinds of "visitors" who are not quite so friendly, or even dangerous in some way?

This could explain why our government officials might have thought it wise to keep information like this from the general public. According to information on the serpo.org site, there are responsible people in and out of government who may now believe that the time is right for more gradual disclosure of information about this situation.

These people, people with compassion and vision, could feel that we might now be ready to obtain some understanding of the situation and react responsibly and with intelligence. Of course, it could all be bunk. There may be no truth to it at all.

Probably not. Right?

CHAPTER 17
THE TRUTH!

1-The truth about ETs through telepathic contact and filtered through God presence
2-The Anunnaki, Sitchin, Amarani, Judaism, the Bible, Archeology, and Channeling Face to Face

There are so many ways of seeing, perceiving, interpreting, understanding and telling the truth. One historical sentence from Blaise Pascal summarizes it: "Vérité au deçà des Pyrénées, erreur au delà." A very a propos ending for this book! I have used this book as a prism reflecting the ideas, opinions and theories of some of the most brilliant minds in ufology, Middle/Near East archeology, paranormal, metaphysics and religion. A great number of their theories was based on facts and meticulous research. Nevertheless, some of their findings remained questionable in the eyes of peers and colleagues. I did not take any stand, nor did I advance a theory. This is not my place, even though, deep down in my heart, I felt sometimes a strong need, and to a certain degree, a duty to honesty and openly express – at least – some of my personal opinions, taking into consideration the fact that I have already written 13 books in the field. But I didn't. My time has not come yet. Some areas or subjects of this field remain a complete mystery for me, an enigma: "Channeling." Especially, the way it has been used by "Channelers" to reveal "THE TRUTH" about UFOs, higher dimensions, supreme beings, extraterrestrials, aliens from planets beyond our reach and discoveries.

OH YES! Channeling is quite a remarkable way to end this book; a work fed with scientific research as strong as the 1,100 ton stones of Baalbeck Temple, and sometimes as fragile as the fading smile of the goddesses who were worshiped on its altar. Sal Rachel and Estelle Nora Harwit Amrani, two channelers and spiritual visionaries will take us there...to the firmament of the Anunnaki, Zeta Reticuli, the gods, vanished civilizations, galactic culture, and beyond. Hopefully, their journey of channeling and contact filtered through their GOD presence and extraterrestrial beings will reveal the truth and bring to our hearts, warmth, joy and peace...

THE TRUTH ABOUT ETS

Regarding the UFO/ET issue: Some of these statements are difficult to verify, but nearly every day I get confirmation that my perceptions are largely accurate. Here's my brief synopsis (received directly through telepathic contact and filtered through my God Presence): Approximately 60% of all UFOs reported are from solar systems outside our own. The majority are from Zeta Reticuli, Alpha Centauri, Rigel & Betelguese (Orion), Sirius A & B, and the Pleiades.

Approximately 20% are above top-secret military tests of experimental craft, often reverse engineered from Zeta craft. Approximately 20% are natural phenomena mistakenly identified as artificial craft. In addition to the above, there are millions of encounters with beings from other dimensions (parallel, higher, etc.), most of whom are benevolent.

We Are All ETs to Some Extent: There is really no difference between ETs and humans, because Earth has been genetically manipulated for aeons by different ET races to the point that almost all of us have genetics from other star systems. There are often some physical genetic markers carried from generation to generation that can help identify one's ET heritage. For example, those carrying genetic material from Nordic Pleaideans are often tall and muscular, with blond hair and blue eyes.. But with all the mixing and blending of our melting pot planet, this is a hard thing to track. For example, I am Venusian, but I do not have any markers that I'm aware of (I'm Italian with dark hair and eyes and olive skin while most Venusians are fair skinned and blond by nature). Actually, if a non-human being were to walk among us (and some do), he/she might not even be noticed. Not only can some alien races disguise themselves, but many already look a lot like us. Approximately 80% of all ETs are benevolent, kind, loving souls who sincerely want to lift humanity and welcome them back into the cosmic family. About 20% of ETs are malevolent, power-hungry beings with total disregard or even disdain of humans. Of course, there's some neutral middle ground (mostly alien scientists who have no ill feelings toward humanity but are not evolved enough spiritually to be in a position to decide what's best for us). In the name of research, they might dissect a human to learn more about him/her. The problem is, most of the negative ETs are vibrating in the 3D and 4D realms and so are often visible to 3D and 4D humans. Many of the higher, more loving races exist in 5D, 6D and 7D and can only be contacted by humans who are attuned to those densities. So it APPEARS there are a lot of negative ETs involved with Earth. And of course, most of the world's rulers are controlled by negative ETs (because of their lust for power.)

There are many different "species" of aliens. Here's my latest assessment including those in human embodiment:

STAR SYSTEM	EARTH GROUP	PERCENTAGE OF TOTAL
Orion Constellation	Councils of Rigel & Betelguese, Incarnates from Mars and Maldek	80%
Pleiades System 7D	Adamic Race (original earthlings) from Lyra/Vega DNA, Atlantean Priest-Kings	15%
Sirius B Binary System	Biblical Gods, Greek Gods, descendants of Israel & the Middle East	2%
Venus, 6th Density	Generally blond-haired, blue-eyed, fair-skinned humans	1%
Pleiades System 4D	Nordic-type tall muscular humans (original Vikings, Scandinavian races)	1%
Andromedan 4D	Oriental-type humans with small slanted eyes	0.5%
Antares 4D	Red giant race mentioned in Genesis, Nordic-types, stocky European	0.3%
Zeta Reticuli 3D	Human incarnates of original Zeta race before hybridization	0.1%
Zeta Reticuli 3D Hybrid	Human incarnates derived from breeding programs	less than 0.1%
Andromedan 3D Hybrid	Human incarnates derived from breeding programs	less than 0.1%
Tau Ceti, Alpha Centauri, Polaris	Human incarnates from these star systems (mostly 6D-8D)	less than 0.1%
Arcturus 7D-9D	Emissaries incarnate in human form	less than one

		million
Nibiru (Planet X)	Nibiruan Council members, on and off-planet incarnations	about 80,000
ETs in alien bodies	Humanoids with off-planet incarnations	about 32,000
Walk-ins (soul transfers)	Various races taking over human bodies through soul transfer	about 6,000
Other categories (3D-12D)	Humans from star systems not mentioned above	about 50 million
Other entities (7D or higher)	Spiritual masters from higher dimensions (avatars in manufactured bodies)	about 300

Population percentage breakdown by density (current vibratory level of humans):

3D -- About 78%
4D -- About 22% (includes yours truly at approx. 4.65)
5D -- About 0.1%
6D -- About 0.00001%
7D -- About 0.000000001%

Here is my assessment of the types of craft observed in our skies, including the ones I've seen physically. The percentages are out of the total observed by humans:

TYPE OF CRAFT	SYSTEM OF ORIGIN	PERCENTAGE OF SIGHTINGS
Grey, saucer shaped, 10m-20m diameter	Zeta Reticuli - 3D/4D	50%
Grey, saucer shaped, 10m-20m diameter	Illuminati Black Ops (Earth)	30%
Black, triangular, a few meters across	Alpha Draconis 3D (Reptilian)	10%
Multicolor, saucer-shaped	Pleiades 4D/7D, Venus 6D	3%

Spherical, green glowing	Pleiades 4D/7D	1%
Black, triangular, very large	Illuminati Black Ops (Earth)	1%
Cigar-shaped (mothercraft - very large)	Zeta Reticuli - 3D/4D	1%
Grey, Cylindrical	Andromeda - 3D/4D	1%
Interdimensional, various sizes and colors	Sirius B, Orion, other systems (5D-9D)	about 3%

NOTE: The Orions interbred with humans nearly half a million years ago. To my knowledge they have only a handful of emissaries from the constellation circling our heavens. The same goes for the Sirians. What about an impending invasion? Sorry to be the bearer of bad news, but it already happened over 500,000 years ago and yeah, they won. No new invasion will be successful because Gaia (Mother Earth) is ascending and only those souls on the path of ascension will be allowed to remain on Earth beyond the 2012 - 2030 A.D. window.

This information may or may not even matter. Please use your own divine judgment when dealing with ETs and especially when dealing with humans, as the percentage of negatively vibrating humans is much higher than that of ETs. In fact, if it were up to chance (which it is not), you would stand a better chance of meeting a positive ET than a positive human.

The Orions look like us because almost 80% of us are Orions. The Pleiadeans look like us because they were the original root race of Earth. The Sirians are a bit taller and lighter than the average humans. The Antareans are large, muscular and have reddish-brown skin. The Andromedans tend to incarnate as orientals, but the original ETs are tall and lanky with large heads and small slanted almond eyes. The Zetas come in three main flavors: (1) alabaster white and short with huge black almond eyes; (2) short and grey with large black almond eyes (the most common); and (3) tall, blue-skinned hybrids with small slanted almond eyes. The other races are higher dimensional and can change their appearance at will. The Venusians are fair-skinned, blond and translucent. The Arcturians are large, blue-skinned translucent beings. The higher-dimensional Pleiadeans are shimmering golden figures of light. The highest level Pleiadeans look like the blue-white stars in the visible Pleiades star cluster.

ETs in Our Solar System

Jupiter has advanced civilizations in the etheric atmosphere of the giant planet, vibrating at 5th and 6th density levels. They are not completely free of service-to-self (STS) vibrations and there is some kind of hierarchy to their government. They are large translucent beings originating in many local sectors of the galaxy. They were called to Jupiter to learn and grow spiritually with the assistance of Arcturians and Venusians. These beings have developed the power side of their nature more than the love side, although they are generally of a positive energy. However, that energy is somewhat harsh compared to the Venusians. Their biggest lesson appears to be finding balance between love, wisdom and power and integrating the mistakes they made during the Mars experience hundreds of thousands of years ago.

The **Orions** (who have controlled Earth for the last half million years) sometimes incarnate etherically in the atmosphere of Jupiter once they have ascended from the warrior-masculine-aggressive Martian paradigm. Most of the rulers of the Jupiter conclave (about 1,000 rulers and 150,000 entities) are being tutored from higher realms in the ways of unconditional love, and how to govern a planet without ego superiority issues (a tough lesson).

The **Venusians** are a sixth density race from which the goddess mythology arose. They look very much as pictured in visionary paintings – long flowing golden hair, flowing robes and translucent bodies of light, some with wings.

The **Martians** are really the Orions prior to coming to Earth. They began their incarnations on the surface of Mars and later went underground when their atmosphere was destroyed by warfare.

The **Maldekians** are really Orions that once inhabited Maldek, the planet between Mars and Jupiter. They blew their planet apart with warfare and what's left is the asteroid belt. The souls incarnated on Mars and Earth after the destruction of Maldek. The destruction of this planet threw the other planets out of their original orbits and created problems far beyond the solar system. For this reason, the Divine Councils of the higher dimensions have intervened and will not allow the total destruction of any more planets in this sector.The Saturn Tribunal is a council of higher-dimensional entities from various systems that use etheric Saturn as their base of operations.-Sal Rachel

*** *** ***

Who Has The Final Word?

The Anunnaki, Sitchin, Amarani, Judaism, the Bible, Archeology, and Channeling Face to Face

---

What a way to end this book!!!

> Estelle Nora Harwit Amrani with Enki's assistance strongly stated that she does not agree with all of Sitchen's data and theories about the Anunnaki. She wrote a fascinating and very impressive thesis on the subject, in which she strongly defended her arguments, points and beliefs. Dr. Sitchin works with historical tablets. Amrani works with a great entity; she channels. On what and which side are you? Archeology or channeling? Science or the Bible? You decide after reading Amrani's thesis. It is an outstanding piece. Here are her arguments and points.

For those of you who are Sitchin fans, you may notice some similarities between his information and mine. I respect the exhaustive research he has done, and the great scholar that he is. He contributed to opening up our planet's memory of the Anunnaki. Scholastic and intellectual viewpoints and written documents are of value and add one part to understanding who we are. However, I feel we must not rule out our holographic, multidimensional viewpoints as being of equal value. This is what I present to you.

I don't agree with all of Sitchin's data, and I include a lot that he does not. There have been many viewpoints from many different writers about the Anunnaki. Most of my information comes from personal memories and channeled information. And, similarities will also exist between certain channels because deeper truth is consistent; those who can channel or tap into universal energies on their own will also receive many parallels to this story. I have something I'd like to add here - the Anunnaki had bases around the world, but primarily in the Middle East - Lebanon, Israel, Egypt, Iraq - and in India and South Africa. There are many artifacts that still exist in Iraq but are not allowed to be seen, and the West has not had much access at all to these artifacts of the Anunnaki. It is my understanding that Saddam Hussein has hoarded many of these and kept many in private vaults under the ground. It is my hope that governments will encourage the Iraqi people who have access to these artifacts to bring them out and share them with the world. Much still lies beneath the sands and it would be fantastic for humanity to be able to uncover the past in this region. Ur, between the Tigris and Euphrates Rivers, was the birthplace of humanity in modern times on Plan-ET Earth, the Garden of Eden, and everyone is entitled to have safe access to it.

Therein lies many eophysical keys to remembering who we all are. Humans were not only created by G-d, but are also genetically, symbolically and literally, related to a few off-planet civilizations; one particularly known on Earth as the Anunnaki.

If you believe humans evolved solely from apes, why, then, are there still apes?

Our story, (a term which replaces "history", because "our story" belongs to all of us), of human life on Earth is often told as creation myths, the planets in the heavens. But these myths were based on something...fact. This is why, around the world, we see the same tales of how one 'god' was instrumental in assisting humanity during creation, the great flood, bringing knowledge to humanity. All cultures have their own creation stories of the 'gods and goddesses,' beings on ships that came from the skies (often wearing masks or strange clothing and possessed some amazing abilities), giants (Anakim), war epochs between two sides of a family, and all over the Earth we also share very similar artwork, music and technology, largely based on extraterrestrial activity and intervention. From Lemuria to Atlantis to Sumeria to Egypt. These portray the story of our cosmos, the constellations, sun and moon, and put into human and "god" forms. Personally, I feel that much of what we attribute to the Anunnaki was not their own doing. For instance, I think that the Anunnaki were limited in their abilities, yet were given credit for doing things that were done by other alien species. But, as human beings saw the Anunnaki as gods and goddesses, they naturally transferred credit to the Annunaki, because they were more tangible, something they could see, make an image of, and so forth. In this article you will see some comparisons between B'raisheet (Genesis) and the written history the Anunnaki.

Although this may not be for everybody (because some people simply aren't interested or curious about any of this stuff), why could it be of value to examine our past in this particular way, with our connections to extraterrestrials, as well as with our past lifetimes? Because when we re-member more of who we are, why we continue to repeat patterns without understanding them, then we can be more of our whole selves in a way that is free from old baggage. We can have clear knowledge of ourselves, accept ourselves, heal what needs healing, and create what we want to have for our future. Or, to quote from a popular TV show ("Kung Fu: The Legend Continues"): "The seeds of destiny are nurtured by our roots in the past." If you want to know what the Anunnaki looked like, one easy way is to see the crop circle from 2001 called the first Chilbolton Face in Hampshire.

Mention the name Anunnaki to some people and deep within them something stirs; a memory of Earth and Mars - and often there is anger, fear, pain, and confusion about the Anunnaki. People seem to like to blame them for all of Earth's problems. Some people remember being part of their family, for better or worse. And yet others don't want to hear anything about them because it dredges up feelings they'd rather avoid or deny. I even hear stories from people who think that the Anunnaki are vicious reptilians who have been battling for control over the Earth for the last half a million years, and they call all of the shots while we sit here like helpless pawns.

I feel that A LOT of what we've learned about the Anunnaki was via bad press due to incorrect translations and the need to have a scapegoat. Do I agree with everything the Anunnaki did, or they way in which they did things? No. They had good sides and also some really awful sides. There were different Anunnaki factions, and there were aliens who gave the impression they were Anunnakis. This article presents some of each. What they did was their responsibility and I'm not about to excuse or even attempt the impossible, which would be to vindicate their actions.

The Anunnaki are archetypal, symbolic, and mythic, too. So, we may each feel a certain personal identification with one or more of them, which is a very interesting phenomenon to investigate. Because people feel a reaction to the Anunnaki, it is a HUGE key that our personal feelings and memories (emotional and cellular) about the Anunnaki still influence us today. In other words, these archetypes are within ourselves. Joseph Campbell stated that, "myths are clues to the spiritual potentialities of the human life." We seek the experience, the rapture of life, and myths help us as guides through life, show us what we are capable of, and mirroring what we feel. We can use the mythology of the Anunnaki as a way to understand and heal ourselves.

From Enki and Enlil, Cain and Abel, Jacob and Esau, Joseph and his brothers, Moses and Ramses, Hatshepsut and Tuthmose, Akhenaten's one god versus the many deities; Inanna (with her insatiable greed for power and adoration who still failed to realize that without her possessions she was nothing); Jehovah and Adoni; Sin (a.k.a. Nanna, Allah); the war over who controls Israel. We have seen brother go against brother (the main theme), religions and governments against others, men against women and women against men up into current times. I feel it's time to get over the past (not necessarily forget it), and heal a lot. It is my hope that through such understanding of who we are, we can resolve ancient battles between nations and heal bitterness and hurts that have held us back from fully enjoying our lives and being the creators that we are RIGHT NOW. It's time to remember who the false gods were and who the real G-d is....the One that is in charge of it all, that is within us; the one that transcends definition.

The return of love/G-d (and the G-d as the common source within us all that is synchronicity, wisdom - love and light) is not only required for our survival, I feel it is eminent. Examining the deep, dark secrets within and healing them can help us accomplish this faster, I think. The most important event that took place when the Anunnakis ruled the Earth was that man rebelled against slavery and demanded sovereignty, and received it. The Anunnaki left. At the end of this article is more information along these lines about what this means for us as a civilization. My thanks go to my higher self, and Enki for helping me, for all of his love and care he gives to me and to all of life. When the Source (G-d) created souls in order to be able to reflect back to itself what it was, beings later manifested in the constellation of Lyra. These were the first "creator gods" (the Council of Twelve and Elohim) who knew how to create matter from light. And create they did - planets, stars, universes, life forms for themselves, and eventually others.

The Lyran's physical lifetimes lasted for approximately one thousand years. In time, however, their life span decreased. They sought out something that would enable them to live longer lives so that they could experience the wonder and miracle of existence. They found that gold not only increased their longevity, but provided them with a superconductivity which gave them the ability to be very telepathic and experience their multidimensionality. Many thousands of years passed, and the beings from Lyra spread out into the cosmos and created new civilizations. Some went to Vega, others the Pleiades, and yet others Sirius. But, they knew (more or less) of their roots in Lyra/Vega and Sirius and that they were creator gods, at that point a.k.a. the Watchers. The search for gold to maintain their longevity continued because, unfortunately, their source for this magical substance was not forever lasting. Their planet (part of Sirius) was destroyed and their lives were doomed. They had to find another way of living - elsewhere.

The following universal history information is from Bashar (channeled by Darryl Anka), and Enki [through myself]: "Approximately 4.6 billion years ago in our solar system there existed: Mercury, Venus, Mars (no moons), a 4th planet (larger than Earth with many moons, including a large one), Jupiter, Saturn (no rings), Uranus, Neptune and Pluto (which was a satellite of Saturn). "4 billion years ago, another planet came into our still forming solar system. This planet had its own moons. It arrived at approximately the same orbit as the 4th planet called Maldek - the one that existed beyond Mars. Mars was then the 3rd planet. (Please read the Sumerian Epic of Creation - the Enuma Elish, as this says it all and explains the importance of the Tablets of Destiny.)

"This planet's moons impacted the 4th planet shattering it so that part of it became the Asteroid Belt. The remnant of the impact (as it cooled and moved into a tighter orbit around the sun) became the Earth and brought with it the large planet that was the moon of the 4th planet. This is our moon. Approx. 67% of the former planet is Earth. Earth brought with it water - but there was water on the other planet, as well. As it reformed and became a sphere again, the rift where the shattering took place is now the Pacific Ocean area.

"This other planet was responsible for shattering the moons gravitationally that caused Saturn's rings and for turning Uranus on its side, so that it has a highly inclined axis. And - this also caused Pluto to release from Saturn and come into its own orbit." This planet, of course, that caused all the havoc was/is Nibiru. It is our 10th planet - not really the 12th. In the late 1980's it was about halfway back. Bases were set up on the Moon. Mars' moons - Phobos and Deimos, are remnants of that original impact that created the Asteroid Belt. These moons have been used for bases and minerals and water. (The above information on the solar system is recorded in ancient texts, and has been accessed through memory and channelings by myself, in sessions by Bashar, and other entities.)

Next phase: The group of beings who originated in Lyra later split up and evolved into Vegans, Sirians and Pleiadeans, are known as the Anunnaki. This particular group is attributed to having their own satellite. Their "planet" (which is partially artificial) was considered to be Nibiru. However, Nibiru is not really the home of the Anunnaki. Sirius was. Nibiru was made up of what I'd call space pirates who imitated other beings, and sometimes a few from one planet would join them, including the Anunnaki. I've seen these pirates - they're not at all like the real Anunnaki. The story of the Anunnaki has been mixed up with these pirates through time so some see the Anunnaki as being only evil. Some of the Anunnaki also were present on Mars before it was destroyed,

The name "Anunnaki" can mean many different things [based on Hebrew interpretations] - it is rich with meaning.

- "An" is short for "anachnu," which means "we"
- "An" also means "heaven"
- "Naki" means "clean"

So, the name can mean "We are clean" and "heaven is clean," clean as in "pure." "Ki" means "Earth," so "We are here on Earth." "Heaven is on Earth." "Anu is here on Earth." The "we" is also meant as a collective oneness, of the Source. They were tall, giant, (in Hebrew the word for giants is "Anakim") and have also been called the Nordics or Blonds, even though not all of them had blond hair or blue eyes. It is easy to see their Lyran and Sirian roots in their appearance. They also glowed a golden color. Their symbol is the winged disk, which not only represents their starships, but also symbolic of the ability of the spirit to fly free while remembering it's wise, divine source. These Anunnaki were later called the Elohim, and Nephilim (those who descended, came down). However, they were NOT "the" Elohim, but Elohim became the word used for the plural of god. In B'raisheet (Genesis) 6:4 it is written: "The Lord said, "My breath shall not abide in man forever, since he too is flesh; let the days be allowed him be one hundred and twenty years." It was then, and later too, that the Nephilim appeared on earth - when the divine beings cohabited with the daughters of men, who bore them offspring. They were the heroes of old, men of renown." It is thought, by some, that the Nephilim were sinful gods who "fell from grace." They fell, alright, in their spaceships. This can also be seen as symbolic. The "fall" having to do with lowering one's frequency from spirit into physical matter, which is slower and denser. "Fall" also meaning forgetting one's true Source. As life forms choose to come to Earth their vibration goes through changes so that they are more matched to the frequency of Earth, their new home. Now these ETs literally came down from space, but souls choosing to incarnate upon the earth also had to change their vibrational frequencies. Enlil was first to come to Earth and was there even before mankind was created. The Sumerian texts called mankind the "Black-Headed People."

If anyone doubts the location of Eden, or why it was chosen by the Anunnaki as a locale, please read on from Genesis: "Then, before there was any rain, he formed man, from the dust of the earth. He blew into his nostrils the breath of life, and man became a living being.

The Lord God planted a garden in Eden, in the east, and placed there the man whom He had formed...", and then all the other life forms came into being, water, animals, minerals. Genesis does say that the first river in Eden was Pishon and winds through the whole land of Havilah, where the gold is - the gold of that land is good; bdellium is there, and lapis lazuli. The name of the second river is Gihon, the one that winds through the whole land of Cush. The name of the third river is Tigris, the one that flows east of Asshur. And the fourth river is the Euphrates.

[For more Biblical references to the Anakim, Anakites, Anunnaki, Nephilim, etc., please see:

- Numbers: 13:22; 13:28-33;
- Deut: 1:28; 2:1-; 9:2;
- Joshua: 11:21-22; 14:12; 14:15; 15:13-14;
- Judges: 1:20. Many of these giants were the result of Anunnaki and human reproduction, such as Gilgamesh]

Being a dreamtime medicine person, I traveled to this place of human's origins and saw the space pirates who gave the impression of being the Anunnaki. This was on the border of Iran and Iraq at Lake Zaga. This lake no longer exists, as it has been covered up by sand, but it exists inside the earth and interdimensionally. To date no one else has ever talked about Lake Zaga or knows where it is - that is, aside from myself and channeled entities who have confirmed my visions and memories of it. I would like to find someone who can provide me with archaeological, geological evidence that this place once existed. I also know the language of the place, and how there are underground facilities, passageways, there. It was once controlled by the Anunnaki. There are many interesting details of how this place once looked, but I am preserving this information for another time. This is part of Earth's story and occurred after there already was life on Earth, hominid beings. Hominids are distinctly human-like creatures, different from apes or chimpanzees. The Anunnaki came to Earth (some of their crafts had crashed in the process), for a haven for themselves, and found it rich with gold, copper, silver and other minerals. They felt that here was their last chance for longevity, survival and the gold was the best conductor of energy which had many important uses. They mined gold for a very long time - hundreds of thousands of years by our standards; for theirs only a few weeks have passed.

What, according to the Old Testament happened? God said, "Now that the man has become like one of us, knowing good and bad, what if he should stretch out his hand and take also from the tree of life and eat, and live forever!" So man was banished from Eden to work the soil from which he was taken. Further on in Genesis, we read: "The Lord saw how great was man's wickedness on earth, and how every plan devised by his mind was nothing but evil all the time. And the Lord regretted that He had made man on earth, and His heart was saddened. The Lord said, "I will blot out from the earth the men whom I created - men together with beasts, creeping things, and birds of the sky; for I regret that I made them." But Noah found favor with the Lord....For My part, I am about to bring the Flood - waters upon the earth - to destroy all flesh under the sky in which there is breath of life; everything on earth shall perish. But I will establish

My covenant with you, and you shall enter the ark, with your sons..." This ark was symbolic and literal, not only a ship, but a covenant.

Stephanie Dalley, author and translator, states from her book "Myths From Mesopotamia: Creation, The Flood, Gilgamesh and Others" (1991) that in the "Epic of Creation" (the epic which explains the history of the cosmos, and the Anunnaki as creator gods), the key element involves the possession of the Tablets of Destinies (which I will discuss at a later time because it's very relevant to today). There also could have been several different versions spread around retelling the Epic. About the Epic, Ms. Dally writes: "Here is no struggle against fate, no mortal heroes, no sense of suspense over the outcome of events. The success of the hero-god Marduk is a foregone conclusion. None of the good gods is injured or killed; no tears are shed. Yet cosmic events are narrated: the earliest generations of the gods are recounted leading up to the birth of the latest hero-god; the forces of evil and chaos are overcome, whereupon the present order of the universe can be established, with its religious centers, its divisions of time, its celestial bodies moving according to proper rules, and with mankind invented to serve the does. The gods themselves behave in an orderly fashion: they assemble, discuss, agree, and elect their leaders in a gathering of males; after Tiamat's primeval parturition and the spawning of monsters, goddesses play no part in creating the civilized world, not even in creating mankind." [p. 228]

However, I find this hard to believe because without a female donor, beings could not procreate, not give birth, and so on. There have been many women I have personally met who remember being birth goddesses, used by the aliens to have embryos implanted within them, to go through the pregnancies and give birth, then raise the children - if they survived.

Dalley also writes that in the Atrahasis, the mother goddess, Ninhursag-Ninharsag-Ki, (Mami, Nintu, who I abbreviate as "Nin"), with Ea, make man out of clay, mixed with the blood from a god slain by Nin, Geshtu-e: "A ghost came into existence from the god's flesh, And she (Nin) proclaimed it as his living sign. The ghost existed so as not to forget (the slain god)."

Mixing and concocting continues and the "womb-goddesses" (creator of fate) were assembled. When birthing time arrived, Nin served as the mid-wife. The ghost is the spirit, the breath, divine life force, that was NOT created by the Anunnaki. This is only created by The Source.

(Personal note: My spelling of Ninhursag is how the name is spoken, and how it is in my memory. When analyzed numerologically, it has a number of 111, which according to Norma Smith, Expert Analyst and Ph.D. in Universal Harmonics Analysis, is a master triple number, and its meaning is DNA template for humanity. I think Sitchin's spelling of the name as Ninharsag is to justify his translation of the name through Hebrew - "har" meaning "mountain." Ninharsag has a value of 91 and means "spirit" and "oneness." So, it is more of a spiritual name for Ninhursag.)

In Dalley's own translation of the Epic, Tiamat is a female who is plotted against by her own family, and then has the tables turned on her by her lover Kingu (Qingu, or Zu) and the Anunnaki, after she gives him the Tablets of Destiny - the Anu power. Ea, married to Damkina, overhears the plot and takes the fate into his own hands, slaying Apsu and Mummu. Afterwards he rested in his own quarters and named them Apsu and made his home there. Here is where he and Damkina created their son Marduk, and Marduk was raised by a nurse and he was suckled by the goddesses.

What follows in the Epic is a war (created by accusations and conspiracies back and forth) between the forces of Anshar, his son Anu, his son EA, and his son Marduk against Tiamat and Kingu. Marduk slays Tiamat - of womankind - the gods rejoice and make Marduk their leader. Marduk took back the Tablets of Destinies and became the king of the entire universe. Let's remember that we're talking about extraterrestrials here, (symbolic and literal); not THE Source. Some of these beings were very wise and knew how to transform energy/light into matter. They were/are seeders. Basically, the Anunnaki who came to Earth were not terribly different from where we are today in terms of scientific development. According to the Enuma Elish, the idea occurred to Marduk that they could create a being that would mine the gold for them and then the gods could take it easy. They used the blood (DNA) of slain Kingu and combined it with a humanoid being on Earth. After many various experiments in which they created other races, (and they had many horrible failures, as well), they created a hybrid being (Adam, Adapa) which evolved into modern human. It is written: "He created mankind from his blood, Imposed the toil of the gods (on man) and released the gods from it. When Ea the wise had created mankind, Had imposed the toil of the gods on them - That deed is impossible to describe..." In both the Enuma Elish and Atrahasis the reason for creating man is the same - to relieve the gods of hard labor. Why there are different versions of this story of creation is more speculative than concretely known. But we can assume that a couple of reasons could be the era in which the Epics were written, who was in power at the time, and who wanted to praise one god over another god or goddess. Actually, the name "human" can be traced to Enki (a.k.a. EA). HU is a transliteration of the ancient Sumerian EA (Grimms' law of interchangeable letters and sounds). Isis (pronounced Ish-Ish, which is interesting, because in Hebrew 'Ish' means 'man') was Enki's mother. Isis was not Nibiruan; she was Sirian, with some Orion connections. His father was Anu. (Anu and his official wife, Antu, had a son named Enlil.)

HU was also Horus, by the way, therefore another connection to Ninhursag, a.k.a. Hathor. What about EArth? EN.KI is "lord of earth." In the early days on Earth, Enki's symbol was the crescent moon with a bearded, olden god surrounded with flowing water. The crescent moon relates to science, measuring, the oceans/tides - Enki's specialties. In later years, the crescent moon developed another association - keep reading. In other ancient "mythology" Enki is known as Oannes, Ptah, Quezecotl, even as his own son, Thoth.

The Anunnaki (who some call the Nephilim) later procreated with the beings who were on Earth at that time. The souls of those who became human came to Earth by their own free will to experience physicality. Several other extraterrestrial civilizations later contributed their own input into human DNA and created many races of humans and other creatures (a couple of which have since left this planet - such as the dinosaurs). However, these hybrids (our missing link in our evolution) helped the Anunnaki mine their gold. As seems pretty obvious thus far, the Anunnaki were pattern-makers, the creators of archetypes and a part of the template for human life on Earth. Throughout all cultures on Earth the same story of these gods (albeit with different names depending on where you are), their gifts to humanity, their failures, their characteristics, their loves, their battles and the results of such warfare are recorded in literature, ritual, art, oral tradition and religion. Astrology is one of the major sciences they brought to Earth, and each main god/goddess had their own constellation. The Anunnaki gave the humans knowledge of how to be this human being, how to take care of themselves, gave them guidelines, rules, for proper living. And yet, at times they were also manipulators, and as long as people didn't upset the "gods" they were safe and provided for. After some time, the humans evolved to a point where they began to question their purpose and their future. They rebelled against their "creators," the Anunnaki. The humans wanted to have the nectar of the gods for themselves. Why shouldn't they be able to have their free will, live as long as their gods did? Why shouldn't they have power and wealth or whatever they felt they lacked? And then the sad realization that they were NOT like "the gods." Read the early sad epics of Enkidu and Gilgamesh who desperately wanted to be divine and have everlasting life, only to find out that their mortal side won out. You will also find out more about the flood and the Anunnaki from the Epic of Gilgamesh. The Anunnaki discussed the possible consequences if they shared the gold (the process of alchemy) with the humans.

Some of the Anunnaki, such as the Sirian leader, Enki, were in favor of letting humans be free and equal to them. Other Anunnaki were angry because of the blending of the two life forms and the continual complaints humans had to the Anunnaki. One of the Anunnaki leaders who had no patience for humans was EN.LIL. Enlil was the Prince of heaven and Earth. He was in charge of airspace, he was chief of the gods and Lord of Sumer. Enki and Enlil were half brothers through the same father, Anu, who was the leader of this Anunnaki group. They also had to contend with Marduk (one of Enki's sons) who was proclaimed the greatest king of the gods. In later years, the symbol of the crescent moon was associated with Nanna/Sin (Enlil's and Ninlil's son), who Sinai was named for, and who became known as Allah. Note the symbol (with the star) is used in Islam and is directly related to Enlil's side of the family. This is proof of the battle for power by the two camps of Anunnaki, those of Enki versus those of Enlil - actually a terrible, nuclear war between the Anunnaki took place in the Sinai, and at the Great Pyramid, for control over the region. Ninhursag acted as mediator and brought the two sides to a peace agreement. (But, in fact, there were many more camps that evolved out of Enki and Enlil's lineages.)

The Anunnaki had two factions fighting one another over humanity's future. This was coded in the books as the Garden of Eden (a genetic metaphor and a literal place). Enlil didn't want the humans to be equal to them. Enki was in favor of allowing humans self-rulership, respect and equality. In order to ensure that humans would be able to, in the long run, benefit from their ancestry, Enki (the serpent of wisdom and healing) suggested those who came to be called Adam and Eve to eat from the Tree of Knowledge.

Had they eaten only from the Tree of Life, humans would have lived a very long time, but not have been the wiser. Nor would humans have reached their own intellectual and spiritual evolution in which they would realize that they are equal to the 'gods' who created them as new humans by virtue of their DNA. This "trick" enraged Enlil who, from that point onward, was furious that humans mated with the Anunnaki, and he wanted to punish humanity. We see this reflected in our societies ever since as the wild drive towards materialism, or racism, or shame, or the focus on doing anything which keeps people from remembering who they are, being in denial of who they are, or angry with life - blaming The G-d.

Civilizations and religions were created by Enki and Enlil (and later their offspring). Egypt, for example, was developed by Enki and his lineage. The areas of the Sinai, Jerusalem, Sumer, India and more were fought over by the two families of Enki and Enlil, changing hands back and forth through different Pyramid Wars.

[This was the of battles of Ra/Marduk, Horus, Thoth, Inanna, Set, Osiris, and mediated into peace by Nin.]

The battle Horus fought for Ra against Seth was the first that used humans in a war with weapons, and this began wars mankind fought against itself. The war between the factions of the Anunnaki continued between humans with claims such as, "There is only One god," or "There are many gods," or "My god is THE god, but yours isn't," or "We are the chosen people, or the superior race - God told us so!" This wasn't from The G-d, the love-energy source of all life: instead this was more reflective of "the creator gods" who had their own beliefs, agendas. The battle between Egypt and Israel goes way back, and it was due to the control and confusion set into motion by many of these factors; extraterrestrials, angels (and messages from THE G-d), humans, mixed messages, control and fear, between worshipping Enki's family or Enlil's family.

Atlantis' finally sinking was due to astronomical events combined with those humans and Anunnakis experimenting with sound technology. They didn't plan on destroying the place - they just miscalculated. The last great flood, approximately 13,000 years ago, became a legend when Enki went against the other Anunnaki and saved humans (the Noahs of Earth) when this accident occurred. The first flood was in Lemuria and then there were others in Atlantis (several times). Those with Enki forced Enlil to help save whatever humans they could.

Enki, having felt completely disgusted and disappointed by Enlil's fierce control, (refer to the Tower of Babel here) left Earth during the Exodus. Moses in confusion as to who he was speaking with on the mountain.

He heard The G-d, messengers (Elohim and Nephilim) as a mixture. The Ten Commandments were supposedly dictated to Moses and he wrote it down, after he was taught the Hebrew alphabet and language, which he would later teach to his people. Have you ever noticed how, at this point in the Hebrew Bible, Adonai is no longer mentioned, and YHWH, Jehovah, Yahweh, is? And yet, everyone thinks they're the same G-d. Just who is this Jehovah, YHWH? Jehovah was an agent of Enlil!

Not long after the Exodus, the other Anunnaki left their Earthly influence, and their secrets of transforming gold into the powerful substance that allowed their longevity and spiritual abilities also vanished. Their knowledge about life was held in the hands of very few who began to abuse it and became greedy. Then, in time, humans who remembered died or disappeared. A lot of knowledge was lost. And yet, people kept trying to capture that special essence of gold in the form of statues or other such items, mistakenly believing that power equated to violence and destruction and hoarding wealth. They felt it was their key to immortality - that which would make them THE G-d. Powdered gold has beneficial properties, but the real gold is within - remembering one's self and connection to Source. This is really what Enki had tried to infuse into people.

The Anunnaki left the Earth, in a sense, but not without creating counterparts or aspects of themselves who would reincarnate as humans in order to share the human experience with them, their oversouls. Some of these continued the lineage through King David and Jesus. Some of these counterparts or aspects have stubbornly stuck to what they presume was Enlil's and Marduk's agenda to control the Earth for their own purposes, keeping humans more fearful, dependent, ignorant. Yet, others continue to share the ancient wisdom from other Anunnaki, encouraging humanity to remember their source which they can access from within their individual and collective cellular/spiritual memories in order to break the ancient and false bonds of slavery, fear and ignorance and reclaim what they feel is rightfully theirs. Any way you look at it, the confusing, chaotic battle continues - and it doesn't have to.

What happens now, on the flip side? Are these Anunnaki "gods" returning to Earth via Nibiru? (Remember - Nibiru really wasn't the home of the Anunnaki.) "They" have never really left! First of all, they exist in many of us as a reincarnation or as aspects of them. (And boy, that's created some sad, major identity crises.) And as a human civilization, we have finally reached the understanding that we are more than ETs or humans, and we do have free will and choice. We can decide how WE want our experiences to be. Secondly, time exists in the third dimension but not beyond, so one can argue that everything is happening right now, but honestly, that doesn't always change what already happened in our "past." All that matters is NOW.

Please don't make a big deal about the "return of Nibiru." If you're looking for a savior, look to yourselves. I know that the family of Anu is helping us. We are also helping the few Anunnaki and humans who are still tuck in old, negative paradigms. Whatever we, or they, do effects the whole (all of life in the cosmos). Regardless, we all have to be self-responsible. And, if one day the Anunnaki, will we still be playing out old dramas and wars? Will we be able to greet them as equals? Will we even want them to be here? Will we care, either way? Is it even possible for these old Anunnaki to return here and be as they once were?

If we want our lives to be destructive or a joyous creation, the choice is ours - truly it is. However, we have to know that our thoughts and feelings are manifesting instantaneously as our reality, so we have to be more aware than ever of what we focus on and choose what we want for ourselves. We have to know who WE are, what our own energy is like versus what another's is like. Using our individual and collective power of choice is our means of attaining complete independence from the limitations and illusions we, or others, have imposed upon us/ourselves. After all, if we, as souls, didn't want to be part of the Anunnaki experience, in a physical life on Earth, we wouldn't have been. It was always a co-creation.

Some of the Anunnaki games, such as that of the needy toddler or dysfunctional adolescent, are still being played by people on Earth: who is more godly, who is more deserving, who is evil, who is powerful, who has to be punished, who gets to own that land, or "I want it, just because I want it, or because he has one!" These "gods" wanted things only "their" way. Some people feel so badly for what they did as Anunnaki that they cover it up or punish themselves, over and over, never letting go of the past. Then there are others won't give up on blaming the Anunnaki for making their current lives miserable, always saying, "It's their fault. I hate them. Poor me."

It's time to have forgiveness, compassion, and gratitude, for them, for ourselves - all of our Selves, and become very clear what we're doing, and why. If we are repeating old patterns, relating to any one of these Anunnaki archetypes, we have to become aware of how destructive these patterns can be. And it's in us - from Enki to Enlil to Sin, from Marduk to Inanna, from those masquerading as the Anunnaki. We have been repeating battles (worldwide), holding on to ancient and unhealthy grudges and dramas, martyring ourselves, fearful of letting go (because these old patterns are comfortable and familiar) and moving forward.

*** *** ***

Note from the publishers:

The author can be reached at delafayette@internationalnewsagency.org

Each month we publish two books by Maximillien de Lafayette.

To read more about his books (current and forthcoming), please visit these websites: www.ufozetareticuli.com   and   www.delafayettebibliography.com

NOTES